Max-Planck-Institut
für ausländisches öffentliches Recht
und Völkerrecht

Max Planck Institute
for Comparative Public Law
and International Law

Under the Direction of

Rudolf Bernhardt · Helmut Steinberger
Jochen Abr. Frowein

WORLD COURT DIGEST

Formerly Fontes Iuris Gentium

Volume 1
1986–1990

Prepared by

Rainer Hofmann · Juliane Kokott
Karin Oellers-Frahm
Stefan Oeter · Andreas Zimmermann

Springer-Verlag

Berlin Heidelberg New York London Paris
Tokyo Hong Kong Barcelona Budapest

To be cited as:
Max-Planck-Institute for International Law,
World Court Digest

ISBN 3-540-56141-2 Springer-Verlag Berlin Heidelberg New York
ISBN 0-387-56141-2 Springer-Verlag New York Berlin Heidelberg

42/3130-5 4 3 2 1 0 – Printed on acid-free paper

PREFACE

This is a new start of an old activity of the Max-Planck-Institute for foreign public law and international law in Heidelberg. Since 1931 a Digest of the Decisions of the Permanent Court and later the International Court of Justice has been published. The last volume appeared in 1990 covering the period 1976–1985. The general title was "Fontes Iuris Gentium" and the subtitle "Digest of the Decisions of the International Court of Justice". The Institute has now decided to publish the Digest under the short title "World Court Digest", in English only.

The general pattern of the earlier volumes has been maintained but a few important changes should be noted. The parts of the judgments or separate opinions reproduced are frequently longer, to make it easier for the reader to see the context of a specific statement. Separate opinions are being reproduced in a restrictive manner, only where they concern essential points of a judgment. The order of presentation has been changed to allow for a better possibility to work with the Digest.

The most important change for the production of the Digest is the use of a scanner in the Institute to read the excerpts of the decisions into a computer. By this method it has been possible to reduce the price of the volume considerably. However, this reduction can only be maintained if the sale of the volume will be increased. The editors hope that many international lawyers should wish to get their own copy of the World Court Digest.

The Digest has been prepared by a working group in the Institute composed of Rainer Hofmann, Juliane Kokott, Karin Oellers-Frahm, Stefan Oeter, Andreas Zimmermann.

Jochen Abr. Frowein
Director at the Institute

TABLE OF CONTENTS

I. Substantive International Law - First Part

1. THE FOUNDATIONS OF INTERNATIONAL LAW 1

1.1. Good Faith 1
1.2. Equity 1
1.3. Estoppel and Acquiescence 6

2. SOURCES OF INTERNATIONAL LAW 7

2.1. General Questions

*2.1.1. Formation of Rules of International Law
*2.1.2. Historic Rights
*2.1.3. Rules of International Law of Regional and Local Application
2.1.4. Ius cogens 7
2.1.5. Relation between the Sources of International Law 9

2.2. Customary International Law 15
2.2.1. Formation of Customary International Law 15
2.2.2. Evidence of Customary International Law 22

*2.3. Treaties
*2.4. General Principles of Law
2.5. Unilateral Acts 24

3. INTERNATIONAL LAW AND MUNICIPAL LAW 27

4. SUBJECTS OF INTERNATIONAL LAW 28

. 4.1. General Questions
4.2. States 28

*4.2.1. Jurisdiction of States
*4.2.2. Territory
*4.2.3. Nationality
4.2.4. Fundamental Rights and Obligations 28

---

*Indicates sections without case excerpts

4.2.4.1. Sovereignty 28
*4.2.4.2. Equality
4.2.4.3. Peaceful Settlement of Disputes 31
*4.2.4.4. Obligations of Cooperation and Negotiation
4.2.5. Succession of States 32
4.3. International Organisations 32
*4.3.1. General Questions
*4.3.2. Legal Position of Member States
*4.3.3. Internal Law
4.3.4. "Implied Powers" 32
*4.4. Other Subjects of International Law
*4.5. Individuals
5. THE UNITED NATIONS 33
*5.1 General Questions
5.2. General Assembly 33
*5.3. Security Council
*5.4. Secretary-General
*5.5. Other Organs
5.6. Interpretation of the Charter 34
*5.7. Maintenance of International Peace and Security
*5.8. Specialized Agencies
5.9. United Nations Administrative Tribunal 37
6. USE OF FORCE AND RELATED PROBLEMS 40
6.1. Use of Force 40
6.2. Self defence 48
6.3. Intervention 69
7. LAW OF TREATIES 69
*7.1. General Questions
*7.2. Conclusion
*7.3. Reservations
*7.4. Invalidity
*7.5. Suspension and Termination
7.6. Interpretation 69
7.7. Specific Treaties 73
7.7.1. Convention on the Privileges and Immunities of the United Nations of 1946 73

* Indicates sections without case excerpts

7.7.2. Inter-American Treaty of Reciprocal Assistance of 1947 77
7.7.3. Geneva Convention on the Protection of Victims of War of 1949 ... 78
7.7.4. Treaty of Friendship Commerce and Navigation of 1956 between the United States and Nicaragua ... 79

8. VIOLATIONS OF INTERNATIONAL LAW AND RESPONSIBILITY OF STATES ... 85
8.1. General Questions ... 85
*8.2. Violation of International Law
8.3. Treaty Violations ... 85
8.4. Imputability ... 88
*8.5. Fault and due Diligence
8.6. Participation ... 92
*8.7. Violation of Duty to Prevent Damage
*8.8. Circumstances Precluding Wrongfulness

II. Substantive International Law - Second Part

1. TERRITORY OF STATES ... 92
*1.1. Acquisition and Loss
1.2. Boundaries ... 92
1.2.1. Land Boundaries ... 92
*1.2.2. Maritime Boundaries
*1.2.3. Air and Space
1.2.4. Principle of "uti possidetis" ... 95

2. LAW OF THE SEA ... 99
2.1. General Questions ... 99
2.2. Determination of Maritime Boundaries ... 100
2.3. Freedom of Navigation ... 100

3. AIR AND SPACE LAW

4. SELF-DETERMINATION ... 102

*5. NATIONALITY
5.1. General Questions
5.2. Acquisition and Loss
5.3. Diplomatic Protection

*6. MINORITIES

---

* Indicates sections without case excerpts

7. LAW OF ALIENS 104
7.1. General Questions 104
7.2. Protection of Property 105
8. HUMAN RIGHTS 107
9. LAW OF ARMED CONFLICTS 108
10. DISPUTE SETTLEMENT 111
*11. DIPLOMACY AND CONSULAR MATTERS
12. INTERNATIONAL ECONOMIC LAW 115
*13. INTERNATIONAL ENVIRONMENTAL LAW

III. The International Court of Justice

1. FUNDAMENTAL PRINCIPLES 117
1.1. General Questions 117
1.2. Consent of States 118
1.3. Equality of Parties 119
1.4. Political Questions/Determination of the Existence of a Dispute 120
*1.5. Ius standi
1.6. Applicable Law 128
1.7. Jura novit curia 129
2. THE JURISDICTION OF THE INTERNATIONAL COURT OF JUSTICE 130
2.1. General Rules 130
2.2. Conditions for a Decision on the Merits 133
2.2.1. Exhaustion of Local Remedies 133
2.2.2. Necessity of Diplomatic Negotiations 138
2.2.3. Jurisdiction in Case of Continuing Negotiations between the Parties 140
2.2.4. Admissibility
2.3. The Optional Clause
2.3.1. General Questions
*2.3.2. Transfer of Acceptances of the Compulsory Jurisdiction of the Permanent Court of International Justice (Article 36, Paragraph 5, of the Statue of the International Court of Justice)

* Indicates sections without case excerpts

2.3.3. Reservations
*2.3.4. Interpretation of a Declaration made under Article 36, Paragraph 5, of the Statute
*2.3.5. Reciprocity

2.4. Jurisdiction on the Basis of a Special Agreement 162
2.5. Jurisdiction on the Basis of Treaties 164

2.5.1. General Questions 164
*2.5.2. Transfer of Competences of the Permanent Court of International Justice
2.5.3. Specific Treaties 165

2.6. Agreement in Regard to Jurisdiction in the Course of the Proceedings
2.7. Concurring Jurisdictions

3. THE PROCEDURE OF THE INTERNATIONAL COURT OF JUSTICE 171

*3.1. General Questions
3.2. Procedure before a Chamber Dealing with a Particular Case (Article 26, Paragraph 2, of the Statute) 171
3.3. Judges ad hoc 189
*3.4. The Submissions
3.5. Preliminary Objections 189
3.6. The Procedure in Default of Appearance 195
3.7. Evidence 199
3.8 Duty of the Court to Seek Further Classification 210
3.9. Relevant Facts 211
3.10. Provisional Measures 211

3.10.1. General Questions 211
*3.10.2. Questions of Procedure
3.10.3. Provisional Measures and Jurisdiction 216
3.10.4. Provisional Measures and Merits 217

3.11. Intervention

3.11.1. General Questions (Article 62 and 63 of the Statute) 220
3.11.2. Article 62, Prerequisites in General 225
3.11.3. Article 62, Jurisdictional Link 233
3.11.4. Procedural Rights of the Intervening State 236
*3.11.5. Article 63

*3.12. Counter-Claim
*3.13. Withdrawal of Suit
*3.14. Question of Costs

* Indicates sections without case excerpts

4. JUDGMENTS OF THE INTERNATIONAL COURT OF JUSTICE 237
4.1. General Questions 237
4.2. Res judicata 239
*4.3. Interpretation of Decisions
*4.4. Revision of Judgments

5. ADVISORY OPINIONS OF THE INTERNATIONAL COURT OF JUSTICE 241
5.1. General Questions
5.2. Request for Advisory Opinion 241
5.3. Jurisdictional Questions and Denial of the Request for Advisory Opinion 245
5.4. Procedure 245
5.5. Review of Decision of the United Nations Administrative Tribunal .. 246

Summary of the Decisions and Advisory Opinions 259
Frontier Dispute (Burkina Faso v. Mali) 260
Military and Paramilitary Activites in and against Nicaragua (Nicaragua v. United States of America) 264
Review of Judgment No. 333 of the United Nations Administrative Tribunal Advisory Opinion 274
Applicability of the Obligation to Arbitrate under Section 21 of the United Nations headquarters Agreement of 26 June 1947, Advisory Opinion 280
Border and Transborder Armed Actions (Nicaragua v. Honduras) 282
Elettronica Sicula S.p.A. (ELSI) case (United States of America v. Italy) ... 286
Case Concerning the Aerial Incident of 3 July 1988 (Islamic Republic of Iran v. United States of America) 289
Applicability of Article VI, Section 22, of the Convention on the Privileges and Immunities of the United Nations, Advisory Opinion 289
Land, Island and Maritime Frontier Dispute (El Salvador v. Honduras) 294
Case Concerning the Arbitral Award of 31 July 1989 (Guinea-Bissau v. Senegal) 295

The Judges of the International Court of Justice, 1986–1990 297

Judges ad hoc 298

General Index 299

* Indicates sections without case excerpts

ABBREVIATIONS

A.O.	=	Advisory Opinion
D.	=	Declaration
D.O.	=	Dissenting Opinion
J.	=	Judgment
J.S.O.	=	Joint Separate Opinion
O.	=	Order

1. THE FOUNDATIONS OF INTERNATIONAL LAW

1.1. Good Faith

Border and Transborder Armed Actions (Nicaragua/Honduras), Jurisdiction and Admissibility, Judgment, I.C.J. Reports 1988, p. 69

[p. 105] The Court has also to deal with the contention of Honduras that Nicaragua is precluded not only by Article IV of the Pact of Bogotá but also "by elementary considerations of good faith" from commencing any other procedure for pacific settlement until such time as the Contadora process has been concluded. The principle of good faith is, as the Court has observed, "one of the basic principles governing the creation and performance of legal obligations" (*Nuclear Tests, I.C.J. Reports 1974*, p. 268, para. 46; p. 473, para. 49); it is not in itself a source of obligation where none would otherwise exist.

Elettronica Sicula S.p.A. (ELSI) Judgment of 20 July 1989 I.C.J. Reports 1989, p. 15

[pp. 76-77] Arbitrariness is not so much something opposed to a rule of law, as something opposed to the rule of law. This idea was expressed by the Court in the Asylum case, when it spoke of "arbitrary action" being "substituted for the rule of law" (*Asylum, Judgment, I.C.J. Reports 1950*, p. 284). It is a wilful disregard of due process of law, an act which shocks, or at least surprises, a sense of juridical propriety. Nothing in the decision of the Prefect, or in the judgment of the Court of Appeal of Palermo, conveys any indication that the requisition order of the Mayor was to be regarded in that light.

The United States argument is not of course based solely on the findings of the Prefect or of the local courts. United States counsel felt able to describe the requisition generally as being an "unreasonable or capricious exercise of authority". Yet one must remember the situation in Palermo at the moment of the requisition, with the threatened sudden unemployment of some 800 workers at one factory. It cannot be said to have been unreasonable or merely capricious for the Mayor to seek to use the powers conferred on him by the law in an attempt to do something about a difficult and distressing situation. Moreover, if one looks at the requisition order itself, one finds an instrument which in its terms recites not only the reasons for its being made but also the provisions of the law on which it is based: one finds that, although later annulled by the Prefect because "the intended purpose of the requisition could not in practice be achieved by the order itself" (paragraph 125 above), it was nonetheless within the competence of the Mayor of Palermo, according to the very provisions of the law cited in it; one finds the Court of Appeal of Palermo, which did not differ from the conclusion that the requisition was *intra vires*, ruling that it was unlawful as falling into the recognized category of administrative law of acts of "*eccesso di potere*". Furthermore, here was an act belonging to a category of public acts from which appeal on juridical grounds was provided in law (and indeed in the event used, not without success). Thus, the Mayor's order was consciously made in the context of an operating system of law and of appropriate remedies of appeal, and treated as such by the superior administrative authority and the local courts. These are not at all the marks of an "arbitrary" act.

The Chamber does not, therefore, see in the requisition a measure which could reasonably be said to earn the qualification "arbitrary", as it is employed in Article I of the Supplementary Agreement. Accordingly, there was no violation of that Article.

[pp. 114-115 **D.O. Schwebel**] It has, it is believed, been shown in the foregoing section that the measure of requisition was unreasonable and capricious since, cumulatively:
- the legal bases on which the Mayor's order relied were justified only in theory;
- the order was incapable of achieving its purported purposes;
- the order did not achieve its purported purposes;
- the order, issued, as it specified, "also" because "the local press is taking a very great interest in the situation and... the press is being very critical toward the authorities and is accusing them of indifference to this serious civic problem", was in part designed to give an impression of the Mayor confronting the problem "in one way or another", rather than prescribing a measure which could have been responsive to the problem;
- the order accordingly was not simply unlawful but "a typical case of excess of power";
- a paramount purpose of the requisition was to prevent the liquidation of ELSI's assets by ELSI, a purpose pursued without regard to treaty obligations of contrary tenor (and the Treaty's obligations, Italy maintains, bound it not only externally but were self-executing internally);
- the Mayor transgressed the terms of his own order by failing to issue a decree for indemnification for the requisition and by failing to offer or pay that indemnification.

By its nature, what is unreasonable or capricious is subject in a given instance to a range of appreciation; these are terms which, while having a sense in customary international law, have no invariable, plain meaning but which are capable of application only in the particular context of the facts of a case. Given the facts of this case, it is concluded, for the reasons stated, that the order of requisition as motivated, issued and implemented was unreasonable and capricious and hence arbitrary.

Military and Paramilitary Activities
(Nicaragua/United States of America
Merits. J. 27.6.1986,
I.C.J. Reports 1986, p. 14

[p. 272 **D.O. Schwebel**] In contemporary international law, the State which first undertakes specified unprovoked, unlawful uses of force against another State - such as substantial involvement in the sending of armed bands onto its territory - is, prima facie, the aggressor. On examination, Nicaragua's status as the prima facie aggressor can only be definitively confirmed. Moreover, Nicaragua has compounded its delictual behaviour by pressing false testimony on the Court in a deliberate effort to conceal it. Accordingly, on both grounds, Nicaragua does not come before the Court with clean hands. Judgment in its favour is thus unwarranted, and would be unwarranted even if it should be concluded - as it should not be - that the responsive actions of the United States were unnecessary or disproportionate.

[pp. 392-394 **D.O. Schwebel**] Nicaragua has not come to Court with clean hands. On the contrary, as the aggressor, indirectly responsible - but ultimately responsible - for large numbers of deaths and widespread destruction in El Salvador apparently much exceeding that which Nicaragua has sustained, Nicaragua's hands are odiously unclean. Nicaragua has compounded its sins by misrepresenting them to the Court. Thus both on the grounds of its unlawful armed intervention in El Salvador, and its deliberately seeking to mislead the Court about the facts of that intervention through false testimony of its Ministers, Nicaragua's claims against the United States should fail.

As recalled in paragraph 240 of this opinion, the Permanent Court of International Justice applied a variation of the "clean hands" doctrine in the *Diversion of Water from the Meuse* case. The basis for its so doing was affirmed by Judge Anzilotti "in a famous statement which has never been objected to: 'The principle ... (*inadimplenti non est adimplendum*) is so just, so equitable, so universally recognized that it must be applied in international relations ...'"(Elisabeth Zoller, *Peacetime Unilateral Remedies: An Analysis of Countermeasures*, 1984, pp. 16-17). That principle was developed at length by Judge Hudson. As Judge Hudson observed in reciting maxims of equity which exercised "great influence in the creative period of the development of Anglo-American law", "Equality is equity", and "He who seeks equity must do equity". A court of equity "refuses relief to a plaintiff whose conduct in regard to the subject-matter of the litigation has been improper" (citing Halsbury's *Laws of England*, 2nd ed., 1934, p. 87). Judge Hudson noted that, "A very similar principle was received into Roman law ... The *exceptio non adimpleti contractus* ..." He shows that it is the basis of articles of the German Civil Code, and is indeed "a general principle" of law. Judge Hudson was of the view that Belgium could not be ordered to discontinue an activity while the Netherlands was left free to continue a like activity - an enjoinder which should have been found instructive for the current case. He held that, "The Court is asked to decree a kind of specific performance of a reciprocal obligation which the demandant is not performing. It must clearly refuse to do so." (*Loc. cit.*, pp. 77-78. And see the Court's holding, at p. 25.) Equally, in this case Nicaragua asks the Court to decree a kind of specific performance of a reciprocal obligation which it is not performing, and, equally, the Court clearly should have refused to do so.

The "clean hands" doctrine finds direct support not only in *the Diversion of Water from the Meuse* case but a measure of support in the holding of the Court in the *Mavrommatis Palestine Concessions* case, *P.C.I.J., Series A, No. 5*, page 50, where the Court held that: "M. Mavrommatis was bound to perform the acts which he actually did perform *in order to preserve his contracts from lapsing as they would otherwise have done.*" (Emphasis supplied.) Still more fundamental support is found in Judge Anzilotti's conclusion in the *Legal Status of Eastern Greenland P.C.I.J., Series A/B, No. 53*, page 95, that "an unlawful act cannot serve as the basis of an action at law". In their dissenting opinions to the Judgment in *United States Diplomatic and Consular Staff in Tehran, I.C.J. Reports 1980*, pages 53-55, 62-63, Judges Morozov and Tarazi invoked a like principle. (The Court also gave the doctrine a degree of analogous support in the *Factory at Chorzów case, P.C.I.J., Series A, No. 9*, p. 31, when it held that "one party cannot avail himself of the fact that the other has not fulfilled some obligation ... if the former party has, by some illegal act, prevented the latter from fulfilling the obligation in question ...") The principle that an unlawful action cannot serve as the basis of an action at law, according to Dr. Cheng, "is generally upheld by international tribunals" (Bin Cheng, *General Princples of Law as Applied by International Courts and Tribunals,* 1958, p. 155). Cheng cites, among other cases, the Clark Claim, 1862, where the American Commissioner disallowed the claim on behalf of an American citizen in asking: "Can he be allowed, so far as the United States are concerned, to profit by his own wrong? ... A party who asks for redress must present himself with clean hands ..." (John Bassett Moore, *History and Digest of the International Arbitrations to which the United States has been a Party*, 1898, Vol. III, at pp. 2738, 2739). Again, in the *Pelletier* case, 1885, the United States Secretary of State "peremptorily and immediately" dropped pursuit of a claim of one Pelletier against Haiti - though it had been sustained in an arbitral award - on the ground of Pelletier's wrongdoing:

"*Ex turpi causa non oritur*: by innumerable rulings under Roman common law, as held by nations holding Latin traditions, and under the common law as held in England and the United States, has this principle been applied." (*Foreign Relations of the United States*, 1887, p. 607.)

The Secretary of State further quoted Lord Mansfield as holding that: "The principle of public policy is this: *ex dolo malo non oritur actio.*" (At p. 607.)

More recently, Sir Gerald Fitzmaurice - then the Legal Adviser of the Foreign Office, shortly to become a judge of this Court - recorded the application in the international sphere of the common law maxims: "He who seeks equity must do equity" and "He who comes to equity for relief must come with clean hands", and concluded:

"Thus a State which is guilty of illegal conduct may be deprived of the necessary *locus standi in judicio* for complaining of corresponding illegalities on the part of other States, especially if these were consequential on or were embarked upon in order to counter its own illegality - in short were provoked by it." ("The General Principles of International Law", 92 *Collected Courses*, Academy of International Law, The Hague, (1957-II), p. 119. For further recent support of the authority of the Court to apply a "clean hands" doctrine, see Oscar Schachter, "International Law in the Hostage Crisis", *American Hostages in Iran*, 1985, p. 344.)

1.2. Equity

Frontier Dispute, Judgment
(Burkina Faso/Republic of Mali)
I.C.J. Reports 1986, p. 554

[pp. 567-568] It is clear that the Chamber cannot decide *ex aequo et bono* in this case. Since the Parties have not entrusted it with the task of carrying out an adjustment of their respective interests, it must also dismiss any possibility of resorting to equity *contra legem*. Nor will the Chamber apply equity *praeter legem*. On the other hand, it will have regard to equity *infra legem*, that is, that form of equity which constitutes a method of interpretation of the law in force, and is one of its attributes. As the Court has observed: "It is not a matter of finding simply an equitable solution, but an equitable solution derived from the applicable law." (*Fisheries Jurisdiction, I.C.J. Reports 1974*, p. 33, para. 78; p. 202, para. 69.) How in practice the Chamber will approach recourse to this kind of equity in the present case will emerge from its application throughout this Judgment of the principles and rules which it finds to be applicable.

[pp. 632-633] It should again be pointed out that the Chamber's task in this case is to indicate the line of the frontier inherited by both States from the colonizers on their accession to independence. For the reasons explained above, this task amounts to ascertaining and defining the lines which formed the administrative boundaries of the colony of Upper Volta on 31 December 1932. Admittedly, the Parties could have modified the frontier existing on the critical date by a subsequent agreement. If the competent authorities had endorsed the agreement of 15 January 1965, it would have been unnecessary for the purpose of the present case to ascertain whether that agreement was of a declaratory or modifying character in relation to the 1932 boundaries. But this did not happen, and the Chamber has received no mandate from the Parties to substitute its own free choice of an appropriate frontier for theirs. The Chamber must not lose sight either of the Court's function, which is to decide in accordance with international law such disputes as are submitted to it, nor of the fact that the Chamber was requested by the Parties in their Special Agreement not to give indications to guide them in determining their common frontier, but to draw a line, and a precise line.

As it has explained, the Chamber can resort to that equity *infra legem*, which both Parties have recognized as being applicable in this case (see paragraph 27 above). In this respect the guiding concept is simply that "Equity as a legal concept is a direct emanation of the idea of justice" (*Continental Shelf (Tunisia/Libyan Arab Jamahiriya), I.C.J. Reports 1982*, p. 60, para. 71). The Chamber would however stress more generally that to resort to the concept of equity in order to modify an established frontier would be quite unjustified. Especially in the African context, the obvious deficiencies of many frontiers inherited from colonization, from the ethnic, geographical or administrative standpoint, cannot support an assertion that the modification of these frontiers is necessary or justifiable on the ground of considerations of equity. These frontiers, however unsatisfactory they may be, possess the authority of the uti possidetis and are thus fully in conformity with contemporary international law. Apart from the case of a decision ex aequo et bono reached with the assent of the Parties, "it is not a matter of finding simply an equitable solution, but an equitable solution derived from the applicable law" (*Fisheries Jurisdiction, I.C.J. Reports 1974*, p. 33, para. 78). It is with a view to achieving a solution of this kind that the Chamber has to take account, not of the agreement of 15 January 1965, but of the circumstances in which that agreement was concluded.

1.3. Estoppel and Acquiescence

Land, Island and
Maritime Frontier Dispute
(El Salvador/Honduras)
Application to Intervene,
Judgment of 13 September 1990,
I.C.J. Reports 1990, p. 92

[pp. 118-119] Nicaragua has presented a particular argument whereby it would apparently be dispensed from producing evidence of the existence of the legal interests on which it relies, by reason of the assertions of the Parties. This argument has at times been denominated "equitable estoppel" and at times "recognition"; in its clearest form it was put forward at the hearings as follows :

"In the submission of the Government of Nicaragua the assertions of fact and law on the part of El Salvador and Honduras in the course of these proceedings constitute recognition of the existence of major legal interests pertaining to Nicaragua which form an inherent part of the parcel of legal questions placed in front of the Chamber by the Special Agreement."

So far as Nicaragua relies on estoppel, the Chamber will only say that it sees no evidence of some essential elements required by estoppel: a statement or representation made by one party to another and reliance upon it by that other party to his detriment or to the advantage of the party making it. The indications to be found in the pleadings of the views of the Parties as to the existence or nature of Nicaraguan interests within or without the Gulf, no doubt amount to some evidence which the Chamber can take into account. None of these however amounts to an admission, recognition or statement that, in the view of the Party concerned, there are interests of Nicaragua such that they may be affected by the decision of the Chamber in the case.

2. SOURCES OF INTERNATIONAL LAW

2.1. General Questions

2.1.4. Ius cogens

Military and Paramilitary Activities
(Nicaragua/United States of America)
Merits. J. 27.6.1986
I.C.J. Reports 1986, p. 14

[pp. 100-101] As regards the United States in particular, the weight oof an expression of *opinio juris* can similarly be attached to its support of the resolution of the Sixth International Conference of American States condemning aggression (18 February 1928) and ratification of the Montevideo Convention on Rights and Duties of States (26 December 1933), Article 11 of which imposes the obligation not to recognize territorial acquisitions or special advantages which have been obtained by force. Also significant is United States acceptance of the principle of the prohibition of the use of force which is contained in the declaration on principles governing the mutual relations of State participating in the Conference on Security and Co-operation in Europe (Helsinki, 1 August 1975), whereby the participating States undertake to "refrain in their mutual relations, *as well as in their international relations in general*," (emphasis added) from the threat or use of force. Acceptance of a text in these terms confirms the existence of an *opinio juris* of the participating States prohibiting the use of force in international relations.

A further confirmation of the validity as customary international law of the principle of the prohibition of the use of force expressed in Article 2, paragraph 4, of the Charter of the United Nations may be found in the fact that it is frequently referred to in statements by State representatives as being not only a principle of customary international law but also a fundamental or cardinal principle of such law. The International Law Commission, in the course of its work on the codification of the law of treaties, expressed the view that "the law of the Charter concerning the prohibition of the use of force in itself constitutes a conspicuous example of a rule in international law having the character of *jus cogens*" (paragraph (1) of the commentary of the Commission to Article 50 of its draft Articles on the Law of Treaties, *ILC Yearbook*, 1966-II, p. 247). Nicaragua in its Memorial on the Merits submitted in the present case states that the principle prohibiting the use of force embodied in Article 2, paragraph 4, of the Charter of the United Nations "has come to be recognized as *jus cogens*". The United States, in its Counter-Memorial on the questions of jurisdiction and admissibility, found it material to quote the views of scholars that this principle is a "universal norm", a "universal international law", a "universally recognized principle of international law", and a "principle of *jus cogens*".

[pp. 152-153 **S.O. Singh**] In this context the Court's approach has indeed been cautious. For example, the requirement "to report" under Article 51 of the Charter is not insisted upon as an essential condition of the concept of self-defence but mentioned by the Court as an indication of the attitude of the State which is invoking the right of self-defence but certainly not closely following the treaty. The Court's observations in paragraph 200 of the Judgment are indeed to the point in this connection. In the present case therefore the Court's approach has been a logical one, inasmuch as it has decided not to apply the multilateral treaties to the resolution of this dispute but to confine its observations to the basis of customary international law, ruling that it had jurisdiction to apply customary law for the settlement of the case before the Court. It is felt that this is not only the correct approach in the circumstances of this case for many reasons, but also that it represents the contribution of the Court in emphasizing that the principle of non-use of force belongs to the realm of *jus cogens*, and is the very cornerstone of the human effort to promote peace in a world torn by strife. This aspect does need to be emphasized.

[pp. 199-200 **S.O. Sette-Camara**] I fully concur with the rest of the Judgment, as I firmly believe that the non-use of force as well as non-intervention - the latter as a corollary of equality of States and self-determination - are not only cardinal principles of customary international law but could in addition be recognized as peremptory rules of customary international law which impose obligations on all States.

With regard to the non-use of force, the International Law Commission in its commentaries on the final articles on the Law of Treaties said:

"the law of the Charter concerning the prohibition of the use of force in itself constitutes a conspicuous example of a rule in international law having the character of *jus cogens*" (*International Law Commission Yearbook*, 1966, Vol. II, p. 247).

As far as non-intervention is concerned, in spite of the uncertainties which still prevail in the matter of identifying norms of *jus cogens*, I submit that the prohibition of intervention would certainly qualify as such, if the test of Article 53 of the Vienna Convention on the Law of Treaties is applied. A treaty containing provisions by which States agree to intervene, directly or indirectly, in the internal or external affairs of any other State would certainly fall within the purview of Article 53, and should consequently be considered void as conflicting with a peremptory norm of general international law.

2.1.5. Relation between the Sources of International Law

Military and Paramilitary Activities
(Nicaragua/United States of America)
Merits. J. 27.6.1986
I.C.J. Reports 1986, p. 14

[pp. 93-94] The Court would observe that, according to the United States argument, it should refrain from applying the rules of customary international law because they have been "subsumed" and "supervened" by those of international treaty law, and especially those of the United Nations Charter. Thus the United States apparently takes the view that the existence of principles in the United Nations Charter precludes the possibility that similar rules might exist independently in customary international law, either because existing customary rules had been incorporated into the Charter, or because the Charter influenced the later adoption of customary rules with a corresponding content.

The Court does not consider that, in the areas of law relevant to the present dispute, it can be claimed that all the customary rules which may be invoked have a content exactly identical to that of the rules contained in the treaties which cannot be applied by virtue of the United States reservation. On a number of points, the areas governed by the two sources of law do not exactly overlap, and the substantive rules in which they are framed are not identical in content. But in addition, even if a treaty norm and a customary norm relevant to the present dispute were to have exactly the same content, this would not be a reason for the Court to take the view that the operation of the treaty process must necessarily deprive the customary norm of its separate applicability. Nor can the multilateral treaty reservation be interpreted as meaning that, once applicable to a given dispute, it would exclude the application of any rule of customary international law the content of which was the same as, or analogous to, that of the treaty-law rule which had caused the reservation to become effective.

[pp. 94-96] As regards the suggestion that the areas covered by the two sources of law are identical, the Court observes that the United Nations Charter, the convention to which most of the United States argument is directed, by no means covers the whole area of the regulation of the use of force in international relations. On one essential point, this treaty itself refers to pre-existing customary international law; this reference to customary law is contained in the actual text of Article 5l, which mentions the "inherent right" (in the French text the "droit naturel") of individual or collective self-defence, which "nothing in the present Charter shall impair" and which applies in the event of an armed attack. The Court therefore finds that Article 51 of the Charter is only meaningful on the basis that there is a "natural" or "inherent" right of self-defence, and it is hard to see how this can be other than of a customary nature, even if its present content has been confirmed and influenced by the Charter. Moreover the Charter, having itself recognized the existence of this right, does not go on to regulate directly all aspects of its content. For example, it does not contain any specific rule whereby self-defence would warrant only measures which are proportional to the armed attack and necessary to respond to it, a rule well established in customary international law. Moreover, a definition of the "armed attack" which, if found to exist, authorizes the exercise of the "inherent right" of self-defence, is not provided in the Charter, and is not part of treaty law. It cannot therefore be held that Article 51 is a provision which "subsumes and supervenes" customary international law. It rather demonstrates that in the field in question, the importance of which for the present dispute need hardly be stressed, customary international law continues to exist alongside treaty law. The areas governed by the two sources of law thus do not overlap exactly, and the rules do not have the same content. This could also be demonstrated for other subjects, in particular for the principle of non-intervention.

But as observed above (paragraph 175), even if the customary norm and the treaty norm were to have exactly the same content, this would not be a reason for the Court to hold that the incorporation of the customary norm into treaty-law must deprive the customary norm of its applicability as distinct from that of the treaty norm. The existence of identical rules in international treaty law and customary law has been clearly recognized by the Court in the *North Sea Continental Shelf* cases. To a large extent, those cases turned on the question whether a rule enshrined in a treaty also existed as a customary rule, either because the treaty had merely codified the custom, or caused it to "crystallize", or because it had influenced its subsequent adoption. The Court found that this identity of content in treaty law and in customary international law did not exist in the case of the rule invoked, which appeared in one article of the treaty, but did not suggest that such identity was debarred as a matter of principle: on the contrary, it considered it to be clear that certain other articles of the treaty in question "were ... regarded as reflecting, or as crystallizing, received or at least emergent rules of customary international law" (*I.C.J. Reports 1969*, p. 39. para. 63). More generally, there are no grounds for holding that when customary international law is comprised of rules identical to those of treaty law, the latter "supervenes" the former, so that the customary international law has no further existence of its own.

There are a number of reasons for considering that, even if two norms belonging to two sources of international law appear identical in content, and even if the States in question are bound by these rules both on the level of treaty-law and on that of customary international law, these norms retain a separate existence. This is so from the standpoint of their applicability. In a legal dispute affecting two States, one of them may argue that the applicability of a treaty rule to its own conduct depends on the other State's conduct in respect of the application of other rules, on other subjects, also included in the same treaty. For example, if a State exercises its right to terminate or suspend the operation of a treaty on the ground of the violation by the other party of a "provision essential to the accomplishment of the object or purpose of the treaty" (in the words of Art. 60, para. 3 (b), of the Vienna Convention on the Law of Treaties), it is exempted, vis-à-vis the other State, from a rule of treaty-law because of the breach by that other State of a different rule of treaty-law. But if the two rules in question also exist as rules of customary international law, the failure of the one State to apply the one rule does not justify the other State in declining to apply the other rule. Rules which are identical in treaty law and in customary international law are also distinguishable by reference to the methods of interpretation and application. A State may accept a rule contained in a treaty not simply because it favours the application of the rule itself, but also because the treaty establishes what that State regards as desirable institutions or mechanisms to ensure implementation of the rule. Thus, if that rule parallels a rule of customary international law, two rules of the same content are subject to separate treatment as regards the organs competent to verify their implementation, depending on whether they are customary rules or treaty rules. The present dispute illustrates this point.

It will therefore be clear that customary international law continues to exist and to apply, separately from international treaty law, even where the two categories of law have an identical content. Consequently, in ascertaining the content of the customary international law applicable to the present dispute, the Court must satisfy itself that the Parties are bound by the customary rules in question; but the Court is in no way bound to uphold these rules only in so far as they differ from the treaty rules which it is prevented by the United States reservation from applying in the present dispute.

[pp. 96-97] The question raised by this argument is whether the provisions of the multilateral treaties in question, particularly the United Nations Charter, diverge from the relevant rules of customary international law to such an extent that a judgment of the Court as to the rights and obligations of the parties under customary law, disregarding the content of the multilateral treaties binding on the parties, would be a wholly academic exercise, and not "susceptible of any compliance or execution whatever" (*Northern Cameroons, I.C.J. Reports* 1963, p. 37). The Court does not consider that this is the case. As already noted, on the question of the use of force, the United States itself argues for a complete identity of the relevant rules of customary international law with the provisions of the Charter. The Court has not accepted this extreme contention, having found that on a number of points the areas governed by the two sources of law do not exactly overlap, and the substantive rules in which they are framed are not identical in content (paragraph 174 above). However, so far from having constituted a marked departure from a customary international law which still exists unmodified, the Charter gave expression in this field to principles already present in customary international law, and that law has in the subsequent four decades developed under the influence of the Charter, to such an extent that a number of rules contained in the Charter have acquired a status independent of it. The essential consideration is that both the Charter and the customary international law flow from a common fundamental principle outlawing the use of force in international relations. The differences which may exist between the specific content of each are not, in the Court's view, such as to cause a judgment confined to the field of customary international law to be ineffective or inappropriate, or a judgment not susceptible of compliance or execution.

[p. 207 **S.O. Ni**] However, it is certain that when principles of customary international law are incorporated into a multilateral treaty like the United Nations Charter, these principles of customary international law do not thereby become extinct. The same principles continue to be operative and binding on States, sometimes alongside or in conjunction with treaty law, in their international relations with one another. Article 38, paragraph 1, of the Statute enumerates, as applicable by the Court, the various sources of international law which, in the course of application, usually support, rather than preclude, each other. But it would be inconceivable that application of one should exclude that of any other.

[p. 303 **D.O. Schwebel**] The argument that the principles if not the provisions of the United Nations Charter governing the use of force in international relations have been incorporated into the body of customary international law is widely and authoritatively accepted, despite the fact that the practice of States manifests such irregular support for the principles of law which the Charter proclaims. Indeed, it could even be argued that the practice, in contrast to the preachment, of States indicates that the restrictions on the use of force in international relations found in the Charter are not part of customary international law.

[p. 305 **D.O. Schwebel**] ... the Court is bound to give substantive effect to the multilateral treaty reservation. It is not free to avoid its application by an argument which, if technically defensible, in real terms would vitiate a limitation which the United States has imposed upon the jurisdiction of the Court. Accordingly, while recognizing that there is room for the contrary conclusion which the Court has reached, I conclude that the generally accepted essential, even if incomplete, identity of Charter principles and principles of customary international law on the use of force in international relations, rather than authorizing the Court to apply those customary principles to the central issues of this case, precludes the Court from doing so by reason of the limitations imposed upon the Court's jurisdiction by the multilateral treaty reservation.

[p. 531 **D.O. Jennings**] If, then, the Charter was not a codification of existing custom about force and self-defence, the question must then be asked whether a general customary law, replicating the Charter provisions, has developed as a result of the influence of the Charter provisions, coupled presumably with subsequent and consonant States' practice; so that it might be said that these Charter provisions:

"generated a rule which, while only conventional or contractual in its origin, has since passed into the general corpus of international law, and is now accepted as such by the *opinio juris*, so as to have become binding even for countries which have never, and do not, become parties to the Convention" (*I.C.J. Reports 1969*, p. 41, para. 71).

But there are obvious difficulties about extracting even a scintilla of relevant "practice" on these matters from the behaviour of those few States which are not parties to the Charter; and the behaviour of all the rest, and the *opinio juris* which it might otherwise evidence, is surely explained by their being bound by the Charter itself [1].

There is, however, a further problem: the widely recognized special status of the Charter itself. This is evident from paragraph 6 of Article 2, that:

"The Organization shall ensure that States which are not Members of the United Nations act in accordance with these Principles so far as may be necessary for the maintenance of international peace and security."

1 For an assessment of this important question, especially in relation to the Declaration of Principles of Friendly Relations, see Professor Arangio-Ruiz, 137 Collected Courses, The Hague (1972-III), Chap. IV.

This contemplates obligations for non-members arising immediately upon the coming into operation of the Charter, which obligations could at that time only be derived, like those for Members, directly from the Charter itself. Even "instant" custom, if there be such a thing, can hardly be simultaneous with the instrument from which it develops. There is, therefore, no room and no need for the very artificial postulate of a customary law paralleling these Charter provisions.

[pp. 532-533 **D.O. Jennings**] This use of treaty provisions as "evidence" of custom, takes the form of an interpretation of the treaty text. Yet the Court itself acknowledges that treaty-law and customary law can be distinguished precisely because the canons of interpretation are different (para. 178). To indulge the treaty interpretation process, in order to determine the content of a posited customary rule, must raise a suspicion that it is in reality the treaty itself that is being applied under another name. Of course this way of going about things may be justified where the treaty text was, from the beginning, designed to be a codification of custom; or where the treaty is itself the origin of a customary law rule. But, as we have already seen, this could certainly not be said of Article 2, paragraph 4, or even Article 51, of the United Nations Charter; nor indeed of most of the other relevant multilateral treaty provisions.

The reader cannot but put to himself the question whether the Judgment would, in its main substance, have been noticeably different in its content and argument, had the application of the multilateral treaty reservation been rejected.

There is no need to pursue further the relationship of the United Nations Charter and customary law; for even if a different view of this question could be adopted, there remains, quite independently, a most cogent objection to any attempt to decide the issues of force and self-defence without the Charter of the United Nations or other relevant treaties. Although the multilateral treaty reservation qualifies the jurisdiction of this Court, it does not qualify the substantive law governing the behaviour of the Parties at the material times. Article 38 of the Court's own Statute requires it first to apply "international conventions, general" as well as "particular" ones, "establishing rules expressly recognized by the contesting States"; and the relevant provisions of the Charter - and indeed also of the Charter of the Organization of American States, and of the Rio Treaty - have at all material times been principal elements of the applicable law governing the conduct, rights and obligations of the Parties. It seems, therefore, eccentric, if not perverse, to attempt to determine the central issues of the present case, after having first abstracted these principal elements of the law applicable to the case, and which still obligate both the Parties.

Elettronica Sicula S.p.A. (ELSI)
Judgment of 20 July 1989
I.C.J. Reports 1989, p. 15

[p. 42] The United States questioned whether the rule of the exhaustion of local remedies could apply at all to a case brought under Article XXVI of the FCN Treaty. That Article, it was pointed out, is categorical in its terms, and unqualified by any reference to the local remedies rule; and it seemed right, therefore, to conclude that the parties to the FCN Treaty, had they intended the jurisdiction conferred upon the Court to be qualified by the local remedies rule in cases of diplomatic protection, would have used exess words to that effect; as was done in an Economic Co-operation Agreement between Italy and the United States of America also concluded in 1948. The Chamber has no doubt that the parties to a treaty can therein either agree that the local remedies rule shall not apply to claims based on alleged breaches of that treaty; or confirm that it shall apply. Yet the Chamber finds itself unable to accept that an important principle of customary international law should be held to have been tacitly dispensed with, in the absence of any words making clear an intention to do so. This part of the United States response to the Italian objection must therefore be rejected.

[p. 86 **S.O. Oda**] That general principle of law concerning the rights or status of shareholders, which underlies not only Italian company law but also the company law of some other civil law countries, may not be altered by any treaty aimed at the protection of investments unless that treaty contains some express provision to that end. A question which should therefore be asked is whether Italy and the United States agreed, by means of the 1948 FCN Treaty or the 1951 Supplementary Agreement, to modify such a general principle of law or to grant any additional rights to foreign shareholders. It is difficult to see how an affirmative answer can be given to this question.

2.2. Customary International Law

2.2.1. Formation of Customary International Law

Military and Paramilitary Activities
(Nicaragua/United States of America)
Merits. J. 27.6.1986
I.C.J. Reports 1986, p. 14

[pp. 97-98] In view of this conclusion, the Court has next to consider what are the rules of customary international law applicable to the present dispute. For this purpose, it has to direct its attention to the practice and *opinio juris* of States; as the Court recently observed,

"It is of course axiomatic that the material of customary international law is to be looked for primarily in the actual practice and *opinio juris* of States, even though multilateral conventions may have an important role to play in recording and defining rules deriving from custom, or indeed in developing them." (*Continental Shelf (Libyan Arab Jamahiriya/Malta), I.C.J. Reports 1985*, pp. 29-30, para. 27.)

In this respect the Court must not lose sight of the Charter of the United Nations and that of the Organization of American States, notwithstanding the operation of the multilateral treaty reservation. Although the Court has no jurisdiction to determine whether the conduct of the United States constitutes a breach of those conventions, it can and must take them into account in ascertaining the content of the customary international law which the United States is also alleged to have infringed.

The Court notes that there is in fact evidence, to be examined below, of a considerable degree of agreement between the Parties as to the content of the customary international law relating to the non-use of force and non-intervention. This concurrence of their views does not however dispense the Court from having itself to ascertain what rules of customary international law are applicable. The mere fact that States declare their recognition of certain rules is not sufficient for the Court to consider these as being part of customary international law, and as applicable as such to those States. Bound as it is by Article 38 of its Statute to apply, *inter alia*, international custom "as evidence of a general practice accepted as law", the Court may not disregard the essential role played by general practice. Where two States agree to incorporate a particular rule in a treaty, their agreement suffices to make that rule a legal one, binding upon them; but in the field of customary international law, the shared view of the Parties as to the content of what they regard as the rule is not enough. The Court must satisfy itself that the existence of the rule in the *opinio juris* of States is confirmed by practice ...

It is not to be expected that in the practice of States the application of the rules in question should have been perfect, in the sense that States should have refrained, with complete consistency, from the use of force or from intervention in each other's internal affairs. The Court does not consider that, for a rule to be established as customary, the corresponding practice must be in absolutely rigorous conformity with the rule. In order to deduce the existence of customary rules, the Court deems it sufficient that the conduct of States should, in general, be consistent with such rules, and that instances of State conduct inconsistent with a given rule should generally have been treated as breaches of that rule, not as indications of the recognition of a new rule. If a State acts in a way prima facie incompatible with a recognized rule, but defends its conduct by appealing to exceptions or justifications contained within the rule itself, then whether or not the State's conduct is in fact justifiable on that basis, the significance of that attitude is to confirm rather than to weaken the rule.

[pp. 99-101] The Court thus finds that both Parties take the view that the principles as to the use of force incorporated in the United Nations Charter correspond, in essentials, to those found in customary international law. The Parties thus both take the view that the fundamental principle in this area is expressed in the terms employed in Article 2, paragraph 4, of the United Nations Charter. They therefore accept a treaty-law obligation to refrain in their international relations from the threat or use of force against the territorial integrity or political independence of any State, or in any other manner inconsistent with the purposes of the United Nations. The Court has however to be satisfied that there exists in customary international law an *opinio juris* as to the binding character of such abstention. This *opinio juris* may, though with all due caution, be deduced from, *inter alia*, the attitude of the Parties and the attitude of States towards certain General Assembly resolutions, and particularly resolution 2625 (XXV) entitled "Declaration on Principles of International Law concerning Friendly Relations and Co-operation among States in accordance with the Charter of the United Nations". The effect of consent to the text of such resolutions cannot be understood as merely that of a "reiteration or elucidation" of the treaty commitment undertaken in the Charter. On the contrary, it may be understood as an acceptance of the validity of the rule or set of rules declared by the resolution by themselves. The principle of non-use of force, for example, may thus be regarded as a principle of customary international law, not as such conditioned by provisions relating to collective security, or to the facilities or armed contingents to be provided under Article 43 of the Charter. It would therefore seem apparent that the attitude referred to expresses an *opinio juris* respecting such rule (or set of rules), to be thenceforth treated separately from the provisions, especially those of an institutional kind, to which it is subject on the treaty-law plane of the Charter.

As regards the United States in particular, the weight of an expression of *opinio juris* can similarly be attached to its support of the resolution of the Sixth International Conference of American States condemning aggression (18 February 1928) and ratification of the Montevideo Convention on Rights and Duties of States (26 December 1933), Article 11 of which imposes the obligation not to recognize territorial acquisitions or special advantages which have been obtained by force. Also significant is United States acceptance of the principle of the prohibition of the use of force which is contained in the declaration on principles governing the mutual relations of States participating in the Conference on Security and Co-operation in Europe (Helsinki, 1 August 1975), whereby the participating States undertake to "refrain in their mutual relations, *as well as in their international relations in general*," (emphasis added) from the threat or use of force. Acceptance of a text in these terms confirms the existence of an *opinio juris* of the participating States prohibiting the use of force in international relations.

A further confirmation of the validity as customary international law of the principle of the prohibition of the use of force expressed in Article 2, paragraph 4, of the Charter of the United Nations may be found in the fact that it is frequently referred to in statements by State representatives as being not only a principle of customary international law but also a fundamental or cardinal principle of such law. The International Law Commission, in the course of its work on the codification of the law of treaties, expressed the view that "the law of the Charter concerning the prohibition of the use of force in itself constitutes a conspicuous example of a rule in international law having the character of *jus cogens*" (paragraph (1) of the commentary of the Commission to Article 50 of its draft Articles on the Law of Treaties, *ILC Yearbook*, 1966-II, p. 247). Nicaragua in its Memorial on the Merits submitted in the present case states that the principle prohibiting the use of force embodied in Article 2, paragraph 4, of the Charter of the United Nations "has come to be recognized as *jus cogens*". The United States, in its Counter-Memorial on the questions of jurisdiction and admissibility, found it material to quote the views of scholars that this principle is a "universal norm", a "universal international law", a "universally recognized principle of international law", and a "principle of *jus cogens*".

As regards certain particular aspects of the principle in question, it will be necessary to distinguish the most grave forms of the use of force (those constituting an armed attack) from other less grave forms. In determining the legal rule which applies to these latter forms, the Court can again draw on the formulations contained in the Declaration on Principles of International Law concerning Friendly Relations and Co-operation among States in accordance with the Charter of the United Nations (General Assembly resolution 2625 (XXV), referred to above). As already observed, the adoption by States of this text affords an indication of their *opinio juris* as to customary international law on the question. Alongside certain descriptions which may refer to aggression, this text includes others which refer only to less grave forms of the use of force.

[pp. 106-109] The principle of non-intervention involves the right of every sovereign State to conduct its affairs without outside interference; though examples of trespass against this principle are not infrequent, the Court considers that it is part and parcel of customary international law. As the Court has observed: "Between independent States, respect for territorial sovereignty is an essential foundation of international relations" (*I.C.J. Reports 1949*, p. 35), and international law requires political integrity also to be respected. Expressions of an *opinio juris* regarding the existence of the principle of non-intervention in customary international law are numerous and not difficult to find. Of course, statements whereby States avow their recognition of the principles of international law set forth in the United Nations Charter cannot strictly be interpreted as applying to the principle of non-intervention by States in the internal and external affairs of other States, since this principle is not, as such, spelt out in the Charter. But it was never intended that the Charter should embody written confirmation of every essential principle of international law in force. The existence in the *opinio juris* of States of the principle of non-intervention is backed by established and substantial practice. It has moreover been presented as a corollary of the principle of the sovereign equality of States. A particular instance of this is General Assembly resolution 2625 (XXV), the Declaration on the Principles of International Law concerning Friendly Relations and Co-operation among States. In the *Corfu Channel* case, when a State claimed a right of intervention in order to secure evidence in the territory of another State for submission to an international tribunal (*I.C.J. Reports 1949*, p. 34), the Court observed that:

"the alleged right of intervention as the manifestation of a policy of force, such as has, in the past, given rise to most serious abuses and such as cannot, whatever be the present defects in international organization, find a place in international law. Intervention is perhaps still less admissible in the particular form it would take here; for, from the nature of things, it would be reserved for the most powerful States, and might easily lead to perverting the administration of international justice itself." (*I.C.J. Reports 1949*, p. 35.)

The principle has since been reflected in numerous declarations adopted by international organizations and conferences in which the United States and Nicaragua have participated, e.g., General Assembly resolution 2131 (XX), the Declaration on the Inadmissibility of Intervention in the Domestic Affairs of States and the Protection of their Independence and Sovereignty. It is true that the United States, while it voted in favour of General Assembly resolution 2131 (XX), also declared at the time of its adoption in the First Committee that it considered the declaration in that resolution to be "only a statement of political intention and not a formulation of law" (*Official Records of the General Assembly, Twentieth Session*, First Committee, A/C.1/SR. 1423, p. 436). However, the essentials of resolution 2131 (XX) are repeated in the Declaration approved by resolution 2625 (XXV), which set out principles which the General Assembly declared to the "basic principles" of international law, and on the adoption of which no analogous statement was made by the United States representative.

As regards inter-American relations, attention may be drawn to, for example, the United States reservation to the Montevideo Convention on Rights and Duties of States (26 December 1933), declaring the opposition of the United States Government to "interference with the freedom, the sovereignty or other internal affairs, or processes of the Governments of other nations"; or the ratification by the United States of the Additional Protocol relative to Non-Intervention (23 December 1936). Among more recent texts, mention may be made of resolutions AG/RES.78 and AG/RES. 128 of the General Assembly of the Organization of American States. In a different context, the

United States expressly accepted the principles set forth in the declaration, to which reference has already been made, appearing in the Final Act of the Conference on Security and Co-operation in Europe (Helsinki, 1 August 1975), including an elaborate statement of the principle of non-intervention; while these principles were presented as applying to the mutual relations among the participating States, it can be inferred that the text testifies to the existence, and the acceptance by the United States, of a customary principle which has universal application.

Notwithstanding the multiplicity of declarations by States accepting the principle of non-intervention, there remain two questions: first, what is the exact content of the principle so accepted, and secondly, is the practice sufficiently in conformity with it for this to be a rule of customary international law? As regards the first problem - that of the content of the principle of non-intervention - the Court will define only those aspects of the principle which appear to be relevant to the resolution of the dispute. In this respect it notes that, in view of the generally accepted formulations, the principle forbids all States or groups of States to intervene directly or indirectly in internal or external affairs of other States. A prohibited intervention must accordingly be one bearing on matters in which each State is permitted, by the principle of State sovereignty, to decide freely. One of these is the choice of a political, economic social, and cultural system, and the formulation of foreign policy. Intervention is wrongful when it uses methods of coercion in regard to such choices, which must remain free ones. The element of coercion, which defines, and indeed forms the very essence of, prohibited intervention, is particularly obvious in the case of an intervention which uses force, either in the direct form of military action, or in the indirect form of support for subversive or terrorist armed activities within another State. As noted above (paragraph 191), General Assembly resolution 2625 (XXV) equates assistance of this kind with the use of force by the assisting State when the acts committed in another State "involve a threat or use of force". These forms of action are therefore wrongful in the light of both the principle of non-use of force, and that of non-intervention. In view of the nature of Nicaragua's complaints against the United States, and those expressed by the United States in regard to Nicaragua's conduct towards El Salvador, it is primarily acts of intervention of this kind with which the Court is concerned in the present case.

However, before reaching a conclusion on the nature of prohibited intervention, the Court must be satisfied that State practice justifies it. There have been in recent years a number of instances of foreign intervention for the benefit of forces opposed to the government of another State. The Court is not here concerned with the process of decolonization; this question is not in issue in the present case. It has to consider whether there might be indications of a practice illustrative of belief in a kind of general right for States to intervene, directly or indirectly, with or without armed force, in support of an internal opposition in another State, whose cause appeared particularly worthy by reason of the political and moral values with which it was identified. For such a general right to come into existence would involve a fundamental modification of the customary law principle of non-intervention.

In considering the instances of the conduct above described, the Court has to emphasize that, as was observed in the *North Sea Continental Shelf* cases, for a new customary rule to be formed, not only must the acts concerned "amount to a settled practice", but they must be accompanied by the *opinio juris* sive necessitatis. Either the States taking such action or other States in a position to react to it, must have behaved so that their conduct is

"evidence of a belief that this practice is rendered obligatory by the existence of a rule of law requiring it. The need for such a belief, i.e., the existence of a subjective element, is implicit in the very notion of the *opinio juris sive necessitatis*." (*I.C.J. Reports 1969*, p. 44, para. 77.)

The Court has no jurisdiction to rule upon the conformity with international law of any conduct of States not parties to the present dispute, or of conduct of the Parties unconnected with the dispute nor has it authority to ascribe to States legal views which they do not themselves advance. The significance for the Court of cases of State conduct prima facie inconsistent with the principle of non-intervention lies in the nature of the ground offered as justification. Reliance by a State on a novel right or an unprecedented exception to the principle might, if shared in principle by other States, tend towards a modification of customary international law. In fact however the Court finds that States have not justified their conduct by reference to a new right of intervention or a new exception to the principle of its prohibition. The United States authorities have on some occasions clearly stated their grounds for intervening in the affairs of a foreign State for reasons connected with, for example, the domestic policies of that country, its ideology, the level of its armaments, or the direction of its foreign policy. But these were statements of international policy, and not an assertion of rules of existing international law.

[pp. 110-111] Furthermore, the Court has to recall that the United States itself is relying on the "inherent right of self-defence" (paragraph 126 above), but apparently does not claim that any such right exists as would, in respect of intervention, operate in the same way as the right of collective self-defence in respect of an armed attack. In the discharge of its duty under Article 53 of the Statute, the Court has nevertheless had to consider whether such a right might exist ; but in doing so it may take note of the absence of any such claim by the United States as an indication of *opinio juris*.

2.2.2. Evidence of Customary International Law

Military and Paramilitary Activities
(Nicaragua/United States of America)
Merits. J. 27.6.1986
I.C.J. Reports 1986, p. 14

[p. 97] In this respect the Court must not lose sight of the Charter of the United Nations and that of the Organization of American States, notwithstanding the operation of the multilateral treaty reservation. Although the Court has no jurisdiction to determine whether the conduct of the United States constitutes a breach of those conventions, it can and must take them into account in ascertaining the content of the customary international law which the United States is also alleged to have infringed.

[pp. 104-105] The question remains whether the lawfulness of the use of collective self-defence by the third State for the benefit of the attacked State also depends on a request addressed by that State to the third State. A provision of the Charter of the Organization of American States is here in point : and while the Court has no jurisdiction to consider that instrument as applicable to the dispute, it may examine it to ascertain what light it throws on the content of customary international law. The Court notes that the Organization of American States Charter includes, in Article 3 (f), the principle that: "an act of aggression against one American State is an act of aggression against all the other American States" and a provision in Article 27 that:

"Every act of aggression by a State against the territorial integrity or the inviolability of the territory or against the sovereignty or political independence of an American State shall be considered an act of aggression against the other American States."

Furthermore, by Article 3, paragraph 1, of the Inter-American Treaty of Reciprocal Assistance, signed at Rio de Janeiro on 2 September 1947, the High-Contracting Parties

"agree that an armed attack by any State against an American State shall be considered as an attack against all the American States and, consequently, each one of the said Contracting Parties undertakes to assist in meeting the attack in the exercise of the inherent right of individual or collective self-defence recognized by Article 51 of the charter of the United Nations";

and under paragraph 2 of that Article,
"On the request of the State or States directly attacked and until the decision of the Organ of Consultation of the Inter-American System, each one of the Contracting Parties may determine the immediate measures which it may individually take in ful

filment of the obligation contained in the preceding paragraph and in accordance with the principle of continental solidarity."

(The 1947 Rio Treaty was modified by the 1975 Protocol of San José, Costa Rica, but that Protocol is not yet in force.)

The Court observes that the Treaty of Rio de Janeiro provides that measures of collective self-defence taken by each State are decided "on the request of the State or States directly attacked". It is significant that this requirement of a request on the part of the attacked State appears in the treaty particularly devoted to these matters of mutual assistance; it is not found in the more general text (the Charter of the Organization of American States), but Article 28 of that Charter provides for the application of the measures and procedures laid down in "the special treaties on the subject".

At all events, the Court finds that in customary international law, whether of a general kind or that particular to the inter-American legal system, there is no rule permitting the exercise of collective self-defence in the absence of a request by the State which regards itself as the victim of an armed attack. The Court concludes that the requirement of a request by the State which is the victim of the alleged attack is additional to the requirement that such a State should have declared itself to have been attacked.

At this point, the Court may consider whether in customary international law there is any requirement corresponding to that found in the treaty law of the United Nations Charter, by which the State claiming to use the right of individual or collective self-defence must report to an international body, empowered to determine the conformity with international law of the measures which the State is seeking to justify on that basis. Thus Article 51 of the United Nations Charter requires that measures taken by States in exercise of this right of self-defence must be "immediately reported" to the Security Council. As the Court has observed above, a principle enshrined in a treaty, if reflected in customary international law, may well be so unencumbered with the conditions and modalities surrounding it in the treaty. Whatever influence the Charter may have had on customary international law in these matters, it is clear that in customary international law it is not a condition of the lawfulness of the use of force in self-defence that a procedure so closely dependent on the content of a treaty commitment and of the institutions established by it, should have been followed. On the other hand, if self-defence is advanced as a justification for measures which would otherwise be in breach both of the principle of customary international law and of that contained in the Charter, it is to be expected that the conditions of the Charter should be respected. Thus for the purpose of enquiry into the customary law position, the absence of a report may be one of the factors indicating whether the State in question was itself convinced that it was acting in self-defence.

[p. 305 D.O. Schwebel] Nor can it be persuasively argued that the sweeping provisions of the OAS Charter concerning intervention constitute customary and general international law. There is no universal treaty which has incorporated those provisions into the body of general international law. There is hardly sign of custom - of the practice of States - which suggests, still less demonstrates, a practice accepted as law which equates with the standards of non-intervention prescribed by the OAS Charter. State practice in the Americas - by States of Latin America as by others - does not begin to form a customary rule of non-intervention which is as categoric and comprehensive as are the provisions of the OAS Charter. Thus it may be contended that, in this case, the Court can apply such customary international law of non-intervention as there is, a customary international law which is much narrower than that which the OAS Charter enacts for the parties to it.

Military and Paramilitary Activities
(Nicaragua/United States of America)
Merits. J. 27.6.1986
I.C.J. Reports 1986, p. 14

[p. 133] The Court has also emphasized the importance to be attached, in other respects, to a text such as the Helsinki Final Act, or, on another level, to General Assembly resolution 2625 (XXV) which, as its name indicates, is a declaration on "Principles of International Law concerning Friendly Relations and Co-operation among States in accordance with the Charter of the United Nations". Texts like these, in relation to which the Court has pointed to the customary content of certain provisions such as the principles of the non-use of force and non-intervention, envisage the relations among States having different political, economic and social systems on the basis of coexistence among their various ideologies; the United States not only voiced no objection to their adoption, but took an active part in bringing it about.

2.5. Unilateral Acts

Military and Paramilitary Activities
(Nicaragua/United States of America)
Merits. J. 27.6.1986
I.C.J. Reports 1986, p. 14

[pp. 132-133] Moreover, the Junta made it plain in one of these documents that its invitation to the Organization of American States to supervise Nicaragua's political life should not be allowed to obscure the fact that it was the Nicaraguans themselves who were to decide upon and conduct the country's domestic policy. The resolution of 23 June 1979 also declares that the solution of their problems is a matter "exclusively" for the Nicaraguan people, while stating that that solution was to be based (in Spanish,

debería inspirarse) on certain foundations which were put forward merely as recommendations to the future government. This part of the resolution is a mere statement which does not comprise any formal offer which if accepted would constitute a promise in law, and hence a legal obligation. Nor can the Court take the view that Nicaragua actually undertook a commitment to organize free elections, and that this commitment was of a legal nature. The Nicaraguan Junta of National Reconstruction planned the holding of free elections as part of its political programme of government, following the recommendation of the XVIIth Meeting of Consultation of Foreign Ministers of the Organization of American States. This was an essentially political pledge, made not only to the Organization, but also to the people of Nicaragua, intended to be its first beneficiaries. But the Court cannot find an instrument with legal force, whether unilateral or synallagmatic, whereby Nicaragua has committed itself in respect of the principle or methods of holding elections. The Organization of American States Charter has already been mentioned, with its respect for the political independence of the member States; in the field of domestic policy, it goes no further than to list the social standards to the application of which the Members "agree to dedicate every effort", including:
"The incorporation and increasing participation of the marginal sectors of the population, in both rural and urban areas, in the economic, social, civic, cultural, and political life of the nation, in order to achieve the full integration of the national community, acceleration of the process of social mobility, and the consolidation of the democratic system." (Art. 43 (*f*).)

It is evident that provisions of this kind are far from being a commitment as to the use of particular political mechanisms.

Moreover, even supposing that such a political pledge had had the force of a legal commitment, it could not have justified the United States insisting on the fulfilment of a commitment made not directly towards the United States, but towards the Organization, the latter being alone empowered to monitor its implementation. The Court can see no legal basis for the "special responsibility regarding the implementation of the commitments made" by the Nicaraguan Government which the United States considers itself to have assumed in view of "its role in the installation of the current Government of Nicaragua" (see paragraph 170 above). Moreover, even supposing that the United States were entitled to act in lieu of the Organization, it could hardly make use for the purpose of methods which the Organization could not use itself; in particular, it could not be authorized to use force in that event. Of its nature, a commitment like this is one of a category which, if violated, cannot justify the use of force against a sovereign State.

Frontier Dispute, Judgment
(Burkina Faso/Republic of Mali)
I.C.J.Reports 1986, p. 554

[pp. 573-574] The statement of Mali's Head of State on 11 April 1975 [2] was not made during negotiations or talks between the two Parties; at most, it took the form of a unilateral act by the Government of Mali. Such declarations "concerning legal or factual situations" may indeed "have the effect of creating legal obligations" for the State on whose behalf they are made, as the Court observed in the *Nuclear Tests* cases (*I.C.J. Reports 1974*, pp. 267,472). But the Court also made clear in those cases that it is only "when it is the intention of the State making the declaration that it should become bound according to its terms" that "that intention confers on the declaration the character of a legal undertaking" (*ibid.*). Thus it all depends on the intention of the State in question, and the Court emphasized that it is for the Court to "form its own view of the meaning and scope intended by the author of a unilateral declaration which may create a legal obligation" (*ibid.*, pp. 269,474). In the case concerning *Military and Paramilitary Activities in and against Nicaragua (Nicaragua v. United States of America)*, the Court examined a communication transmitted by the Junta of National Reconstruction of Nicaragua to the Organization of American States, in which the Junta listed its objectives; but the Court was unable to find anything in that communication "from which it can be inferred that any legal undertaking was intended to exist" (*I.C.J. Reports 1986*, p. 132, para. 261). The Chamber considers that it has a duty to show even greater caution when it is a question of a unilateral declaration not directed to any particular recipient.

In order to assess the intentions of the author of a unilateral act, account must be taken of all the factual circumstances in which the act occurred. For example, in the *Nuclear Tests* cases, the Court took the view that since the applicant States were not the only ones concerned at the possible continuance of atmospheric testing by the French Government, that Government's unilateral declarations had "conveyed to the world at large, including the Applicant, its intention effectively to terminate these tests" (*I.C.J. Reports 1974*, p. 269, para. 51; p. 474, para. 53). In the particular circumstances of those cases, the French Government could not express an intention to be bound otherwise than by unilateral declarations. It is difficult to see how it could have accepted the terms of a negotiated solution with each of the applicants without thereby jeopardizing its contention that its conduct was lawful. The circumstances of the present case are

---

2 On 11 April 1975, the head of State of Mali granted an interview to the France-Presse agency, during which he stated that:

"Mali extends over 1,240,000 square kilometres, and we cannot justify fighting for a scrap of territory 150 kilometres long. Even if the Organization of African Unity Commission decides objectively that the frontier line passes through Bamako, my Government will comply with the decision."

radically different. Here, there was nothing to hinder the Parties from manifesting an intention to accept the binding character of the conclusions of the Organization of African Unity Mediation Commission by the normal method: a formal agreement on the basis of reciprocity. Since no agreement of this kind was concluded between the Parties, the Chamber finds that there are no grounds to interpret the declaration made by Mali's head of State on 11 April 1975 as a unilateral act with legal implications in regard to the present case.

3. INTERNATIONAL LAW AND MUNICIPAL LAW

Applicability of the Obligation to Arbitrate under Section 21 of the United Nations Headquarters Agreement of 26 June 1947
Advisory Opinion of 26 April 1988
I.C.J.Reports 1988, p. 12

[pp. 34-35] The fact remains however that, as the Court has already observed, the United States has declared (letter from the Permanent Representative, 11 March 1988) that its measures against the PLO Observer Mission were taken "irrespective of any obligations the United States may have under the [Headquarters] Agreement". If it were necessary to interpret that statement as intended to refer not only to the substantive obligations laid down in, for example, sections 11, 12 and 13, but also to the obligation to arbitrate provided for in section 21, this conclusion would remain intact. It would be sufficient to recall the fundamental principle of international law that international law prevails over *domestic law*. This principle was endorsed by judicial decision as long ago as the arbitral award of 14 September 1872 in the *Alabama* case between Great Britain and the United States, and has frequently been recalled since, for example in the case concerning the *Greco-Bulgarian "Communities"* in which the Permanent Court of International Justice laid it down that
"it is a generally accepted principle of international law that in the relations between Powers who are contracting Parties to a treaty, the provisions of municipal law cannot prevail over those of the treaty (*P.C.I.J., Series B, No. 17*, p. 32).

[p. 42 **S.O. Schwebel**] It is axiomatic that, on the international legal plane, national law cannot derogate from international law, that a State cannot avoid its international responsibility by the enactment of domestic legislation which conflicts with its international obligations. It is evident that a party to an agreement containing an obligation to arbitrate any dispute over its interpretation or application cannot legally avoid that obligation by denying the existence of a dispute or by maintaining that arbitration of it would not serve a useful purpose.

Elettronica Sicula S.p.A. (ELSI)
Judgment of 20 July 1989
I.C.J.Reports 1989, p. 15

[p. 51] The question still remains, therefore, whether the requisition was or was not a violation of Article III, paragraph 2. This question arises irrespective of the position in municipal law. Compliance with municipal law and compliance with the provisions of a treaty are different questions. What is a breach of treaty may be lawful in the municipal law and what is unlawful in the municipal law may be wholly innocent of violation of a treaty provision. Even had the Prefect held the requisition to be entirely justified in Italian law, this would not exclude the possibility that it was a violation of the FCN Treaty.

[p. 74] Yet it must be borne in mind that the fact that an act of a public authority may have been unlawful in municipal law does not necessarily mean that that act was unlawful in international law, as a breach of treaty or otherwise. A finding of the local courts that an act was unlawful may well be relevant to an argument that it was also arbitrary; but by itself, and without more, unlawfulness cannot be said to amount to arbitrariness. It would be absurd if measures later quashed by higher authority or a superior court could, for that reason, be said to have been arbitrary in the sense of international law. To identify arbitrariness with mere unlawfulness would be to deprive it of any useful meaning in its own right. Nor does it follow from a finding by a municipal court that an act was unjustified, or unreasonable, or arbitrary, that that act is necessarily to be classed as arbitrary in international law, though the qualification given to the impugned act by a municipal authority may be a valuable indication.

4. SUBJECTS OF INTERNATIONAL LAW

4.2. States

4.2.4. Fundamental Rights and Obligations

4.2.4.1. Sovereignty

Military and Paramilitary Activities
(Nicaragua/United States of America)
Merits. I. 27.6.1986
I.C.I.Reports 1986, p. 14

[p. 111] The Court should now mention the principle of respect for State sovereignty, which in international law is of course closely linked with the principles of the prohibition of the use of force and of non-intervention. The basic legal concept of State sovereignty in customary international law, expressed in, *inter alia*, Article 2, paragraph 1, of the United Nations Charter, extends to the internal waters and territorial sea of every State and to the air space above its territory. As to superjacent air space, the 1944 Chicago Convention on Civil Aviation (Art. 1) reproduces the established principle of the complete and exclusive sovereignty of a State over the air space above its territory. That convention, in conjunction with the 1958 Geneva Convention on the Territorial Sea, further specifies that the sovereignty of the coastal State extends to the territorial sea and to the air space above it, as does the United Nations Convention on the Law of the Sea adopted on 10 December 1982. The Court has no doubt that these prescriptions of treaty-law merely respond to firmly established and longstanding tenets of customary international law.

[p. 111] The duty of every State to respect the territorial sovereignty of others is to be considered for the appraisal to be made of the facts relating to the mining which occurred along Nicaragua's coasts. The legal rules in the light of which these acts of mining should be judged depend upon where they took place. The laying of mines within the ports of another State is governed by the law relating to internal waters, which are subject to the sovereignty of the coastal State. The position is similar as regards mines placed in the territorial sea. It is therefore the sovereignty of the coastal State which is affected in such cases. It is also by virtue of its sovereignty that the coastal State may regulate access to its ports.

[p. 128] The effects of the principle of respect for territorial sovereignty inevitably overlap with those of the principles of the prohibition of the use of force and of non-intervention. Thus the assistance to the *contras*, as well as the direct attacks on Nicaraguan ports, oil installations, etc., referred to in paragraphs 81 to 86 above, not only amount to an unlawful use of force, but also constitute infringements of the territorial sovereignty of Nicaragua, and incursions into its territorial and internal waters. Similarly, the mining operations in the Nicaraguan ports not only constitute breaches of the principle of the non-use of force, but also affect Nicaragua's sovereignty over certain maritime expanses. The Court has in fact found that these operations were carried on in Nicaragua's territorial or internal waters or both (paragraph 80), and accordingly they constitute a violation of Nicaragua's sovereignty. The principle of respect for territorial sovereignty is also directly infringed by the unauthorized overflight of a State's territory by aircraft belonging to or under the control of the government of another State. The Court has found above that such overflights were in fact made (paragraph 91 above).

These violations cannot be justified either by collective self-defence, for which, as the Court has recognized, the necessary circumstances are lacking, nor by any right of the United States to take counter-measures involving the use of force in the event of intervention by Nicaragua in El Salvador, since no such right exists under the applicable international law. They cannot be justified by the activities in El Salvador attributed to the Government of Nicaragua. The latter activities, assuming that they did in fact occur, do not bring into effect any right belonging to the United States which would justify the actions in question. Accordingly, such actions constitute violations of Nicaragua's sovereignty under customary international law.

[p. 131] A State's domestic policy falls within its exclusive jurisdiction, provided of course that it does not violate any obligation of international law. Every State possesses a fundamental right to choose and implement its own political, economic and social systems. Consequently, there would normally be no need to make any enquiries, in a matter outside the Court's jurisdiction, to ascertain in what sense and along what lines Nicaragua has actually exercised its right.

However, the assertion of a commitment raises the question of the possibility of a State binding itself by agreement in relation to a question of domestic policy, such as that relating to the holding of free elections on its territory. The Court cannot discover, within the range of subjects open to international agreement, any obstacle or provision to hinder a State from making a commitment of this kind. A State, which is free to decide upon the principle and methods of popular consultation within its domestic order, is sovereign for the purpose of accepting a limitation of its sovereignty in this field. This is a conceivable situation for a State which is bound by institutional links to a confederation of States, or indeed to an international organization. Both Nicaragua and the United States are members of the Organization of American States. The Charter of that Organization however goes no further in the direction of an agreed limitation on sovereignty of this kind than the provision in Article 3 (*d*) that

"The solidarity of the American States and the high aims which are sought through it require the political organization of those States on the basis of the effective exercise of representative democracy";

on the other hand, it provides for the right of every State "to organize itself as it sees fit" (Art. 12), and to "develop its cultural, political and economic life freely and naturally" (Art. 16).

[p. 133] The finding of the United States Congress also expressed the view that the Nicaraguan Government had taken "significant steps towards establishing a totalitarian Communist dictatorship". However the regime in Nicaragua be defined, adherence by a State to any particular doctrine does not constitute a violation of customary international law; to hold otherwise would make nonsense of the fundamental principle of State sovereignty, on which the whole of international law rests, and the freedom of choice of the political, social, economic and cultural system of a State. Consequently, Nicaragua's domestic policy options, even assuming that they correspond to the description given of them by the Congress finding, cannot justify on the legal plane the various actions of the Respondent complained of. The Court cannot contemplate the creation of a new rule opening up a right of intervention by one State against another on the ground that the latter has opted for some particular ideology or political system.

[p. 135]... in international law there are no rules, other than such rules as may be accepted by the State concerned, by treaty or otherwise, whereby the level of armaments of a sovereign State can be limited, and this principle is valid for all States without exception.

4.2.4.3. Peaceful Settlement of Disputes

Military and Paramilitary Activities
(Nicaragua/United States of America)
Merits. J. 27.6.1986
I.C.J.Reports 1986, p. 14

[p. 145] The Court has however also to recall a further principle of international law, one which is complementary to the principles of a prohibitive nature examined above, and respect for which is essential in the world of today: the principle that the parties to any dispute, particularly any dispute the continuance of which is likely to endanger the maintenance of international peace and security, should seek a solution by peaceful means. Enshrined in Article 33 of the United Nations Charter, which also indicates a number of peaceful means which are available, this principle has also the status of customary law.

In its Order indicating provisional measures, the Court took note of the Contadora Process, and of the fact that it had been endorsed by the United Nations Security Council and General Assembly (*I.C.J. Reports 1984*, pp. 183-184, para. 34). During that phase of the proceedings as during the phase devoted to jurisdiction and admissibility, both Nicaragua and the United States have expressed full support for the Contadora Process, and praised the results achieved so far. Therefore, the Court could not but take cognizance of this effort, which merits full respect and consideration as a unique contribution to the solution of the difficult situation in the region. The Court is aware that considerable progress has been achieved on the main objective of the process, namely agreement on texts relating to arms control and reduction, exclusion of foreign military bases or military interference and withdrawal of foreign advisers, prevention of arms traffic, stopping the support of groups aiming at the destabilization of any of the Governments concerned, guarantee of human rights and enforcement of democratic processes, as well as on cooperation for the creation of a mechanism for the verification of the agreements concerned. The work of the Contadora Group may facilitate the delicate and difficult negotiations, in accord with the letter and spirit of the United

Nations Charter, that are now required. The Court recalls to both Parties to the present case the need to cooperate with the Contadora efforts in seeking a definitive and lasting peace in Central America, in accordance with the principle of customary international law that prescribes the peaceful settlement of international disputes.

4.2.5. Succession of States

Frontier Dispute, Judgment
(Burkina Faso/Republic of Mali)
I.C.J. Reports 1986, p. 554

[p. 566] The territorial boundaries which have to be respected may also derive from international frontiers which previously divided a colony of one State from a colony of another, or indeed a colonial territory from the territory of an independent State, or one which was under protectorate, but had retained its international personality. There is no doubt that the obligation to respect pre-existing international frontiers in the event of a State succession derives from a general rule of international law, whether or not the rule is expressed in the formula *uti possidetis*. Hence the numerous solemn affirmations of the intangibility of the frontiers existing at the time of the independence of African States, whether made by senior African statesmen or by organs of the Organization of African Unity itself are evidently declaratory rather than constitutive: they recognize and confirm an existing principle; and do not seek to consecrate a new principle or the extension to Africa of a rule previously applied only in another continent.

4.3. International Organisations

4.3.4. "Implied Powers"

Land, Island and
Maritime Frontier Dispute
(El Salvador/Honduras)
Application to Intervene,
Order of 28 February 1990,
I.C.J. Reports 1990, p. 3

[pp. 40-41 **D.O. Shahabuddeen**] The whole nature of the Court, as a court of justice, constitutes a prohibition, no less clear for being implied, against giving the parties any say in the selection of judges to hear a case, whether through the Rules of Court or otherwise, and whether in whole or in part, except in the case of *ad hoc* judges. So fundamental was that prohibition to the character of the Court as a court of justice, as distinguished from an arbitral body, that it was no more necessary to express it in its Statute than it would have been to do so in the constitution of any other "court of justice" within the normal acceptation of the meaning of this expression.

This implied prohibition is not neutralized by approaching the matter from the point of view of the doctrine of implied powers. True, the fact that specific powers are conferred on a body does not necessarily imply the non-existence of others. But the latter do not float around at large. In the last analysis, all the powers of a body must be conferred by its constituent instrument, whether expressly or impliedly.

[pp. 41-42 **D.O. Shahabuddeen]** However elastic may be the test to be applied in determining the existence and extent of implied powers - and undue rigidity is surely to be avoided - it seems in any event clear that a constituent instrument cannot be read as implying the existence of powers which contradict the essential nature of the organization which it creates to exercise them. Powers of that kind could not be described as "required" or "essential" (within the meaning of the *Reparation* case) to enable the organization effectively to discharge the functions laid upon it by its organic text.

5. THE UNITED NATIONS

5.2. General Assembly

Military and Paramilitary Activities
(Nicaragua/United States of America)
Merits. J. 27.6.1986
I.C.J. Reports 1986, p. 14

[p. 100] This *opinio juris* may, though with all due caution, be deduced from, *inter alia*, the attitude of the Parties and the attitude of States towards certain General Assembly resolutions, and particularly resolution 2625 (XXV) entitled "Declaration on Principles of International Law concerning Friendly Relations and Co-operation among States in accordance with the Charter of the United Nations". The effect of consent to the text of such resolutions cannot be understood as merely that of a "reiteration or elucidation" of the treaty commitment undertaken in the Charter. On the contrary, it may be understood as an acceptance of the validity of the rule or set of rules declared by the resolution by themselves.

[p. 345 **D.O. Schwebel]** The significance of the Definition of Aggression - or of any definition of aggression - should not be magnified. It is not a treaty text. It is a resolution of the General Assembly which rightly recognizes the supervening force of the United Nations Charter and the supervening authority in matters of aggression of the Security Council. The Definition has its conditions, its flaws, its ambiguities and uncertainties. It is open-ended. Any definition of aggression must be, because aggression can only be ultimately defined and found in the particular case in the light of its particular facts. At the same time, the Definition of Aggression is not a resolution of the General Assembly which purports to declare principles of customary international law not regulated by the United Nations Charter. The legal significance of such resolutions is controversial, a controversy which is not relevant for immediate purposes. This resolution rather is an interpretation by the General Assembly of the meaning of the provisions of the United Nations Charter governing the use of armed force - the use of armed force "in contravention of the Charter". As such, of itself it is significant. Weighed as it should be in the light of the practice and the doctrine which the Nicaraguan Memorial assembles - which may be extensively amplified to the same effect - the Definition cannot be dismissed. In substance, however, the Court's Judgment - while affirming that the Definition of Aggression reflects customary international law - does dismiss both the import of the Definition of Aggression and the State practice and doctrine which on this paramount point is reflected by the Definition.

5.6. Interpretation of the Charter

Application for Review of Judgment No. 333 of the United Nations Administrative Tribunal, Advisory Opinion Advisory Opinion 27.5.1987

[p. 63] It is clear that the expression "the paramount consideration" (in French, *la considération dominante*) in Article 101 of the Charter is not synonymous with "the sole consideration"; it is simply a consideration to which greater weight is normally to be given than to any other. Nor does it mean that "efficiency, competence and integrity" together constitute a sufficient consideration, in the sense that a high enough standard of each gives rise to an entitlement to appointment. It is also clear, since paragraph 1 of the Article provides that "The staff shall be appointed by the Secretary-General under regulations established by the General Assembly", that the task of balancing the various considerations, in cases where they incline in different directions, is for the Secretary-General, subject to any general directions which might be given to him by the General Assembly. Resolution 37/126 itself constitutes such a direction, and one which operated in favour of the Applicant as compared with any outside candidate, or one without his record of more than "five years' continuing good service". Both on this basis, and on the basis of Article 101, paragraph 3, of the Charter, it is material to observe that the Applicant's efficiency and competence were highly spoken of by his superiors. The Tribunal did not make any finding reflecting on his integrity; it did however discuss the consequences of a change of nationality by a staff member in another connection - to be considered below.

The decision was that of the Secretary-General; and it was not for the Tribunal, nor indeed for the Court, to substitute its own appreciation of the problem for that of the

Secretary-General. The Court could only find that the Tribunal had in this respect "erred on a question of law relating to the provisions of the Charter" if it found that the Tribunal had upheld a decision of the Secretary-General which could not be reconciled with the relevant article of the Charter. That does not appear to the Court to be the case. The decision of the Secretary-General cannot be said to have failed to respect the "paramount" character of the considerations mentioned in Article 101, paragraph 3, simply because he took into account "all the circumstances" enumerated in his Answer (paragraph 80 above) in order to give effect to "the interests of the Organization".

[pp. 118-119 **D.O. Schwebel**] While the critical error of law relating to a provision of the United Nations Charter in this case lies in the Tribunal's failure to find that the Secretary-General had not given Mr. Yakimetz's candidacy every reasonable consideration, and in its consequent failure to require the Secretary-General to comply with a regulation binding upon him, established by the General Assembly in pursuance of Article 101, paragraph 1, of the Charter, still another error of law relates to Article 101, paragraph 3, of the Charter. That provision in effect establishes three "paramount" considerations in the employment of staff: efficiency, competence, and integrity. It further provides that: "Due regard shall be paid to the importance of recruiting staff on as wide a geographical basis as possible." That lesser consideration in no way imports that a change in the nationality of a staff member, much less actions manifesting an intent to seek a change in nationality, are considerations relevant to the suitability for continued service of such a staff member. The Administrative Tribunal held in the *Estabial* case (Judgment No. 310) that considerations of geographical distribution may not be given precedence over an employment decision which is to be reached on the basis of an assessment of an official's efficiency, competence and integrity. No less must the paramount considerations of efficiency, competence and integrity govern considerations of nationality, which are not even mentioned in the Charter.

[pp. 142-143 **D.O. Jennings**] As concerns paragraph 1 of Article 101 of the Charter, it is entirely clear that it is the Secretary-General, under the appropriate regulations, to whom alone is given the competence to appoint staff. The decision in a particular case is in his discretion and subject to his judgment of the matter. Neither the Tribunal, nor this Court, may usurp that discretion. It was without doubt for the Secretary-General to decide whether to give further employment to Mr. Yakimetz or not.

Yet this discretion must be exercised within and in conformity with "regulations established by the General Assembly", and any failure to conform to the legal requirements of the exercise of the discretion is a matter which comes within the jurisdiction of the Tribunal, and where accordingly it is possible that the Tribunal in its Judgement may commit an error relating to the provisions of the Charter, which error is subject to review and reformation by this Court. Is there then, in the case of Mr. Yakimetz, evidence of any such failure to act in accordance with the corpus of Charter law and derivatory regulations adopted by the General Assembly; and if so did the Tribunal's Judgement err in not detecting such a failure? This is the question to which this Court has to address itself.

First it is necessary to dispose of the argument that the effect of paragraph 3 of Article 101 - certainly a provision of the greatest possible importance for the efficiency and integrity of the United Nations staff - has the effect that a person with reports indicating that he has displayed the highest standards of efficiency, competence and integrity, can hardly be refused further employment. Thus the Applicant, in his letter of 13 December to the Secretary-General, avers that:

"To deny me the right to reasonable consideration for a career appointment for any reason unrelated to merit - efficiency, competence, integrity - would, I believe, be a violation of Article 100 [?101] of the Charter."

This is to go too far (quite apart from the interpolation of the notion of "merit", which does not appear in Article 101.3). Efficiency, competence and integrity are surely a paramount consideration but this does not mean that this is the *only* consideration permitted by the Charter; in fact the very word "paramount" implies that there are other relevant and permissible grounds. And if considerations other than efficiency, competence and integrity, may sometimes have to be taken into account besides the paramount consideration, it must be assumed that there can be cases where considerations other than the paramount consideration may prevail.

[pp. 165-166 **D.O. Evensen**] It follows from Article 101, paragraph 1, of the Charter that not only has the Secretary-General been imbued with the power to appoint the United Nations staff, but the Secretary-General must *exercise* his discretionary power. He cannot abide by or be unduly influenced by the orders or wishes of governments, organizations or other external forces. Secondly, and especially important, is that the Secretary-General's discretionary power is not synonymous with unlimited or absolute powers. Under general principles of law, this discretionary power has to be exercised in accordance with accepted governing procedures.

On the other hand, it is clear under Staff Rule 104.12 (*b*) that a fixed term appointment does not carry any legal expectancy of renewal or conversion to a career appointment. Consequently, the discretionary power of the Secretary-General is of major importance for the appointment and composition of the Secretariat. It is equally clear that, in exercising his discretionary power, the Secretary-General must apply certain established standards and norms.

5.9. United Nations Administrative Tribunal

Application for Review of Judgement No. 333 of the United Nations Administrative Tribunal, Advisory Opinion Advisory Opinion 27.5.1987

[pp. 52-53] It is essential to keep clearly in mind the distinction between the Secretary-General's discharge of his duties and the performance by the Tribunal of its judicial functions, even though the same considerations may have had to be taken into account for both. It was the duty of the Secretary-General to give "every reasonable consideration" to the Applicant as a candidate for a career appointment; if he failed to do so, he failed to comply with General Assembly resolution 37/126. In order to do so, or in the course of doing so, he had to weigh up all relevant considerations, including the fact of the Applicant's secondment, in a reasonable manner in order to arrive at a conclusion. The Tribunal, when seised of the question, did not have to follow the Secretary General through this process, checking every step of the sequence. It had to decide whether there had been "non-observance" of any of the relevant texts, including General Assembly resolution 37/126; it had therefore to determine whether "every reasonable consideration" had been given. It clearly had the power and the duty to re-examine the question of secondment as a legal impediment, to satisfy itself that the Secretary-General had not committed an error of law on the point, and this it did. It had then to assess the question of reasonableness; but this did not, in the Court's view, involve the Tribunal in an attempt to make its own decision as to whether the Applicant should be given a career appointment.

Once the Tribunal had found that the Applicant did not possess a "legal expectancy" of further employment, involving a corresponding obligation on the United Nations to "provide continuing employment" (see paragraphs 33 and 34 above), his entitlement was only to receive "every reasonable consideration". Such consideration must by definition involve latitude for the exercise of the Secretary-General's discretion; and the Tribunal in fact found that "the Respondent had the sole authority to decide ... whether the Applicant could be given a probationary appointment" and that he "exercised his discretion properly" (para. XVIII). The consistent jurisprudence of the Tribunal itself is to the effect that where the Secretary-General has been invested with discretionary powers, the Tribunal will in principle not enquire into their exercise, provided however that "Such discretionary powers must be exercised without improper motive so that there shall be no misuse of power, since any such misuse of power would call for the rescinding of the decision" (Judgement No. 50 (*Brown*).

[p. 57] However while it is true that the Secretary-General made no claim to an unfettered discretion, and the Tribunal nowhere stated that he possessed one, the Tribunal did in effect accept as sufficient a statement by the Secretary-General that the "reasonable consideration" required by resolution 37/126 had been given, and did not require him to furnish any details of when and how it was given, let alone calling for evidence to that effect. The view might therefore be advanced that the Tribunal did not properly discharge its function of judicial review of administrative action, since the practical effect of an unquestioning acceptance of the Secretary-General's assertion that he had given "every reasonable consideration" would, it is suggested, be that he would enjoy such an unfettered discretion. It is however necessary to recall once again that the question before the Court is a different one: whether the Tribunal erred on a question of law relating to the provisions of the Charter of the United Nations. It is only if the Tribunal can be said, by the course of action it is alleged to have adopted, to have erred on a question of law of that kind, that it becomes the duty of the Court to examine the matter.

[pp. 153-154 **D.O. Jennings**] Turning now to what seems to be the actual *ratio decidendi* of the Tribunal's Judgement, what it amounts to is simply this: the Respondent has stated to the Tribunal that he gave every reasonable consideration, in accordance with the resolution, to the possibility of a career grade appointment of the Applicant, and if the Respondent says he has done so, his assertion must be accepted to be true, at least in the absence of proof to the contrary. To this way of deciding the matter there are two objections: the first is one of juridical principle; and the second is that the Respondent's assertion is irreconcilable with the documents presented to the Tribunal.

The objection of juridical principle may be very shortly stated. The UNAT Statute - itself an enactment of the General Assembly in pursuance of the relevant provisions of the Charter - establishes a system of judicial control of administrative discretions of the sort familiar in administrative law generally. The essence of such a system is that the judicial tribunal's task is to ensure that administrative decisions are made within the applicable legal framework. Thus, in the present case, whilst it is no part of the Tribunal's functions to usurp the discretion which the Respondent alone can exercise, it is for the Tribunal to ensure that, in making his decision, the Respondent did comply with the law; which everybody agrees included the resolution 37/126, IV, paragraph 5.

Such a system of judicial control of administrative discretion is subverted if the Tribunal simply accepts the assertion of the administrator, after the event, that his decision was made in accordance with the legal requirements. There is no purpose in having an administrative tribunal at all if it accepts as sufficient the administrator's assurances, made not even to the objecting applicant at the material time, but subsequently, and to the Tribunal; and, moreover, in the absence of evidence at the material time that the law was indeed complied with, and in the absence of reasons for the decision. This situation is incompatible with a system of judicial control of administrative discretion.

Application for Review of Judgement No. 333 of the United Nations Administrative Tribunal, Advisory Opinion Advisory Opinion 27.5.1987

[pp. 78-79 **S.O. Elias**] It is clear that the Court may sometimes find itself in a strait-jacket if it follows closely the limit set in Article 11; nevertheless, to allow the Court to raise any legal issue analogous, but not strictly relevant, to the ones specifically asked of it by the Committee might not always give satisfaction. A flexible procedure is, therefore, called for which enables the Court to raise *all* legal issues considered by it to be relevant and necessary for the proper disposal of the problem at issue, so long as it satisfies the requirement of the judicial process.

A sensible way out will be for the preliminary problems arising in a given case to be dealt with first by a tribunal of first instance and then for legal issues to be raised later on appeal to the Administrative Tribunal in the normal system of adjudication, which the latter would be obliged to deal with as a court of appeal. The whole question would then turn on the judicial rather than on the present almost non-judicial manner of the Committee on Applications for Review. The political overtone of the Committee's deliberations would be minimized, if not completely eliminated, because the present composition of the Committee does not lend itself to strictly legal adjudications of issues. At present, the framing of questions to be put to the Court is often tinged with meta-legal conceptions of particular State Members of the Committee, which are often reflected in the manner of the categorization of the questions to be asked of the Court. The result has often been to make the question in the end either irrelevant or patently obscure. The Court has accordingly been put to the trouble of having to find out what the Committee did in fact mean by the questions as put to it, thereby wasting judges' time and effort, before coming round to the real issues involved in a particular case. The new procedure of using a tribunal of first instance would entail a recast of the present Statute of the Administrative Tribunal, *inter alia*, to require its members to possess legal qualifications. The present Article 11 would in particular need to be modified. The body operating at this level should do so as a court. For the purpose the General Assembly might establish a study group to submit necessary changes, which must allow appeals to the Administrative Tribunal, the functions of which might have to be suitably modified.

[pp. 135-136 **D.O. Jennings**] What then is the Committee's role when an objection to a judgement of the Tribunal comes before it? This is stated in paragraph 2 of the same

Article, namely to "decide whether or not there is a substantial basis for the application". Presumably this means that, provided that the application raises one or more of the valid grounds of legal challenge set out in Article 11.1, the Committee must then decide whether the case is important enough, and sufficiently substantiated by the evidence, to justify being referred to the International Court of Justice. Such an assessment is appropriate for an essentially political body like the Committee. It is more doubtful whether it is also part of the task of the Committee to determine whether the Applicant's objection or objections to the Tribunal's Judgement properly fall within the particular categories of Article 11.1 in which he himself has expressed them. That is, ultimately at least, the task of this Court; furthermore, being an essentially juridical task and a technically difficult one at that, it would be a curious task for a committee whose procedures are neither judicial nor even quasi-judicial in character.

However that may be, the present questions seem to exhibit a tendency to assume that the questions to be put to this Court should themselves be couched in, or very nearly couched in, the language of one or more of the categories of grounds of valid objection set out in Article 11.1. The grounds of objection, expressed inevitably in the most general terms, have thus become in practice the language of permissible questions to the Court. It is rather as if, to take an analogous series of grounds of jurisdiction, an applicant to the Court's contentious jurisdiction under paragraph 2 of Article 36 of the Court's Statute were to assume that his case must not only fall within that provision, but that his submissions should finally be reduced to the actual language of the famous list in that paragraph of Article 36.

The effect of this interpretation of Article 11 is that questions are put to this Court, not in the terms of the applicant's specific grievance, but in abstract and conceptual terms of the list of grounds of objection in Article 11.1. This manner of proceeding can easily transform a simple grievance into a jurisprudential problem of some complexity and doubt.

6. USE OF FORCE AND RELATED PROBLEMS

6.1. Use of Force

Military and Paramilitary Activities
(Nicaragua/United States of America)
Merits. J. 27.6.1986
I.C.J. Reports 1986, p. 14

[pp.100-103] As regards the United States in particular, the weight of an expression of *opinio juris* can similarly be attached to its support of the resolution of the Sixth International Conference of American States condemning aggression (18 February 1928) and ratification of the Montevideo Convention on Rights and Duties of States (26 December 1933), Article 11 of which imposes the obligation not to recognize territorial acquisitions or special advantages which have been obtained by force. Also significant is United States acceptance of the principle of the prohibition of the use of force which is contained in the declaration on principles governing the mutual relations of States participating in the Conference on Security and co-operation in Europe (Helsinki, 1 August 1975), whereby the participating States undertake to "refrain in their mutual relations, *as well as in their international relations in general*," (emphasis added) from the threat or use of force. Acceptance of a text in these terms confirms the existence of an *opinio juris* of the participating States prohibiting the use of force in international relations. A further confirmation of the validity as customary international law of the principle of the prohibition of the use of force expressed in Article 2, paragraph 4, of the Charter of the United Nations may be found in the fact that it is frequently referred to in statements by State representatives as being not only a principle of customary international law but also a fundamental or cardinal principle of such law. The International Law Commission, in the course of its work on the codification of the law of treaties, expressed the view that "the law of the Charter concerning the prohibition of the use of force in itself constitutes a conspicuous example of a rule in international law having the character of *jus cogens*" (paragraph (1) of the commentary of the Commission to Article 50 of its draft Articles on the Law of Treaties, *ILC Yearbook*, 1966-II, p. 247). Nicaragua in its Memorial on the Merits submitted in the present case states that the principle prohibiting the use of force embodied in Article 2, paragraph 4, of the Charter of the United Nations "has come to be recognized as *jus cogens*". The United States, in its Counter-Memorial on the questions of jurisdiction and admissibility, found it material to quote the views of scholars that this principle is a "universal norm", a "universal international law", a "universally recognized principle of international law", and a "principle of *jus cogens*".

As regards certain particular aspects of the principle in question, it will be necessary to distinguish the most grave forms of the use of force (those constituting an armed attack) from other less grave forms. In determining the legal rule which applies to these latter forms, the Court can again draw on the formulations contained in the Declaration on Principles of International Law concerning Friendly Relations and Co-operation among States in accordance with the Charter of the United Nations (General Assembly resolution 2625 (XXV), referred to above). As already observed, the adoption by States of this text affords an indication of their *opinio juris* as to customary international law on the question. Alongside certain descriptions which may refer to aggression, this text includes others which refer only to less grave forms of the use of force. In particular, according to this resolution:

"Every State has the duty to refrain from the threat or use of force to violate the existing international boundaries of another State or as a means of solving international disputes, including territorial disputes and problems concerning frontiers of States.

....

States have a duty to refrain from acts of reprisal involving the use of force.

....

Every State has the duty to refrain from any forcible action which deprives peoples referred to in the elaboration of the principle of equal rights and self-determination of that right to self-determination and freedom and independence.

Every State has the duty to refrain from organizing or encouraging the organization of irregular forces or armed bands, including mercenaries, for incursion into the territory of another State.

Every State has the duty to refrain from organizing, instigating, assisting or participating in acts of civil strife or terrorist acts in another State or acquiescing in organized activities within its territory directed towards the commission of such acts, when the acts referred to in the present paragraph involve a threat or use of force."

Moreover, in the part of this same resolution devoted to the principle of non-intervention in matters within the national jurisdiction of States, a very similar rule is found:

"Also, no State shall organize, assist, foment, finance, incite or tolerate subversive, terrorist or armed activities directed towards the violent overthrow of the regime of another State, or interfere in civil strife in another State."

In the context of the inter-American system, this approach can be traced back at least to 1928 (Convention on the Rights and Duties of States in the Event of Civil Strife, Art. I (1)); it was confirmed by resolution 78 adopted by the General Assembly of the Organization of American States on 21 April 1972. The operative part of this resolution reads as follows:

"The General Assembly Resolves:

1. To reiterate solemnly the need for the member states of the Organization to observe strictly the principles of nonintervention and self-determination of peoples as a means of ensuring peaceful coexistence among them and to refrain from committing any direct or indirect act that might constitute a violation of those principles.

2. To reaffirm the obligation of those states to refrain from applying economic, political, or any other type of measures to coerce another state and obtain from it advantages of any kind.

3. Similarly, to reaffirm the obligation of these states to refrain from organizing, supporting, promoting, financing, instigating, or tolerating subversive, terrorist, or armed activities against another state and from intervening in a civil war in another state or in its internal struggles."

The general rule prohibiting force allows for certain exceptions. In view of the arguments advanced by the United States to justify the acts of which it is accused by Nicaragua, the Court must express a view on the content of the right of self-defence, and more particularly the right of collective self-defence. First, with regard to the existence of this right, it notes that in the language of Article 51 of the United Nations Charter, the inherent right (or "droit naturel") which any State possesses in the event of an armed attack, covers both collective and individual self-defence. Thus, the Charter itself testifies to the existence of the right of collective self-defence in customary international law. Moreover, just as the wording of certain General Assembly declarations adopted by States demonstrates their recognition of the principle of the prohibition of force as definitely a matter of customary international law, some of the wording in those declarations operates similarly in respect of the right of self-defence (both collective and individual). Thus, in the declaration quoted above on the Principles of International Law concerning Friendly Relations and Co-operation among States in accordance with the Charter of the United Nations, the reference to the prohibition of force is followed by a paragraph stating that:

"nothing in the foregoing paragraphs shall be construed as enlarging or diminishing in any way the scope of the provisions of the Charter concerning cases in which the use of force is lawful".

This resolution demonstrates that the States represented in the General Assembly regard the exception to the prohibition of force constituted by the right of individual or collective self-defence as already a matter of customary international law.

[p. 108] Intervention is wrongful when it uses methods of coercion in regard to such choices, which must remain free ones. The element of coercion, which defines, and indeed forms the very essence of, prohibited intervention, is particularly obvious in the case of an intervention which uses force, either in the direct form of military action, or in the indirect form of support for subversive or terrorist armed activities within another State. As noted above (paragraph 191), General Assembly resolution 2625 (XXV) equates assistance of this kind with the use of force by the assisting State when the acts committed in another State "involve a threat or use of force". These forms of action are therefore wrongful in the light of both the principle of non-use of force, and that of non-intervention.

[pp. 118-119] As to the claim that United States activities in relation to the *contras* constitute a breach of the customary international law principle of the non-use of force, the Court finds that, subject to the question whether the action of the United States might be justified as an exercise of the right of self-defence, the United States has committed a prima facie violation of that principle by its assistance to the *contras* in Nicaragua, by "organizing or encouraging the organization of irregular forces or armed bands ... for incursion into the territory of another State", and "participating in acts of civil strife ... in another State", in the terms of General Assembly resolution 2625 (XXV). According to that resolution, participation of this kind is contrary to the principle of the prohibition of the use of force when the acts of civil strife referred to "involve a threat or use of force". In the view of the Court, while the arming and training of the *contras* can certainly be said to involve the threat or use of force against Nicaragua, this is not necessarily so in respect of all the assistance given by the United States Government. In particular, the Court considers that the mere supply of funds to the *contras* while undoubtedly an act of intervention in the internal affairs of Nicaragua, as will be explained below, does not in itself amount to a use of force.

[p. 127] On the legal level the Court cannot regard response to an intervention by Nicaragua as such a justification. While an armed attack would give rise to an entitlement to collective self-defence, a use of force of a lesser degree of gravity cannot, as the Court has already observed (paragraph 211 above), produce any entitlement to take collective counter-measures involving the use of force. The acts of which Nicaragua is accused, even assuming them to have been established and imputable to that State, could only have justified proportionate counter-measures on the part of the State which had been the victim of these acts, namely El Salvador, Honduras or Costa Rica. They could not justify counter-measures taken by a third State, the United States, and particularly could not justify intervention involving the use of force.

[p. 128] The effects of the principle of respect for territorial sovereignty inevitably overlap with those of the principles of the prohibition of the use of force and of non-intervention. Thus the assistance to the *contras*, as well as the direct attacks on Nicaraguan ports, oil installations, etc., referred to in paragraphs 81 to 86 above, not only amount to an unlawful use of force, but also constitute infringements of the territorial sovereignty of Nicaragua, and incursions into its territorial and internal waters. Similarly, the mining operations in the Nicaraguan ports not only constitute breaches of the principle of the non-use of force, but also affect Nicaragua's sovereignty over certain maritime expanses. The Court has in fact found that these operations were carried on in Nicaragua's territorial or internal waters or both (paragraph 80), and accordingly they constitute a violation of Nicaragua's sovereignty. The principle of respect for territorial sovereignty is also directly infringed by the unauthorized overflight of a State's territory by aircraft belonging to or under the control of the government of another State. The Court has found above that such overflights were in fact made (paragraph 91 above).

These violations cannot be justified either by collective self-defence, for which, as the Court has recognized, the necessary circumstances are lacking, nor by any right of the United States to take counter-measures involving the use of force in the event of intervention by Nicaragua in El Salvador, since no such right exists under the applicable international law. They cannot be justified by the activities in El Salvador attributed to the Government of Nicaragua. The latter activities, assuming that they did in fact occur, do not bring into effect any right belonging to the United States which would justify the actions in question. Accordingly, such actions constitute violations of Nicaragua's sovereignty under customary international law.

[pp. 151-152 **S.O. Singh**] A major consideration in the resolution of the dispute in this case has been the principle of non-use of force. It is indeed a well-established tenet of modern international law that the lawful use of force is circumscribed by proper regulation, and this is so from whichever angle one looks at it, whether the customary viewpoint or that of the conventional international law on the subject. However the customary aspect does visualize the exceptional need for the provision of the "inherent right" to use force in self-defence. The aforesaid concepts of the principle and its exception do have an existence independent of treaty-law as contained in the United Nations Charter or the Inter-American system of conventional law on the subject. In this context it appears necessary to emphasize certain aspects, which is attempted below.

In fact this cardinal principle of non-use of force in international relations has been the pivotal point of a time-honoured legal philosophy that has evolved particularly after the two World Wars of the current century. It has thus been deliberately extended to cover the illegality of recourse to armed reprisals or other forms of armed intervention not amounting to war which aspect may not have been established by the law of the League of Nations, or by the Nuremberg or Tokyo Trials, but left to be expressly developed and codified by the United Nations Charter. The logic behind this extension of the principle of non-use of force to reprisals has been that if use of force was made permissible not as a lone restricted measure of self-defence, but also for other minor provocations demanding counter-measures, the day would soon dawn when the world would have to face the major catastrophe of a third World War - an event so dreaded in 1946 as to have justified concrete measures being taken forthwith to eliminate such a contingency arising in the future.

There can be no doubt therefore of the innate legal existence of this basic reasoning, irrespective of the later developments which have now found a place in the treaty provisions as reflected in Article 2, paragraph 4, and Article 51 of the United Nations Charter. However it is pertinent that the origin of legal regulation of use of force is much older than the United Nations Charter and this has been acknowledged to be so. If an issue was raised whether the concepts of the principle of non-use of force and the exception to it in the form of use of force for self-defence are to be characterized as either part of customary international law or that of conventional law, the answer would appear to be that both the concepts are inherently based in customary international law in their origins, but have been developed further by treaty-law. In any search to determine whether these concepts belong to customary or conventional international law it would appear to be a fallacy to try to split any concept to ascertain what part or percentage of it belongs to customary law and what fraction belongs to conventional law. There is no need to try to separate the inseparable, because the simple logical approach would be that if the concept in its origin was a customary one, as in this case, and later built up by treaty law, the Court would be right in ruling that the present dispute before the Court does not arise under a multilateral treaty, so as to fall outside the Court's jurisdiction because of the Vandenberg Reservation invoked by the Respondent.

[p. 176 **S.O. Ruda**] If, juridically, assistance to rebels cannot, *per se*, be justified on grounds of self-defence, I do not see why the Court feels bound to analyse in detail the facts of the case relating to such assistance. Neither do I perceive the need for entering, in the Judgment, into the questions of the requirements, in the case of collective self-defence, of a request by a State which regards itself as the victim of an armed attack, or a declaration by that State that it has been attacked or of its submission of an immediate report on the measure taken in the exercise of this right of self-defence.

From my point of view it would have been sufficient to say, just as the Court does in its conclusions, that even if there was such assistance and flow of arms, that is not a sufficient excuse for invoking self-defence because, juridically, the concept of "armed attack" does not include assistance to rebels.

[pp. 530-531 **D.O. Jennings**] Let us look first, therefore, at the relationship between customary international law, and Article 2, paragraph 4, and Article 51 of the United Nations Charter. There is no doubt that there was, prior to the United Nations Charter, a customary law which restricted the lawful use of force, and which correspondingly provided also for a right to use force in self-defence; as indeed the use of the term "inherent" in Article 51 of the United Nations Charter suggests. The proposition, however, that, after the Charter, there exists alongside those Charter provisions on force and self-defence, an independent customary law that can be applied as alternative to Articles 2, paragraph 4, and 51 of the Charter, raises questions about how and when this correspondence came about, and about what the differences, if any, between customary law and the Charter provisions, may be.

A multilateral treaty may certainly be declaratory of customary international law either:

"as incorporating and giving recognition to a rule of customary international law that existed prior to the conclusion of the treaty or, on the other hand, as being the *fons et origo* of a rule of international law which subsequently secured the general assent of States and thereby was transformed into customary law" (see *Baxter, British Year Book of International Law,* Vol. XLI, 1965-1966, p. 277).

It could hardly be contended that these provisions of the Charter were merely a codification of the existing customary law. The literature is replete with statements that Article 2, paragraph 4, - for example in speaking of "force" rather than war, and providing that even a "threat of force" may be unlawful - represented an important innovation in the law. The late Sir Humphrey Waldock, in a passage dealing with matters very much in issue in the present case, put it this way:

"The illegality of recourse to armed reprisals or other forms of armed intervention not amounting to war was not established beyond all doubt by the law of the League, or by the Nuremberg and Tokyo Trials. That was brought about by the law of the Charter ..." (106 *Collected Courses*, Academy of International Law, The Hague (1962-II), p. 231.)

Even Article 51, though referring to an "inherent" and therefore supposedly pre-existing, right of self-defence, introduced a novel concept in speaking of "collective self-defence" [3]. Article 51 was introduced into the Charter at a late stage for the specific purpose of clarifying the position in regard to collective understandings - multilateral treaties - for mutual self-defence, which were part of the contemporary scene.

---

3 Cf. Aréchaga, 159 Collected Courses, The Hague (1978-I), at p. 87, and p. 96 where he goes so far as to assert: "The so-called customary law of self-defence supposedly pre-existing the Charter, and dependent on this single word [inherent] simply did not exist."

6.2. Self-defence

Military and Paramilitary Activities
(Nicaragua/United States of America)
Merits. J. 27.6.1986
I.C.J. Reports 1986, p. 14

[pp. 35-36] Both Article 51 of the United Nations Charter and Article 21 of the Organization of American States Charter refer to self-defence as an exception to the principle of the prohibition of the use of force. Unlike the United Nations Charter, the Organization of American States Charter does not use the expression "collective self-defence", but refers to the case of "self-defence in accordance with existing treaties or in fulfillment thereof", one such treaty being the United Nations Charter. Furthermore it is evident that if actions of the United States complied with all requirements of the United Nations Charter so as to constitute the exercise of the right of collective self-defence, it could not be argued that they could nevertheless constitute a violation of Article 21 of the Organization of American States Charter. It therefore follows that the situation of El Salvador with regard to the assertion by the United States of the right of collective self-defence is the same under the Organization of American States Charter as it is under the United Nations Charter.

[p. 45] The Court would observe that the normal purpose of an invocation of self-defence is to justify conduct which would otherwise be wrongful. If advanced as a justification in itself, not coupled with a denial of the conduct alleged, it may well imply both an admission of that conduct, and of the wrongfulness of that conduct in the absence of the justification of self-defence.

[p. 71] In the Court's view, however, if Nicaragua has been giving support to the armed opposition in El Salvador, and if this constitutes an armed attack on El Salvador and the other appropriate conditions are met, collective self-defence could be legally invoked by the United States, even though there may be the possibility of an additional motive, one perhaps even more decisive for the United States, drawn from the political orientation of the present Nicaraguan Government. The existence of an additional motive, other than that officially proclaimed by the United States, could not deprive the latter of its right to resort to collective self-defence. The conclusion to be drawn is that special caution is called for in considering the allegations of the United States concerning conduct by Nicaragua which may provide a sufficient basis for self-defence.

[p. 94] As regards the suggestion that the areas covered by the two sources of law are identical, the Court observes that the United Nations Charter, the convention to which most of the United States argument is directed, by no means covers the whole area of the regulation of the use of force in international relations. On one essential point, this treaty itself refers to pre-existing customary international law; this reference to customary law is contained in the actual text of Article 5l, which mentions the "inherent right" (in the French text the "droit naturel") of individual or collective self-defence, which "nothing in the present Charter shall impair" and which applies in the event of an armed attack. The Court therefore finds that Article 51 of the Charter is only meaningful on the basis that there is a "natural" or "inherent" right of self-defence, and it is hard to see how this can be other than of a customary nature, even if its present content has been confirmed and influenced by the Charter. Moreover the Charter, having itself recognized the existence of this right, does not go on to regulate directly all aspects of its content. For example, it does not contain any specific rule whereby self-defence would warrant only measures which are proportional to the armed attack and necessary to respond to it, a rule well established in customary international law. Moreover, a definition of the "armed attack" which, if found to exist, authorizes the exercise of the "inherent right" of self-defence, is not provided in the Charter, and is not part of treaty law. It cannot therefore be held that Article 51 is a provision which "subsumes and supervenes" customary international law. It rather demonstrates that in the field in question, the importance of which for the present dispute need hardly be stressed, customary international law continues to exist alongside treaty law. The areas governed by the two sources of law thus do not overlap exactly, and the rules do not have the same content. This could also be demonstrated for other subjects, in particular for the principle of non-intervention.

[pp. 102-105] The general rule prohibiting force allows for certain exceptions. In view of the arguments advanced by the United States to justify the acts of which it is accused by Nicaragua, the Court must express a view on the content of the right of self-defence, and more particularly the right of collective self-defence. First, with regard to the existence of this right, it notes that in the language of Article 51 of the United Nations Charter, the inherent right (or "droit naturel") which any State possesses in the event of an armed attack, covers both collective and individual self-defence. Thus, the Charter itself testifies to the existence of the right of collective self-defence in customary international law. Moreover, just as the wording of certain General Assembly declarations adopted by States demonstrates their recognition of the principle of the prohibition of force as definitely a matter of customary international law, some of the wording in those declarations operates similarly in respect of the right of self-defence (both collective and individual). Thus, in the declaration quoted above on the Principles of International Law concerning Friendly Relations and Co-operation among States in accordance with the Charter of the United Nations, the reference to the prohibition of force is followed by a paragraph stating that:

"nothing in the foregoing paragraphs shall be construed as enlarging or diminishing in any way the scope of the provisions of the Charter concerning cases in which the use of force is lawful".

This resolution demonstrates that the States represented in the General Assembly regard the exception to the prohibition of force constituted by the right of individual or collective self-defence as already a matter of customary international law.

With regard to the characteristics governing the right of self-defence, since the Parties consider the existence of this right to be established as a matter of customary international law, they have concentrated on the conditions governing its use. In view of the circumstances in which the dispute has arisen, reliance is placed by the Parties only on the right of self-defence in the case of an armed attack which has already occurred, and the issue of the lawfulness of a response to the imminent threat of armed attack has not been raised. Accordingly the Court expresses no view on that issue. The Parties also agree in holding that whether the response to the attack is lawful depends on observance of the criteria of the necessity and the proportionality of the measures taken in self-defence. Since the existence of the right of collective self-defence is established in customary international law, the Court must define the specific conditions which may have to be met for its exercise, in addition to the conditions of necessity and proportionality to which the Parties have referred.

In the case of individual self-defence, the exercise of this right is subject to the State concerned having been the victim of an armed attack. Reliance on collective self-defence of course does not remove the need for this. There appears now to be general agreement on the nature of the acts which can be treated as constituting armed attacks. In particular, it may be considered to be agreed that an armed attack must be understood as including not merely action by regular armed forces across an international border, but also "the sending by or on behalf of a State of armed bands, groups, irregulars or mercenaries, which carry out acts of armed force against another State of such gravity as to amount to" (*inter alia*) an actual armed attack conducted by regular forces, "or its substantial involvement therein". This description, contained in Article 3, paragraph (*g*), of the Definition of Aggression annexed to General Assembly resolution 3314 (XXIX), may be taken to reflect customary international law. The Court sees no reason to deny that, in customary law, the prohibition of armed attacks may apply to the sending by a State of armed bands to the territory of another State, if such an operation, because of its scale and effects, would have been classified as an armed attack rather than as a mere frontier incident had it been carried out by regular armed forces. But the Court does not believe that the concept of "armed attack" includes not only acts by armed bands where such acts occur on a significant scale but also assistance to rebels in the form of the provision of weapons or logistical or other support. Such assistance may be regarded as a threat or use of force, or amount to intervention in the internal or external affairs of other States. It is also clear that it is the State which is the victim of an armed attack which must form and declare the view that it has been so attacked. There is no rule in customary international law permitting another State to exercise the right of collective self-defence on the basis of its own assessment of the situation. Where collective self-defence is invoked, it is to be expected that the State for whose benefit this right is used will have declared itself to be the victim of an armed attack.

The question remains whether the lawfulness of the use of collective self-defence by the third State for the benefit of the attacked State also depends on a request addressed by that State to the third State. A provision of the Charter of the Organization of American States is here in point : and while the Court has no jurisdiction to consider that instrument as applicable to the dispute, it may examine it to ascertain what light it throws on the content of customary international law. The Court notes that the Organization of American States Charter includes, in Article 3 the principle that: "an act of aggression against one American State is an act of aggression against all the other American States" and a provision in Article 27 that:

"Every act of aggression by a State against the territorial integrity or the inviolability of the territory or against the sovereignty or political independence of an American State shall be considered an act of aggression against the other American States."

Furthermore, by Article 3, paragraph 1, of the Inter-American Treaty of Reciprocal Assistance, signed at Rio de Janeiro on 2 September 1947, the High-Contracting Parties

"agree that an armed attack by any State against an American State shall be considered as an attack against all the American States and, consequently, each one of the said Contracting Parties undertakes to assist in meeting the attack in the exercise of the inherent right of individual or collective self-defence recognized by Article 51 of the Charter of the United Nations";

and under paragraph 2 of that Article,

"On the request of the State or States directly attacked and until the decision of the Organ of Consultation of the Inter-American System, each one of the Contracting Parties may determine the immediate measures which it may individually take in fulfilment of the obligation contained in the preceding paragraph and in accordance with the principle of continental solidarity."

(The 1947 Rio Treaty was modified by the 1975 Protocol of San José, Costa Rica, but that Protocol is not yet in force.)

The Court observes that the Treaty of Rio de Janeiro provides that measures of collective self-defence taken by each State are decided "on the request of the State or States directly attacked". It is significant that this requirement of a request on the part of the attacked State appears in the treaty particularly devoted to these matters of mutual assistance; it is not found in the more general text (the Charter of the Organization of American States), but Article 28 of that Charter provides for the application of the measures and procedures laid down in "the special treaties on the subject".

At all events, the Court finds that in customary international law, whether of a general kind or that particular to the inter-American legal system, there is no rule permitting the exercise of collective self-defence in the absence of a request by the State which regards itself as the victim of an armed attack. The Court concludes that the requirement of a request by the State which is the victim of the alleged attack is additional to the requirement that such a State should have declared itself to have been attacked.

At this point, the Court may consider whether in customary international law there is any requirement corresponding to that found in the treaty law of the United Nations Charter, by which the state claiming to use the right of individual or collective self-defence must report to an international body, empowered to determine the conformity with international law of the measures which the state is seeking to justify on that basis. Thus Article 51 of the United Nations Charter requires that measures taken by States in exercise of this right of self-defence must be "immediately reported" to the Security Council. As the Court has observed above, a principle enshrined in a treaty, if reflected in customary international law, may well be so unencumbered with the conditions and modalities surrounding it in the treaty. Whatever influence the Charter may have had on customary international law in these matters, it is clear that in customary international law it is not a condition of the lawfulness of the use of force in the self-defence that a procedure so closely dependent on the content of a treaty commitment and of the institutions established by it, should have been followed. On the other hand, if self-defence is advanced as a justification for measures which would otherwise be in breach both of the principle of customary international law and of that contained in the Charter, it is to be expected that the conditions of the Charter should be respected. Thus for the purpose of enquiry into the customary law position, the absence of a report may be one of the factors indicating whether the State in question was itself convinced that it was acting in self-defence.

[p. 110] When dealing with the rule of prohibition of the use of force, the Court considered the exception to it constituted by the exercise of the right of collective self-defence in the event of armed attack. Similarly, it must now consider the following question: if one State acts towards another State in breach of the principle of non-intervention, may a third State lawfully take such action by way of counter-measures against the first State as would otherwise constitute an intervention in its internal affairs? A right to act in this way in the case of intervention would be analogous to the right of collective self-defence in the case of an armed attack, but both the act which gives rise to the reaction, and that reaction itself, would in principle be less grave. Since the Court is here dealing with a dispute in which a wrongful use of force is alleged, it has primarily to consider whether a State has a right to respond to intervention with intervention going so far as to justify a use of force in reaction to measures which do not constitute an armed attack but may nevertheless involve a use of force. The question is itself undeniably relevant from the theoretical viewpoint. However, since the Court is bound to confine its decision to those points of law which are essential to the settlement of the dispute before it, it is not for the Court here to determine what direct reactions are lawfully open to a State which considers itself the victim of another State's acts of intervention, possibly involving the use of force. Hence it has not to determine whether, in the event of Nicaragua's having committed any such acts against El Salvador, the latter was lawfully entitled to take any particular counter-measure. It might however be suggested that, in such a situation, the United States might have been permitted to intervene in Nicaragua in the exercise of some right analogous to the right of collective self-defence, one which might be resorted to in a case of intervention short of armed attack.

The Court has recalled above (paragraphs 193 to 195) that for one State to use force against another, on the ground that that State has committed a wrongful act of force against a third State, is regarded as lawful, by way of exception, only when the wrongful act provoking the response was an armed attack. Thus the lawfulness of the use of force by a State in response to a wrongful act of which it has not itself been the victim is not admitted when this wrongful act is not an armed attack. In the view of the Court, under international law in force today - whether customary international law or that of the United Nations system - States do not have a right of "collective" armed response to acts which do not constitute an "armed attack".

[pp. 116-117] As to subparagraph 1 (d) [4], clearly "measures... necessary to fulfill the obligations of a Party for the maintenance or restoration of international peace and security" must signify measures which the State in question must take in performance of an international commitment of which any evasion constitutes a breach. A commitment of this kind is accepted by Members of the United Nations in respect of Security Council decisions taken on the basis of Chapter VII of the United Nations Charter (Art. 25), or, for members of the Organization of American States, in respect of decisions taken by the Organ of Consultation of the Inter-American system, under Articles 3 and 20 of the

4 Subparagraph 1 (d) of Article XXI of the 1956 FCN-Treaty.

Inter-American Treaty of Reciprocal Assistance (Rio de Janeiro, 1947). The Court does not believe that this provision of the 1956 Treaty can apply to the eventuality of the exercise of the right of individual or collective self-defence.

On the other hand, action taken in self-defence, individual or collective, might be considered as part of the wider category of measures qualified in Article XXI as "necessary to protect" the "essential security interests" of a party. In its Counter-Memorial on jurisdiction and admissibility, the United States contended that : "Any possible doubts as to the applicability of the FCN Treaty to Nicaragua's claims is dispelled by Article XXI of the Treaty ..." After quoting paragraph 1 (*d*) (set out in paragraph 221 above), the Counter-Memorial continues:

"Article XXI has been described by the Senate Foreign Relations Committee as containing 'the usual exceptions relating ... to traffic in arms, ammunition and implements of war and to measures for collective or individual self-defense'."

It is difficult to deny that self-defence against an armed attack corresponds to measures necessary to protect essential security interests. But the concept of essential security interests certainly extends beyond the concept of an armed attack, and has been subject to very broad interpretations in the past.

[p. 119] As regards El Salvador, the Court has found (paragraph 160 above) that it is satisfied that between July 1979 and the early months of 1981, an intermittent flow of arms was routed via the territory of Nicaragua to the armed opposition in that country. The Court was not however satisfied that assistance has reached the Salvadorian armed opposition, on a scale of any significance, since the early months of 1981, or that the Government of Nicaragua was responsible for any flow of arms at either period. Even assuming that the supply of arms to the opposition in El Salvador could be treated as imputable to the Government of Nicaragua, to justify invocation of the right of collective self-defence in customary international law, it would have to be equated with an armed attack by Nicaragua on El Salvador. As stated above, the Court is unable to consider that, in customary international law, the provision of arms to the opposition in another State constitutes an armed attack on that State. Even at a time when the arms flow was at its peak, and again assuming the participation of the Nicaraguan Government, that would not constitute such armed attack.

[pp. 120-121] The exercise of the right of collective self-defence presupposes that an armed attack has occurred; and it is evident that it is the victim State, being the most directly aware of that fact, which is likely to draw general attention to its plight. It is also evident that if the victim State wishes another State to come to its help in the exercise of the right of collective self-defence, it will normally make an express request to that effect. Thus in the present instance, the Court is entitled to take account, in judging the asserted justification of the exercise of collective self-defence by the United States, of the actual conduct of El Salvador, Honduras and Costa Rica at the relevant time, as indicative of a belief by the State in question that it was the victim of an armed attack by Nicaragua, and of the making of a request by the victim State to the United States for help in the exercise of collective self-defence.

The Court has seen no evidence that the conduct of those States was consistent with such a situation, either at the time when the United States first embarked on the activities which were allegedly justified by self-defence, or indeed for a long period subsequently.

[pp. 121-122] There is also an aspect of the conduct of the United States which the Court is entitled to take into account as indicative of the view of that State on the question of the existence of an armed attack. At no time, up to the present, has the United States Government addressed to the Security Council, in connection with the matters the subject of the present case, the report which is required by Article 51 of the United Nations Charter in respect of measures which a State believes itself bound to take when it exercises the right of individual or collective self-defence. The Court, whose decision has to be made on the basis of customary international law, has already observed that in the context of that law, the reporting obligation enshrined in Article 51 of the Charter of the United Nations does not exist. It does not therefore treat the absence of a report on the part of the United States as the breach of an undertaking forming part of the customary international law applicable to the present dispute. But the Court is justified in observing that this conduct of the United States hardly conforms with the latter's avowed conviction that it was acting in the context of collective self-defence as consecrated by Article 51 of the Charter. This fact is all the more noteworthy because, in the Security Council, the United States has itself taken the view that failure to observe the requirement to make a report contradicted a State's claim to be acting on the basis of collective self-defence (S/PV. 2187).

[pp. 122-123] Since the Court has found that the condition *sine qua non* required for the exercise of the right of collective self-defence by the United States is not fulfilled in this case, the appraisal of the United States activities in relation to the criteria of necessity and proportionality takes on a different significance. As a result of this conclusion of the Court, even if the United States activities in question had been carried on in strict compliance with the canons of necessity and proportionality, they would not thereby become lawful. If however they were not, this may constitute an additional ground of wrongfulness. On the question of necessity, the Court observes that the United States measures taken in December 1981 (or, at the earliest, March of that year - paragraph 93 above) cannot be said to correspond to a "necessity" justifying the United States action against Nicaragua on the basis of assistance given by Nicaragua to the armed opposition in El Salvador. First, these measures were only taken, and began to produce their effects, several months after the major offensive of the armed opposition against the Government of El Salvador had been completely repulsed (January 1981), and the actions of the opposition considerably reduced in consequence. Thus it was possible to eliminate the main danger to the Salvadorian Government without the United States embarking on activities in and against Nicaragua. Accordingly, it cannot be held that these activities were undertaken in the light of necessity. Whether or not the assistance to the *contras* might meet the criterion of proportionality, the Court cannot regard the United States activities summarized in paragraphs 80, 81 and 86, i.e., those relating to the mining of the Nicaraguan ports and the attacks on ports, oil installations, etc., as satisfying that criterion. Whatever uncertainty may exist as to the exact scale of the aid received by the Salvadorian armed opposition from Nicaragua, it is clear that these latter United States activities in question could not have been proportionate to that aid. Finally on this point, the Court must also observe that the reaction of the United States in the context of what it regarded as self-defence was continued long after the period in which any presumed armed attack by Nicaragua could reasonably be contemplated.

[p. 127] On the legal level the Court cannot regard response to an intervention by Nicaragua as such a justification. While an armed attack would give rise to an entitlement to collective self-defence, a use of force of a lesser degree of gravity cannot, as the Court has already observed (paragraph 211 above), produce any entitlement to take collective counter-measures involving the use of force. The acts of which Nicaragua is accused, even assuming them to have been established and imputable to that State, could only have justified proportionate counter-measures on the part of the State which had been the victim of these acts, namely El Salvador, Honduras or Costa Rica. They could not justify counter-measures taken by a third State, the United States, and particularly could not justify intervention involving the use of force.

[pp. 268-269 **D.O. Schwebel**] The delictual acts of the Nicaraguan Government have not been confined to provision of very large quantities of arms, munitions and supplies (an act which of itself might be viewed as not tantamount to an armed attack); Nicaragua (and Cuba) have joined with the Salvadoran rebels in the organization, planning and training for their acts of insurgency; and Nicaragua has provided the Salvadoran insurgents with command-and-control facilities, bases, communications and sanctuary, which have enabled the leadership of the Salvadoran insurgency to operate from Nicaraguan territory. Under both customary and conventional international law, that scale of Nicaraguan subversive activity not only constitutes unlawful intervention in the affairs of El Salvador; it is cumulatively tantamount to an armed attack upon El Salvador. (It is striking that both Nicaragua and the United States, in their pleadings before the Court, agree that significant material support by a State of foreign armed irregulars who endeavour forcibly to overthrow the Government of another State is tantamount to armed attack upon the latter State by the former State.) Not only is El Salvador entitled to defend itself against this armed attack; it can, and has, called upon the United States to assist it in the exercise of collective self-defence. The United States is legally entitled to respond. It can lawfully respond to Nicaragua's covert attempt to overthrow the Government of El Salvador by overt or covert pressures, military and other, upon the Government of Nicaragua, which are exerted either directly upon the Government, territory and people of Nicaragua by the United States, or indirectly through the actions of Nicaraguan rebels - the "*contras*" - supported by the United States.

[p. 269 **D.O. Schwebel**] While United States pressure upon Nicaragua is essentially lawful, nevertheless questions about the legality of aspects of United States conduct remain. In my view, the fundamental question is this. Granting that the United States can join El Salvador in measures of collective self-defence (even if, contrary to Article 51 of the United Nations Charter, they were not reported to the United Nations Security Council, as, by their nature, covert defensive measures will not be), those measures must be necessary, and proportionate to the delicts - the actions tantamount to armed attack - of Nicaragua. And they must in their nature be fundamentally measures of self-defence.

By these standards, the unannounced mining by the United States of Nicaraguan ports was a violation of international law. That mining could affect and did affect third States as against whom no rationale of self-defence could apply in these circumstances. As against Nicaragua, however, the mining was no less lawful than other measures of pressure.

[p. 270 **D.O. Schwebel**] To say, as did Nicaraguan counsel, that action designed to overthrow a government cannot be defensive, is evident error, which would have come as a surprise to Roosevelt and Churchill (and Stalin), who insisted on the unconditional surrender of the Axis Powers. In the largest-scale international hostilities currently in progress, one State, which maintains that it is the victim of armed attack, proclaims as its essential condition for peace that the government of the alleged aggressor be overthrown - a condition which some may find extreme, others not, but which in any event has not aroused the legal condemnation of the international community. Moreover, I agree with the Court that, if Nicaragua has been giving support to the armed opposition in El Salvador, and if this constitutes an armed attack upon El Salvador, collective self-defence may be legally invoked by the United States, even though the United States may possibly have an additional and perhaps more decisive motive drawn from the political orientation of the Nicaraguan Government.

[p. 332 **D.O. Schwebel**] In my view, the Judgment of the Court on the critical question of whether aid to irregulars may be tantamount to an armed attack departs from accepted - and desirable - law. Far from contributing, as so many of the Court's judgments have, to the progressive development of the law, on this question the Court's Judgment implies a regressive development of the law which fails to take account of the realities of the use of force in international relations: realities which have unfortunately plagued the world for years and give every sign of continuing to do so - whether they are recognized by the Court or not. I regret to say that I believe that the Court's Judgment on this profoundly important question may detract as much from the security of States as it does from the state of the law.

[p. 344 **D.O. Schwebel**] It accordingly follows not only that the multiple acts of subversive intervention by Nicaragua against El Salvador are acts of aggression, and that those acts fall within the proscriptions of the Definition of Aggression. It is also important to note that the Definition - contrary to the Thirteen-Power proposals - designedly says nothing about prohibiting a State from having recourse to the right of individual or collective self-defence when that State "is a victim in its own territory of subversive and/or terrorist acts by irregular, volunteer or armed bands organized or supported by another State". That prohibitive proposal proved unacceptable to the international community. Rather, it is plain that, under the Definition, and customary international law, and in the practice of the United Nations and of States, a State is entitled in precisely these circumstances to act in individual and collective self-defence. To be entitled to do so, it is not required to show that the irregulars operating on its territory act as the agents of the foreign State or States which support them. It is enough to show that those States are "substantially involved" in the sending of those irregulars on to its territory.

[pp. 347-348 **D.O. Schwebel**] I do not agree with a construction of the United Nations Charter which would read Article 51 as if it were worded: "Nothing in the present Charter shall impair the inherent right of individual or collective self-defence if, and only if, an armed attack occurs ..." I do not agree that the terms or intent of Article 51 eliminate the right of self-defence under customary international law, or confine its entire scope to the express terms of Article 51. While I recognize that the issue is controversial and open to more than one substantial view.

[pp. 372-373 **D.O. Schwebel**] What matters in this context is not whether one agrees or disagrees with the legality of the cited acts of the United Nations, Israel, France, the United Kingdom, the United States, China, Viet Nam, Iraq, the Soviet Union, Afghanistan and Nicaragua. It is by no means suggested that all of these actions are of the same legal value; some were clearly lawful, others clearly not. But what is significant is that these actions, whose legality has been affirmed by those carrying them out, provide ample and significant State practice indicating that what is proposed as a limitation upon self-defence and counter-intervention is not today applied as a rule of international law. It is not generally accepted State practice.

Nevertheless, if the proposed rule is not the accepted rule, should it be? Should the response of a victim of direct or indirect aggression, and a State or States lending it support in its resistance to that aggression, be confined to the territory of the victim? The purpose of such a principle would be to constrict conflict by reducing the actuality of and potential for its territorial expansion. That is an appealing purpose. But the drawbacks of implementing such a principle appear to outweigh its attractions. For a result of confining hostilities to the territory of the victim would be to encourage victimization; potential aggressors would be the likelier to estimate that their aggression will be free of significant cost. The potential aggressor might reason that it has little to lose in launching covert aggression, as by concealed support of insurgents operating against the government of a neighbouring State. If the aggression succeeds, the aggressor's purposes are achieved; if not, the aggressor cannot suffer in its territory. If it has done no more than lend substantial support to foreign insurgents, it is those insurgents alone who will take the punishment. The aggressor may lose its material investment in the foreign insurgency but no more; it will not suffer deterrence of its forces, on its territory, with incidental damage to its people and possessions. Thus if one attempt at foreign armed subversion fails, another can be attempted at a more propitious time. Or, indeed, the aggressor can carry on its support of a foreign insurgency continuously, relatively secure in the "rule" of international law that it is immune from a defensive response on its territory directed at its forces. In short, such a rule would encourage rather than deter aggression. Thus it would not succeed even in its purpose of confining the potential for the territorial expansion of hostilities. International law is better left as it is, confining the scope of permissible self-defence, individual and collective, by the provisions of the United Nations Charter and the norms of necessity and proportionality.

[p. 376 **D.O. Schwebel**] It must be recalled, however, that, if the legality of the actions of the United States in this case are to be adjudged not under the United Nations Charter and the other treaties on which Nicaragua has relied, but, by reason of the multilateral treaty reservation of the United States, under customary international law, customary international law knows nothing of an obligation of a State to report to the Security Council.

[pp. 379-380 **D.O. Schwebel**] The use of mines in hostilities is not of itself unlawful. That today is so whether the hostilities are declared or undeclared; a state of war or of belligerency need not exist. If the use of force by the United States against Nicaragua is lawful, then the use of mining as a measure of such use of force may, in principle, be lawful, provided that its usage comports with measures taken in the exercise of the right of collective self-defence.

...

However, as against third States whose shipping was damaged or whose nationals were injured by mines laid by or on behalf of the United States, the international responsibility of the United States may arise. Third States were and are entitled to carry on commerce with Nicaragua and their ships are entitled to make use of Nicaraguan ports. If the United States were to be justified in taking blockade-like measures against Nicaraguan ports, as by mining, it could only be so if its mining of Nicaraguan ports were publicly and officially announced by it and if international shipping were duly warned by it about the fact that mines would be or had been laid in specified waters. However, no such announcement was made by the United States in advance of or upon the laying of mines; international shipping was not duly warned by it in a timely, official manner.

[p. 535 **D.O. Jennings**] One is, however, immediately faced with the difficulty that a plea of collective self-defence is obviously a possible justification of intervention and that this is the justification which the United States has pleaded. So it is again a dispute arising under Article 51 of the United Nations Charter. If one turns to the Inter-American system of law, the same problem arises. Article 18 of the Charter of the Organization of American States deals with intervention in peculiarly comprehensive terms, in that it prohibits intervention "for any reason whatever"; it also, in Article 21, deals with force and self-defence, but in specifically treaty terms. Thus, by that article, the American States "bind themselves in their international relations not to have recourse to the use of force, except in the case of self-defense *in accordance with existing treaties or in fulfillment thereof*" (emphasis added).

[pp. 543-544 **D.O. Jennings**] It may readily be agreed that the mere provision of arms cannot be said to amount to an armed attack. But the provision of arms may, nevertheless, be a very important element in what might be thought to amount to armed attack, where it is coupled with other kinds of involvement. Accordingly, it seems to me that to say that the provision of arms, coupled with "logistical or other support" is not armed attack is going much too far. Logistical support may itself be crucial. According to the dictionary, logistics covers the "art of moving, lodging, and supplying troops and equipment" (*Concise Oxford English Dictionary*, 7th ed., 1982). If there is added to all this "other support", it becomes difficult to understand what it is, short of direct attack by a State's own forces, that may not be done apparently without a lawful response in the form of collective self-defence nor indeed may be responded to at all by the use of force or threat of force, for, to cite the Court again, "States do not have a right of 'collective' armed response to acts which do not constitute an 'armed attack'" (see para. 211).

This looks to me neither realistic nor just in the world where power struggles are in every continent carried on by destabilization, interference in civil strife, comfort, aid and encouragement to rebels, and the like. The original scheme of the United Nations Charter, whereby force would be deployed by the United Nations itself, in accordance with the provisions of Chapter VII of the Charter, has never come into effect. Therefore an essential element in the Charter design is totally missing. In this situation it seems dangerous to define unnecessarily strictly the conditions for lawful self-defence, so as to leave a large area where both a forcible response to force is forbidden, and yet the United Nations employment of force, which was intended to fill that gap, is absent.

[pp. 544-546 **D.O. Jennings**] Obviously the notion of collective self-defence is open to abuse and it is necessary to ensure that it is not employable as a mere cover for aggression disguised as protection, and the Court is therefore right to define it somewhat strictly. Even so, it may be doubted whether it is helpful to suggest that the attacked State must in some more or less formal way have "declared" itself the victim of an attack and then have, as an additional "requirement", made a formal request to a particular third State for assistance. Thus the Court says:

"The Court concludes that the requirement of a request by the State which is the victim of the alleged attack is additional to the requirement that such a State should have declared itself to have been attacked." (Para. 199.)

It may readily be agreed that the victim State must both be in real need of assistance and must want it and that the fulfilment of both these conditions must be shown. But to ask that these requirements take the form of some sort of formal declaration and request might sometimes be unrealistic.

But there is another objection to this way of looking at collective self-defence. It seems to be based almost upon an idea of vicarious defence by champions: that a third State may lawfully come to the aid of an authenticated victim of armed attack provided that the requirements of a declaration of attack and a request for assistance are complied with. But whatever collective self-defence means, it does not mean vicarious defence; for that way the notion is indeed open to abuse. The assisting State is not an authorized champion, permitted under certain conditions to go to the aid of a favoured State. The assisting State surely must, by going to the victim State's assistance, be also, and in addition to other requirements, in some measure defending itself. There should even in "collective self-defence" be some real element of self [5] involved with the notion of defence. This is presumably also the philosophy which underlies mutual security arrangements, such as the system of the Organization of American States, for which indeed Article 51 was specifically designed. By such a system of collective security, the security of each member State is meant to be involved with the security of the others; not merely as a result of a contractual arrangement but by the real consequences of the System and its organization. Thus, Article 27 of the Charter of the Organization of American States provides that:

"Every act of aggression by a State against the territorial integrity or the inviolability of the territory or against the sovereignty or political independence of an American State shall be considered an act of aggression against the other American States."

This, I believe, should not be regarded as a mere contractual arrangement for collective defence - a legal fiction used as a device for arranging for mutual defence -; it is to be regarded as an organized system of collective security by which the security of each member is made really and truly to have become involved with the security of the others, thus providing a true basis for a system of collective self-defence.

6.3. Intervention

Military and Paramilitary Activities
(Nicaragua/United States of America)
Merits. J. 27.6.1986
I.C.J. Reports 1986, p. 14

[pp. 106-108] The principle of non-intervention involves the right of every sovereign State to conduct its affairs without outside interference; though examples of trespass against this principle are not infrequent, the Court considers that it is part and parcel of customary international law. As the Court has observed: "Between independent States, respect for territorial sovereignty is an essential foundation of international relations" (*I.C.J. Reports 1949*, p. 35), and international law requires political integrity also to be respected. Expressions of an *opinio juris* regarding the existence of the principle of non-intervention in customary international law are numerous and not difficult to find. Of course, statements whereby States avow their recognition of the principles of international law set forth in the United Nations Charter cannot strictly be interpreted as

5 It may be objected that the very term "self-defence" is a common law notion, and that, for instance, the French equivalent of "légitime défense" does not mention "self". Here, however, the French version is for once, merely unhelpful; it does no more than beg the question of what is "légitime".

applying to the principle of non-intervention by States in the internal and external affairs of other States, since this principle is not, as such, spelt out in the Charter. But it was never intended that the Charter should embody written confirmation of every essential principle of international law in force. The existence in the *opinio juris* of States of the principle of non-intervention is backed by established and substantial practice. It has moreover been presented as a corollary of the principle of the sovereign equality of States. A particular instance of this is General Assembly resolution 2625 (XXV), the Declaration on the Principles of International Law concerning Friendly Relations and Co-operation among States. In the *Corfu Channel* case, when a State claimed a right of intervention in order to secure evidence in the territory of another State for submission to an international tribunal (*I.C.J. Reports 1949*, p. 34), the Court observed that:

"the alleged right of intervention as the manifestation of a policy of force, such as has, in the past, given rise to most serious abuses and such as cannot, whatever be the present defects in international organization, find a place in international law. Intervention is perhaps still less admissible in the particular form it would take here; for, from the nature of things, it would be reserved for the most powerful States, and might easily lead to perverting the administration of international justice itself." (*I.C.J. Reports 1949*, p. 35.)

The principle has since been reflected in numerous declarations adopted by international organizations and conferences in which the United States and Nicaragua have participated, e.g., General Assembly resolution 2131 (XX), the Declaration on the Inadmissibility of Intervention in the Domestic Affairs of States and the Protection of their Independence and Sovereignty. It is true that the United States, while it voted in favour of General Assembly resolution 2131 (XX), also declared at the time of its adoption in the First Committee that it considered the declaration in that resolution to be "only a statement of political intention and not a formulation of law" (*Official Records of the General Assembly, Twentieth Session*, First Committee, A/C.1/SR. 1423, p. 436). However, the essentials of resolution 2131 (XX) are repeated in the Declaration approved by resolution 2625 (XXV), which set out principles which the General Assembly declared to the "basic principles" of international law, and on the adoption of which no analogous statement was made by the United States representative.

As regards inter-American relations, attention may be drawn to, for example, the United States reservation to the Montevideo Convention on Rights and Duties of States (26 December 1933), declaring the opposition of the United States Government to "interference with the freedom, the sovereignty or other internal affairs, or processes of the Governments of other nations"; or the ratification by the United States of the Additional Protocol relative to Non-Intervention (23 December 1936). Among more recent texts, mention may be made of resolutions AG/RES.78 and AG/RES. 128 of the General Assembly of the Organization of American States. In a different context, the United States expressly accepted the principles set forth in the declaration, to which reference has already been made, appearing in the Final Act of the Conference on Security and Co-operation in Europe (Helsinki, 1 August 1975), including an elaborate statement of the principle of non-intervention; while these principles were presented as applying to the mutual relations among the participating States, it can be inferred that the text testifies to the existence, and the acceptance by the United States, of a customary principle which has universal application.

Notwithstanding the multiplicity of declarations by States accepting the principle of non-intervention, there remain two questions: first, what is the exact content of the principle so accepted, and secondly, is the practice sufficiently in conformity with it for this to be a rule of customary international law? As regards the first problem - that of the content of the principle of non-intervention - the Court will define only those aspects of the principle which appear to be relevant to the resolution of the dispute. In this respect it notes that, in view of the generally accepted formulations, the principle forbids all States or groups of States to intervene directly or indirectly in internal or external affairs of other States. A prohibited intervention must accordingly be one bearing on matters in which each State is permitted, by the principle of State sovereignty, to decide freely. One of these is the choice of a political, economic, social and cultural system, and the formulation of foreign policy. Intervention is wrongful when it uses methods of coercion in regard to such choices, which must remain free ones. The element of coercion, which defines, and indeed forms the very essence of, prohibited intervention, is particularly obvious in the case of an intervention which uses force, either in the direct form of military action, or in the indirect form of support for subversive or terrorist armed activities within another State. As noted above (paragraph 191), General Assembly resolution 2625 (XXV) equates assistance of this kind with the use of force by the assisting State when the acts committed in another State "involve a threat or use of force". These forms of action are therefore wrongful in the light of both the principle of non-use of force, and that of non-intervention. In view of the nature of Nicaragua's complaints against the United States, and those expressed by the United States in regard to Nicaragua's conduct towards El Salvador, it is primarily acts of intervention of this kind with which the Court is concerned in the present case.

However, before reaching a conclusion on the nature of prohibited intervention, the Court must be satisfied that State practice justifies it. There have been in recent years a number of instances of foreign intervention for the benefit of forces opposed to the government of another State. The Court is not here concerned with the process of decolonization; this question is not in issue in the present case. It has to consider whether there might be indications of a practice illustrative of belief in a kind of general right for States to intervene, directly or indirectly, with or without armed force, in support of an internal opposition in another State, whose cause appeared particularly worthy by reason of the political and moral values with which it was identified. For such a general right to come into existence would involve a fundamental modification of the customary law principle of non-intervention.

[pp. 109-110] The Court therefore finds that no such general right of intervention, in support of an opposition within another State, exists in contemporary international law. The Court concludes that acts constituting a breach of the customary principle of non-intervention will also, if they directly or indirectly involve the use of force, constitute a breach of the principle of non-use of force in international relations.

[p. 119] In the view of the Court, while the arming and training of the *contras*, can certainly be said to involve the threat or use of force against Nicaragua, this is not necessarily so in respect of all the assistance given by the United States Government. In particular, the Court considers that the mere supply of funds to the *contras* while undoubtedly an act of intervention in the internal affairs of Nicaragua, as will be explained below, does not in itself amount to a use of force.

[p. 124] The Court considers that in international law, if one State, with a view to the coercion of another State, supports and assists armed bands in that State whose purpose is to overthrow the government of that State, that amounts to an intervention by the one State in the internal affairs of the other, whether or not the political objective of the State giving such support and assistance is equally far-reaching.

[pp. 124-125] There can be no doubt that the provision of strictly humanitarian aid to persons or forces in another country, whatever their political affiliations or objectives, cannot be regarded as unlawful intervention, or as in any other way contrary to international law. The characteristics of such aid were indicated in the first and second of the fundamental principles declared by the Twentieth International Conference of the Red Cross, that

"The Red Cross, born of a desire to bring assistance without discrimination to the wounded on the battlefield, endeavours - in its international and national capacity - to prevent and alleviate human suffering wherever it may be found. Its purpose is to protect life and health and to ensure respect for the human being. It promotes mutual understanding, friendship, cooperation and lasting peace amongst all peoples"

and that

"It makes no discrimination as to nationality, race, religious beliefs, class or political opinions. It endeavours only to relieve suffering, giving priority to the most urgent cases of distress".

[p. 125] An essential feature of truly humanitarian aid is that it is given "without discrimination" of any kind. In the view of the Court, if the provision of "humanitarian assistance" is to escape condemnation as an intervention in the internal affairs of Nicaragua, not only must it be limited to the purposes hallowed in the practice of the Red Cross, namely "to prevent and alleviate human suffering", and "to protect life and health and to ensure respect for the human being"; it must also, and above all, be given without discrimination to all in need in Nicaragua, not merely to the *contras* and their dependents.

[pp. 125-126] As already noted, Nicaragua has also asserted that the United States is responsible for an "indirect" form of intervention in its internal affairs inasmuch as it has taken, to Nicaragua's disadvantage, certain action of an economic nature. The Court's attention has been drawn in particular to the cessation of economic aid in April 1981; the 90 per cent reduction in the sugar quota for United States imports from Nicaragua in April 1981; and the trade embargo adopted on 1 May 1985. While admitting in principle that some of these actions were not unlawful in themselves, counsel for Nicaragua argued that these measures of economic constraint add up to a systematic violation of the principle of non-intervention.

The Court does not here have to concern itself with possible breaches of such international economic instruments as the General Agreement on Tariffs and Trade, referred to in passing by counsel for Nicaragua; any such breaches would appear to fall outside the Court's jurisdiction, particularly in view of the effect of the multilateral treaty reservation, nor has Nicaragua seised the Court of any complaint of such breaches. The question of the compatibility of the actions complained of with the 1956 Treaty of Friendship, Commerce and Navigation will be examined below, in the context of the Court's examination of the provisions of that Treaty. At this point, the Court has merely to say that it is unable to regard such action on the economic plane as is here complained of as a breach of the customary-law principle of non-intervention.

[p. 126] As the Court has stated, the principle of non-intervention derives from customary international law. It would certainly lose its effectiveness as a principle of law if intervention were to be justified by a mere request for assistance made by an opposition group in another State - supposing such a request to have actually been made by an opposition to the régime in Nicaragua in this instance. Indeed, it is difficult to see what would remain of the principle of non-intervention in international law if intervention, which is already allowable at the request of the government of a State, were also to be allowed at the request of the opposition. This would permit any State to intervene at any moment in the internal affairs of another State, whether at the request of the government or at the request of its opposition. Such a situation does not in the Court's view correspond to the present state of international law.

[p. 128] The effects of the principle of respect for territorial sovereignty inevitably overlap with those of the principles of the prohibition of the use of force and of non-intervention. Thus the assistance to the *contras*, as well as the direct attacks on Nicaraguan ports, oil installations, etc., referred to in paragraphs 81 to 86 above, not only amount to an unlawful use of force, but also constitute infringements of the territorial sovereignty of Nicaragua, and incursions into its territorial and internal waters. Similarly, the mining operations in the Nicaraguan ports not only constitute breaches of the principle of the non-use of force, but also affect Nicaragua's sovereignty over certain maritime expanses. The Court has in fact found that these operations were carried on in Nicaragua's territorial or internal waters or both (paragraph 80), and accordingly they constitute a violation of Nicaragua's sovereignty. The principle of respect for territorial sovereignty is also directly infringed by the unauthorized overflight of a State's territory by aircraft belonging to or under the control of the government of another State. The Court has found above that such overflights were in fact made (paragraph 91 above).

These violations cannot be justified either by collective self-defence, for which, as the Court has recognized, the necessary circumstances are lacking, nor by any right of the United States to take counter-measures involving the use of force in the event of intervention by Nicaragua in El Salvador, since no such right exists under the applicable international law. They cannot be justified by the activities in El Salvador attributed to the Government of Nicaragua. The latter activities, assuming that they did in fact occur, do not bring into effect any right belonging to the United States which would justify the actions in question. Accordingly, such actions constitute violations of Nicaragua's sovereignty under customary international law.

[p. 133] Nicaragua's domestic policy options, even assuming that they correspond to the description given of them by the Congress finding, cannot justify on the legal plane the various actions of the Respondent complained of. The Court cannot contemplate the creation of a new rule opening up a right of intervention by one State against another on the ground that the latter has opted for some particular ideology or political system.

[p. 133] Whatever the impact of individual alliances on regional or international political-military balances, the Court is only competent to consider such questions from the standpoint of international law. From that aspect, it is sufficient to say that State sovereignty evidently extends to the area of its foreign policy, and that there is no rule of customary international law to prevent a State from choosing and conducting a foreign policy in co-ordination with that of another State.

[p. 156 **S.O. Singh**] I cannot conclude this opinion without emphasizing the key importance of the doctrine of non-intervention in the affairs of States which is so vital for the peace and progress of the international community. To ignore this doctrine is to undermine international order and to promote violence and bloodshed which may prove catastrophic in the end. The significant contribution which the Latin American treaty system along with the United Nations Charter make to the essentials of sound public order embraces the clear, unequivocal expression given to the principle of non-intervention, to be treated as a sanctified absolute rule of law whose non-observance could lead to disastrous consequences causing untold misery to humanity.

[pp. 199-200 **S.O. Sette-Camara**] I fully concur with the rest of the Judgment, as I firmly believe that the non-use of force as well as non-intervention - the latter as a corollary of equality of States and self-determination - are not only cardinal principles of customary international law but could in addition be recognized as peremptory rules of customary international law which impose obligations on all States.

With regard to the non-use of force, the International Law Commission in its commentaries on the final articles on the Law of Treaties said:

"the law of the Charter concerning the prohibition of the use of force in itself constitutes a conspicuous example of a rule in international law having the character of *jus cogens*" (*International Law Commission Yearbook*, 1966, Vol. II, p. 247).

As far as non-intervention is concerned, in spite of the uncertainties which still prevail in the matter of identifying norms of *jus cogens*, I submit that the prohibition of intervention would certainly qualify as such, if the test of Article 53 of the Vienna Convention on the Law of Treaties is applied. A treaty containing provisions by which States agree to intervene, directly or indirectly, in the internal or external affairs of any other State would certainly fall within the purview of Article 53, and should consequently be considered void as conflicting with a peremptory norm of general international law.

[pp. 534-535 **D.O. Jennings**] There can be no doubt that the principle of non-intervention is an autonomous principle of customary law; indeed it is very much older than any of the multilateral treaty regimes in question. It is, moreover, a principle of law which in the inter-American System has its own peculiar development, interpretation and importance.

[p. 273 **D.O. Schwebel**] Moreover, the Court has in my view further compromised its Judgment by its inference that there may be double standard in the law governing the use of force in international relations: intervention is debarred, except, it appears, in "the process of decolonization". I deeply regret to be obliged to say that, in my submission, far from the Court, in pursuance of the requirements of its Statute, satisfying itself as to the facts and the law, it has stultified itself.

[pp. 305-306 **D.O. Schwebel**] But it may be argued to the contrary that, where, as here, the United States and Nicaragua (and the "affected" States) are bound by the terms of the OAS Charter, and where the provisions of that Charter embrace not only dictatorial interference but much more pervasive proscription of intervention, the greater includes the lesser; that, since the OAS Charter sets out between the Parties, and as among them and the States affected, the specific and governing legal standards, and since the multilateral treaty reservation debars the Court from application of those standards, it withholds from the Court jurisdiction to pass upon complaints of intervention in this case, all of which must fall within the capacious terms of the OAS Charter. In my view, the latter argument, while open to challenge, is the stronger. Moreover, the complaints of intervention in this case are so intimately involved with the complaints of the unlawful use of force - the facts that underlie both causes of action correspond so closely - that the artificiality of treating the Court as having jurisdiction to deal with charges of intervention and not having jurisdiction to deal with charges of the unlawful use of force reinforces this conclusion.

7. LAW OF TREATIES

7.6. Interpretation

Border and Transborder Armed Actions Nicaragua/Honduras), Jurisdiction and Admissibility, Judgment, I.C.J. Reports 1988, p. 69

[pp. 85-86] Further confirmation of the Court's reading of Article XXXI [6] is to be found in the *travaux préparatoires*. In this case these must of course be resorted to only with caution, as not all the stages of the drafting of the texts at the Bogotá Conference

6 Article XXXI of the Pact of Bogotá.

were the subject of detailed records. The proceedings of the Conference were however published, in accordance with Article 47 of the Regulations of the Conference, in Spanish, and certain recorded discussions of Committee III of the Conference throw light particularly upon the contemporary conception of'the relationship between Article XXXI and declarations under Article 36 of the Statute.

The text which was to become Article XXXI was discussed at the meeting of Committee III held on 27 April 1948. The representative of the United States reminded the meeting that his country had previously, under Article 36, paragraph 2, of the Statute, made a declaration of acceptance of compulsory jurisdiction that included reservations; he made it clear that the United States intended to maintain those reservations in relation to the application of the Pact of Bogotá. The representative of Mexico replied that States which wished to maintain such reservations in their relations with the other parties to the Pact would have to reformulate them as reservations to the Pact, under Article LV. The representatives of Colombia and Ecuador, members of the drafting group, confirmed that interpretation. The representative of Peru asked whether an additional Article should not be added to the draft in order to specify that adhesion to the treaty would imply, as between the parties to it, the automatic removal of any reservations to declarations of acceptance of compulsory jurisdiction. The majority of Committee III considered, however, that such an Article was not necessary and the representative of Peru went on to say, after the vote, that "we should place on record what has been said here, to the effect that it is understood that adhesion is unconditional and that reservations are automatically removed" [7] *(translation by the Registry)*.

[pp. 88-90] The second objection of Honduras to jurisdiction is based on Article XXXII of the Pact of Bogotá, which reads as follows:

"When the conciliation procedure previously established in the present Treaty or by agreement of the parties does not lead to a solution, and the said parties have not agreed upon an arbitral procedure, either of them shall be entitled to have recourse to the International Court of Justice in the manner prescribed in Article 40 of the Statute thereof. The Court shall have compulsory jurisdiction in accordance with Article 36, paragraph 1, of the said Statute."

It is the contention of Honduras that Articles XXXI and XXXII must be read together. The first is said to define the extent of the Court's jurisdiction and the second to determine the conditions under which the Court may be seised. According to Honduras it follows that the Court could only be seised under Article XXXI if, in accordance with Article XXXII, there had been a prior recourse to conciliation and lack of agreement to

7 "Pero deben constar en actas las palabras pronunciadas aquí, acerca de que se entiende que es adhesión incondicional y que quedan removidas, automáticamente, las reservas." (*Novena Conferencia Internacional Americana, Actas y Documentos*, Vol. IV, p. 167).

arbitrate, which is not the situation in the present case.

Nicaragua on the other hand contends that Article XXXI and Article XXXII are two autonomous provisions, each of which confers jurisdiction upon the Court in the cases for which it provides. It claims that Article XXXI covers all juridical disputes which, before the conclusion of the Pact, would have been subject to arbitration under the General Treaty of Inter-American Arbitration of 5 January 1929; and that Article XXXII relates to disputes, whatever their nature, previously in the domain of conciliation under the General Convention of Inter-American Conciliation of the same date. It maintains accordingly that the Court can be seised, under Article XXXI, in the cases covered by that text, without there being any requirement to ascertain whether the procedural conditions laid down, in other cases, by Article XXXII have or have not been satisfied.

Honduras's interpretation of Article XXXII runs counter to the terms of that Article. Article XXXII makes no reference to Article XXXI; under that text the parties have, in general terms, an entitlement to have recourse to the Court in cases where there has been an unsuccessful conciliation.

It is true that one qualification of this observation is required, with regard to the French text of Article XXXII, which provides that, in the circumstances there contemplated, the party has "le droit de porter *la question* devant la Cour". That expression might be thought to refer back to the question which might have been the subject of the dispute referred to the Court under Article XXXI. It should, however, be observed that the text uses the word "*question*", which leaves room for uncertainty, rather than the word "*différend* (dispute)", used in Article XXXI, which would have been perfectly clear. Moreover, the Spanish, English and Portuguese versions speak, in general terms, of an entitlement to have recourse to the Court and do not justify the conclusion that there is a link between Article XXXI and Article XXXII.

Moreover, Article XXXII, unlike Article XXXI, refers expressly to the jurisdiction which the Court has under Article 36, paragraph 1, of the Statute. That reference would be difficult to understand if, as Honduras contends, the sole purpose of Article XXXII were to specify the procedural conditions for bringing before the Court disputes for which jurisdiction had already been conferred upon it by virtue of the declaration made in Article XXXI, pursuant to Article 36, paragraph 2.

It is, moreover, quite clear from the Pact that the purpose of the American States in drafting it was to reinforce their mutual commitments with regard to judicial settlement. This is also confirmed by the *travaux préparatoires*: the discussion at the meeting of Committee III of the Conference held on 27 April 1948 has already been referred to in paragraph 37 above. At that meeting, furthermore, the delegate of Colombia explained to the Committee the general lines of the system proposed by the Sub-Committee which had prepared the draft; the Sub-Committee took the position "that the principal procedure for the peaceful settlement of conflicts between the American States had to be judicial procedure before the International Court of Justice" [8] (*translation by the Registry*). Honduras's interpretation would however imply that the commitment, at first sight firm and unconditional, set forth in Article XXXI would, in fact, be emptied of all content if, for any reason, the dispute were not subjected to prior conciliation. Such a solution would be clearly contrary to both the object and the purpose of the Pact.

In short, Articles XXXI and XXXII provide for two distinct ways by which access may be had to the Court. The first relates to cases in which the Court can be seised directly and the second to those in which the parties initially resort to conciliation.

In the present case, Nicaragua has relied upon Article XXXI, not Article XXXII. It is accordingly not pertinent whether the dispute submitted to the Court has previously been the subject of an attempted conciliation, nor what interpretation is given to Article XXXII in other respects, in particular as regards the nature and the subject-matter of the disputes to which that text applies. It is sufficient for the Court to find that the second objection put forward by Honduras is based upon an incorrect interpretation of that Article and, for that reason, cannot be accepted.

Article XXXI of the Pact of Bogotá thus confers jurisdiction upon the Court to entertain the dispute submitted to it. For that reason, the Court does not need to consider whether it might have jurisdiction by virtue of the declarations of acceptance of compulsory jurisdiction by Nicaragua and Honduras set out in paragraphs 23 to 25 above.

[pp. 94-95] Before proceeding further, the Court notes that the Parties have drawn attention to a discrepancy between the four texts of Article II of the Pact (English, French, Portuguese and Spanish). In the French text, what is required is that, "de l'avis de l'une des parties", i.e., "in the opinion of one of the parties", the dispute should not be susceptible of settlement by negotiation. In the English, Portuguese and Spanish texts, the corresponding phrase is "in the opinion of the parties", or the equivalent in the other two languages. For reasons which will appear, the Court's reasoning does not require the resolution of the problem posed by this textual discrepancy, and it will therefore not rehearse all the arguments that have been put forward by the Parties to explain it or to justify the preferring of one version to another.

For the purpose of determining the application in this case of Article II of the Pact, the Court will proceed on the hypothesis that the stricter interpretation should be used, i.e., that it would be necessary to consider whether the "opinion" of both Parties was that it was not possible to settle the dispute by negotiation. For this purpose the Court does not consider that it is bound by the mere assertion of the one Party or the other that its opin-

8 "La Subcomisión estimó que el procedimiento principal para el arreglo pacífico de los conflictos entre los Estados Americanos ha de ser el procedimiento judicial ante la Corte Internacional de Justicia; ..." (*Novena Conferencia Internacional Americana, Actas y Documentos*, Vol. IV, p. 156).

ion is to a particular effect: it must, in the exercise of its judicial function, be free to make its own determination of that question on the basis of such evidence as is available to it.

Elettronica Sicula S.p.A. (ELSI)
Judgment of 20 July 1989
I.C.J. Reports 1989, p. 15

[p. 97 **D.O. Schwebel**] In the current case, the Parties attached radically different interpretations to the provisions of the Treaty and its Supplementary Agreement which were at issue between them. It is undeniable that, when their conflicting arguments are matched together, the meaning of some of the Treaty's provisions are ambiguous or obscure; indeed, each of the Parties maintained that the opposing interpretation led to results which, if not manifestly absurd, were unreasonable. Thus, according to the Vienna Convention, this is a case in which recourse to the preparatory work and circumstances of the Treaty's conclusion was eminently in order.

7.7. Specific Treaties

7.7.1. Convention on the Privileges and Immunities of the United Nations of 1946

Applicability of Article VI, Section 22,
of the Convention on the Privileges and
Immunities of the United Nations,
Advisory Opinion of 15 December 1989
I.C.J. Reports 1989, p. 177

[pp. 193-196] The Court will examine the applicability of Section 22 [9] *ratione*

---

9 Section 22 provides as follows:

"Experts (other than officials coming within the scope of Article V) performing missions for the United Nations shall be accorded such privileges and immunities as are necessary for the independent exercise of their functions during the period of their missions, including the time spent on journeys in connection with their missions. In particular they shall be accorded:

(a) immunity from personal arrest or detention and from seizure of their personal baggage;
(b) in respect of words spoken or written and acts done by them in the course of the performance of their mission, immunity from legal process of every kind. This immunity from legal process shall continue to be accorded notwithstanding that the persons concerned are no longer employed on missions for the United Nations;
(c) inviolability for all papers and documents;
(d) for the purpose of their communications with the United Nations, the right to use codes and to receive papers or correspondence by courier or in sealed bags;
(e) the same facilities in respect of currency or exchange restrictions as are

personae, ratione temporis and ratione loci, that is to say it will consider first what is meant by "experts on missions" for the purposes of Section 22, and then the meaning to be attached to the expression "period of [the] missions", before considering the position of experts in their relations with the States of which they are nationals or on the territory of which they reside.

The General Convention gives no definition of "experts on missions". All it does is to clarify two points, one negative and the other positive. From Section 22 it is clear, first that the officials of the Organization, even if chosen in consideration of their technical expertise in a particular field, are not included in the category of experts within the meaning of that provision; and secondly that only experts performing missions for the United Nations are covered by Section 22. The Section does not, however, furnish any indication of the nature, duration or place of these missions.

Nor is there really any guidance in this respect to be found in the *travaux préparatoires* of the General Convention. The Convention was initially drafted and submitted to the General Assembly by the Preparatory Commission set up at San Francisco in June 1945; that initial draft did not contain anything corresponding to the present Article VI. That article was added by the Sub-Commission on Privileges and Immunities established by the Sixth Committee to examine the draft, but the contemporary official records do not make it possible to ascertain the reasons for the addition.

The purpose of Section 22 is nevertheless evident, namely, to enable the United Nations to entrust missions to persons who do not have the status of an official of the Organization, and to guarantee them "such privileges and immunities as are necessary for the independent exercise of their functions". The experts thus appointed or elected may or may not be remunerated, may or may not have a contract, may be given a task requiring work over a lengthy period or a short time. The essence of the matter lies not in their administrative position but in the nature of their mission.

In practice, according to the information supplied by the Secretary-General, the United Nations has had occasion to entrust missions - increasingly varied in nature - to persons not having the status of United Nations officials. Such persons have been entrusted with mediation, with preparing reports, preparing studies, conducting investigations or finding and establishing facts. They have participated in certain peace-keeping forces, technical assistance work, and a multitude of other activities. In addition, many committees, commissions or similar bodies whose members serve, not as representatives of States, but in a personal capacity, have been set up within the Organization; for example the International Law Commission, the Advisory Committee on Administrative and Budgetary Questions, the International Civil Service

---

accorded to representatives of foreign governments on temporary official missions;

(f) the same immunities and facilities in respect of their personal baggage as are accorded to diplomatic envoys."

Commission, the Human Rights Committee established for the implementation of the International Covenant on Civil and Political Rights, and various other committees of the same nature, such as the Committee on the Elimination of Racial Discrimination or the Committee on the Elimination of All Forms of Discrimination Against Women. In all these cases, the practice of the United Nations shows that the persons so appointed, and in particular the members of these committees and commissions, have been regarded as experts on missions within the meaning of Section 22.

According to that Section, experts enjoy the privileges and immunities therein provided for "during the period of their missions, including the time spent on journeys". The question thus arises whether experts are covered by Section 22 only during missions requiring travel or whether they are also covered when there is no such travel or apart from such travel. To answer this question, it is necessary to determine the meaning of the word "*mission*" in French and "mission" in English, the two languages in which the General Convention was adopted. Initially, in keeping with its Latin derivation, the word referred to a task entrusted to a person only if that person was sent somewhere to perform it. It implied a journey. The same connotation is apparent in the words, of the same derivation, "emissary", "missionary" and "missive". The French word "*mission*"; and the English word "mission", have however long since acquired a broader meaning and nowadays embrace in general the tasks entrusted to a person, whether or not those tasks involve travel.

The Court considers that Section 22, in its reference to experts performing missions for the United Nations, uses the word "mission" in a general sense. While some experts have necessarily to travel in order to perform their tasks, others can perform them without having to travel. In either case, the intent of Section 22 is to ensure the independence of such experts in the interests of the Organization by according them the privileges and immunities necessary for the purpose. In some cases these privileges and immunities are designed to facilitate the travel of experts and their stay abroad, for instance those concerning seizure or searching of personal baggage. In other cases, however, they are of a far more general nature, particularly with respect to communications with the United Nations or the inviolability of papers and documents. Accordingly, Section 22 is applicable to every expert on mission, whether or not he travels.

The question whether experts on missions can invoke these privileges and immunities against the States of which they are nationals or on the territory of which they reside has also been raised. In this connection, the Court notes that Section 15 of the General Convention provides that the terms of Article IV, Sections 11,12 and 13, relating to the representatives of Members "are not applicable as between a representative and the authorities of the State of which he is a national or of which he is or has been the representative". Article V, concerning officials of the Organization, and Article VI, concerning experts on missions for the United Nations, do not, however, contain any comparable rule. This difference of approach can readily be explained. The privileges and immunities of Articles V and VI are conferred with a view to ensuring the independence of international officials and experts in the interests of the Organization. This independence must be respected by all States including the State of nationality and the State of residence. Some States parties to the General Convention (Canada, the Lao People's Democratic Republic, Nepal, Thailand, Turkey and the United States of America) have indeed entered reservations to certain provisions of Article V, or of Article VI itself (Mexico and the United States of America), as regards their nationals or persons habitually resident on their territory. The very fact that it was felt necessary to make such reservations confirms the conclusion that, in the absence of such reservations, experts on missions enjoy the privileges and immunities provided for under the Convention in their relations with the States of which they are nationals or on the territory of which they reside.

To sum up, the Court takes the view that Section 22 of the General Convention is applicable to persons (other than United Nations officials) to whom a mission has been entrusted by the Organization and who are therefore entitled to enjoy the privileges and immunities provided for in this Section with a view to the independent exercise of their functions. During the whole period of such missions, experts enjoy these functional privileges and immunities whether or not they travel. They may be invoked as against the State of nationality or of residence unless a reservation to Section 22 of the General Convention has been validly made by that State.

[pp. 196-197] The members of the Sub-Commission, since their status is neither that of a representative of a member State nor that of a United Nations official, and since they perform independently for the United Nations functions contemplated in the remit of the Sub-Commission, must be regarded as experts on missions within the meaning of Section 22.

In accordance with the practice followed by many United Nations bodies, the Sub-Commission has from time to time appointed rapporteurs or special rapporteurs with the task of studying specified subjects. These rapporteurs or special rapporteurs are normally selected from among members of the Sub-Commission. However, over the past ten years, special rapporteurs have, on at least three occasions, been appointed from outside the Sub-Commission. Furthermore, in numerous cases, special rapporteurs appointed from among members of the Sub-Commission have completed their reports only after their membership of the Sub-Commission had expired. In any event, rapporteurs or special rapporteurs are entrusted by the Sub-Commission with a research mission. Their functions are diverse, since they have to compile, analyse and check the existing documentation on the problem to be studied, prepare a report making appropriate recommendations, and present the report to the Sub-Commission. Since their status is neither that of a representative of a member State nor that of a United Nations official, and since they carry out such research independently for the United Nations, they must be regarded as experts on missions within the meaning of Section 22, even in the event that they are not, or are no longer, members of the Sub-Commission. Consequently they enjoy, in accordance with Section 22, the privileges and immunities necessary for the exercise of their functions, and in particular for the establishment of any contacts which may be useful for the preparation, the drafting and the presentation of their reports to the Sub-Commission.

[pp. 210-211 **S.O. Evensen**] It seems obvious that the protection provided for in Article VI, Section 22, of the 1946 Convention cannot be confined only to the "expert Mazilu" but must apply to a reasonable extent to his family. This seems self-evident and has been touched upon in one special relation in Article V, Section 18 (*d*), of the Convention. It states that officials of the United Nations shall "be immune, together with their spouses and relatives dependent on them, from immigration restrictions and alien registration".

The integrity of a person's family and family life is a basic human right protected by prevailing principles of international law which derive not only from conventional international law or customary international law but from "general principles of law recognized by civilized nations".

Thus in the Universal Declaration of Human Rights adopted by the United Nations General Assembly on 10 December 1948 the integrity of family and family life was laid down as a basic human right in Article 16, paragraph 3, as follows: "The family is the natural and fundamental group unit of society and is entitled to protection by society and the State." This principle, which is a concrete expression of an established principle of human rights in the modern law of nations, has been similarly expressed in other international law instruments. Thus the European Convention on Human Rights (the Rome Convention) of 4 November 1950 provides in Article 8, paragraph 1: "Everyone has the right to respect for his private and family life, his home and his correspondence."

The respect for a person's family and family life must be considered as integral parts of the "privileges and immunities" that are necessary for "the independent exercise of their functions" under Article VI, Section 22, of the 1946 Convention on the Privileges and Immunities of the United Nations.

7.7.2. Inter-American Treaty of Reciprocal Assistance of 1947

[p. 359 **D.O. Schwebel**] In implementation of the Rio Treaty, as well as its inherent right recognized by Article 51 of the United Nations Charter, El Salvador has resisted Nicaragua's armed attack by acting in self-defence, and, equally, the United States has determined "the immediate measures which it may individually take in fulfillment of the obligation" it has undertaken to treat an attack on any American State as an attack on all (including itself). By the terms and intent of the Rio Pact, the United States is entitled individually to determine such measures until the OAS and the United Nations Security Council have acted; it does not require the prior authorization either of the OAS or of the Security Council. In so doing, the United States fulfils an obligation which it has undertaken to act in collective self-defence.

7.7.3. Geneva Convention on the Protection of Victims of War of 1949

Military and Paramilitary Activities
(Nicaragua/United States of America)
Merits. J. 27.6.1986
I.C.J. Reports 1986, p. 14

[pp. 113-114] ... the conduct of the United States may be judged according to the fundamental general principles of humanitarian law; in its view, the Geneva Conventions are in some respects a development, and in other respects no more than the expression, of such principles. It is significant in this respect that, according to the terms of the Conventions, the denunciation of one of them

"shall in no way impair the obligations which the Parties to the conflict shall remain bound to fulfil by virtue of the principles of the law of nations, as they result from the usages established among civilized peoples, from the laws of humanity and the dictates of the public conscience" (Convention I, Art. 63; Convention II, Art. 62; Convention III, Art. 142; Convention IV, Art. 158).

Article 3 which is common to all four Geneva Conventions of 12 August 1949 defines certain rules to be applied in the armed conflicts of a non-international character. There is no doubt that, in the event of international armed conflicts, these rules also constitute a minimum yardstick, in addition to the more elaborate rules which are also to apply to international conflicts; and they are rules which, in the Court's opinion, reflect what the Court in 1949 called "elementary considerations of humanity" (*Corfu Channel, Merits, I.C.J. Reports 1949*, p. 22; paragraph 215 above). The Court may therefore find them applicable to the present dispute, and is thus not required to decide what role the United States multilateral treaty reservation might otherwise play in regard to the treaties in question.

The conflict between the *contras'* forces and those of the Government of Nicaragua is an armed conflict which is "not of an international character". The acts of the *contras* towards the Nicaraguan Government are therefore governed by the law applicable to conflicts of that character; whereas the actions of the United States in and against

Nicaragua fall under the legal rules relating to international conflicts. Because the minimum rules applicable to international and to non-international conflicts are identical, there is no need to address the question whether those actions must be looked at in the context of the rules which operate for the one or for the other category of conflict. The relevant principles are to be looked for in the provisions of Article 3 of each of the four Conventions of 12 August 1949, the text of which, identical in each Convention, expressly refers to conflicts not having an international character.

The Court considers that there is an obligation on the United States Government, in the terms of Article 1 of the Geneva Conventions, to "respect" the Conventions and even "to ensure respect" for them "in all circumstances", since such an obligation does not derive only from the Conventions themselves, but from the general principles of humanitarian law to which the Conventions merely give specific expression. The United States is thus under an obligation not to encourage persons or groups engaged in the conflict in Nicaragua to act in violation of the provisions of Article 3 common to the four 1949 Geneva Conventions.

7.7.4. Treaty of Friendship Commerce and Navigation of 1956 between the United States and Nicaragua

[pp. 115-116] In its Judgment of 26 November 1984, the Court concluded that, in so far as the claims presented in Nicaragua's Application revealed the existence of a dispute as to the interpretation or application of the Articles of the 1956 Treaty of Friendship, Commerce and Navigation between the Parties mentioned in paragraph 82 of that Judgment (that is, Arts. XIX, XIV, XVII, XX, I), it had jurisdiction to deal with them under Article XXIV, paragraph 2, of that Treaty. Having thus established its jurisdiction to entertain the dispute between the Parties in respect of the interpretation and application of the Treaty in question, the Court must determine the meaning of the various provisions which are relevant for its judgment. In this connection, the Court has in particular to ascertain the scope of Article XXI, paragraphs 1 (*c*) and 1 (*d*), of the Treaty. According to that clause

"the present Treaty shall not preclude the application of measures:

(c) regulating the production of or traffic in arms, ammunition and implements of war, or traffic in other materials carried on directly or indirectly for the purpose of supplying a military establishment;

(d) necessary to fulfill the obligations of a Party for the maintenance or restoration of international peace and security, or necessary to protect its essential security interests".

In the Spanish text of the Treaty (equally authentic with the English text) the last phrase is rendered as "sus intereses esenciales y seguridad".

This article cannot be interpreted as removing the present dispute as to the scope of the Treaty from the Court's jurisdiction. Being itself an article of the Treaty, it is covered by the provision in Article XXIV that any dispute about the "interpretation or application" of the Treaty lies within the Court's jurisdiction. Article XXI defines the instances in which the Treaty itself provides for exceptions to the generality of its other provisions, but it by no means removes the interpretation and application of that article from the jurisdiction of the Court as contemplated in Article XXIV. That the Court has jurisdiction to determine whether measures taken by one of the Parties fall within such an exception, is also clear *a contrario* from the fact that the text of Article XXI of the Treaty does not employ the wording which was already to be found in Article XXI of the General Agreement on Tariffs and Trade. This provision of GATT, contemplating exceptions to the normal implementation of the General Agreement, stipulates that the Agreement is not to be construed to prevent any contracting party from taking any action which it "considers necessary for the protection of its essential security interests", in such fields as nuclear fission, arms, etc. The 1956 Treaty, on the contrary, speaks simply of "necessary" measures, not of those considered by a party to be such.

[pp. 116-117] As to subparagraph 1 (*d*) [10], clearly "measures... necessary to fulfill the obligations of a Party for the maintenance or restoration of international peace and security" must signify measures which the State in question must take in performance of an international commitment of which any evasion constitutes a breach. A commitment of this kind is accepted by Members of the United Nations in respect of Security Council decisions taken on the basis of Chapter VII of the United Nations Charter (Art. 25), or, for members of the Organization of American States, in respect of decisions taken by the Organ of Consultation of the Inter-American system, under Articles 3 and 20 of the Inter-American Treaty of Reciprocal Assistance (Rio de Janeiro, 1947). The Court does not believe that this provision of the 1956 Treaty can apply to the eventuality of the exercise of the right of individual or collective self-defence.

On the other hand, action taken in self-defence, individual or collective, might be considered as part of the wider category of measures qualified in Article XXI as "necessary to protect" the "essential security interests" of a party. In its Counter-Memorial on jurisdiction and admissibility, the United States contended that : "Any possible doubts as to the applicability of the FCN Treaty to Nicaragua's claims is dispelled by Article XXI of the Treaty ..." After quoting paragraph 1 (*d*) (set out in paragraph 221 above), the Counter-Memorial continues:

---

10 Subparagraph 1 (*d*) of Article XXXI of the 1956 FCN Treaty.

"Article XXI has been described by the Senate Foreign Relations Committee as containing 'the usual exceptions relating ... to traffic in arms, ammunition and implements of war and to measures for collective or individual self-defense'."

It is difficult to deny that self-defence against an armed attack corresponds to measures necessary to protect essential security interests. But the concept of essential security interests certainly extends beyond the concept of an armed attack, and has been subject to very broad interpretations in the past.

[p. 138] In respect of the claim that the United States activities have been such as to deprive the 1956 FCN Treaty of its object and purpose, the Court has to make a distinction. It is unable to regard all the acts complained of in that light; but it does consider that there are certain activities of the United States which are such as to undermine the whole spirit of a bilateral agreement directed to sponsoring friendship between the two States parties to it. These are: the direct attacks on ports, oil installations, etc., referred to in paragraphs 81 to 86 above; and the mining of Nicaraguan ports, mentioned in paragraph 80 above. Any action less calculated to serve the purpose of "strengthening the bonds of peace and friendship traditionally existing between" the Parties, stated in the Preamble of the Treaty, could hardly be imagined.

While the acts of economic pressure summarized in paragraphs 123_to 125 above are less flagrantly in contradiction with the purpose of the Treaty, the Court reaches a similar conclusion in respect of some of them. A State is not bound to continue particular trade relations longer than it sees fit to do so, in the absence of a treaty commitment or other specific legal obligation; but where there exists such a commitment, of the kind implied in a treaty of friendship and commerce, such an abrupt act of termination of commercial intercourse as the general trade embargo of 1 May 1985 will normally constitute a violation of the obligation not to defeat the object and purpose of the treaty. The 90 per cent cut in the sugar import quota of 23 September 1983 does not on the other hand seem to the Court to go so far as to constitute an act calculated to defeat the object and purpose of the Treaty. The cessation of economic aid, the giving of which is more of a unilateral and voluntary nature, could be regarded as such a violation only in exceptional circumstances. The Court has also to note that, by the very terms of the legislation authorizing such aid (the Special Central American Assistance Act, 1979), of which the Government of Nicaragua must have been aware, the continuance of aid was made subject to the appreciation of Nicaragua's conduct by the President of the United States. As to the opposition to the grant of loans from international institutions, the Court cannot regard this as sufficiently linked with the 1956 FCN Treaty to constitute an act directed to defeating its object and purpose.

[pp. 139-142] Nicaragua claims that the United States has violated the provisions of the Treaty relating to freedom of communication and commerce. For the reasons indicated in paragraph 253 above, the Court must uphold the contention that the mining of the Nicaraguan ports by the United States is in manifest contradiction with the freedom of navigation and commerce guaranteed by Article XIX, paragraph I, of the 1956 Treaty; there remains the question whether such action can be justified under Article XXI (see paragraphs 280 to 282 below). In the commercial context of the Treaty, Nicaragua's claim is justified not only as to the physical damage to its vessels, but also the consequential damage to its trade and commerce. Nicaragua however also contended that all the activities of the United States in and against Nicaragua are "violative of the 1956 Treaty":

"Since the word 'commerce' in the 1956 Treaty must be understood in its broadest sense, all of the activities by which the United States has deliberately inflicted on Nicaragua physical damage and economic losses of all types, violate the principle of freedom of commerce which the Treaty establishes in very general terms."

It is clear that considerable economic loss and damage has been inflicted on Nicaragua by the actions of the *contras*: apart from the economic impact of acts directly attributable to the United States, such as the loss of fishing boats blown up by mines, the Nicaraguan Minister of Finance estimated loss of production in 1981-1984 due to inability to collect crops, etc., at some US$ 300 million. However, as already noted (paragraph 277 above) the Court has not found the relationship between the *contras* and the United States Government to have been proved to be such that the United States is responsible for all acts of the *contras*.

The trade embargo declared by the United States Government on 1 May 1985 has already been referred to in the context of Nicaragua's contentions as to acts tending to defeat the object and purpose of the 1956 FCN Treaty. The question also arises of its compatibility with the letter and the spirit of Article XIX of the Treaty. That Article provides that "Between the territories of the two Parties there shall be freedom of commerce and navigation" (para. 1) and continues

"3. Vessels of either Party shall have liberty, on equal terms with vessels of the other Party and on equal terms with vessels of any third country, to come with their cargoes to all ports, places and waters of such other Party open to foreign commerce and navigation..."

By the Executive Order dated 1 May 1985 the President of the United States declared "I hereby prohibit vessels of Nicaraguan registry from entering into United States ports, and transactions relating thereto". The Court notes that on the same day the United States gave notice to Nicaragua to terminate the Treaty under Article XXV, paragraph 3, thereof; but that Article requires "one year's written notice" for the termination to take effect. The freedom of Nicaraguan vessels, under Article XIX, paragraph 3, "to come with their cargoes to all ports, places and waters" of the United States could not therefore be interfered with during that period of notice, let alone terminated abruptly by the declaration of an embargo. The Court accordingly finds that the embargo constituted a measure in contradiction with Article XIX of the 1956 FCN Treaty.

The Court has thus found that the United States is in breach of a duty not to deprive the 1956 FCN Treaty of its object and purpose, and has committed acts which are in contradiction with the terms of the Treaty, subject to the question whether the exceptions in Article XXI, paragraphs 1 (*c*) and 1 (*d*), concerning respectively "traffic in arms and measures ... necessary to fulfill" obligations "for the maintenance or restoration of international peace and security" or necessary to protect the "essential security interests" of a party, may be invoked to justify the acts complained of. In its Counter-Memorial on jurisdiction and admissibitity, the United States relied on paragraph 1 (*c*) as showing the inapplicability of the 1956 FCN Treaty to Nicaragua's claims. This paragraph appears however to be relevant only in respect of the complaint of supply of arms to the *contras*, and since the Court does not find that arms supply to be a breach of the Treaty, or an act calculated to deprive it of its object and purpose, paragraph 1 (*c*) does not need to be considered further. There remains the question of the relationship of Article XXI, paragraph 1 (*d*), to the direct attacks on ports, oil installations, etc.; the mining of Nicaraguan ports; and the general trade embargo of 1 May 1985 (paragraphs 275 to 276 above).

In approaching this question, the Court has first to bear in mind the chronological sequence of events. If the activities of the United States are to be covered by Article XXI of the Treaty, they must have been, at the time they were taken, measures necessary to protect its essential security interests. Thus the finding of the President of the United States on 1 May 1985 that "the policies and actions of the Government of Nicaragua constitute an unusual and extraordinary threat to the national security and foreign policy of the United States", even if it be taken as sufficient evidence that that was so, does not justify action by the United States previous to that date.

Secondly, the Court emphasizes the importance of the word "necessary" in Article XXI: the measures taken must not merely be such as tend to protect the essential security interests of the party taking them, but must be "necessary" for that purpose. Taking into account the whole situation of the United States in relation to Central America, so far as the Court is informed of it (and even assuming that the justification of self-defence, which the Court has rejected on the legal level, had some validity on the political level), the Court considers that the mining of Nicaraguan ports, and the direct attacks on ports and oil installations, cannot possibly be justified as "necessary" to protect the essential security interests of the United States. As to the trade embargo, the Court has to note the express justification for it given in the Presidential finding quoted in paragraph 125 above, and that the measure was one of an economic nature, thus one which fell within the sphere of relations contemplated by the Treaty. But by the terms of the Treaty itself, whether a measure is necessary to protect the essential security interests of a party is not, as the Court has emphasized (paragraph 222 above), purely a question for the subjective judgment of the party; the text does not refer to what the party "considers necessary" for that purpose. Since no evidence at all is available to show how Nicaraguan policies had in fact become a threat to "essential security interests" in May 1985, when those policies had been consistent, and consistently criticized by the United States, for four years previously, the Court is unable to find that the embargo was "necessary" to protect those interests. Accordingly, Article XXI affords no defence for the United States in respect of any of the actions here under consideration.

[p. 541 **D.O. Jennings**] The question arising under Article XXI is not, however, whether such measures are justified in international law as action taken in self-defence, or as justified counter-measures in general international law; the question is whether the measures in question are, or are not, in breach of the Treaty. Any operation that comes squarely within Article XXI, as a measure taken by one party to the Treaty, as being "necessary to protect its essential security interests", cannot be in breach of the Treaty. I do not see what other meaning can be given to a clause which simply states that "The present Treaty shall not preclude the application" of such measures, and thus is a proviso to the entire Treaty.

[p. 541 **D.O. Jennings**] The question, however, in relation to the 1956 Treaty, is not whether the United States acted in breach of "elementary considerations of humanity", but whether it acted also in breach of the bilateral treaty relationship with Nicaragua, having regard to the general proviso in Article XXI? Again it must be emphasized that the issue here is not simply the lawfulness or unlawfulness of the act in general international law, but whether it was also in breach of the terms of the Treaty? Certainly it is prima facie a breach of Article XIX, providing for freedom of navigation; but is it a "measure" excepted by the proviso clause of Article XXI? Although not without some remaining doubts, I have come to the conclusion that Article XXI cannot have contemplated a measure which cannot, under general international law, be justified even as being part of an operation in legitimate self-defence.

8. VIOLATIONS OF INTERNATIONAL LAW AND RESPONSIBILITY OF STATES

8.1. General Questions

Military and Paramilitary Activities
(Nicaragua/United States of America)
Merits. J. 27.6.1986
I.C.J. Reports 1986, p. 14

[p. 136] In the view of the Court, an act cannot be said to be one calculated to deprive a treaty of its object and purpose, or to impede its due performance, if the possibility of that act has been foreseen in the treaty itself, and it has been expressly agreed that the treaty "shall not preclude" the act, so that it will not constitute a breach of the express terms of the treaty. Accordingly, the Court cannot entertain either the claim of Nicaragua alleging conduct depriving the treaty of its object and purpose, or its claims of breach of specific articles of the treaty, unless it is first satisfied that the conduct complained of is not "measures ... necessary to protect" the essential security interests of the United States.

[p. 250 **D.O. Oda**] Thus the Court appears to have misinterpreted the words "the object and purpose" of a treaty, as introduced by the 1969 Convention on the Law of Treaties in a completely different context. Independently of that Convention, it is noted that the Court attributes to Nicaragua an argument to the effect that abstention from conduct likely to defeat the object and purpose of a treaty is an obligation implicit in the principle *pacta sunt servanda*. However, the Judgment does not make it clear whether it is espousing this point of view. In any case, I would like to take this opportunity of indicating my own understanding of this principle, which to my mind requires compliance with the letter of obligations subscribed to, and not necessarily the avoidance of conduct not expressly precluded by the terms of the given treaty. It may furthermore be asked where the jurisdiction granted by a treaty clause would ever end if it were held to entitle the Court to scrutinize any act remotely describable as inimical to the object and purpose of the treaty in question. The ultimate result of so sweeping an assumption could only be an increasing reluctance on the part of States to support the inclusion of such clauses in their treaties.

8.3. Treaty Violations

Military and Paramilitary Activities
(Nicaragua/United States of America)
Merits. J. 27.6.1986
I.C.J. Reports 1986, p. 14

[pp. 136-137] In other words, the Court is asked to rule that a State which enters into a treaty of friendship binds itself, for so long as the Treaty is in force, to abstain from any act toward the other party which could be classified as an unfriendly act, even if such act is not in itself the breach of an international obligation. Such a duty might of course be expressly stipulated in a treaty, or might even emerge as a necessary implication from the text; but as a matter of customary international law, it is not clear that the existence of such a far-reaching rule is evidenced in the practice of States. There must be a distinction, even in the case of a treaty of friendship, between the broad category of unfriendly acts, and the narrower category of acts tending to defeat the object and purpose of the Treaty. That object and purpose is the effective implementation of friendship in the specific fields provided for in the Treaty, not friendship in a vague general sense.

Elettronica Sicula S.p.A. (ELSI)
Judgment of 20 July 1989
I.C.J. Reports 1989, p. 15

[p. 51] The question still remains, therefore, whether the requisition was or was not a violation of Article III, paragraph 2 [11]. This question arises irrespective of the position in municipal law. Compliance with municipal law and compliance with the provisions of a treaty are different questions. What is a breach of treaty may be lawful in the municipal law and what is unlawful in the municipal law may be wholly innocent of violation of a treaty provision. Even had the Prefect held the requisition to be entirely justified in Italian law, this would not exclude the possibility that it was a violation of the FCN Treaty.

[pp. 76-77] Arbitrariness is not so much something opposed to a rule of law, as something opposed to the rule of law. This idea was expressed by the Court in the *Asylum* case, when it spoke of "arbitrary action" being "substituted for the rule of law" (*Asylum,*

---

11 Article III paragraph 2 FCN Treaty reads as follows:

"The nationals, corporations and associations of either High Contracting Party shall be permitted, in conformity with the applicable laws and regulations within the territories of the other High Contracting Party, to organize, control and manage corporations and associations of such other High Contracting Party for engaging in commercial, manufacturing, processing, mining, educational, philanthropic, religious and scientific activities. Corporations and associations, controlled by nationals, corporations and associations of either High Contracting Party and created or organized under the applicable laws and regulations within the territories of the other High Contracting Party, shall be permitted to engage in the afore-mentioned activities therein, in conformity with the applicable laws and regulations, upon terms no less favorable than those now or hereafter accorded to corporations and associations of such other High Contracting Party controlled by its own nationals, corporations and associations."

Judgment, I.C.J. Reports 1950, p. 284). It is a wilful disregard of due process of law, an act which shocks, or at least surprises, a sense of juridical propriety. Nothing in the decision of the Prefect, or in the judgment of the Court of Appeal of Palermo, conveys any indication that the requisition order of the Mayor was to be regarded in that light.

The United States argument is not of course based solely on the findings of the Prefect or of the local courts. United States counsel felt able to describe the requisition generally as being an "unreasonable or capricious exercise of authority". Yet one must remember the situation in Palermo at the moment of the requisition, with the threatened sudden unemployment of some 800 workers at one factory. It cannot be said to have been unreasonable or merely capricious for the Mayor to seek to use the powers conferred on him by the law in an attempt to do something about a difficult and distressing situation. Moreover, if one looks at the requisition order itself, one finds an instrument which in its terms recites not only the reasons for its being made but also the provisions of the law on which it is based: one finds that, although later annulled by the Prefect because "the intended purpose of the requisition could not in practice be achieved by the order itself" (paragraph 125 above), it was nonetheless within the competence of the Mayor of Palermo, according to the very provisions of the law cited in it; one finds the Court of Appeal of Palermo, which did not differ from the conclusion that the requisition was *intra vires*, ruling that it was unlawful as falling into the recognized category of administrative law of acts of "*eccesso di potere*". Furthermore, here was an act belonging to a category of public acts from which appeal on juridical grounds was provided in law (and indeed in the event used, not without success). Thus, the Mayor's order was consciously made in the context of an operating system of law and of appropriate remedies of appeal, and treated as such by the superior administrative authority and the local courts. These are not at all the marks of an "arbitrary" act.

The Chamber does not, therefore, see in the requisition a measure which could reasonably be said to earn the qualification "arbitrary", as it is employed in Article I of the Supplementary Agreement. Accordingly, there was no violation of that Article.

Military and Paramilitary Activities
(Nicaragua/United States of America)
Merits. J. 27.6.1986
I.C.J. Reports 1986, p. 14

[pp. 142-143] The Court considers appropriate the request of Nicaragua for the nature and amount of the reparation due to it to be determined in a subsequent phase of the proceedings. While a certain amount of evidence has been provided, for example, in the testimony of the Nicaraguan Minister of Finance, of pecuniary loss sustained, this was based upon contentions as to the responsibility of the United States which were more far-reaching than the conclusions at which the Court has been able to arrive. The opportunity should be afforded Nicaragua to demonstrate and prove exactly what injury was suffered as a result of each action of the United States which the Court has found contrary to international law. Nor should it be overlooked that, while the United States has chosen not to appear or participate in the present phase of the proceedings, Article 53 of the Statute does not debar it from appearing to present its arguments on the question of reparation if it so wishes. On the contrary, the principle of the equality of the Parties requires that it be given that opportunity. It goes without saying, however, that in the phase of the proceedings devoted to reparation, neither Party may call in question such findings in the present Judgment as have become *res judicata*.

There remains the request of Nicaragua (paragraph 15 above) for an award, at the present stage of the proceedings, of $ 370,200,000 as the "minimum (and in that sense provisional) valuation of direct damages". There is no provision in the Statute of the Court either specifically empowering the Court to make an interim award of this kind, or indeed debarring it from doing so. In view of the final and binding character of the Court's judgments under Articles 59 and 60 of the Statute, it would however only be appropriate to make an award of this kind, assuming that the Court possesses the power to do so, in exceptional circumstances, and where the entitlement of the State making the claim was already established with certainty and precision. Furthermore, in a case in which the respondent State is not appearing, so that its views on the matter are not known to the Court, the Court should refrain from any unnecessary act which might prove an obstacle to a negotiated settlement. It bears repeating that

"the judicial settlement of international disputes, with a view to which the Court has been established, is simply an alternative to the direct and friendly settlement of such disputes between the Parties; as consequently it is for the Court to facilitate, so far as is compatible with its Statute, such direct and friendly settlement ..." (*Free Zones of Upper Savoy and the District of Gex, Order of 19 August 1929, P.C.I.J., Series A, No. 22*, p. 13).

Accordingly, the Court does not consider that it can accede at this stage to the request made in the Fourth Submission of Nicaragua.

8.4. Imputability

Military and Paramilitary Activities
(Nicaragua/United States of America)
Merits. J. 27.6.1986
I.C.J. Reports 1986, p. 14

[p. 62] What the Court has to determine at this point is whether or not the relationship of the *contras* to the United States Government was so much one of dependence on the one side and control on the other that it would be right to equate the *contras*, for legal purposes, with an organ of the United States Government, or as acting on behalf of that Government. Here it is relevant to note that in May 1983 the assessment of the Intelligence Committee, in the Report referred to in paragraph 95 above, was that the *contras* "constitute[d] an independent force" and that the "only element of control that could be exercised by the United States" was "cessation of aid". Paradoxically this assessment serves to underline, *a contrario*, the potential for control inherent in the degree of the *contras*' dependence on aid. Yet despite the heavy subsidies and other support provided to them by the United States, there is no clear evidence of the United States having actually exercised such a degree of control in all fields as to justify treating the *contras* as acting on its behalf.

[p. 63] In the view of the Court it is established that the contra force has, at least at one period, been so dependent on the United States that it could not conduct its crucial or most significant military and paramilitary activities without the multi-faceted support of the United States. This finding is fundamental in the present case. Nevertheless, adequate direct proof that all or the great majority of contra activities during that period received this support has not been, and indeed probably could not be, advanced in every respect. It will suffice the Court to stress that a degree of control by the United States Government, as described above, is inherent in the position in which the contra force finds itself in relation to that Government.

[pp. 64-65] The Court has taken the view (paragraph 110 above) that United States participation, even if preponderant or decisive, in the financing, organizing, training, supplying and equipping of the *contras*, the selection of its military or paramilitary targets, and the planning of the whole of its operation, is still insufficient in itself, on the basis of the evidence in the possession of the Court, for the purpose of attributing to the United States the acts committed by the *contras* in the course of their military or paramilitary operations in Nicaragua. All the forms of United States participation mentioned above, and even the general control by the respondent State over a force with a high degree of dependency on it, would not in themselves mean, without further evidence, that the United States directed or enforced the perpetration of the acts contrary to human rights and humanitarian law alleged by the applicant State. Such acts could well be committed by members of the *contras* without the control of the United States. For this conduct to give rise to legal responsibility of the United States, it would in principle have to be proved that that State had effective control of the military or paramilitary operations in the course of which the alleged violations were committed.

The Court does not consider that the assistance given by the United States to the *contras* warrants the conclusion that these forces are subject to the United States to such an extent that any acts they have committed are imputable to that State. It takes the view that the *contras* remain responsible for their acts, and that the United States is not responsible for the acts of the *contras*, but for its own conduct vis-à-vis Nicaragua, including conduct related to the acts of the *contras*. What the Court has to investigate is not the complaints relating to alleged violations of humanitarian law by the *contras*, regarded by Nicaragua as imputable to the United States, but rather unlawful acts for which the United States may be responsible directly in connection with the activities of the *contras*. The lawfulness or otherwise of such acts of the United States is a question different from the violations of humanitarian law of which the *contras* may or may not have been guilty. It is for this reason that the Court does not have to determine whether the violations of humanitarian law attributed to the *contras* were in fact committed by them. At the same time, the question whether the United States Government was, or must have been, aware at the relevant time that allegations of breaches of humanitarian law were being made against the *contras* is relevant to an assessment of the lawfulness of the action of the United States. In this respect the material facts are primarily those connected with the issue in 1983 of a manual of psychological operations.

[pp. 83-84] Secondly, even supposing it well established that military aid is reaching the armed opposition in El Salvador from the territory of Nicaragua, it still remains to be proved that this aid is imputable to the authorities of the latter country. Indeed, the applicant State has in no way sought to conceal the possibility of weapons en route to the armed opposition in El Salvador crossing its territory but it denies that this is the result of any deliberate official policy on its part. As the Court observed in 1949:

"it cannot be concluded from the mere fact of the control exercised by a State over its territory and waters that that State necessarily knew, or ought to have known, of any unlawful act perpetrated therein, nor yet that it necessarily knew, or should have known, the authors. This fact, by itself and apart from other circumstances, neither involves *prima facie* responsibility nor shifts the burden of proof." (*Corfu Channel, I.C.J. Reports 1949*, p. 18.)

[p 85] ... if the flow of arms is in fact reaching El Salvador without either Honduras or El Salvador or the United States succeeding in preventing it, it would clearly be unreasonable to demand of the Government of Nicaragua a higher degree of diligence than is achieved by even the combined efforts of the other three States. In particular, when Nicaragua is blamed for allowing consignments of arms to cross its territory, this is tantamount, where El Salvador is concerned, to an admission of its inability to stem the flow. This is revealing as to the predicament of any government, including that of Nicaragua, faced with this arms traffic: its determination to put a stop to it would be likely to fail. More especially, to the extent that some of this aid is said to be successfully routed through Honduras, this accusation against Nicaragua would also signify that Honduras, which is not suspected of seeking to assist the armed opposition in El Salvador, is providing involuntary proof that it is by no means certain that Nicaragua can combat this clandestine traffic any better than Honduras. As the means at the disposal of the governments in the region are roughly comparable, the geographical obstacles, and the intrinsic character of any clandestine arms traffic, simply show that this traffic may be carried on successfully without any complicity from governmental authorities, and even when they seek to put a stop to it. Finally, if it is true that the exceptionally extensive resources deployed by the United States have been powerless to prevent this traffic from keeping the Salvadorian armed opposition supplied, this suggests even more clearly how powerless Nicaragua must be with the much smaller resources at its disposal for subduing this traffic if it takes place on its territory and the authorities endeavour to put a stop to it.

Confining itself to the regional States concerned, the Court accordingly considers that it is scarcely possible for Nicaragua's responsibility for an arms traffic taking place on its territory to be automatically assumed while the opposite assumption is adopted with regard to its neighbours in respect of similar traffic. Having regard to the circumstances characterizing this part of Central America, the Court considers it more realistic, and consistent with the probabilities, to recognize that an activity of that nature, if on a limited scale, may very well be pursued unbeknown to the territorial government.

[pp. 188-189 **S.O. Ago**] On the other hand, the negative answer returned by the Court to the Applicant's suggestion that the misdeeds committed by some members of the contra forces should be considered as acts imputable to the United States of America is likewise in conformity with the provisions of the International Law Commission's draft [12]. It would indeed be inconsistent with the principles governing the question to regard members of the contra forces as persons or groups acting in the name and on behalf of the United States of America. Only in cases where certain members of those forces happened to have been specifically charged by United States authorities to commit a particular act, or carry out a particular task of some kind on behalf of the United States, would it be possible so to regard them. Only in such instances does international law recognize, as a rare exception to the rule, that the conduct of persons or groups which are neither agents nor organs of a State, nor members of its apparatus even in the broadest acceptation of that term, may be held to be acts of that State.

---

12 I refer to Articles 11 (Conduct of persons not acting on behalf of the State) and 8 (Attribution to the State of the conduct of persons acting in fact on behalf of the State), read together.

8.6. Participation

Military and Paramilitary Activities
(Nicaragua/United States of America)
Merits. J. 27.6.1986
I.C.J. Reports 1986, p. 14

[p. 130] It is also appropriate to recall the circumstances in which the manual of psychological operations was issued. When considering whether the publication of such a manual, encouraging the commission of acts contrary to general principles of humanitarian law, is unlawful, it is material to consider whether that encouragement was offered to persons in circumstances where the commission of such acts was likely or foreseeable. The Court has however found (paragraph 121) that at the relevant time those responsible for the issue of the manual were aware of, at the least, allegations that the behaviour of the *contras* in the field was not consistent with humanitarian law; it was in fact even claimed by the CIA that the purpose of the manual was to "moderate" such behaviour. The publication and dissemination of a manual in fact containing the advice quoted above must therefore be regarded as an encouragement, which was likely to be effective, to commit acts contrary to general principles of international humanitarian law reflected in treaties.

[pp. 388-389 **D.O. Schwebel**] Customary international law does not know the delict of "encouragement". There appears to be no precedent for holding a State responsible for breach of the Geneva Conventions for the Protection of War Victims of 1949 by reason of its advocacy of violations of humanitarian law, though it may reasonably be maintained that a State which encourages violations of that law fails to "ensure respect" for the Geneva Conventions, as by their terms it is obliged to do.

II. Substantive International Law - Second Part

1. TERRITORY OF STATES

1.2. Boundaries

1.2.1. Land Boundaries

Cf. also: The principle of *uti possidetis*

Frontier Dispute, Judgment
(Burkina Faso/Republic of Mali)
I.C.J. Reports 1986, p. 554

[pp. 563-564] The Parties have argued at length over how the present dispute is to be classified in terms of a distinction sometimes made by legal writers between "frontier disputes" or "delimitation disputes", and "disputes as to attribution of territory". According to this distinction, the former refer to delimitation operations affecting what has been described as "a portion of land which is not geographically autonomous" whereas the object of the latter is the attribution of sovereignty over the whole of a geographical entity. Both Parties seem ultimately to have accepted that the present dispute belongs rather to the category of delimitation disputes, even though they fail to agree on the conclusions to be drawn from this. In fact, however, in the great majority of cases, including this one, the distinction outlined above is not so much a difference in kind but rather a difference of degree as to the way the operation in question is carried out. The effect of any delimitation, no matter how small the disputed area crossed by the line, is an apportionment of the areas of land lying on either side of the line. In the present case, it may be noted that the Special Agreement, in Article I, refers not merely to a line to be drawn, but to a disputed "area", which it defines as consisting of a "band" of territory encompassing the "region" of the Béli. Moreover, the effect of any judicial decision rendered either in a dispute as to attribution of territory or in a delimitation dispute, is necessarily to establish a frontier. It is not without interest that certain recent codifying conventions have used formulae such as a treaty which "establishes a boundary" or a "boundary established by a treaty" to cover both delimitation treaties and treaties ceding or attributing territory (cf. Vienna Convention on the Law of Treaties, Art. 62; Vienna Convention on Succession of States in respect of Treaties, Art. 11). In both cases, a clarification is made of a given legal situation with declaratory effect from the date of the legal title upheld by the court. This clarification is itself a new element; it was because the parties wished to see that element introduced that they went to court at all. If there had been no dispute or uncertainty, they would not have wished to do so. Hence it is not so much the nature and qualification of the present dispute as the Statute of the Court and the terms of the Special Agreement which must determine the nature and extent of the Chamber's task and functions in this case.

[p. 582] At the present stage of its reasoning the Chamber can confine itself to the statement of a principle. Whether in frontier delimitations or in international territorial conflicts, maps merely constitute information which varies in accuracy from case to case; of themselves, and by virtue solely of their existence, they cannot constitute a territorial title, that is, a document endowed by international law with intrinsic legal force for the purpose of establishing territorial rights. Of course, in some cases maps may acquire such legal force, but where this is so the legal force does not arise solely from their intrinsic merits: it is because such maps fall into the category of physical expressions of the will of the State or States concerned. This is the case, for example, when maps are annexed to an official text of which they form an integral part. Except in this clearly defined case, maps are only extrinsic evidence of varying reliability or unreliability which may be used, along with other evidence of a circumstantial kind, to establish or reconstitute the real facts.

[pp. 632-633] It should again be pointed out that the Chamber's task in this case is to indicate the line of the frontier inherited by both States from the colonizers on their accession to independence. For the reasons explained above, this task amounts to ascertaining and defining the lines which formed the administrative boundaries of the colony of Upper Volta on 31 December 1932. Admittedly, the Parties could have modified the frontier existing on the critical date by a subsequent agreement. If the competent authorities had endorsed the agreement of 15 January 1965, it would have been unnecessary for the purpose of the present case to ascertain whether that agreement was of a declaratory or modifying character in relation to the 1932 boundaries. But this did not happen, and the Chamber has received no mandate from the Parties to substitute its own free choice of an appropriate frontier for theirs. The Chamber must not lose sight either of the Court's function, which is to decide in accordance with international law such disputes as are submitted to it, nor of the fact that the Chamber was requested by the Parties in their Special Agreement not to give indications to guide them in determining their common frontier, but to draw a line, and a precise line.

As it has explained, the Chamber can resort to that equity *infra legem*, which both Parties have recognized as being applicable in this case (see paragraph 27 above). In this respect the guiding concept is simply that "Equity as a legal concept is a direct emanation of the idea of justice" (*Continental Shelf (Tunisia/Libyan Arab Jamahiriya), I.C.J. Reports 1982*, p. 60, para. 71). The Chamber would however stress more generally that to resort to the concept of equity in order to modify an established frontier would be quite unjustified. Especially in the African context, the obvious deficiencies of many frontiers inherited from colonization, from the ethnic, geographical or administrative standpoint, cannot support an assertion that the modification of these frontiers is necessary or justifiable on the ground of considerations of equity. These frontiers, however unsatisfactory they may be, possess the authority of the *uti possidetis* and are thus fully in conformity with contemporary international law. Apart from the case of a decision *ex aequo et bono* reached with the assent of the Parties, "it is not a matter of finding simply an equitable solution, but an equitable solution derived from the applicable law" (*Fisheries Jurisdiction, I.C.J. Reports 1974*, p. 33, para. 78). It is with a view to achieving a solution of this kind that the Chamber has to take account, not of the agreement of 15 January 1965, but of the circumstances in which that agreement was concluded.

1.2.4. Principle of "*uti possidetis*"

Frontier Dispute, Judgment
(Burkina Faso/Republic of Mali)
I.C.J. Reports 1986, p. 554

[pp. 565-567] Since the two Parties have, as noted above, expressly requested the Chamber to resolve their dispute on the basis, in particular, of the "principle of the intangibility of frontiers inherited from colonization", the Chamber cannot disregard the principle of *uti possidetis juris*, the application of which gives rise to this respect for intangibility of frontiers. Although there is no need, for the purposes of the present case, to show that this is a firmly established principle of international law where decolonization is concerned, the Chamber nonetheless wishes to emphasize its general scope, in view of its exceptional importance for the African continent and for the two Parties. In this connection it should be noted that the principle of *uti possidetis* seems to have been first invoked and applied in Spanish America, inasmuch as this was the continent which first witnessed the phenomenon of decolonization involving the formation of a number of sovereign States on territory formerly belonging to a single metropolitan State. Nevertheless the principle is not a special rule which pertains solely to one specific system of international law. It is a general principle, which is logically connected with the phenomenon of the obtaining of independence, wherever it occurs. Its obvious purpose is to prevent the independence and stability of new States being endangered by fratricidal struggles provoked by the challenging of frontiers following the withdrawal of the administering power.

It was for this reason that, as soon as the phenomenon of decolonization characteristic of the situation in Spanish America in the 19th century subsequently appeared in Africa in the 20th century, the principle of *uti possidetis*, in the sense described above, fell to be applied. The fact that the new African States have respected the administrative boundaries and frontiers established by the colonial powers must be seen not as a mere practice contributing to the gradual emergence of a principle of customary international law, limited in its impact to the African continent as it had previously been to Spanish America, but as the application in Africa of a rule of general scope.

The elements of *uti possidetis* were latent in the many declarations made by African leaders in the dawn of independence. These declarations confirmed the maintenance of the territorial status quo at the time of independence, and stated the principle of respect both for the frontiers deriving from international agreements, and for those resulting from mere internal administrative divisions. The Charter of the Organization of African Unity did not ignore the principle of *uti possidetis*, but made only indirect reference to it in Article 3, according to which member States solemnly affirm the principle of respect for the sovereignty and territorial integrity of every State. However, at their first summit conference after the creation of the Organization of African Unity, the African Heads of State, in their Resolution mentioned above (AGH/ Res. 16 (I)), adopted in Cairo in July 1964, deliberately defined and stressed the principle of *uti possidetis juris* contained only in an implicit sense in the Charter of their organization.

There are several different aspects to this principle, in its well-known application in Spanish America. The first aspect, emphasized by the Latin genitive *juris*, is found in the pre-eminence accorded to legal title over effective possession as a basis of sovereignty. Its purpose, at the time of the achievement of independence by the former Spanish colonies of America, was to scotch any designs which non-American colonizing powers might have on regions which had been assigned by the former metropolitan State to one division or another, but which were still uninhabited or unexplored. However, there is more to the principle of *uti possidetis* than this particular aspect. The essence of the principle lies in its primary aim of securing respect for the territorial boundaries at the moment when independence is achieved. Such territorial boundaries might be no more than delimitations between different administrative divisions or colonies all subject to the same sovereign. In that case, the application of the principle of *uti possidetis* resulted in administrative boundaries being transformed into international frontiers in the full sense of the term. This is true both of the States which took shape in the regions of South America which were dependent on the Spanish Crown, and of the States Parties to the present case, which took shape within the vast territories of French West Africa. *Uti possidetis*, as a principle which upgraded former administrative delimitations, established during the colonial period, to international frontiers, is therefore a principle of a general kind which is logically connected with this form of decolonization wherever it occurs.

The territorial boundaries which have to be respected may also derive from international frontiers which previously divided a colony of one State from a colony of another, or indeed a colonial territory from the territory of an independent State, or one which was under protectorate, but had retained its international personality. There is no doubt that the obligation to respect pre-existing international frontiers in the event of a State succession derives from a general rule of international law, whether or not the rule is expressed in the formula *uti possidetis*. Hence the numerous solemn affirmations of the intangibility of the frontiers existing at the time of the independence of African States, whether made by senior African statesmen or by organs of the Organization of African Unity itself are evidently declaratory rather than constitutive: they recognize and confirm an existing principle, and do not seek to consecrate a new principle or the extension to Africa of a rule previously applied only in another continent.

However, it may be wondered how the time-hallowed principle has been able to withstand the new approaches to international law as expressed in Africa, where the successive attainment of independence and the emergence of new States have been accompanied by a certain questioning of traditional international law. At first sight this principle conflicts outright with another one, the right of peoples to self-determination. In fact, however, the maintenance of the territorial status quo in Africa is often seen as the wisest course, to preserve what has been achieved by peoples who have struggled for their independence, and to avoid a disruption which would deprive the continent of the gains achieved by much sacrifice. The essential requirement of stability in order to survive, to develop and gradually to consolidate their independence in all fields, has induced African States judiciously to consent to the respecting of colonial frontiers, and to take account of it in the interpretation of the principle of self-determination of peoples.

Thus the principle of *uti possidetis* has kept its place among the most important legal principles, despite the apparent contradiction which explained its coexistence alongside the new norms. Indeed it was by deliberate choice that African States selected, among all the classic principles, that of *uti possidetis*. This remains an undeniable fact. In the light of the foregoing remarks, it is clear that the applicability of *uti possidetis* in the present case cannot be challenged merely because in 1960, the year when Mali and Burkina Faso achieved independence, the Organization of African Unity which was to proclaim this principle did not yet exist, and the above-mentioned resolution calling for respect for the preexisting frontiers dates only from 1964.

[p. 568] By becoming independent, a new State acquires sovereignty with the territorial base and boundaries left to it by the colonial power. This is part of the ordinary operation of the machinery of State succession. International law - and consequently the principle of *uti possidetis* - applies to the new State (as a State) not with retroactive effect, but immediately and from that moment onwards. It applies to the State as *it is*, i.e., to the "photograph" of the territorial situation then existing. The principle of *uti possidetis* freezes the territorial title; it stops the clock, but does not put back the hands. Hence international law does not effect any renvoi to the law established by the colonizing State, nor indeed to any legal rule unilaterally established by any State whatever; French law - especially legislation enacted by France for its colonies and *territoires d'outre-mer* - may play a role not in itself (as if there were a sort of *continuum juris*, a legal relay between such law and international law), but only as one factual element among others, or as evidence indicative of what has been called the "colonial heritage", i.e., the "photograph of the territory" at the critical date.

[pp. 586-587] Apart from the texts and maps listed above, the Parties have invoked in support of their respective contentions the "colonial *effectivités*", in other words, the conduct of the administrative authorities as proof of the effective exercise of territorial jurisdiction in the region during the colonial period. For Burkina Faso, the *effectivités* can support an existing title, whether written or cartographical, but when their probative value has to be assessed they must be systematically compared with the title in question; in no circumstances can they be substituted for the title. For its part, Mali admits that in principle the *effectivités* cannot be brought into operation where they are contrary to the text of a treaty, but argues that in a situation where there is no boundary described in conventional or legislative form, it is necessary to ascertain the boundary by other methods, and an investigation of the *effectivités* then becomes essential. The role played in this case by such *effectivités* is complex, and the Chamber will have to weigh carefully the legal force of these in each particular instance. It must however state forthwith, in general terms, what legal relationship exists between such acts and the titles on which the implementation of the principle of *uti possidetis* is grounded. For this purpose, a distinction must be drawn among several eventualities. Where the act corresponds exactly to law, where effective administration is additional to the *uti possidetis juris*, the only role of *effectivité* is to confirm the exercise of the right derived from a legal title. Where the act does not correspond to the law, where the territory which is the subject of the dispute is effectively administered by a State other than the one possessing the legal title, preference should be given to the holder of the title. In the event that the *effectivité* does not co-exist with any legal title, it must invariably be taken into consideration. Finally, there are cases where the legal title is not capable of showing exactly the territorial expanse to which it relates. The *effectivités* can then play an essential role in showing how the title is interpreted in practice.

[pp. 661-662 **S.O. Abi-Saab**] The purpose of this frantic search for a "written legal title", turning anything and everything into account, is to satisfy a particular conception of the *uti possidetis* principle.

However, this principle, like any other, is not to be conceived in the absolute; it has always to be interpreted in the light of its function within the international legal order.

At first sight, it may indeed seem paradoxical that peoples that have struggled for their independence should set so much store by their "colonial heritage". At the beginning, however, at the time when the Latin American countries were achieving independence, the principle of *uti possidetis* was formulated to serve a dual purpose: first, a defensive purpose towards the rest of the world, in the form of an outright denial that there was any land without a sovereign (or *terra nullius*) in the decolonized territories, even in unexplored areas or those beyond the control of the colonizers; secondly, a preventive purpose: to avoid or at least to minimize conflict occurring in the relationships among the successors, by freezing the carved-up territory in the format it exhibited at the moment of independence.

These two objectives therefore postulate the existence of a boundary, an impermeable territorial division, at the moment of independence. This hypothesis can only be factually verified in each case if a boundary is taken to mean a "line" in the geometric sense of the word. Otherwise it will be the inevitable fate of the principle of *uti possidetis* to operate as a mere fiction that jars with reality.

This is because a minimum of two points will always suffice for the definition of a line if one starts from the geometric concept of a "line" as "generated by the motion of a point" (*Encyclopaedia Britannica*, 11th ed.). In this sense there would always be a line to satisfy the logical requirements for the functioning of the *uti possidetis* principle. But if one starts from the common idea of a line as a concrete trace every point on which is specifically identifiable, it is far from likely that the postulate could be shown as realized in every instance.

By proceeding from the geometric concept of a line, which is alone capable of reconciling the principle of *uti possidetis* with the facts, we can state that there is always a line which defines the outer limit of lawful possession. But the scope of a court's role in identifying that line will vary inversely to the extent of its having taken concrete shape. The fewer the points (or points of reference) involved in its definition, the greater the court's "degrees of freedom" (in the statistical sense). And it is here that considerations of equity *infra legem* (mentioned in paragraph 28 of the Judgment) come into play, to guide the court in the exercise of this freedom when interpreting and applying the law and the legal titles involved.

2. LAW OF THE SEA

2.1. General Questions

Land, Island and
Maritime Frontier Dispute
(El Salvador/Honduras)
Application to Intervene,
Judgment of 13 September 1990,
I.C.J. Reports 1990, p. 92

[pp. 126-127] Whether a State is entitled to a territorial sea, continental shelf, or exclusive economic zone is a question to be decided by application of the principles and rules of the law of the sea on those matters. As observed above (paragraph 76), an interest in the application of general legal rules and principles is not the kind of interest which will justify an application for permission to intervene. In the present case, the legal regime within the Gulf - whatever it may be found by the Chamber to be - will no doubt also be relevant to any decision delimiting the waters outside the Gulf; but this, in the view of the Chamber, tends solely to strengthen Nicaragua's claim to intervene in relation to the legal régime of the maritime spaces inside the Gulf, not to justify an" intervention in relation to the legal situation of the maritime spaces outside.

2.2. Determination of Maritime Boundaries

Land, Island and
Maritime Frontier Dispute
(El Salvador/Honduras)
Application to Intervene,
Judgment of 13 September 1990,
I.C.J. Reports 1990, p. 92

[p. 124] It occurs frequently in practice that a delimitation between two States involves taking account of the coast of a third State; but the taking into account of all the coasts and coastal relationships within the Gulf as a geographical fact for the purpose of effecting an eventual delimitation as between two riparian States - El Salvador and Honduras in the instant case - in no way signifies that by such an operation itself the legal interest of a third riparian State of the Gulf, Nicaragua, may be affected.

2.3. Freedom of Navigation

Military and Paramilitary Activities
(Nicaragua/United States of America)
Merits. J. 27.6.1986
I.C.J. Reports 1986, p. 14

[pp. 111-112] It is also by virtue of its sovereignty that the coastal State may regulate access to its ports.

On the other hand, it is true that in order to enjoy access to ports, foreign vessels possess a customary right of innocent passage in territorial waters for the purposes of entering or leaving internal waters; Article 18, paragraph 1 (b), of the United Nations Convention on the Law of the Sea of 10 December 1982, does no more than codify customary international law on this point. Since freedom of navigation is guaranteed, first in the exclusive economic zones which may exist beyond territorial waters (Art. 58 of the Convention), and secondly, beyond territorial waters and on the high seas (Art. 87), it follows that any State which enjoys a right of access to ports for its ships also enjoys all the freedom necessary for maritime navigation. It may therefore be said that, if this right of access to the port is hindered by the laying of mines by another State, what is infringed is the freedom of communications and of maritime commerce. At all events, it is certain that interference with navigation in these areas prejudices both the sovereignty of the coastal State over its internal waters and the right of free access enjoyed by foreign ships.

[pp. 128-129] As the Court has indicated in paragraph 214 above, where the vessels of one State enjoy a right of access to ports of another State, if that right of access is hindered by the laying of mines, this constitutes an infringement of the freedom of communications and of maritime commerce. This is clearly the case here. It is not for the Court to pass upon the rights of States which are not parties to the case before it; but it is clear that interference with a right of access to the ports of Nicaragua is likely to have an adverse effect on Nicaragua's economy and its trading relations with any State whose vessels enjoy the right of access to its ports. Accordingly, the Court finds, in the context of the present proceedings between Nicaragua and the United States, that the laying of mines in or near Nicaraguan ports constituted an infringement, to Nicaragua's detriment, of the freedom of communications and of maritime commerce.

[p. 536 **D.O. Jennings**] The dispute concerning the responsibility of the United States for the unnotified mining of Nicaraguan ports, which apparently resulted in damage to a number of merchant ships, some under the flags of third States, seems to be a matter which does not arise out of the provisions of multilateral treaties, and is therefore within the jurisdiction of the Court. When this Court had to consider the laying of mines in a seaway in the Corfu Channel case, it did not find it necessary, in connection with the responsibility for damage caused by the mines, to invoke the provisions of the United Nations Charter, but based its decision on the obligation to notify the existence of the mines "for the benefit of shipping in general"; an obligation:

"based, not on the Hague Convention of 1907, No. VIII, which is applicable in time of war, but on certain general and well-recognized principles, namely: elementary considerations of humanity, even more exacting in peace than in war; the principle of freedom of maritime communication; and every State's obligation not to allow knowingly its territory to be used for acts contrary to the rights of other States" (*I.C.J. Reports 1949*, p. 22).

This law would seem to apply *a fortiori* where a State lays mines in another State's ports or port approaches, and fails to notify shipping. Nor does this conclusion depend upon a construction of Article 51 of the Charter, for even supposing the United States were acting in legitimate self-defence, failure to notify shipping would still make the mine-laying unlawful.

No doubt that the Court is right, therefore, in finding that the United States has, in this matter, acted unlawfully.

4. SELF-DETERMINATION

Frontier Dispute, Judgment
(Burkina Faso/Republic of Mali)
I.C.J. Reports 1986, p. 554

[pp. 566-567] However, it may be wondered how the time-hallowed principle has been able to withstand the new approaches to international law as expressed in Africa, where the successive attainment of independence and the emergence of new States have been accompanied by a certain questioning of traditional international law. At first sight this principle conflicts outright with another one, the right of peoples to self-determination. In fact, however, the maintenance of the territorial status quo in Africa is often seen as the wisest course, to preserve what has been achieved by peoples who have struggled for their independence, and to avoid a disruption which would deprive the continent of the gains achieved by much sacrifice. The essential requirement of stability in order to survive, to develop and gradually to consolidate their independence in all fields, has induced African States judiciously to consent to the respecting of colonial frontiers, and to take account of it in the interpretation of the principle of self-determination of peoples.

[pp. 652-654 **S.O. Luchaire**] In legal discourse, the term "decolonization" should be used only with great caution and must above all not be confused with accession to independence.

On the one hand, it would be wrong to ignore a certain opinion - which like all opinions, whether one shares them or not, is deserving of some respect - to the effect that independence is not the opposite of colonization but rather its crowning achievement, especially in cases where it has been obtained, without fighting, from an administering authority which has facilitated the cultural, economic, social and political progress of the inhabitants, such progress being fundamental to any genuine independence.

On the other hand, it is the right of peoples to determine their own future which has received the blessing of international law: a right which is expressly enshrined in the French constitution of 1958 in regard to what were then the French overseas territories, including French Sudan (now the Republic of Mali) and Upper Volta (now Burkina Faso). What the Declaration made by the General Assembly of the United Nations on 14 December 1960 (1514 (XV)) specifies, in recognizing the right of self-determination possessed by all peoples, is that they "freely determine their political status"; but the exercise of that right does not necessarily lead to the independence of a State with the same frontiers as a former colony. It may lead (see the list of factors annexed to General Assembly resolution 648 (VII) of 10 December 1952) either to:

- independence within the aforesaid geographical framework or
- integration into the territory of the administering power with strict equality of rights as between individuals, irrespective of whether their origins lie in the former colony or the former metropolitan state, or merger with a neighbouring State on the same conditions of equality,

  or
- the voluntary association of the ex-colony with the former metropolis on terms including unqualified respect for the former's personality.

Finally, the exercise of the right of self-determination may evidently lead certain plainly individualized parts of the former colony to a different option from that followed by the other parts.

The history of the last few decades provides numerous examples of very different options being preferred from among these solutions. The area of Togo that used to be under British trusteeship was integrated with the State of Ghana; the northern part of that area of Cameroon which used to be under British trusteeship was merged with the State of Nigeria, and the southern part with the territory of Cameroon formerly under French trusteeship; British and Italian Somaliland became one State of Somalia; some of the trust territories under United States strategic administration chose independence, while the others opted for association with the United States; and so on.

Several conclusions can be drawn from this:

First, the frontiers of an independent State emerging from colonization may differ from the frontiers of the colony which it replaces, and this may actually result from the exercise of the right of self-determination.

Second, the colonial process must be regarded as finally over once the inhabitants of a colony have been able to exercise this right of self-determination. So far as the French overseas territories are concerned, and French Sudan and Upper Volta in particular, this means that the colonial phenomenon disappeared on 28 September 1958 when, by an act of self-determination - accomplished through a referendum the authenticity of which has not been challenged by anyone -, those territories chose their status. At the time, some wished to remain overseas territories receiving similar status to the other territorial entities of the French Republic, while others - including French Sudan and Upper Volta - opted for the status of member States of the *Communauté*, i.e., for the solution of association. Lastly, another - Guinea - chose independence. As from that date, the French overseas territories could therefore no longer be considered as colonies, and that they were fully free was confirmed by the fact that those having chosen the status of member States of the *Communauté* became independent in 1960, while this was later also the case with some of those that had opted for keeping the status of an overseas territory (e.g. the Republic of Djibouti).

These considerations undoubtedly present several points of interest where the settlement of the problem referred to the Chamber is concerned, for on the day of their independence Mali and Upper Volta acceded both to the powers the *Communauté* had been exercising in their regard and to the powers which they themselves had been exercising as member States of that *Communauté*; they therefore succeeded in large measure to themselves. Consequently, by virtue of the theory of State succession, they remain bound by the deliberate or implicit decisions they took or may be deemed to have taken within the framework of the very broad powers they enjoyed before the day of their accession to independence.

7. LAW OF ALIENS

7.1. General Questions

Elettronica Sicula S.p.A. (ELSI)
Judgment of 20 July 1989
I.C.J. Reports 1989, p. 15

[p. 65] In any event, considering that it is not established that any deterioration in the plant and machinery was due to the presence of the workers, and that the authorities were able not merely to protect the plant but even in some measure to continue production, the protection provided by the authorities could not be regarded as falling below "the full protection and security required by international law"; or indeed as less than the national or third-State standards. The mere fact that the occupation was referred to by the Court of Appeal of Palermo as unlawful does not, in the Chamber's view, necessarily mean that the protection afforded fell short of the national standard to which the FCN Treaty refers. The essential question is whether the local law, either in its terms or its application, has treated United States nationals less well than Italian nationals. This, in the opinion of the Chamber, has not been shown.

[pp. 66-67] The primary standard laid down by Article V is "the full protection and security required by international law", in short the "protection and security" must conform to the minimum international standard. As noted above, this is supplemented by the criteria of national treatment and most-favoured-nation treatment. The Chamber is here called upon to apply the provisions of a treaty which sets standards in addition to the reference to general international law which may go further in protecting nationals of the High Contracting Parties than general international law requires; but the United States has not - save in one respect - suggested that these requirements do in this respect set higher standards than the international standard. It must be doubted whether in all the circumstances, the delay in the Prefect's ruling in this case can be regarded as falling below that standard. Certainly, the Applicant's use of so serious a charge as to call it a "denial of procedural justice" might be thought exaggerated.

7.2. Protection of Property

Elettronica Sicula S.p.A. (ELSI)
Judgment of 20 July 1989
I.C.J. Reports 1989, p. 15

[pp. 70-71] The argument that there was a "taking" involving transfer of title gives rise to a number of difficulties. Even assuming, though without deciding, that "*espropriazione*" might be wide enough to include not only formal and open expropriation, but also a disguised expropriation, there would still be a question whether the paragraph can be extended to include even a "taking" of an Italian corporation in Italy, of which, strictly speaking, Raytheon and Machlett only held the shares. This, however, is where account must also be taken of the first paragraph of the Protocol appended to the FCN Treaty, which provides:

"1. The provisions of paragraph 2 of Article V, providing for the payment of compensation, shall extend to interests held directly or indirectly [*si estenderanno ai diritti spettanti direttamente od indirettamente ai cittadini...*] by nationals, corporations and associations of either High Contracting Party in property which is taken within the territories of the other High Contracting Party."

The English text of this provision suggests that it was designed precisely to resolve the doubts just described. The interests of shareholders in the assets of a company, and in their residuary value on liquidation, would appear to fall in the category of the "interests" to be protected by Article V, paragraph 2, and the Protocol. Italy has however drawn attention to the use in the Italian text - which is equally authentic - of the narrower term "*diritti*" (rights), and has argued that, on the basis of the principle expressed in Article 33, paragraph 4, of the Vienna Convention on the Law of Treaties, the correct interpretation of the Protocol must be in the more restrictive sense of the Italian text.

In the view of the Chamber, however, neither this question of interpretation of the two texts of the Protocol, nor the questions raised as to the possibilities of disguised expropriation or of a "taking" amounting ultimately to expropriation, have to be resolved in the present case, because it is simply not possible to say that the ultimate result was the consequence of the acts or omissions of the Italian authorities, yet at the same time to ignore the most important factor, namely ELSI's financial situation, and the consequent decision of its shareholders to close the plant and put an end to the company's activities. As explained above (paragraphs 96-98), the municipal courts considered that ELSI, if not already insolvent in Italian law before the requisition, was in so precarious a state that bankruptcy was inevitable. The Chamber cannot regard any of the acts complained of which occurred subsequent to the bankruptcy as breaches of Article V, paragraph 2, in the absence of any evidence of collusion, which is now no longer even alleged. Even if it were possible to see the requisition as having been designed to bring about bankruptcy, as a step towards disguised expropriation, then, if ELSI was already under an obligation to file a petition of bankruptcy, or in such a financial state that such a petition could not be long delayed, the requisition was an act of supererogation. Furthermore this requisition, independently of the motives which allegedly inspired it, being by its terms for a limited period, and liable to be overturned by administrative appeal, could not, in the Chamber's view, amount to a "taking" contrary to Article V unless it constituted a significant deprivation of Raytheon and Machlett's interest in ELSI's plant; as might have been the case if, while ELSI remained solvent, the requisition had been extended and the hearing of the administrative appeal delayed. In fact the bankruptcy of ELSI transformed the situation less than a month after the requisition. The requisition could therefore only be regarded as significant for this purpose if it caused or triggered the bankruptcy. This is precisely the proposition which is irreconcilable with the findings of the municipal courts, and with the Chamber's conclusions in paragraphs 99-100 above.

[p. 120 **D.O. Schwebel**] May the measure and amount of compensation awarded by the Court of Appeal of Palermo be viewed as "full and complete compensation" which provides an equivalent result to ELSI's never having been requisitioned? Surely not. Whether or not the requisition was the cause of ELSI's bankruptcy - indeed, accepting that it was not "the" cause - the requisition inflicted uncompensated damage upon ELSI and its creditors, including (*a*) ELSI's practical inability to sell its accounts receivable for 100 per cent of their face value; (*b*) ELSI's actual inability to complete its work-in-progress and sell that work and its inventory for their value (in the event, work-in-progress was sold for materially less than its appraised value); and (*c*) ELSI's actual inability to arrange the showing and sale of its plant, product lines and equipment and its inability to bring to bear its knowledge of its assets and of the industry so as to raise the maximum return from the sale of those assets (including intangible assets).

8. HUMAN RIGHTS

Military and Paramilitary Activities
(Nicaragua/United States of America)
Merits. J. 27.6.1986
I.C.J. Reports 1986, p. 14

[pp. 134-135] The Court also notes that Nicaragua is accused by the 1985 finding of the United States Congress of violating human rights. This particular point requires to be studied independently of the question of the existence of a "legal commitment" by Nicaragua towards the Organization of American States to respect these rights ; the absence of such a commitment would not mean that Nicaragua could with impunity violate human rights. However, where human rights are protected by international conventions, that protection takes the form of such arrangements for monitoring or ensuring respect for human rights as are provided for in the conventions themselves. The political pledge by Nicaragua was made in the context of the Organization of American States, the organs of which were consequently entitled to monitor its observance. The Court has noted above (paragraph 168) that the Nicaraguan Government has since 1979 ratified a number of international instruments on human rights, and one of these was the American Convention on Human Rights (the Pact of San José, Costa Rica). The mechanisms provided for therein have functioned. The Inter-American Commission on Human Rights in fact took action and compiled two reports (OEA/Ser.L/V/11.53 and 62) following visits by the Commission to Nicaragua at the Government's invitation. Consequently, the Organization was in a position, if it so wished, to take a decision on the basis of these reports.

In any event, while the United States might form its own appraisal of the situation as to respect for human rights in Nicaragua, the use of force could not be the appropriate method to monitor or ensure such respect. With regard to the steps actually taken, the protection of human rights, a strictly humanitarian objective, cannot be compatible with the mining of ports, the destruction of oil installations, or again with the training, arming and equipping of the *contras*. The Court concludes that the argument derived from the preservation of human rights in Nicaragua cannot afford a legal justification for the conduct of the United States, and cannot in any event be reconciled with the legal strategy of the respondent State, which is based on the right of collective self-defence.

Applicability of Article VI, Section 22,
of the Convention on the Privileges and
Immunities of the United Nations,
Advisory Opinion of 15 December 1989
I.C.J. Reports 1989, p. 177

[pp. 210-211 **S.O. Evensen**] The integrity of a person's family and family life is a basic human right protected by prevailing principles of international law which derive not only from conventional international law or customary international law but from "general principles of law recognized by civilized nations".

Thus in the Universal Declaration of Human Rights adopted by the United Nations General Assembly on 10 December 1948 the integrity of family and family life was laid down as a basic human right in Article 16, paragraph 3, as follows: "The family is the natural and fundamental group unit of society and is entitled to protection by society and the State." This principle, which is a concrete expression of an established principle of human rights in the modern law of nations, has been similarly expressed in other international law instruments. Thus the European Convention on Human Rights (the Rome Convention) of 4 November 1950 provides in Article 8, paragraph 1: "Everyone has the right to respect for his private and family life, his home and his correspondence."

9. LAW OF ARMED CONFLICTS

Military and Paramilitary Activities
(Nicaragua/United States of America)
Merits. J. 27.6.1986
I.C.J. Reports 1986, p. 14

[p. 112] The Court has noted above (paragraph 77 *in fine*) that the United States did not issue any warning or notification of the presence of the mines which had been laid in or near the ports of Nicaragua. Yet even in time of war, the Convention relative to the laying of automatic submarine contact mines of 18 October 1907 (the Hague Convention No. VIII) provides that "every possible precaution must be taken for the security of peaceful shipping" and belligerents are bound

"to notify the danger zones as soon as military exigencies permit, by a notice addressed to ship owners, which must also be communicated to the Governments through the diplomatic channel" (Art. 3).

Neutral Powers which lay mines off their own coasts must issue a similar notification, in advance (Art. 4). It has already been made clear above that in peacetime for one State to lay mines in the internal or territorial waters of another is an unlawful act; but in addition, if a State lays mines in any waters whatever in which the vessels of another State have rights of access or passage, and fails to give any warning or notification whatsoever, in disregard of the security of peaceful shipping, it commits a breach of the principles of humanitarian law underlying the specific provisions of Convention No. VIII of 1907. Those principles were expressed by the Court in the *Corfu Channel* case as follows:

"certain general and well recognized principles, namely: elementary considerations of humanity, even more exacting in peace than in war" (*I.C.J. Reports 1949*, p. 22).

[pp. 113-114] ... the conduct of the United States may be judged according to the fundamental general principles of humanitarian law; in its view, the Geneva Conventions are in some respects a development, and in other respects no more than the expression, of such principles. It is significant in this respect that, according to the terms of the Conventions, the denunciation of one of them

"shall in no way impair the obligations which the Parties to the conflict shall remain bound to fulfil by virtue of the principles of the law of nations, as they result from the usages established among civilized peoples, from the laws of humanity and the dictates of the public conscience" (Convention I, Art. 63; Convention II, Art. 62; Convention III, Art. 142; Convention IV, Art. 158).

Article 3 which is common to all four Geneva Conventions of 12 August 1949 defines certain rules to be applied in the armed conflicts of a non-international character. There is no doubt that, in the event of international armed conflicts, these rules also constitute a minimum yardstick, in addition to the more elaborate rules which are also to apply to international conflicts; and they are rules which, in the Court's opinion, reflect what the Court in 1949 called "elementary considerations of humanity" (*Corfu Channel, Merits, I.C.J. Reports 1949*, p. 22; paragraph 215 above). The Court may therefore find them applicable to the present dispute, and is thus not required to decide what role the United States multilateral treaty reservation might otherwise play in regard to the treaties in question.

The conflict between the *contras*' forces and those of the Government of Nicaragua is an armed conflict which is "not of an international character". The acts of the *contras* towards the Nicaraguan Government are therefore governed by the law applicable to conflicts of that character; whereas the actions of the United States in and against Nicaragua fall under the legal rules relating to international conflicts. Because the minimum rules applicable to international and to non-international conflicts are identical, there is no need to address the question whether those actions must be looked at in the context of the rules which operate for the one or for the other category of conflict. The relevant principles are to be looked for in the provisions of Article 3 of each of the four Conventions of 12 August 1949, the text of which, identical in each Convention, expressly refers to conflicts not having an international character.

The Court considers that there is an obligation on the United States Government, in the terms of Article 1 of the Geneva Conventions, to "respect" the Conventions and even "to ensure respect" for them "in all circumstances", since such an obligation does not derive only from the Conventions themselves, but from the general principles of humanitarian law to which the Conventions merely give specific expression. The United States is thus under an obligation not to encourage persons or groups engaged in the conflict in Nicaragua to act in violation of the provisions of Article 3 common to the four 1949 Geneva Conventions.

[pp. 124-125] There can be no doubt that the provision of strictly humanitarian aid to persons or forces in another country, whatever their political affiliations or objectives, cannot be regarded as unlawful intervention, or as in any other way contrary to international law. The characteristics of such aid were indicated in the first and second of the fundamental principles declared by the Twentieth International Conference of the Red Cross, that

"The Red Cross, born of a desire to bring assistance without discrimination to the wounded on the battlefield, endeavours - in its international and national capacity - to prevent and alleviate human suffering wherever it may be found. Its purpose is to protect life and health and to ensure respect for the human being. It promotes mutual understanding, friendship, cooperation and lasting peace amongst all peoples"

and that

"It makes no discrimination as to nationality, race, religious beliefs, class or political opinions. It endeavours only to relieve suffering, giving priority to the most urgent cases of distress."

[p. 125] An essential feature of truly humanitarian aid is that it is given "without discrimination" of any kind. In the view of the Court, if the provision of "humanitarian assistance" is to escape condemnation as an intervention in the internal affairs of Nicaragua, not only must it be limited to the purposes hallowed in the practice of the Red Cross, namely "to prevent and alleviate human suffering", and "to protect life and health and to ensure respect for the human being"; it must also, and above all, be given without discrimination to all in need in Nicaragua, not merely to the *contras* and their dependents.

10. DISPUTE SETTLEMENT

Applicability of the Obligation to Arbitrate under Section 21 of the United Nations Headquarters Agreement of 26 June 1947
Advisory Opinion of 26 April 1988
I.C.J. Reports 1988, p. 12

[**p. 29**] The Court could not allow considerations as to what might be "appropriate" to prevail over the obligations which derive from section 21 of the Headquarters Agreement, as "the Court, being a Court of justice, cannot disregard rights recognized by it, and base its decision on considerations of pure expediency" (*Free Zones of Upper Savoy and the District of Gex, Order of 6 December 1930, P.C.I.J., Series A, No. 24*, p. 15).

The Court must further point out that the alleged dispute relates solely to what the United Nations considers to be its rights under the Headquarters Agreement. The purpose of the arbitration procedure envisaged by that Agreement is precisely the settlement of such disputes as may arise between the Organization and the host country without any prior recourse to municipal courts, and it would be against both the letter and the spirit of the Agreement for the implementation of that procedure to be subjected to such prior recourse. It is evident that a provision of the nature of section 21 of the Headquarters Agreement cannot require the exhaustion of local remedies as a condition of its implementation.

[p. 43 **S.O. Schwebel**] My difference of perspective with the Court turns on whether the dispute between the United Nations and the United States at this juncture concerns "the interpretation or application" of the Headquarters Agreement. The nub of my appreciation of the facts of the case is that there is essential agreement between the United Nations and the United States on the interpretation of the Headquarters Agreement. Whether there currently is a dispute over its application is not so clear.

It can be concluded, as the Court concludes, that, by the course of conduct which the Government of the United States has followed with respect to the continued functioning of the office in New York City of the Observer Mission to the United Nations of the Palestine Liberation Organization, a dispute has arisen between the United Nations and the United States "concerning the ... application of this Agreement...". But, in my view, the facts of the case alternatively allow the conclusion that, since the effective application of the United States Act at issue - the Anti-Terrorism Act - to the PLO's New York office has been deferred pending the outcome of litigation now in progress in the United States District Court for the Southern District of New York, a dispute over the application of the Headquarters Agreement will arise if and when the result of that litigation is effectively to apply that Act to the PLO's office.

[pp. 51-52 **S.O. Schwebel**] In view of the demonstrated consistency of the views of the United Nations and the United States on the interpretation of the Headquarters Agreement, I am unpersuaded by the Court's conclusion that "the opposing attitudes of the parties" give rise to a dispute "concerning the interpretation or application" of the Headquarters Agreement. In so far as that conclusion relates to application, it is not without force; in so far as it relates to interpretation, the above recitation of the facts of the case in my view demonstrates that it is not wholly convincing.

It is of course true that, where the breach by a State of its obligations under a treaty is manifest and undenied, such breach does not escape a jurisdictional clause which affords a court - such as this Court - the authority to decide disputes over that treaty's interpretation or application. Counsel for the United States so argued in the case of *United States Diplomatic and Consular Staff in Tehran (I.C.J. Pleadings*, p. 279), and that argument, apparently accepted by the Court, remains persuasive. But it does not follow that, in a particular case, the existence or non-existence of a dispute over the interpretation of a treaty is unaffected by the articulated concordance of views of the parties concerning its interpretation. In the case before the Court, if the question of application of the Headquarters Agreement is for purposes of analysis put aside, it does appear that the views of the parties on its interpretation "coincide" (to use the term employed by the Secretary-General).

That being said, I nevertheless recognize that there is logic in and authority for the position that every allegation by a party of a breach of a treaty provision - however manifest and admitted by the other party - necessarily entails elements of interpretation (by the parties and by any court adjudging them), because an application or misapplication of a treaty, however clear, is rooted in an interpretation of it. But when a party actually alleges, if not in form then in substance, only a failure to apply the treaty, and makes clear that there is no dispute over its interpretation, is there, for purposes of dispute settlement, a dispute over the treaty's interpretation? I have my doubts.

The essential question at issue in this case is whether there is a dispute over the application of the Headquarters Agreement. The Court acknowledges that there may be question about whether the Anti-Terrorism Act has been applied or whether the Act will only have received effective application when or if, on completion of current United states judicial proceedings, the PLO Mission is in fact closed. It maintains, however, that this is not decisive as regards section 21 of the Headquarters Agreement, since that Agreement refers to any dispute concerning its interpretation or application and not the application of measures taken in the municipal law of the United States.

[p. 54 **S.O. Schwebel**] The question in the end comes to whether the United States now is bound to arbitrate the dispute, or whether it will only be so bound in the event that the District Court should order that the Act be enforced against the PLO Observer

Mission. Should proceedings before the District Court and any appeals therefrom be maintained, the possibilities of municipal judgment are several. It could be held that the Act applies to the PLO Observer Mission, in which event the United States has inferred that it then will regard arbitration of the resultant dispute as "timely and appropriate". Alternatively, having regard to the reasoning of Senator Pell set out above or on other grounds, it could be held that the Act does not apply to the PLO Observer Mission, in which event, if a dispute requiring arbitration ever existed, it no longer will. Or it could be held that, in view of the Advisory Opinion of this Court, and in view of the fact that the Anti-Terrorism Act does not mention, and accordingly cannot be interpreted as derogating from, arbitral obligations of the United States under the Headquarters Agreement, in any event the United States is bound to arbitrate the dispute. There may be other possibilities as well.

[pp. 58-60 **S.O. Shahabuddeen**] As to whether the dispute in this case related to a question of interpretation of the Agreement, it was indeed the case that the views of the State Department coincided with those of the Secretary-General on the question of the status of the PLO Observer Mission under the Agreement (see the Secretary-General's letter of 13 October 1987 to United States Permanent Representative Ambassador Walters). But then different views on the subject seemingly prevailed with the United States legislature, and these would seem to have been upheld by the President when he assented to the Act adopted by it.

I have, however, considered an argument that, even so, there is still no conflict of views between the United States and the United Nations as to the interpretation of the Agreement for the reason that the United States has taken a position which may be interpreted to mean that, although the Administration is obliged by domestic law to enforce the Act by closing the PLO Observer Mission, it at the same time recognizes that it has no right to do so under international law and will engage international responsibility accordingly if it proceeds to a closure.

The argument is interesting, as much for its refinement as for its consequences, for, if sound, it means that, provided a State is prepared to go on record as admitting that it is consciously embarking on the violation of its accepted treaty obligation - something few States are prepared to do (see S. Rosenne, *Breach of Treaty*, 1984, p. 11) - it can escape its obligation to submit to an agreed procedure for the settlement of disputes concerning the interpretation of the treaty on the ground that it is in fact in agreement with the other party as to the meaning of the treaty, with the consequence that there is no dispute as to its interpretation.

A proposition productive of such strange results may not unreasonably be suspected of supplying its own refutation. I would suspect that, to begin with, the superstructure of the argument bases itself too narrowly on a possibly disjointed reading of the disputes settlement formula prescribed by section 21 of the Agreement.

The phrase "interpretation and application" has occurred in one version or another in a multitude of disputes settlement provisions extending over many decades into the past. In the *Certain German Interests in Polish Upper Silesia* case (*P.C.I.J., Series A, No. 6*, p. 14), it was held that it was not necessary to satisfy both elements of the phrase taken cumulatively, the word "and" falling to be read disjunctively. The phrase in this case happens to be "interpretation or application". Satisfaction of either element will therefore suffice. But, further, since it is not possible to interpret a treaty save with reference to some factual field (even if taken hypothetically) and since it is not possible to apply a treaty except on the basis of some interpretation of it, there is a detectable view that there is little practical, or even theoretical, distinction between the two elements of the formula (see L. B. Sohn, "Settlement of Disputes relating to the Interpretation and Application of Treaties", *Recueil des cours de l'Académie de droit international de La Haye*, Vol. 150, 1976, p. 271). It seems arguable that the two elements constitute a compendious term of art generally covering all disputes as to rights and duties having their source in the controlling treaty (see the language used in the *Chorzów Factory* case, *P.C.I.J., Series A, No. 9*, p. 24). It is, with much respect to the opposite view, not right to adopt an approach which would seek to avoid this conclusion by dissecting the phrase in question, focusing separately on its individual elements, and then reading them as if they did not belong together in a single formula whose force indeed derives from its constituent parts but is not coextensive with their sum [13].

[pp. 61-62 **S.O. Shahabuddeen**] The disputes settlement procedure of section 21 of the Agreement clearly applies to disputes arising out of complaints about an actual breach of the Agreement, but equally clearly it is not limited to such cases only. It extends to disputes arising out of opposition by one party to a course of conduct pursued by the other party, or a threat by it to act, with a view to producing what the complainant considers would be a breach of the Agreement. In the view of the Secretary-General, as I interpret it, such a course of conduct or threat was represented by the enactment of the Anti-Terrorism Act of 1987, this having in fact been assented to by the host country's Head of State whose recognized duty it was to carry out the laws of the State. Failing assurances to the contrary (which were sought but never given) the Secretary-General was entitled to assume that the President, through his appropriate officers, would carry out that duty with consequences which the Secretary-General considered would be at variance with the Agreement. This conflict of both views and interests would give rise to a dispute within the established jurisprudence on the subject, whether or not any actual breach of the Agreement had as yet occurred through the enforced closure of the Mission.

---

13 Footnote omitted.

The framework of the Agreement does not link the concept of a dispute to the concept of an actual breach. A claim by one party that the other party is in actual breach of an obligation under the Agreement is not a precondition to the existence of a dispute. And disputes as to the application of the Agreement comprehend disputes as to its applicability (see the *Chorzów Factory* case, *P.C.I.J., Series A, No. 9*, p. 20).

However, if this is wrong, with the consequence that a claim that there has been an actual breach is required, then it is to be noted that, from the record, it is a reasonably clear interpretation of the Secretary-General's position that it does include a claim that the host State is in current breach of its obligations under the Headquarters Agreement by reason of the enactment of the Act considered either separately from, or cumulatively with, the subsequent actions taken pursuant to it. Such a claim may be contested but cannot be considered so wholly unarguable as to be incapable of giving rise to a real dispute (see the *Nuclear Tests* case, *I.C.J. Reports 1974*, p. 430, per Judge Barwick, dissenting).

12. INTERNATIONAL ECONOMIC LAW

Military and Paramilitary Activities
(Nicaragua/United States of America)
Merits. J. 27.6.1986
I.C.J. Reports 1986, p. 14

[pp. 125-126] As already noted, Nicaragua has also asserted that the United States is responsible for an "indirect" form of intervention in its internal affairs inasmuch as it has taken, to Nicaragua's disadvantage, certain action of an economic nature. The Court's attention has been drawn in particular to the cessation of economic aid in April 1981; the 90 per cent reduction in the sugar quota for United States imports from Nicaragua in April 1981; and the trade embargo adopted on 1 May 1985. While admitting in principle that some of these actions were not unlawful in themselves, counsel for Nicaragua argued that these measures of economic constraint add up to a systematic violation of the principle of non-intervention.

The Court does not here have to concern itself with possible breaches of such international economic instruments as the General Agreement on Tariffs and Trade, referred to in passing by counsel for Nicaragua; any such breaches would appear to fall outside the Court's jurisdiction, particularly in view of the effect of the multilateral treaty reservation, nor has Nicaragua seised the Court of any complaint of such breaches. The question of the compatibility of the actions complained of with the 1956 Treaty of Friendship, Commerce and Navigation will be examined below, in the context of the Court's examination of the provisions of that Treaty. At this point, the Court has merely to say that it is unable to regard such action on the economic plane as is here complained of as a breach of the customary-law principle of non-intervention.

[p. 138] A State is not bound to continue particular trade relations longer than it sees fit to do so, in the absence of a treaty commitment or other specific legal obligation; but where there exists such a commitment, of the kind implied in a treaty of friendship and commerce, such an abrupt act of termination of commercial intercourse as the general trade embargo of 1 May 1985 will normally constitute a violation of the obligation not to defeat the object and purpose of the treaty. The 90 per cent cut in the sugar import quota of 23 September 1983 does not on the other hand seem to the Court to go so far as to constitute an act calculated to defeat the object and purpose of the Treaty.

[pp. 252-253 **D.O. Oda**] I totally fail to understand what the Court has attempted to contend in connection with the trade embargo ordered on 1 May 1985. From my point of view, the United States decision on a trade embargo quite unlike that on laying of mines, is open to justification under Article XXI [14]. Trade is not a duty of a State under general international law but may only be a duty imposed by a treaty to which that State is a party, and can be suspended under certain circumstances expressly specified in that treaty. In fact, the United States, when declaring a trade embargo on 1 May 1985, did not announce its reliance on this particular provision of the Treaty, but, instead, gave notice on the same day to terminate the Treaty. Even so, I am inclined to maintain that, in principle, the trade assured by Article XIX, paragraph 3, of the Treaty, could also justifiably have been suspended in reliance on another provision, Article XXI, of the same Treaty.

"Laying mines" is totally different, in that it is illegal in the absence of any justification recognized in international law, while Article XXI of the Treaty, being simply one provision in a commercial treaty, can in no way be interpreted to justify a State party in derogating from this principle of general international law. I must add that this action did not meet the conditions of necessity and proportionality that may be required as a minimum in resort to the doctrine of self-defence under general and customary international law. I thus conclude that, under the jurisdiction granted to the Court by Article XXIV of the 1956 Treaty, the Court should have found the United States responsible only for violation of Article XIX by laying mines in Nicaraguan waters.

14 Article XXI of the 1956 FCN Treaty.

III. The International Court of Justice

1. FUNDAMENTAL PRINCIPLES

1.1. General Questions

**Military and Paramilitary Activities
(Nicaragua/United States of America)
Merits. J. 27.6.1986
I.C.J. Reports 1986, p. 14**

[pp. 158-159 **S.O. Lachs**] ... even apart from the stipulations of Article 2 of the Court's Statute, two requirements are overriding: integrity and independence.

A judge - as needs no emphasis - is bound to be impartial, objective, detached, disinterested and unbiased. In invoking the assistance of this Court or accepting its jurisdiction, States must feel assured that the facts of the dispute will be properly elicited; they must have the certainty that their jural relationship will be properly defined and that no partiality will result in injustice towards them. Thus those on the bench may represent different schools of law, may have different ideas about law and justice, be inspired by conflicting philosophies or travel on divergent roads - as indeed will often be true of the States parties to a case - and that their characters, outlook and background will widely differ is virtually a corollary of the diversity imposed by the Statute. But whatever philosophy the judges may confess they are bound to "master the facts" and then apply to them the law with utmost honesty.

As human beings, judges have their weaknesses and limitations; however, to be equal to their task they have to try to overcome them. Thus in both their achievements and shortcomings they must be looked upon as individuals: it is their personality that matters.

**Land, Island and
Maritime Frontier Dispute
(El Salvador/Honduras)
Application to Intervene,
Order of 28 February 1990,
I.C.J. Reports 1990, p. 3**

[pp. 40-41 **D.O. Shahabuddeen**] The whole nature of the Court, as a court of justice, constitutes a prohibition, no less clear for being implied, against giving the parties any say in the selection of judges to hear a case, whether through the Rules of Court or otherwise, and whether in whole or in part, except in the case of *ad hoc* judges. So fundamental was that prohibition to the character of the Court as a court of justice, as distinguished from an arbitral body, that it was no more necessary to express it in its Statute than it would have been to do so in the constitution of any other "court of justice" within the normal acceptation of the meaning of this expression.

This implied prohibition is not neutralized by approaching the matter from the point of view of the doctrine of implied powers. True, the fact that specific powers are conferred on a body does not necessarily imply the non-existence of others. But the latter do not float around at large. In the last analysis, all the powers of a body must be conferred by its constituent instrument, whether expressly or impliedly.

[p. 34 **D.O. Shahabuddeen**] The material makes it clear that the concept of judges being selected by the parties was regarded as being a characteristic of arbitral procedures; that, as such, that concept was essentially opposed to the judicial character of the Court; that, on special grounds, it was, after anxious debate, nevertheless allowed a limited operation within the constitution of the Court in relation to *ad hoc* judges; but that this limited operation could not be extended consistently with the judicial character of the Court without an appropriate enabling amendment of its Statute.

[p. 55 **D.O. Shahabuddeen**] In my opinion, reached with reluctance but with conviction, the methods by which the members of the Chamber have been selected do not satisfy the criteria required to enable it to discharge the judicial mission of the International Court of Justice, considered as a court of justice, in relation to the Applicant; and the fundamental reason for this is that the Chamber has been constituted not in accordance with the Statute, but in accordance with an unauthorized arrangement under which the Court has been essaying to transform itself into the Permanent Court of Arbitration, or something akin to it. This represents a major flaw which the Court, as the avowed guardian of its own judicial integrity, cannot correctly overlook. The existing practice may well continue unabated. My views may make no difference. It was nevertheless my duty to state them.

1.2. Consent of States

Military and Paramilitary Activities
(Nicaragua/United States of America)
Merits. J. 27.6.1986
I.C.J. Reports 1986, p. 14

[p. 32] The Court's jurisdiction, as it has frequently recalled, is based on the consent of States, expressed in a variety of ways including declarations made under Article 36, paragraph 2, of the Statute. It is the declaration made by the United States under that Article which defines the categories of dispute for which the United States consents to the Court's jurisdiction. If therefore that declaration, because of a reservation contained in it, excludes from the disputes for which it accepts the Court's jurisdiction certain disputes arising under multilateral treaties, the Court must take that fact into account. The final decision on this point, which it was not possible to take at the jurisdictional stage, can and must be taken by the Court now when coming to its decision on the merits. If this were not so, the Court would not have decided whether or not the objection was well-founded, either at the jurisdictional stage, because it did not possess an exclusively preliminary character, or at the merits stage, because it did to some degree have such a character.

[p. 183 **S.O. Ago**] It can never be sufficiently emphasized that acceptance of the Court's compulsory jurisdiction on the basis of Article 36, paragraph 2, of its Statute is a sovereign, voluntary act the effects of which are strictly confined to the limits within which it was conceived and intended. The Court therefore proceeded correctly in holding itself obliged to conclude that the jurisdiction conferred upon it by the declaration of acceptance which the United States made in 1946 under Article 36, paragraph 2, of the Statute did not enable it to entertain the complaints submitted by Nicaragua concerning the violation of the treaties in question.

1.3. Equality of Parties

Military and Paramilitary Activities
(Nicaragua/United States of America)
Merits. J. 27.6.1986
I.C.J. Reports 1986, p. 14

[pp. 25-26] On the other hand, the Court has to emphasize that the equality of the parties to the dispute must remain the basic principle for the Court. The intention of Article 53 was that in a case of non-appearance neither party should be placed at a disadvantage; therefore the party which declines to appear cannot be permitted to profit from its absence, since this would amount to placing the party appearing at a disadvantage. The provisions of the Statute and Rules of Court concerning the presentation of pleadings and evidence are designed to secure a proper administration of justice, and a fair and equal opportunity for each party to comment on its opponent's contentions. The treatment to be given by the Court to communications or material emanating from the absent party must be determined by the weight to be given to these different considerations, and is not susceptible of rigid definition in the form of a precise general rule. The vigilance which the Court can exercise when aided by the presence of both parties to the proceedings has a counterpart in the special care it has to devote to the proper administration of justice in a case in which only one party is present.

1.4. Political Questions/ Determination of the Existence of a Dispute

Military and Paramilitary Activities
(Nicaragua/United States of America)
Merits. J. 27.6.1986
I.C.J. Reports 1986, p. 14

[pp. 26-27] In the first place, it has been suggested that the present dispute should be declared non-justiciable because it does not fall into the category of "legal disputes" within the meaning of Article 36, paragraph 2, of the Statute. It is true that the jurisdiction of the Court under that provision is limited to "legal disputes" concerning any of the matters enumerated in the text. The question whether a given dispute between two States is or is not a "legal dispute" for the purposes of this provision may itself be a matter in dispute between those two States and if so, that dispute is to be settled by the decision of the Court in accordance with paragraph 6 of Article 36. In the present case, however, this particular point does not appear to be in dispute between the Parties. The United States, during the proceedings devoted to questions of jurisdiction and admissibility, advanced a number of grounds why the Court should find that it had no jurisdiction, or that the claim was not admissible. It relied *inter alia* on proviso (*c*) to its own declaration of acceptance of jurisdiction under Article 36, paragraph 2, without ever advancing the more radical argument that the whole declaration was inapplicable because the dispute brought before the Court by Nicaragua was not a "legal dispute" within the meaning of that paragraph. As a matter of admissibility, the United States objected to the application of Article 36, paragraph 2, not because the dispute was not a "legal dispute", but because of the express allocation of such matters as the subject of Nicaragua's claims to the political organs under the United Nations Charter, an argument rejected by the Court in its Judgment of 26 November 1984 (*I.C.J. Reports 1984*, pp. 431-436). Similarly, while the United States contended that the nature of the judicial function precludes its application to the substance of Nicaragua's allegations in this case - an argument which the Court was again unable to uphold (*ibid.*, pp. 436-438)-, it was careful to emphasize that this did not mean that it was arguing that international law was not relevant or controlling in a dispute of this kind. In short, the Court can see no indication whatsoever that, even in the view of the United States, the present dispute falls outside the category of "legal disputes" to which Article 36, paragraph 2, of the Statute applies.

[p. 220 **D.O. Oda**] I believe that the Nicaraguan Application should be declared non-justiciable, since in my view the dispute at issue is one which does not fall into the category of "legal" disputes within the meaning and intention of Article 36, paragraph 2, of the Statute. It may be argued (and the present Judgment deliberately attempts to do so, see para. 32) that the interpretation of the competence of the Court as conferred in accordance with that provision has been settled by a determination of jurisdiction. However, the question as to whether this dispute should be considered as justiciable in terms of the concept of "legal disputes" within the meaning of the Statute is related to the merits of the dispute. Accordingly, it deserves and requires reconsideration at the present stage (see Section B below).

Furthermore, even if my contention were not well founded, it would in my view have been prudent for the Court, in the light of the merits of the present case, to find it a matter of judicial propriety not to proceed with a case so highly charged with issues central to the sensitive political relations of many States: a circumstance that undoubtedly accounts for much of the vigour with which the Respondent has first challenged, then been seen to defy, the Court's jurisdiction (see Section C below).

[p. 221 **D.O. Oda**] Looking back at the history of the settlement of international disputes by arbitration or adjudication, one may clearly see that the "legal disputes" subject to such settlement were limited in scope and, more basically, that their referral to such a settlement was always to depend ultimately on the assent of the States in dispute.

[p. 236 **D.O. Oda**] In consequence, the fact that the Court or its predecessor entertained a handful of previous cases submitted on the basis of Article 36, paragraph 2, of the Statute affords absolutely no ground for concluding that voluntary acceptance of the obligation for submission of legal disputes to the Court's jurisdiction under that Article equates with the submission of all disputes however politically charged they may be. The United States, though having voluntarily accepted the Optional Clause, appears to be of the view that the present dispute does not fall within the meaning of what is a "legal dispute" under Article 36, paragraph 2. Even if it did not explicitly contend this during the proceedings on jurisdiction, which were largely devoted to the jurisdictional position of the Applicant, its reliance on the "ongoing armed conflict" argument furnished a clear indication that the Respondent viewed the dispute as "not susceptible of decision by the application of the principles of law" - or, in other words, that the sense of "legal dispute" had not evolved so far as to embrace the subject-matter of the application. Whether this view is right or wrong is beside the point in considering a *voluntary* acceptance of jurisdiction.

In sum, the Court should note that the meaning of "legal disputes" is not to be taken separately from the fact that the Court's jurisdiction over "legal disputes" can only be accepted voluntarily. The Court is at present not in a position, as it was in the *Aegean Sea Continental Shelf* case, to apply an extended concept of the law, one not contemplated at the time of the filing of the declaration, because by doing so it would risk imposing its jurisdiction in contravention of the voluntary character of that instrument, whereas in the case referred to it did so in order to be quite sure of respecting that character in the case of the Respondent's declaration.

[p. 238 **D.O. Oda**] ... it has throughout this century been considered that any dispute which a State was prepared voluntarily to submit to judicial settlement should be one where the parties are in conflict as to their respective rights, or where differences arise by virtue of a claim of right made by one against the other; and disputes such as the present one, at least where it concerns allegations of threat or use of force and intervention, have not been deemed to fall into this category. The distinction between "legal" and "non-legal" (or political) is certainly vague inasmuch as, on the one hand, a legal dispute may eventually give rise to political friction and tension and, on the other, any political dispute is almost bound to contain certain aspects of a legal nature; yet in the 60-year history of the past and present Courts, issues regarding matters of an overwhelmingly political nature have never been dealt with by way of adjudication before the Court on the basis of Article 36, paragraph 2, of the Statute.

[pp. 239-240 **D.O. Oda**] While Article 36 of the United Nations Charter states that "legal disputes should as a general rule be referred by the parties to the International Court of Justice", this certainly should not be interpreted as implying that the term "legal disputes" covers disputes which are non-justiciable because of their overwhelmingly political nature. In other words, it is normal to assume that the term "legal disputes" refers to disputes whose primary characteristic it is to be "legal". Otherwise - since practically every dispute has a "legal" aspect as at least a secondary characteristic - there would have been no reason to include the word "legal" in the provision. Furthermore, the qualifying phrase "as a general rule" serves to stress the necessity of not jumping to the conclusion that the presence of a legal element in a dispute attracts the application of the provision. For it is well known that the phrase in question, just like "in principle", functions as a pointer to the possibility of exceptions and borderline cases. Moreover, it may be observed that, in practice, the parties to international legal disputes do not, as a general rule, refer them to the Court, while, for its part, the Security Council has almost invariably failed to make recommendations for such referral; this may be deplored, but should not be ignored as an indication of the relative cogency of the rule.

Under the United Nations system, where the maintenance of international peace and security falls within the functions of the Security Council, resort to force as a means of self-defence is permissible only until such time as the Security Council has taken the necessary measures, and any measures taken by the member State in the exercise of its right of self-defence must be reported immediately to the Security Council. This would mean, in my view, that a dispute in which use of force is resorted to is in essence and *in limine* one most suitable for settlement by a political organ such as the Security Council, but is not necessarily a justiciable dispute such as falls within the proper functions of the judicial organ.

Applicability of the Obligation to Arbitrate under Section 21 of the United Nations Headquarters Agreement of 26 June 1947
Advisory Opinion of 26 April 1988
I.C.J. Reports 1988, p. 12

[p. 27] In order to answer the question put to it, the Court has to determine whether there exists a dispute between the United Nations and the United States, and if so whether or not that dispute is one "concerning the interpretation or application of" the Headquarters Agreement within the meaning of section 21 thereof. If it finds that there is such a dispute it must also, pursuant to that section, satisfy itself that it is one "not settled by negotiation or other agreed mode of settlement".

As the Court observed in the case concerning *Interpretation of Peace Treaties with Bulgaria, Hungary and Romania*, "whether there exists an international dispute is a matter for objective determination" (*I.C.J. Reports 1950*, p. 74). In this respect the Permanent Court of International Justice, in the case concerning *Mavrommatis Palestine Concessions*, had defined a dispute as "a disagreement on a point of law or fact, a conflict of legal views or of interests between two persons" (*P.C.I.J., Series A, No. 2*, p. 11). This definition has since been applied and clarified on a number of occasions. In the Advisory Opinion of 30 March 1950 the Court, after examining the diplomatic exchanges between the States concerned, noted that "the two sides hold clearly opposite views concerning the question of the performance or non-performance of certain treaty obligations" and concluded that "international disputes have arisen" (*Interpretation of Peace Treaties with Bulgaria, Hungary and Romania, First Phase, I.C.J. Reports 1950*, p. 74). Furthermore, in its Judgment of 21 December 1962 in the *South West Africa* cases, the Court made it clear that in order to prove the existence of a dispute

"it is not sufficient for one party to a contentious case to assert that a dispute exists with the other party. A mere assertion is not sufficient to prove the existence of a dispute any more than a mere denial of the existence of the dispute proves its non-existence. Nor is it adequate to show that the interests of the two parties to such a case are in conflict. It must be shown that the claim of one party is positively opposed by the other." (*I.C.J. Reports 1962*, p. 328.)

The Court found that the opposing attitudes of the parties clearly established the existence of a dispute (*ibid.*; see also *Northern Cameroons, I.C.J. Reports 1963*, p. 27).

[p. 28] The United States has never expressly contradicted the view expounded by the Secretary-General and endorsed by the General Assembly regarding the sense of the Headquarters Agreement. Certain United States authorities have even expressed the same view, but the United States has nevertheless taken measures against the PLO Mission to the United Nations. It has indicated that those measures were being taken "irrespective of any obligations the United States may have under the [Headquarters] Agreement" (paragraph 24 above).

In the view of the Court, where one party to a treaty protests against the behaviour or a decision of another party, and claims that such behaviour or decision constitutes a breach of the treaty, the mere fact that the party accused does not advance any argument to justify its conduct under international law does not prevent the opposing attitudes of the parties from giving rise to a dispute concerning the interpretation or application of the treaty.

[pp. 29-30] The United States in its written statement might be implying that neither the signing into law of the Anti-Terrorism Act, nor its entry into force, nor the Attorney General's decision to apply it, nor his resort to court proceedings to close the PLO Mission to the United Nations, would have been sufficient to bring about a dispute between the United Nations and the United States, since the case was still pending before an American court and, until the decision of that court, the United States, according to the Acting Permanent Representative's letter of 11 March 1988, "will not take other actions to close" the Mission. The Court cannot accept such an argument. While the existence of a dispute does presuppose a claim arising out of the behaviour of or a decision by one of the parties, it in no way requires that any contested decision must already have been carried into effect. What is more, a dispute may arise even if the party in question gives an assurance that no measure of execution will be taken until ordered by decision of the domestic courts.

The Anti-Terrorism Act was signed into law on 22 December 1987. It was automatically to take effect 90 days later. Although the Act extends to every PLO office situated within the jurisdiction of the United States and contains no express reference to the office of the PLO Mission to the United Nations in New York, its chief, if not its sole, objective was the closure of that office. On 11 March 1988, the United States Attorney General considered that he was under an obligation to effect such a closure; he notified the Mission of this, and applied to the United States courts for an injunction prohibiting those concerned "from continuing violations of" the Act. As noted above, the

Secretary-General, acting both on his own behalf and on instructions from the General Assembly, has consistently challenged the decisions contemplated and then taken by the United States Congress and the Administration. Under those circumstances, the Court is obliged to find that the opposing attitudes of the United Nations and the United States show the existence of a dispute between the two parties to the Headquarters Agreement.

For the purposes of the present advisory opinion there is no need to seek to determine the date at which the dispute came into existence, once the Court has reached the conclusion that there is such a dispute at the date on which its opinion is given.

[p. 32] To conclude, the United States has taken a number of measures against the PLO Observer Mission to the United Nations in New York. The Secretary-General regarded these as contrary to the Headquarters Agreement. Without expressly disputing that point, the United States stated that the measures in question were taken "irrespective of any obligations the United States may have under the Agreement". Such conduct cannot be reconciled with the position of the Secretary-General. There thus exists a dispute between the United Nations and the United States concerning the application of the Headquarters Agreement, falling within the terms of section 21 thereof.

The question might of course be raised whether in United States domestic law the decisions taken on 11 and 21 March 1988 by the Attorney General brought about the application of the Anti-Terrorism Act, or whether the Act can only be regarded as having received effective application when or if, on completion of the current judicial proceedings, the PLO Mission is in fact closed. This is however not decisive as regards section 21 of the Headquarters Agreement, which refers to any dispute "concerning the interpretation or application" of the Agreement, and not concerning the application of the measures taken in the municipal law of the United States. The Court therefore sees no reason not to find that a dispute exists between the United Nations and the United States concerning the "interpretation or application" of the Headquarters Agreement.

[p. 43 **S.O. Schwebel**] My difference of perspective with the Court turns on whether the dispute between the United Nations and the United States at this juncture concerns "the interpretation or application" of the Headquarters Agreement. The nub of my appreciation of the facts of the case is that there is essential agreement between the United Nations and the United States on the interpretation of the Headquarters Agreement. Whether there currently is a dispute over its application is not so clear.

It can be concluded, as the Court concludes, that, by the course of conduct which the Government of the United States has followed with respect to the continued functioning of the office in New York City of the Observer Mission to the United Nations of the Palestine Liberation Organization, a dispute has arisen between the United Nations and the United States "concerning the ... application of this Agreement...". But, in my view, the facts of the case alternatively allow the conclusion that, since the effective application of the United States Act at issue - the Anti-Terrorism Act - to the PLO's New York office has been deferred pending the outcome of litigation now in progress in the United States District Court for the Southern District of New York, a dispute over the application of the Headquarters Agreement will arise if and when the result of that litigation is effectively to apply that Act to the PLO's office.

[pp. 51-52 **S.O. Schwebel**] In view of the demonstrated consistency of the views of the United Nations and the United States on the interpretation of the Headquarters Agreement, I am unpersuaded by the Court's conclusion that "the opposing attitudes of the parties" give rise to a dispute "concerning the interpretation or application" of the Headquarters Agreement. In so far as that conclusion relates to application, it is not without force; in so far as it relates to interpretation, the above recitation of the facts of the case in my view demonstrates that it is not wholly convincing.

It is of course true that, where the breach by a State of its obligations under a treaty is manifest and undenied, such breach does not escape a jurisdictional clause which affords a court - such as this Court - the authority to decide disputes over that treaty's interpretation or application. Counsel for the United States so argued in the case of *United States Diplomatic and Consular Staff in Tehran (I.C.J. Pleadings*, p. 279), and that argument, apparently accepted by the Court, remains persuasive. But it does not follow that, in a particular case, the existence or non-existence of a dispute over the interpretation of a treaty is unaffected by the articulated concordance of views of the parties concerning its interpretation. In the case before the Court, if the question of application of the Headquarters Agreement is for purposes of analysis put aside, it does appear that the views of the parties on its interpretation "coincide" (to use the term employed by the Secretary-General).

That being said, I nevertheless recognize that there is logic in and authority for the position that every allegation by a party of a breach of a treaty provision - however manifest and admitted by the other party - necessarily entails elements of interpretation (by the parties and by any court adjudging them), because an application or misapplication of a treaty, however clear, is rooted in an interpretation of it. But when a party actually alleges, if not in form then in substance, only a failure to apply the treaty, and makes clear that there is no dispute over its interpretation, is there, for purposes of dispute settlement, a dispute over the treaty's interpretation? I have my doubts.

The essential question at issue in this case is whether there is a dispute over the application of the Headquarters Agreement. The Court acknowledges that there may be question about whether the Anti-Terrorism Act has been applied or whether the Act will only have received effective application when or if, on completion of current United states judicial proceedings, the PLO Mission is in fact closed. It maintains, however, that this is not decisive as regards section 21 of the Headquarters Agreement, since that Agreement refers to any dispute concerning its interpretation or application and not the application of measures taken in the municipal law of the United States.

Border and Transborder Armed Actions Nicaragua/Honduras), Jurisdiction and Admissibility, Judgment, I.C.J. Reports 1988, p. 69

[pp. 91-92] Honduras's first objection to the admissibility of the Application is that "It is a politically-inspired, artificial request which the Court should not entertain consistently with its judicial character"; it claims that Nicaragua is attempting to use the Court, or the threat of litigation before the Court, as a means of exerting political pressure on the other Central American States.

As regards the first aspect of this objection, the Court is aware that political aspects may be present in any legal dispute brought before it. The Court, as a judicial organ, is however only concerned to establish, first, that the dispute before it is a legal dispute, in the sense of a dispute capable of being settled by the application of principles and rules of international law, and secondly, that the Court has jurisdiction to deal with it, and that that jurisdiction is not fettered by any circumstance rendering the application inadmissible. The purpose of recourse to the Court is the peaceful settlement of such disputes; the Court's judgment is a legal pronouncement, and it cannot concern itself with the political motivation which may lead a State at a particular time, or in particular circumstances, to choose judicial settlement. So far as the objection of Honduras is based on an alleged political inspiration of the proceedings, it therefore cannot be upheld.

The second aspect of the first objection of Honduras is its claim that the request is artificial. In its Memorial Honduras explains that in its view the overall result of Nicaragua's action is "an artificial and arbitrary dividing up of the general conflict existing in Central America", which "may have negative consequences for Honduras as a defendant State before the Court", because, it is said, certain facts appertaining to the general conflict "are inevitably absent from the proceedings before the Court", and other facts have already been in issue before the Court in the case concerning *Military and Paramilitary Activities in and against Nicaragua (Nicaragua v. United States of America).* Honduras contends that no real distinction can be made between the general situation of tension in the region and the various bilateral disputes which Nicaragua claims to exist there, and that the "procedural situation" created by Nicaragua's splitting-up of the overall conflict into separate disputes is contrary to the requirements of good faith and the proper functioning of international justice.

The Court cannot uphold this contention. It is not clear why any facts should be "inevitably absent" from the proceedings, since it is open to Honduras to bring to the Court's attention any facts which in its view are relevant to the issues in this case. Nor can it be accepted that once the Court has given judgment in a case involving certain allegations of fact, and made findings in that respect, no new procedure can be commenced in which those, as well as other, facts might have to be considered. In any event, it is for the Parties to establish the facts in the present case taking account of the usual rules of evidence, without it being possible to rely on considerations of *res judicata* in another case not involving the same parties (see Article 59 of the Statute).

There is no doubt that the issues of which the Court has been seised may be regarded as part of a wider regional problem. The Court is not unaware of the difiiculties that may arise where particular aspects of a complex general situation are brought before a Court for separate decision. Nevertheless, as the Court observed in the case concerning *United States Diplomatic and Consular Staff in Tehran*, "no provision of the Statute or Rules contemplates that the Court should decline to take cognizance of one aspect of a dispute merely because that dispute has other aspects, however important" (*I.C.J. Reports 1980*, p. 19, para. 36).

1.6. Applicable Law

Frontier Dispute, Judgment
(Burkina Faso/Republic of Mali)
I.C.J. Reports 1986, p. 554

[p. 575] It must be recalled in this connection that the Chamber, whose judgment "shall be considered as rendered by the Court" (Statute, Art. 27), is bound to settle the present dispute "in accordance with international law" (Art. 38). Accordingly, it is on the basis of international law that the Chamber will have to fix the frontier line, weighing for that purpose the legal force of the respective evidence submitted by the Parties for its appraisal. It is therefore of little significance whether Mali adopted a particular approach, either in the course of negotiations on frontier questions, or with respect to the conclusions of the Legal Sub-Commission of the Organization of African Unity Mediation Commission, and whether that approach may or may not be construed to reflect a specific position, or indeed to signify acquiescence, towards the principles and rules, including those which determine the respective weight of the various kinds of evidence applicable to the dispute. If these principles and rules are applicable as elements of law in the present case, they remain so whatever Mali's attitude. If the reverse is true, the Chamber could only take account of them if the two Parties had requested it to do so, or had given such principles and rules a special place in the Special Agreement, as "rules expressly recognized by the contesting States" (Art. 38, para. 1 (*a*), of the Statute).

"While the Court is... bound to have regard to all the legal sources specified in Article 38, paragraph 1, of the Statute... it is also bound, in accordance with paragraph 1 (*a*), of that Article, to apply the provisions of the Special Agreement." (*I.C.J. Reports 1982*, p. 37; para. 23.)

1.7. Jura novit curia

Military and Paramilitary Activities
(Nicaragua/United States of America)
Merits. J. 27.6.1986
I.C.J. Reports 1986, p. 14

[pp. 24-25] For the purpose of deciding whether the claim is well founded in law, the principle *jura novit curia* signifies that the Court is not solely dependent on the argument of the parties before it with respect to the applicable law (*cf.* *"Lotus", P.C.I.J., Series A, No. 10*, p. 31), so that the absence of one party has less impact. As the Court observed in the *Fisheries Jurisdiction* cases:

"The Court ..., as an international judicial organ, is deemed to take judicial notice of international law, and is therefore required in a case falling under Article 53 of the Statute, as in any other case, to consider on its own initiative all rules of international law which may be relevant to the settlement of the dispute. It being the duty of the Court itself to ascertain and apply the relevant law in the given circumstances of the case, the burden of establishing or proving rules of international law cannot be imposed upon any of the parties, for the law lies within the judicial knowledge of the Court." (*I.C.J. Reports 1974*, p. 9, para. 17; p. 181, para. 18.)

Nevertheless the views of the parties to a case as to the law applicable to their dispute are very material, particularly, as will be explained below (paragraphs 184 and 185), when those views are concordant.

[pp. 97-98] The Court notes that there is in fact evidence, to be examined below, of a considerable degree of agreement between the Parties as to the content of the customary international law relating to the non-use of force and non-intervention. This concurrence of their views does not however dispense the Court from having itself to ascertain what rules of customary international law are applicable. The mere fact that States declare their recognition of certain rules is not sufficient for the Court to consider these as being part of customary international law, and as applicable as such to those States. Bound as it is by Article 38 of its Statute to apply, *inter alia*, international custom "as evidence of a general practice accepted as law", the Court may not disregard the essential role played by general practice. Where two States agree to incorporate a particular rule in a treaty, their agreement suffices to make that rule a legal one, binding upon them; but in the field of customary international law, the shared view of the Parties as to the content of what they regard as the rule is not enough. The Court must satisfy itself that the existence of the rule in the *opinio juris* of States is confirmed by practice.

2. THE JURISDICTION OF THE INTERNATIONAL COURT OF JUSTICE

2.1. General Rules

Military and Paramilitary Activities
(Nicaragua/United States of America)
Merits. J. 27.6.1986
I.C.J. Reports 1986, p. 14

[pp. 23-24] The fact that a State purports to "reserve its rights" in respect of a future decision of the Court, after the Court has determined that it has jurisdiction, is clearly of no effect on the validity of that decision. Under Article 36, paragraph 6, of its Statute, the Court has jurisdiction to determine any dispute as to its own jurisdiction, and its judgment on that matter, as on the merits, is final and binding on the parties under Articles 59 and 60 of the Statute (*cf. Corfu Channel, Judgment of 15 December 1949, I.C.J. Reports 1949*, p. 248).

[p. 28] The Court notes that since the institution of the present proceedings, both bases of jurisdiction have been terminated. On 1 May 1985 the United States gave written notice to the Government of Nicaragua to terminate the Treaty, in accordance with Article XXV, paragraph 3, thereof; that notice expired, and thus terminated the treaty relationship, on 1 May 1986. On 7 October 1985 the United States deposited with the Secretary-General of the United Nations a notice terminating the declaration under the optional clause, in accordance with the terms of that declaration, and that notice expired on 7 April 1986. These circumstances do not however affect the jurisdiction of the Court under Article 36, paragraph 2, of the Statute, or its jurisdiction under Article XXIV, paragraph 2, of the Treaty to determine "any dispute between the Parties as to the interpretation or application" of the Treaty.

[pp. 176-177 **S.O. Ruda]** Once the Court has established its competence, a judge is bound to decide on the merits of the case, even if he was in the minority on the question of jurisdiction. Otherwise, in the event that a judge had voted against both sources of jurisdiction, as has happened in this case, that judge would have no standing for participating in the merits stage, which would be an absurd proposition.

Border and Transborder Armed Actions
Nicaragua/Honduras),
Jurisdiction and Admissibility,
Judgment, I.C.J. Reports 1988, p. 69

[pp. 75-76] The Parties have devoted some argument to a question defined by them as that of the burden of proof: whether it is for Nicaragua to show the existence of jurisdiction for the Court to deal with its claims, or for Honduras to establish the absence of such jurisdiction. Each of them has cited, in support of its contention, the Court's dictum that "it is the litigant seeking to establish a fact who bears the burden of proving it" *(Military and Paramilitary Activities in and against Nicaragua* (*Nicaragua v. United States of America), I.C.J. Reports 1984*, p. 437, para. 101).

The existence of jurisdiction of the Court in a given case is however not a question of fact, but a question of law to be resolved in the light of the relevant facts. The determination of the facts may raise questions of proof. However the facts in the present case - the existence of the Parties' declarations under Article 36 of the Statute, the signature and ratification of the Pact of Bogotá, etc. - are not in dispute; the issue is, what are the legal effects to be attached to them? The question is whether in case of doubt the Court is to be deemed to have jurisdiction or not. This question has already been considered by the Permanent Court of International Justice in the case concerning the *Factory at Chorzów, Jurisdiction*, when it observed:
"It has been argued repeatedly in the course of the present proceedings that in case of doubt the Court should decline jurisdiction. It is true that the Court's jurisdiction is always a limited one, existing only in so far as States have accepted it; consequently, the Court will, in the event of an objection - or when it has automatically to consider the question - only affirm its jurisdiction provided that the force of the arguments militating in favour of it is preponderant. The fact that weighty arguments can be advanced to support the contention that it has no jurisdiction cannot of itself create a doubt calculated to upset its jurisdiction. When considering whether it has jurisdiction or not, the Court's aim is always to ascertain whether an intention on the part of the Parties exists to confer jurisdiction upon it." (*P.C.I.J., Series A, No. 9*, p. 32.)

The Court will therefore in this case have to consider whether the force of the arguments militating in favour of jurisdiction is preponderant, and to "ascertain whether an intention on the part of the Parties exists to confer jurisdiction upon it".

[pp. 124-125 **S.O. Oda**] In conclusion, I would like to add the following comments. It is certainly possible for States jointly to assume the obligation to accept the Court's jurisdiction over certain types of disputes under Article 36, paragraph 1, of the Statute, and they can also jointly declare their acceptance of the Court's jurisdiction over legal disputes, as provided for in Article 36, paragraph 2. In cases of general dispute-settlement treaties, the acceptance of jurisdiction over legal disputes in the framework of Article 36, paragraph 1, of the Statute, can be equated, in effect, with the acceptance of jurisdiction under Article 36, paragraph 2. Such an obligation must, however, be assumed in an unequivocal manner. For example, as previously stated, the 1949 Revised General Act for the Pacific Settlement of International Disputes provides that disputes "shall be submitted for decision [to the Court]" and the 1957 European Convention for the Pacific Settlement of Disputes states that the parties "shall submit [disputes] to the judgment of the... Court".

It cannot be denied that the parties to those two treaties accept the Court's jurisdiction within the limits of Article 36, paragraph 2, of the Statute, though it remains to be seen whether the instruments constituting a declaration of acceptance of the Court's jurisdiction should not have been deposited under Article 36, paragraph 4, of the Statute, or whether the simple registration of the treaties in question with the United Nations Secretariat, pursuant to Article 102 of the United Nations Charter, might be looked upon as a substitute for the requirement of that paragraph of the Statute.

I hesitate to assimilate the Pact of Bogotá to those two treaties for the following reasons: firstly, as I explained above, the existence of Article XXXII complicates the Pact's system of peaceful settlement because this particular Article, by its ambiguous content, casts doubt upon the intention of the parties to accept the Court's compulsory jurisdiction. Secondly, unlike the two other treaties of a general dispute-settlement nature, the Pact of Bogotá, although providing for a general obligation to settle international disputes, does not specify the use of any particular procedure, except for resort to the Court in certain cases, and thus the choice of peaceful settlement procedures is to be made jointly by the parties. Thirdly, and more significantly, it will be clearly apparent from what has been stated above that no delegate at the Bogotá Conference ever expressed his country's readiness to confer compulsory jurisdiction on the Court by virtue of the forthcoming Treaty, although some delegates were aware of the possible implication of the text to be adopted. It is accordingly true to say that the present text of the Pact emerged without any clear indication of the parties' real intention.

The Permanent Court of International Justice, as quoted in the Judgment (para. 16), once mentioned

"the fact that [the Court's] jurisdiction is limited, that it is invariably based on the consent of the respondent and only exists in so far as this consent has been given ..." (case concerning *Mavrommatis Palestine Concessions, 1924, P.C.I.J., Series A, No. 2*, p.

16).

It also stated:
"When considering whether it has jurisdiction or not, the Court's aim is always to ascertain whether an intention on the part of the Parties exists to confer jurisdiction upon it." (Case concerning the *Factory at Chorzów, Jurisdiction, Judgment No. 8,1927, P.C.I.J., Series A, No. 9*, p. 32.)

The present Court accepted the validity of this principle in the *Interpretation of Peace Treaties* case, in which it stated that "[t]he consent of States, parties to a dispute, is the basis of the Court's jurisdiction in contentious cases" (*I.C.J. Reports 1950*, p. 71). The Court, in the case of the *Monetary Gold Removed from Rome in 1943 (Preliminary Question, Judgment, I.C.J. Reports 1954*, p. 32), referred to "a well-established principle of international law embodied in the Court's Statute, namely, that the Court can only exercise jurisdiction over a State with its consent". More recently, the fundamental principle mentioned in the 1950 case was reiterated in the *Application for Revision and Interpretation of the Judgment of 24 February 1982 in the Case concerning the Continental Shelf (Tunisia/Libyan Arab Jamahiriya) (Tunisia v. Libyan Arab Jamahiriya) (I.C.J. Reports 1985*, p. 216).

In sum, one cannot lay too much stress upon the paramount importance of the expression of the acceptance of the Court's jurisdiction, which is invariably required for the Court to entertain a case, as the first and critical task of the Court is always to ascertain the intention of the Parties. I doubt whether this particular point has been given all the weight due to it.

2.2. Conditions for a Decision on the Merits

2.2.1. Exhaustion of Local Remedies

Applicability of the Obligation to Arbitrate under Section 21 of the United Nations Headquarters Agreement of 26 June 1947
Advisory Opinion of 26 April 1988
I.C.J. Reports 1988, p. 12

[p. 29] The Court must further point out that the alleged dispute relates solely to what the United Nations considers to be its rights under the Headquarters Agreement. The purpose of the arbitration procedure envisaged by that Agreement is precisely the settlement of such disputes as may arise between the Organization and the host country without any prior recourse to municipal courts, and it would be against both the letter and the spirit of the Agreement for the implementation of that procedure to be subjected to such prior recourse. It is evident that a provision of the nature of section 21 of the Headquarters Agreement cannot require the exhaustion of local remedies as a condition of its implementation.

Elettronica Sicula S.p.A. (ELSI)
Judgment of 20 July 1989
I.C.J. Reports 1989, p. 15

[pp. 42-44] The United States questioned whether the rule of the exhaustion of local remedies could apply at all to a case brought under Article XXVI of the FCN Treaty. That Article, it was pointed out, is categorical in its terms, and unqualified by any reference to the local remedies rule; and it seemed right, therefore, to conclude that the parties to the FCN Treaty, had they intended the jurisdiction conferred upon the Court to be qualified by the local remedies rule in cases of diplomatic protection, would have used express words to that effect; as was done in an Economic Co-operation Agreement between Italy and the United States of America also concluded in 1948. The Chamber has no doubt that the parties to a treaty can therein either agree that the local remedies rule shall not apply to claims based on alleged breaches of that treaty; or confirm that it shall apply. Yet the Chamber finds itself unable to accept that an important principle of customary international law should be held to have been tacitly dispensed with, in the absence of any words making clear an intention to do so. This part of the United States response to the Italian objection must therefore be rejected.

The United States further argued that the local remedies rule would not apply in any event to the part of the United States claim which requested a declaratory judgment finding that the FCN Treaty had been violated. The argument of the United States is that such a judgment would declare that the United States own rights under the FCN Treaty had been infringed; and that to such a direct injury the local remedies rule, which is a rule of customary international law developed in the context of the espousal by a State of the claim of one of its nationals, would not apply. The Chamber, however, has not found it possible in the present case to find a dispute over alleged violation of the FCN Treaty resulting in direct injury to the United States, that is both distinct from, and independent of, the dispute over the alleged violation in respect of Raytheon and Machlett. The case arises from a dispute which the Parties did not "satisfactorily adjust by diplomacy"; and that dispute was described in the 1974 United States claim made at the diplomatic level as a "claim of the Government of the United States of America on behalf of Raytheon Company and Machlett Laboratories, Incorporated". The Agent of the United States told the Chamber in the oral proceedings that "the United States seeks reparation for injuries suffered by Raytheon and Machlett". And indeed, as will appear later, the question whether there has been a breach of the FCN Treaty is itself much involved with the financial position of the Italian company, ELSI, which was controlled by Raytheon and Machlett.

Moreover, when the Court was, in the *Interhandel* case, faced with a not dissimilar argument by Switzerland that in that case its "principal submission" was in respect of a "direct breach of international law" and therefore not subject to the local remedies rule, the Court, having analysed that "principal submission", found that it was bound up with the diplomatic protection claim, and that the Applicant's arguments "do not deprive the dispute ... of the character of a dispute in which the Swiss Government appears as having adopted the cause of its national ... (*Interhandel, Judgment, I.C.J. Reports 1959*, p. 28). In the present case, likewise, the Chamber has no doubt that the matter which colours and pervades the United States claim as a whole, is the alleged damage to Raytheon and Machlett, said to have resulted from the actions of the Respondent. Accordingly, the Chamber rejects the argument that in the present case there is a part of the Applicant's claim which can be severed so as to render the local remedies rule inapplicable to that part.

There was a further argument of the Applicant, based on estoppel in relation to the application of the local remedies rule, which should be examined. In the "Memorandum of Law" elaborating the United States claim on the diplomatic plane, transmitted to the Italian Government by Note Verbale of 7 February 1974, one finds that the whole of Part VI (pp. 53 *et seq.*) deals generally and at some length with the "Exhaustion of Local Remedies". There were also annexed the opinions of the lawyers advising the Applicant, which dealt directly with the position of Raytheon and Machlett in relation to the local remedies rule. The Memorandum concluded that Raytheon and Machlett had indeed exhausted "every meaningful legal remedy available to them in Italy" (paragraph 46 above). In view of this evidence that the United States was very much aware that it must satisfy the local remedies rule, that it evidently believed that the rule had been satisfied, and that it had been advised that the shareholders of ELSI had no direct action against the Italian Government under Italian law, it was argued by the Applicant that Italy, if it was indeed at that time of the opinion that the local remedies had not been exhausted, should have apprised the United States of its opinion. According to the United States, however, at no time until the filing of the Respondent's Counter-Memorial in the present proceedings did Italy suggest that Raytheon and Machlett should sue in the Italian courts on the basis of the Treaty. The written aide-mémoire of 13 June 1978, by which Italy rejected the 1974 claim, had contained no suggestion that the local remedies had not been exhausted, nor indeed any mention of the matter.

It was argued by the Applicant that this absence of riposte from Italy amounts to an estoppel. There are however difficulties about drawing any such conclusion from the exchanges of correspondence when the matter was still being pursued on the diplomatic level. In the *Interhandel* case, when Switzerland argued that the United States had at one time actually "admitted that *Interhandel* had exhausted the remedies available in the

United States courts", the Court, far from seeing in this admission an estoppel, dismissed the argument by merely observing that "This opinion was based upon a view which has proved unfounded" (*Interhandel, Judgment, I.C.J. Reports 1959*, p. 27). Furthermore, although it cannot be excluded that an estoppel could in certain circumstances arise from a silence when something ought to have been said, there are obvious difficulties in constructing an estoppel from a mere failure to mention a matter at a particular point in somewhat desultory diplomatic exchanges.

[pp. 46-47] With such a deal of litigation in the municipal courts about what is in substance the claim now before the Chamber, it was for Italy to demonstrate that there was nevertheless some local remedy that had not been tried; or at least, not exhausted. This burden Italy never sought to deny. It contended that it was possible for the matter to have been brought before the municipal courts, citing the provisions of the treaties themselves, and alleging their violation. This was never done. In the actions brought before the Court of Palermo, and subsequently the Court of Appeal of Palermo, and the Court of Cassation, the FCN Treaty and its Supplementary Agreement were never mentioned. This is not surprising, for, as Italy recognizes, the way in which the matter was pleaded before the courts of Palermo was not for Raytheon and Machlett to decide but for the trustee. Furthermore, the local remedies rule does not, indeed cannot, require that a claim be presented to the municipal courts in a form, and with arguments, suited to an international tribunal, applying different law to different parties: for an international claim to be admissible, it is sufficient if the essence of the claim has been brought before the competent tribunals and pursued as far as permitted by local law and procedures, and without success.

The question, therefore, reduces itself to this: ought Raytheon and Machlett, suing in their own right, as United States corporations allegedly injured by the requisition of property of an Italian company whose shares they held, have brought an action in the Italian courts, within the general limitation-period (five years), alleging violation of certain provisions of the FCN Treaty between Italy and the United States; this mindful of the fact that the very question of the consequences of the requisition was already in issue in the action brought by its trustee in bankruptcy, and that any damages that might there be awarded would pass into the pool of realized assets, for an appropriate part of which Raytheon and Machlett had the right to claim as creditors?

Italy contends that Raytheon and Machlett could have based such an action before the Italian courts on Article 2043 of the Italian Civil Code, which provides that "Any act committed either wilfully or through fault which causes wrongful damages to another person implies that the wrongdoer is under an obligation to pay compensation for those damages." According to Italy, this provision is frequently invoked by individuals against the Italian State, and substantial sums have been awarded to claimants where appropriate. If Raytheon and Machlett suffered damage caused by violations by Italian public authorities of the FCN Treaty and the Supplementary Agreement, an Italian court would, it was contended, have been bound to conclude that the relevant acts of the public authorities were wrongful acts for the purposes of Article 2043. It is common ground between the Parties that implementing legislation ("*ordini di esecuzione*") was enacted (Law No. 385 of 15 June 1949 and Law No. 910 of 1 August 1960), to give effect in Italy to the FCN Treaty and Supplementary Agreement, but that their provisions cannot be invoked in protection of individual rights before the Italian courts unless those provisions are regarded by the courts as self-executing. In order to show that the relevant provisions would be so regarded, decisions of the Court of Cassation have been cited by Italy in which provisions of the FCN Treaty (not the provisions relied on in the present case) have been applied for the benefit of United States nationals who have invoked them before Italian courts, and a provision of a treaty between Italy and the Federal Republic of Germany, said to be comparable with Article V of the FCN Treaty, was given effect.

However, those decisions were not based on Article 2043 of the Italian Civil Code; and the treaty provisions applied were given effect in conjunction with municipal legislation or the provisions of other treaties through the mechanism of a most-favoured-nation provision. In none of the cases cited was the FCN Treaty provision relied on to establish the wrongfulness of conduct of Italian public officials. When in 1971 Raytheon consulted two Italian jurists on the question of local remedies for the purposes of a diplomatic claim, it apparently did not occur to either of them to refer even as a possibility to action under Article 2043 in conjunction with the FCN Treaty. It thus appears to the Chamber to be impossible to deduce, from the recent jurisprudence cited, what the attitude of the Italian courts would have been had Raytheon and Machlett brought an action, some 20 years ago, in reliance on Article 2043 of the Civil Code in conjunction with provisions of the FCN Treaty and Supplementary Agreement. Where the determination of a question of municipal law is essential to the Court's decision in a case, the Court will have to weigh the jurisprudence of the municipal courts, and "If this is uncertain or divided, it will rest with the Court to select the interpretation which it considers most in conformity with the law" (*Brazilian Loans, P.C.I.J., Series A, Nos. 20/21*, p. 124). In the present case, however, it was for Italy to show, as a matter of fact, the existence of a remedy which was open to the United States stockholders and which they failed to employ. The Chamber does not consider that Italy has discharged that burden.

[p. 94 **D.O. Schwebel**] First, the Judgment applies a rule of reason in its interpretation of the reach of the requirement of the exhaustion of local remedies. It holds not that every possible local remedy must have been exhausted to satisfy the local remedies rule but that, where in substance local remedies have been exhausted, that suffices to meet the requirements of the rule even if it may be that a variation on the pursuit of local remedies in the particular case was not in fact played out. It has of course long been of the essence of the rule of exhaustion of local remedies that local remedies need not be exhausted where there are no effective remedies to exhaust. It may be said that the Chamber has done no more than to reaffirm this established element of the rule. In fact it has reaffirmed it, but in doing so the Judgment makes a contribution to the elucidation of the local remedies rule by indicating that, where the substance of the issues of a case has been definitively litigated in the courts of a State, the rule does not require that those issues also have been litigated by the presentation of every relevant legal argument which any municipal forum might have been able to pass upon, however unlikely in practice the possibilities of reaching another result were. The United States of America submitted that the claims brought by it were admissible since "all reasonable" local remedies had been exhausted; in substance, the Chamber agreed, and rightly so. Its holding thus confines certain prior constructions of the reach of the rule of exhaustion of local remedies to a sensible limit.

2.2.2. Necessity of Diplomatic Negotiations

Applicability of the Obligation to Arbitrate under Section 21 of the United Nations Headquarters Agreement of 26 June 1947 Advisory Opinion of 26 April 1988 I.C.J. Reports 1988, p. 12

[pp. 33-34] In his letter to the United States Permanent Representative dated 14 January 1988, the Secretary-General not only formally invoked the dispute settlement procedure set out in section 21 ofthe Headquarters Agreement, but also noted that "According to section 21 (*a*), an attempt has to be made at first to solve the dispute through negotiations" and proposed that the negotiations phase of the procedure commence on 20 January 1988. According to the Secretary-General's report to the General Assembly, a series of consultations had already begun on 7 January 1988 (A/42/915, para. 6) and continued until 10 February 1988 (*ibid*., para. 10). Technical discussions, on an informal basis, on procedural matters relating to the arbitration contemplated by the Secretary-General, were held between 28 January 1988 and 2 February 1988 (*ibid*., paras. 8-9). On 2 March 1988, the Acting Permanent Representative of the United States stated in the General Assembly that

"we have been in regular and frequent contact with the United Nations Secretariat over the past several months concerning an appropriate resolution of this matter" (A/42/PV.104, p. 59).

The Secretary-General recognizes that "The United States did not consider these contacts and consultations to be formally within the framework of section 21 (*a*) of the Headquarters Agreement" (written statement, para. 44), and in a letter to the United States Permanent Representative dated 2 February 1988, the Secretary-General noted that the United States was taking the position that, pending its evaluation of the situation which would arise from application of the Anti-Terrorism Act, "it cannot enter into the dispute settlement procedure outlined in section 21 of the Headquarters Agreement".

The Court considers that, taking into account the United States attitude, the Secretary-General has in the circumstances exhausted such possibilities of negotiation as were open to him. The Court would recall in this connection the dictum of the Permanent Court of International Justice in the *Mavrommatis Palestine Concessions* case that

"the question of the importance and chances of success of diplomatic negotiations is essentially a relative one. Negotiations do not of necessity always presuppose a more or less lengthy series of notes and despatches; it may suffice that a discussion should have been commenced, and this discussion may have been very short; this will be the case if a deadlock is reached, or if finally a point is reached at which one of the Parties definitely declares himself unable, or refuses, to give way, and there can therefore be no doubt that *the dispute cannot be settled by diplomatic negotiation" (P.C.I.J., Series A, No. 2,* p. 13).

When in the case concerning *United States Diplomatic and Consular Staff in Tehran* the attempts of the United States to negotiate with Iran "had reached a deadlock, owing to the refusal of the Iranian Government to enter into any discussion ofthe matter", the Court concluded that "In consequence, there existed at that date not only a dispute but, beyond any doubt, a 'dispute... not satisfactorily adjusted by diplomacy' within the meaning of" the relevant jurisdictional text (*I.C.J. Reports 1980*, p. 27, para. 51). In the present case, the Court regards it as similarly beyond any doubt that the dispute between the United Nations and the United States is one "not settled by negotiation" within the meaning of section 21, paragraph (*a*), of the Headquarters Agreement.

Nor was any "other agreed mode of settlement" of their dispute contemplated by the United Nations and the United States. In this connection the Court should observe that current proceedings brought by the United States Attorney General before the United States courts cannot be an "agreed mode of settlement" within the meaning of section 21 of the Headquarters Agreement. The purpose of these proceedings is to enforce the Anti-Terrorism Act of 1987; it is not directed to settling the dispute, concerning the application of the Headquarters Agreement, which has come into existence between the United Nations and the United States. Furthermore, the United Nations has never agreed to settlement of the dispute in the American courts; it has taken care to make it clear that it wishes to be admitted only as amicus curiae before the District Court for the Southern District of New York.

Land, Island and
Maritime Frontier Dispute
(El Salvador/Honduras)
Application to Intervene,
Judgment of 13 September 1990,
I.C.J. Reports 1990, p. 92

[pp. 113-114] Finally, El Salvador relies on the fact that there has been "no discussion whatsoever between Nicaragua and either of the original Parties regarding the position of the Gulf of Fonseca". Therefore, it is argued, it is premature to bring such issues before the Chamber, and counter to the established rule "that before proceedings are brought in the Court, there must be a defined dispute which... has matured through the process of negotiation between the parties".

The Chamber does not consider that there is any requirement for the definition of a dispute in prior negotiations before an application can be made for permission to intervene. The function of intervention is, as indicated in the 1984 Judgment on the Application of Italy for permission to intervene in the case concerning the *Continental Shelf (Libyan Arab Jamahiriya/Malta)*, and as explained below, something wholly different from the determination of a further dispute between the State seeking to intervene and one or both of the parties. In that Judgment the Court found that that Application could not be granted because, *inter alia*, to give effect to it "the Court would be called upon... to determine a dispute, or some part of a dispute, between Italy and one or both of the principal Parties" (*I.C.J. Reports 1984*, p. 20, para. 31), without the consent of those parties. It would therefore be inappropriate to require, as a condition of intervention, the existence of such a dispute, defined by prior negotiations.

2.2.3. Jurisdiction in Case of Continuing Negotiations between the Parties

Border and Transborder Armed Actions
Nicaragua/Honduras),
Jurisdiction and Admissibility,
Judgment, I.C.J. Reports 1988, p. 69

[pp. 94-95] Nicaragua has argued, first, that it does not necessarily follow from the text of Article II [15] that recourse to pacific procedures is available only when it is the

15 Article II of the Pact of Bogotá reads as follows:

"The High Contracting Parties recognize the obligation to settle international controversies by regional pacific procedures before referring them to the Security Council of the United Nations.

Consequently, in the event that a controversy arises between two or more signatory States which, in the opinion of the parties [in the French text "de l'avis de l'une des opinion of the parties that the dispute cannot be settled by direct negotiations; that it is perfectly logical to read Article II as setting forth one circumstance - but not the exclusive one - in which the parties bind themselves to use the procedures set forth in the Pact.

The Court does not consider that Article II, in the context of the Pact as a whole, can be read in this sense; that provision constitutes, as was argued by Honduras, a condition precedent to recourse to the pacific procedures of the Pact in all cases. The Court has therefore to consider how that condition applies in the present case.

Nicaragua then rejects the interpretation of Article II advanced by Honduras, that both parties to a dispute should have manifested the opinion that it cannot be settled by negotiations, contending that it would give a recalcitrant party to a dispute a right of veto of judicial or other settlement which would shatter the whole carefully constructed scheme of compulsory jurisdiction established by the Pact. It further contends that the question is not whether one of the parties or both of them must think that the dispute cannot be settled by diplomatic means, but whether the dispute can in fact be settled by such means; in its view the jurisprudence of the Court supports the principle that when there is disagreement between the parties on the point, the issue is to be resolved not so much on the basis of the particular form of words used in the compromissory instrument, but by an objective evaluation by the Court of the possibilities for settlement of the dispute by direct negotiations.

The Court observes however that that jurisprudence concerns cases in which the applicable text referred to the possibility of such settlement; Article II however refers to the opinion of the parties as to such possibility. The Court therefore does not have to make an objective assessment of such possibility, but to consider what is the opinion of the Parties thereon.

Before proceeding further, the Court notes that the Parties have drawn attention to a discrepancy between the four texts of Article II of the Pact (English, French, Portuguese and Spanish). In the French text, what is required is that, "de l'avis de l'une des parties", i.e., "in the opinion of one of the parties", the dispute should not be susceptible of settlement by negotiation. In the English, Portuguese and Spanish texts, the corresponding phrase is "in the opinion of the parties", or the equivalent in the other two languages. For reasons which will appear, the Court's reasoning does not require the resolution of the problem posed by this textual discrepancy, and it will therefore not rehearse all the arguments that have been put forward by the Parties to explain it or to justify the preferring of one version to another.

---

parties"], cannot be settled by direct negotiations through the usual diplomatic channels, the parties bind themselves to use the procedures established in the present Treaty, in the manner and under the conditions provided for in the following articles, or, alternatively, such special procedures as, in their opinion, will permit them to arrive at a solution."

For the purpose of determining the application in this case of Article II of the Pact, the Court will proceed on the hypothesis that the stricter interpretation should be used, i.e., that it would be necessary to consider whether the "opinion" of both Parties was that it was not possible to settle the dispute by negotiation. For this purpose the Court does not consider that it is bound by the mere assertion of the one Party or the other that its opinion is to a particular effect: it must, in the exercise of its judicial function, be free to make its own determination of that question on the basis of such evidence as is available to it.

[p. 99] While there were extensive consultations and negotiations between 1983 and 1986, in different forms, both among the Central American States themselves, and between those States and those belonging to the Contadora Group and the Support Group, these were organized and carried on within the context of the mediation to which they were subordinate. At this time the Contadora process was primarily a mediation, in which third States, on their own initiative, endeavoured to bring together the viewpoints of the States concerned by making specific proposals to them.

That process therefore, which Honduras had accepted, was, as a result of the presence and action of third States, markedly different from a "direct negotiation through the usual diplomatic channels". It thus did not fall within the relevant provisions of Article II of the Pact of Bogotá. Furthermore, no other negotiation which would meet the conditions laid down in that text was contemplated on 28 July 1986, the date of filing of the Nicaraguan Application. Consequently Honduras could not plausibly maintain at that date that the dispute between itself and Nicaragua, as defined in the Nicaraguan Application, was at that time capable of being settled by direct negotiation through the usual diplomatic channels.

The Court therefore considers that the provisions of Article II of the Pact of Bogotá relied on by Honduras do not constitute a bar to the admissibility of Nicaragua's Application.

[pp. 99-100] The fourth and last objection of Honduras to the admissibility of the Nicaraguan Application is that:

"Having accepted the Contadora process as a 'special procedure' within the meaning of Article II of the Pact of Bogotá, Nicaragua is precluded both by Article IV of the Pact and by elementary considerations of good faith from commencing any other procedure for pacific settlement until such time as the Contadora process has been concluded; and that time has not arrived."

Article IV of the Pact of Bogotá, upon which Honduras relies, reads as follows:

"Once any pacific procedure has been initiated, whether by agreement between the parties or in fulfillment of the present Treaty or a previous pact, no other procedure may be commenced until that procedure is concluded."

It is common ground between the Parties that the present proceedings before the Court are a "pacific procedure" as contemplated by the Pact of Bogotá, and that therefore if any other "pacific procedure" under the Pact has been initiated and not concluded, the proceedings were instituted contrary to Article IV and must therefore be found inadmissible. The disagreement between the Parties is whether the Contadora process is or is not a procedure contemplated by Article IV. Honduras contends that the Contadora process is a "special procedure" for the purposes of Article II of the Pact, which refers to "such special procedures as, in their [the parties'] opinion, will permit them to arrive at a solution" of the dispute, as an alternative to "the procedures established in the present Treaty". This special procedure has, in the contention of Honduras, been entered into by agreement between the Parties, and thus must be regarded as a "pacific procedure" for the purposes of Article IV. Nicaragua on the other hand denies that the Contadora process can be treated as a "special procedure" for purposes of Articles II and IV of the Pact, because, *inter alia*, its subject-matter is distinct from the dispute before the Court.

It is clear that the question whether or not the Contadora process can be regarded as a "special procedure" or a "pacific procedure" within the meaning of Articles II and IV of the Pact would not have to be determined if such a procedure had to be regarded as "concluded" by 28 July 1986, the date of filing of the Nicaraguan Application. The date of the institution of proceedings is the date at which the admissibility of a claim has to be assessed (paragraph 66 above); for the application of Article IV, the question is specifically whether any initial pacific procedure which may have been instituted has been "concluded" before any other procedure, including judicial procedure, is "commenced".

For the purposes of Article IV of the Pact, no formal act is necessary before a pacific procedure can be said to be "concluded". The procedure in question does not have to have failed definitively before a new procedure can be commenced. It is sufficient if, at the date on which a new procedure is commenced, the initial procedure has come to a standstill in such circumstances that there appears to be no prospect of its being continued or resumed.

[pp. 104-105] From this account it is clear that the Contadora process was at a standstill at the date on which Nicaragua filed its Application. This situation continued until the presentation of the Arias Plan and the adoption by the five Central American

States of the Esquipulas II Accord, which in August 1987 set in train the procedure frequently referred to as the Contadora-Esquipulas II process. The question therefore arises, for the purposes of Article IV of the Pact, whether this latter procedure should be regarded as having ensured the continuation of the initial procedure without interruption, or whether on 28 July 1986 that initial procedure should be regarded as having "concluded", and a procedure of a different nature as having got under way thereafter. This question is of crucial importance, since on the latter hypothesis, whatever may have been the nature of the initial Contadora process with regard to Article IV, that Article would not have constituted a bar to the commencement of a procedure before the Court on that date.

The views of the Parties in this respect were given in particular in their replies to a question put by a Member of the Court. Nicaragua indicated that "the Contadora process has not been abandoned or suspended at any moment". As for Honduras, it declared that "the Contadora process has not been abandoned" and that, after the non-signature of the Act of Contadora, the Contadora Group and the Support Group continued their efforts up to the time of the approval of the Esquipulas II Accord. Since that time the process, according to Honduras, continued without interruption.

The Court fully appreciates the importance of this concordance of views between the Parties on the subject of regional initiatives which are highly regarded by them. But it cannot see in this a concordance of views as to the interpretation of the term "concluded" in Article IV of the Pact of Bogotá, in relation to the position of the Contadora process at the moment of the filing of the Nicaraguan Application. In the Court's view, on the basis of the facts described above the action of the Contadora Group before June 1986 cannot be regarded, for the purposes of the application of the Pact, as on the same footing as its subsequent action.

While the peacemaking process has continued to bear the name "Contadora", the fact is that that title has become practically a symbol of all the stages traversed and all the multilateral initiatives taken in the last few years to restore peace to Central America. In fact however the Contadora process, as it operated in the first phase, is different from the Contadora-Esquipulas II process initiated in the second phase. The two differ with regard both to their object and to their nature. The Contadora process, as has been explained above, initially constituted a mediation in which the Contadora Group and Support Group played a decisive part. In the Contadora-Esquipulas II process, on the other hand, the Contadora Group of States played a fundamentally different role. The five countries of Central America set up an independent mechanism of multilateral negotiation, in which the role of the Contadora Group was confined to the tasks laid down in Sections 7 and 10 (*a*) of the Esquipulas II Declaration, and has effectively shrunk still further subsequently.

The facts show that the Contadora Group regarded its mission as completed, at least so far as the negotiation of any substantive accord is concerned, with the presentation to the Central American States on 6-7 June 1986 of the final and definitive Act of Contadora. The signature of that Act would have crowned the mediation with a success; its non-signature had the opposite effect. Moreover, it should not be overlooked that there was a gap of several months between the end of the initial Contadora process and the beginning of the Contadora Esquipulas II process; and it was during this gap that Nicaragua filed its Application to the Court.

The Court concludes that the procedures employed in the Contadora process up to 28 July 1986, the date of filing of the Nicaraguan Application, had been "concluded", within the meaning of Article IV of the Pact of Bogotá, at that date. That being so, the submissions of Honduras based on Article IV of the Pact must be rejected, and it is unnecessary for the Court to determine whether the Contadora process was a "special procedure" or a "pacific procedure" for the purpose of Articles II and IV of the Pact, and whether that procedure had the same object as that now in progress before the Court.

[pp. 105-106] The Court has also to deal with the contention of Honduras that Nicaragua is precluded not only by Article IV of the Pact of Bogotá but also "by elementary considerations of good faith" from commencing any other procedure for pacific settlement until such time as the Contadora process has been concluded. The principle of good faith is, as the Court has observed, "one of the basic principles governing the creation and performance of legal obligations" (*Nuclear Tests, I.C.J. Reports 1974*, p. 268, para. 46; p. 473, para. 49); it is not in itself a source of obligation where none would otherwise exist. In this case however the contention of Honduras is that, on the basis of successive acts by Nicaragua culminating in the Esquipulas Declaration of 25 May 1986 (paragraph 81 above), Nicaragua has entered into a "commitment to the Contadora process"; it argues that by virtue of that Declaration, "Nicaragua entered into a commitment with which its present unilateral Application to the Court is plainly incompatible". The Court considers that whether or not the conduct of Nicaragua or the Esquipulas Declaration created any such commitment, the events of June/July 1986 constituted a "conclusion" of the initial procedure both for purposes of Article IV of the Pact and in relation to any other obligation to exhaust that procedure which might have existed independently of the Pact.

[pp. 154-155 **S.O. Shahabuddeen**] It is, in my opinion, equally clear that the Contadora process, though generically a pacific procedure, is not a "pacific procedure" within the meaning of Article IV. The process appears to comprehend a protean amalgam of elements of negotiation, good offices, mediation and possibly conciliation, the proportionate weight of each element varying from phase to phase. Though referred to in the Pact, negotiation is not a procedure established by it. The others are so established, but the prescribed steps relating to mediation and conciliation - no particular ones were prescribed in relation to good offices - were not observed and were not intended to be observed, with the suggested inference that the procedures followed were not those established by the Pact.

2.2.4. Admissibility

Border and Transborder Armed Actions Nicaragua/Honduras), Jurisdiction and Admissibility, Judgment, I.C.J. Reports 1988, p. 69

[pp. 91-92] Honduras's first objection to the admissibility of the Application is that "It is a politically-inspired, artificial request which the Court should not entertain consistently with its judicial character"; it claims that Nicaragua is attempting to use the Court, or the threat of litigation before the Court, as a means of exerting political pressure on the other Central American States.

As regards the first aspect of this objection, the Court is aware that political aspects may be present in any legal dispute brought before it. The Court, as a judicial organ, is however only concerned to establish, first, that the dispute before it is a legal dispute, in the sense of a dispute capable of being settled by the application of principles and rules of international law, and secondly, that the Court has jurisdiction to deal with it, and that that jurisdiction is not fettered by any circumstance rendering the application inadmissible. The purpose of recourse to the Court is the peaceful settlement of such disputes; the Court's judgment is a legal pronouncement, and it cannot concern itself with the political motivation which may lead a State at a particular time, or in particular circumstances, to choose judicial settlement. So far as the objection of Honduras is based on an alleged political inspiration of the proceedings, it therefore cannot be upheld.

The second aspect of the first objection of Honduras is its claim that the request is artificial. In its Memorial Honduras explains that in its view the overall result of Nicaragua's action is "an artificial and arbitrary dividing up of the general conflict existing in Central America", which "may have negative consequences for Honduras as a defendant State before the Court", because, it is said, certain facts appertaining to the general conflict "are inevitably absent from the proceedings before the Court", and other facts have already been in issue before the Court in the case concerning *Military and Paramilitary Activities in and against Nicaragua (Nicaragua v. United States of America).* Honduras contends that no real distinction can be made between the general situation of tension in the region and the various bilateral disputes which Nicaragua claims to exist there, and that the "procedural situation" created by Nicaragua's splitting-up of the overall conflict into separate disputes is contrary to the requirements of good faith and the proper functioning of international justice.

The Court cannot uphold this contention. It is not clear why any facts should be "inevitably absent" from the proceedings, since it is open to Honduras to bring to the Court's attention any facts which in its view are relevant to the issues in this case. Nor can it be accepted that once the Court has given judgment in a case involving certain allegations of fact, and made findings in that respect, no new procedure can be commenced in which those, as well as other, facts might have to be considered. In any event, it is for the Parties to establish the facts in the present case taking account of the usual rules of evidence, without it being possible to rely on considerations of *res judicata* in another case not involving the same parties (see Article 59 of the Statute).

There is no doubt that the issues of which the Court has been seised may be regarded as part of a wider regional problem. The Court is not unaware of the difficulties that may arise where particular aspects of a complex general situation are brought before a Court for separate decision. Nevertheless, as the Court observed in the case concerning *United States Diplomatic and Consular Staff in Tehran*, "no provision of the Statute or Rules contemplates that the Court should decline to take cognizance of one aspect of a dispute merely because that dispute has other aspects, however important" (*I.C.J. Reports 1980*, p. 19, para. 36).

[p. 92] The second Honduran objection to admissibility is that "the Application is vague and the allegations contained in it are not properly particularized, so that the Court cannot entertain the Application without substantial prejudice to Honduras". In support of this Honduras asserts that "a large number of the matters put forward by Nicaragua do not constitute concrete acts or omissions, identifiable by reference to place and to time", but concern "indeterminate situations" or "opinions about intentions", that another large group of these matters are referred to only by the year in which they took place without geographical location; and that the Application confuses facts of a different nature and attributable to different causes.

Article 40, paragraph 1, of the Statute requires that an Application indicate "the subject of the dispute". Under the Rules of Court, an Application is required to specify "the precise nature of the claim", and in support thereof to give no more than "a succinct statement of the facts and grounds on which the claim is based" (Art. 38, para. 2). The Court considers that the Nicaraguan Application in the present case, summarized in paragraph 50 above, meets these requirements.

[p. 95] The critical date for determining the admissibility of an application is the date on which it is filed (cf. *South West Africa, Preliminary Objections, I.C.J. Reports 1962*, p. 344). It may however be necessary, in order to determine with certainty what the situation was at the date of filing of the Application, to examine the events, and in particular the relations between the Parties, over a period prior to that date, and indeed during the subsequent period. Furthermore, subsequent events may render an application without object, or even take such a course as to preclude the filing of a later application in similar terms. In this case, the date at which "the opinion of the parties" has to be ascertained for the application of Article II of the Pact is 28 July 1986, the date of filing of the Nicaraguan Application.

[p. 99] While there were extensive consultations and negotiations between 1983 and 1986, in different forms, both among the Central American States themselves, and between those States and those belonging to the Contadora Group and the Support Group, these were organized and carried on within the context of the mediation to which they were subordinate. At this time the Contadora process was primarily a mediation, in which third States, on their own initiative, endeavoured to bring together the viewpoints of the States concerned by making specific proposals to them.

That process therefore, which Honduras had accepted, was, as a result of the presence and action of third States, markedly different from a "direct negotiation through the usual diplomatic channels". It thus did not fall within the relevant provisions of Article II of the Pact of Bogotá. Furthermore, no other negotiation which would meet the conditions laid down in that text was contemplated on 28 July 1986, the date of filing of the Nicaraguan Application. Consequently Honduras could not plausibly maintain at that date that the dispute between itself and Nicaragua, as defined in the Nicaraguan Application, was at that time capable of being settled by direct negotiation through the usual diplomatic channels.

The Court therefore considers that the provisions of Article II of the Pact of Bogotá relied on by Honduras do not constitute a bar to the admissibility of Nicaragua's Application.

[pp. 99-100] The fourth and last objection of Honduras to the admissibility of the Nicaraguan Application is that:

"Having accepted the Contadora process as a 'special procedure' within the meaning of Article II of the Pact of Bogotá, Nicaragua is precluded both by Article IV of the Pact and by elementary considerations of good faith from commencing any other procedure for pacific settlement until such time as the Contadora process has been concluded; and that time has not arrived."

Article IV of the Pact of Bogotá, upon which Honduras relies, reads as follows:

"Once any pacific procedure has been initiated, whether by agreement between the parties or in fulfillment of the present Treaty or a previous pact, no other procedure may be commenced until that procedure is concluded."

It is common ground between the Parties that the present proceedings before the Court are a "pacific procedure" as contemplated by the Pact of Bogotá, and that therefore if any other "pacific procedure" under the Pact has been initiated and not concluded, the proceedings were instituted contrary to Article IV and must therefore be found inadmissible. The disagreement between the Parties is whether the Contadora process is or is not a procedure contemplated by Article IV. Honduras contends that the Contadora process is a "special procedure" for the purposes of Article II of the Pact, which refers to "such special procedures as, in their [the parties'] opinion, will permit them to arrive at a solution" of the dispute, as an alternative to "the procedures established in the present Treaty". This special procedure has, in the contention of Honduras, been entered into by agreement between the Parties, and thus must be regarded as a "pacific procedure" for the purposes of Article IV. Nicaragua on the other hand denies that the Contadora process can be treated as a "special procedure" for purposes of Articles II and IV of the Pact, because, *inter alia*, its subject-matter is distinct from the dispute before the Court.

It is clear that the question whether or not the Contadora process can be regarded as a "special procedure" or a "pacific procedure" within the meaning of Articles II and IV of the Pact would not have to be determined if such a procedure had to be regarded as "concluded" by 28 July 1986, the date of filing of the Nicaraguan Application. The date of the institution of proceedings is the date at which the admissibility of a claim has to be assessed (paragraph 66 above); for the application of Article IV, the question is specifically whether any initial pacific procedure which may have been instituted has been "concluded" before any other procedure, including judicial procedure, is "commenced".

For the purposes of Article IV of the Pact, no formal act is necessary before a pacific procedure can be said to be "concluded". The procedure in question does not have to have failed definitively before a new procedure can be commenced. It is sufficient if, at the date on which a new procedure is commenced, the initial procedure has come to a standstill in such circumstances that there appears to be no prospect of its being continued or resumed.

[pp. 104-105] From this account it is clear that the Contadora process was at a standstill at the date on which Nicaragua filed its Application. This situation continued until the presentation of the Arias Plan and the adoption by the five Central American States of the Esquipulas II Accord, which in August 1987 set in train the procedure frequently referred to as the Contadora-Esquipulas II process. The question therefore arises, for the purposes of Article IV of the Pact, whether this latter procedure should be regarded as having ensured the continuation of the initial procedure without interruption, or whether on 28 July 1986 that initial procedure should be regarded as having "concluded", and a procedure of a different nature as having got under way thereafter. This question is of crucial importance, since on the latter hypothesis, whatever may have been the nature of the initial Contadora process with regard to Article IV, that Article would not have constituted a bar to the commencement of a procedure before the Court on that date.

The views of the Parties in this respect were given in particular in their replies to a question put by a Member of the Court. Nicaragua indicated that "the Contadora process has not been abandoned or suspended at any moment". As for Honduras, it declared that "the Contadora process has not been abandoned" and that, after the non-signature of the Act of Contadora, the Contadora Group and the Support Group continued their efforts up to the time of the approval of the Esquipulas II Accord. Since that time the process, according to Honduras, continued without interruption.

The Court fully appreciates the importance of this concordance of views between the Parties on the subject of regional initiatives which are highly regarded by them. But it cannot see in this a concordance of views as to the interpretation of the term "concluded" in Article IV of the Pact of Bogotá, in relation to the position of the Contadora process at the moment of the filing of the Nicaraguan Application. In the Court's view, on the basis of the facts described above the action of the Contadora Group before June 1986 cannot be regarded, for the purposes of the application of the Pact, as on the same footing as its subsequent action.

While the peacemaking process has continued to bear the name "Contadora", the fact is that that title has become practically a symbol of all the stages traversed and all the multilateral initiatives taken in the last few years to restore peace to Central America. In fact however the Contadora process, as it operated in the first phase, is different from the Contadora-Esquipulas II process initiated in the second phase. The two differ with regard both to their object and to their nature. The Contadora process, as has been explained above, initially constituted a mediation in which the Contadora Group and Support Group played a decisive part. In the Contadora-Esquipulas II process, on the other hand, the Contadora Group of States played a fundamentally different role. The five countries of Central America set up an independent mechanism of multilateral negotiation, in which the role of the Contadora Group was confined to the tasks laid down in Sections 7 and 10 (*a*) of the Esquipulas II Declaration, and has effectively shrunk still further subsequently.

The facts show that the Contadora Group regarded its mission as completed, at least so far as the negotiation of any substantive accord is concerned, with the presentation to the Central American States on 6-7 June 1986 of the final and definitive Act of Contadora. The signature of that Act would have crowned the mediation with a success; its non-signature had the opposite effect. Moreover, it should not be overlooked that there was a gap of several months between the end of the initial Contadora process and the beginning of the Contadora Esquipulas II process; and it was during this gap that Nicaragua filed its Application to the Court.

The Court concludes that the procedures employed in the Contadora process up to 28 July 1986, the date of filing of the Nicaraguan Application, had been "concluded", within the meaning of Article IV of the Pact of Bogotá, at that date. That being so, the submissions of Honduras based on Article IV of the Pact must be rejected, and it is unnecessary for the Court to determine whether the Contadora process was a "special procedure" or a "pacific procedure" for the purpose of Articles II and IV of the Pact, and whether that procedure had the same object as that now in progress before the Court.

[pp. 126-127 **S.O. Schwebel**] The admissibility of Nicaragua's Application raises more substantial doubts, by reason of the operation of Articles II and IV of the Pact of Bogotá. Believing as I do that jurisdiction in this case can only be founded on the Pact of Bogotá, and that accordingly Nicaragua's Application must be considered subject to the provisions of that Pact, those Articles initially appear to render Nicaragua's Application inadmissible because the substance of that Application is clearly comprehended by the Contadora process. That process, not being a pacific procedure established by the Pact, surely is a "special procedure", agreed upon by Nicaragua and Honduras as well as other States, which, if successfully concluded, would permit them to arrive at a solution of Nicaragua's essential causes of action. Moreover, the Contadora process in any event is a "pacific procedure" (it can hardly be a warlike procedure), from which it follows that, according to Article IV of the Pact, being a pacific procedure which "has been initiated... by agreement between the parties" before the bringing of Nicaragua's Application, "no other procedure may be commenced until that procedure is concluded". The Court avoids confronting more than one knotty problem of the interpretation of Articles II and IV by its holding that the Contadora process was "concluded" at the time when Nicaragua filed its Application. It so holds despite the common view of the Parties that that process "has not been abandoned or suspended at any moment". The Court maintains that it appreciates the importance of this concordance of views between the Parties; nevertheless, it decides that the Contadora process, at any rate in the phase directed towards resolution of the substance of the issues before it, had concluded by 28 July 1986. This is, for the reasons set out by the Court, one plausible interpretation of the facts; one might also arrive at another plausible interpretation as the Parties appear to do; but I do not think that the Court's interpretation is untenable.

[pp. 130-131 **S.O. Schwebel**] On the one hand, the Court concludes that it cannot uphold the contention of Honduras that the procedural situation created by Nicaragua's splitting up of the overall conflict into separate disputes is contrary to the requirements of good faith and the proper functioning of international justice. On the other hand, the Court holds that:
"In any event, it is for the Parties to establish the facts in the present case taking account of the usual rules of evidence, without it being possible to rely on considerations of *res judicata* in another case not involving the same parties (see Article 59 of the Statute)." (Judgment, para. 54.)

It follows from this latter holding that if, at the stage of the merits, a Party to the instant case should endeavour to rely on the findings of fact of the Judgment of 27 June 1986 in *Military and Paramilitary Activities in and against Nicaragua*, the Court will not accept such reliance but will require that Party to establish the facts in the present case taking account of the usual rules of evidence. Despite the fact that that Judgment passed upon causes of action which are found in the instant case, and despite the fact that Honduras is repeatedly specified both in the pleadings of the *Military and Paramilitary Activities in and against Nicaragua* case and in the Court's Judgment, considerations of res judicata cannot apply since that case was another case, to which the Parties were not the same as the Parties to this case.

This says no more than what the terms of Article 59 of the Statute require. Nevertheless, in the circumstances, it is important that the Court says it, and, if the instant case reaches the stage of the merits, it will be crucial for the Court to give full effect to Article 59. In the nature of the situation with which the Parties and the Court are confronted, that will not be simple.

2.3. The Optional Clause

2.3.1. General Questions

Military and Paramilitary Activities
(Nicaragua/United States of America)
Merits. J. 27.6.1986
I.C.J. Reports 1986, p. 14

[p. 142] In general, jurisdiction to determine the merits of a dispute entails jurisdiction to determine reparation. More specifically, the Court notes that in its declaration of acceptance of jurisdiction under the Optional Clause of 26 August 1946, the United States expressly accepted the Court's jurisdiction in respect of disputes concerning "the nature or extent of the reparation to be made for the breach of an international obligation". The corresponding declaration by which Nicaragua accepted the Court's jurisdiction contains no restriction of the powers of the Court under Article 36, paragraph 2 d of its Statute; Nicaragua has thus accepted the "same obligation".

2.3.3. Reservations

Cf. also: Preliminary Objections, infra III, 3.5.

Military and Paramilitary Activities
(Nicaragua/United States of America)
Merits. J. 27.6.1986
I.C.J. Reports 1986, p. 14

[pp. 32-34] The reservation in question is not necessarily a bar to the United States accepting the Court's jurisdiction whenever a third State which may be affected by the decision is not a party to the proceedings. According to the actual text of the reservation, the United States can always disregard this fact if it "specially agrees to jurisdiction". Besides, apart from this possibility, as the Court recently observed: "in principle a State may validly waive an objection to jurisdiction which it might otherwise have been entitled to raise" (*I.C.J. Reports 1985*, p. 216, para. 43). But it is clear that the fact that the United States, having refused to participate at the merits stage, did not have an opportunity to press again at that stage the argument which, in the jurisdictional phase, it founded on its multilateral treaty reservation cannot be tantamount to a waiver of the argument drawn from the reservation. Unless unequivocally waived, the reservation constitutes a limitation on the extent of the jurisdiction voluntarily accepted by the United States and, as the Court observed in the *Aegean Sea Continental Shelf* case,

"It would not discharge its duty under Article 53 of the Statute if it were to leave out of its consideration a reservation, the invocation of which by the Respondent was properly brought to its notice earlier in the proceedings." (*I.C.J. Reports 1978*, p. 20, para. 47.)

The United States has not in the present phase submitted to the Court any arguments whatever, either on the merits proper or on the question - not exclusively preliminary - of the multilateral treaty reservation. The Court cannot therefore consider that the United States has waived the reservation or no longer ascribes to it the scope which the United States attributed to it when last stating its position on this matter before the Court. This conclusion is the more decisive inasmuch as a respondent's non-participation requires the Court, as stated for example in the *Fisheries Jurisdiction* cases, to exercise "particular circumspection and ... special care" (*I.C.J. Reports 1974,* p. 10, para. 17, and p. 181, para. 18).

It has also been suggested that the United States may have waived the multilateral treaty reservation by its conduct of its case at the jurisdictional stage, or more generally by asserting collective self-defence in accordance with the United Nations Charter as justification for its activities vis-à-vis Nicaragua. There is no doubt that the United States, during its participation in the proceedings, insisted that the law applicable to the dispute was to be found in multilateral treaties, particularly the United Nations Charter and the Charter of the Organization of American States; indeed, it went so far as to contend that such treaties supervene and subsume customary law on the subject. It is however one thing for a State to advance a contention that the law applicable to a given dispute derives from a specified source; it is quite another for that State to consent to the Court's having jurisdiction to entertain that dispute, and thus to apply that law to the dispute. The whole purpose of the United States argument as to the applicability of the United Nations and Organization of American States Charters was to convince the Court that the present dispute is one "arising under" those treaties, and hence one which is excluded from jurisdiction by the multilateral treaty reservation in the United States declaration of acceptance of jurisdiction. It is impossible to interpret the attitude of the United States as consenting to the Court's applying multilateral treaty law to resolve the dispute, when what the United States was arguing was that, for the very reason that the dispute "arises under" multilateral treaties, no consent to its determination by the Court has ever been given. The Court was fully aware, when it gave its 1984 Judgment, that the United States regarded the law of the two Charters as applicable to the dispute; it did not then regard that approach as a waiver, nor can it do so now.

[pp. 36-38] It could be argued that the Court, if it found that the situation does not permit the exercise by El Salvador of its right of self-defence, would not be "affecting" that right itself but the application of it by El Salvador in the circumstances of the present case. However, it should be recalled that the condition of the application of the multilateral treaty reservation is not that the "right" of a State be affected, but that the State itself be "affected" - a broader criterion. Furthermore whether the relations between Nicaragua and El Salvador can be qualified as relations between an attacker State and a victim State which is exercising its right of self-defence, would appear to be a question in dispute between those two States. But El Salvador has not submitted this dispute to the Court; it therefore has a right to have the Court refrain from ruling upon a dispute which it has not submitted to it. Thus, the decision of the Court in this case would affect this right of El Salvador and consequently this State itself.

Nor is it only in the case of a decision of the Court rejecting the United States claim to be acting in self-defence that El Salvador would be "affected" by the decision. The multilateral treaty reservation does not require, as a condition for the exclusion of a dispute from the jurisdiction of the Court, that a State party to the relevant treaty be "adversely" or "prejudicially" affected by the decision, even though this is clearly the case primarily in view. In other situations in which the position of a State not before the

Court is under consideration (cf. *Monetary Gold Removed from Rome in 1943, I.C.J. Reports 1954*, p. 32; *Continental Shelf (Libyan Arab Jamahiriya/Malta), Application to Intervene, Judgment, I.C.J. Reports 1984*, p. 20, para. 31) it is clearly impossible to argue that that State may be differently treated if the Court's decision will not necessarily be adverse to the interests of the absent State, but could be favourable to those interests. The multilateral treaty reservation bars any decision that would "affect" a third State party to the relevant treaty. Here also, it is not necessary to determine whether the decision will "affect" that State unfavourably or otherwise; the condition of the reservation is met if the State will necessarily be "affected", in one way or the other.

There may of course be circumstances in which the Court, having examined the merits of the case, concludes that no third State could be "affected" by the decision: for example, as pointed out in the 1984 Judgment, if the relevant claim is rejected on the facts (*I.C.J. Reports 1984*, p. 425, para. 75). If the Court were to conclude in the present case, for example, that the evidence was not sufficient for a finding that the United States had used force against Nicaragua, the question of justification on the grounds of self-defence would not arise, and there would be no possibility of El Salvador being "affected" by the decision. In 1984 the Court could not, on the material available to it, exclude the possibility of such a finding being reached after fuller study of the case, and could not therefore conclude at once that El Salvador would necessarily be "affected" by the eventual decision. It was thus this possibility which prevented the objection based on the reservation from having an exclusively preliminary character.

There remains the claim of Nicaragua that the United States has intervened in the internal and external affairs of Nicaragua in violation of Article 18 of the Organization of American States Charter. That Article provides:

> "No State or group of States has the right to intervene, directly or indirectly, for any reason whatever, in the internal or external affairs of any other State. The foregoing principle prohibits not only armed force but also any other form of interference or attempted threat against the personality of the State or against its political, economic, and cultural elements."

The potential link, recognized by this text, between intervention and the use of armed force, is actual in the present case, where the same activities attributed to the United States are complained of under both counts, and the response of the United States is the same to each complaint - that it has acted in self-defence. The Court has to consider what would be the impact, for the States identified by the United States as likely to be "affected", of a decision whereby the Court would decline to rule on the alleged violation of Article 21 of the Organization of American States Charter, concerning the use of force, but passed judgment on the alleged violation of Article 18. The Court will not here enter into the question whether self-defence may justify an intervention involving armed force, so that it has to be treated as not constituting a breach either of the principle of non-use of force or of that of non-intervention. At the same time, it concludes that in the particular circumstances of this case, it is impossible to say that a ruling on the alleged breach by the United States of Article 18 of the Organization of American States Charter would not "affect" El Salvador.

The Court therefore finds that El Salvador, a party to the United Nations Charter and to the Charter of the Organization of American States, is a State which would be "affected" by the decision which the Court would have to take on the claims by Nicaragua that the United States has violated Article 2, paragraph 4, of the United Nations Charter and Articles 18, 20 and 21 of the Organization of American States Charter. Accordingly, the Court, which under Article 53 of the Statute has to be "satisfied" that it has jurisdiction to decide each of the claims it is asked to uphold, concludes that the jurisdiction conferred upon it by the United States declaration of acceptance of jurisdiction under Article 36, paragraph 2, of the Statute does not permit the Court to entertain these claims. It should however be recalled that, as will be explained further below, the effect of the reservation in question is confined to barring the applicability of the United Nations Charter and Organization of American States Charter as multilateral treaty law, and has no further impact on the sources of international law which Article 38 of the Statute requires the Court to apply.

[p. 197 **S.O. Sette-Camara**] Therefore the decision of the Court as it stands in the operative part of the Judgment could in no way "affect" El Salvador such as to warrant application of the multilateral treaty reservation. In this sense I do not concur with paragraph 51 of the reasoning. Nor do I agree with the argument contained in paragraph 53. The distinction between "adversely" affecting and otherwise, is irrelevant and beside the point. Nothing in the operative clause of the Judgment could, I submit, "affect" the rights or obligations of El Salvador either "adversely" or "favourably".

[p. 198 **S.O. Sette-Camara**] The Court concludes that it must regard itself as without competence to deal with either of the two claims of breach of the OAS Charter. As to the alleged violation of Article 18 of the OAS Charter by the United States intervention in the internal or external affairs of Nicaragua, a subject disposed of by subparagraph (3) of the operative part, I fail to see by what stretch of imagination such a decision could be said to affect El Salvador.

The so-called Vandenberg Amendment applies to disputes under multilateral treaties which are also multilateral disputes. The current case is between the Applicant - Nicaragua - and the Respondent - the United States of America. Any other State which has any reason to consider that it might be affected by a Judgment of the Court, and which has jurisdictional links with the Parties in the case, and with the Applicant in particular, is free to initiate proceedings of its own or to intervene under Articles 62 and 63 of the Statute. The only relevance of the multilateral treaty reservation in the merits phase of the proceedings is, I submit, that the Court cannot ignore the problem of third States parties to multilateral treaties which might be affected by the Judgment, and should deal with it in the proper terms, namely that they are free to come before the Court to defend their rights and interests if they so desire.

[pp. 217-219 **S.O. Oda**] It may well be contended that principles such as the non-use of force and the non-intervention now exist independently as customary and general international law. However, I cannot agree with the Judgment in its contention that the Court may entertain the Nicaraguan Application under Article 36, paragraph 2, of the Statute on the alleged assumption that the United States reservation regarding "disputes arising under a multilateral treaty" simply excludes from the jurisdiction conferred on the Court under that provision of the Statute legal disputes concerning "the interpretation of a [multilateral] treaty", or that, since the present case involves a "question of international law", the Court's entertainment of it should not be affected by that reservation inasmuch as the Court, independently of "the interpretation of a treaty", can confine itself to the application of the principles of customary and general international law.

I believe that the issue - which relates to applicable law - of whether, once the Court assumes jurisdiction over a case, it can apply the rules of customary and general international law apart from any applicable treaty rules, is quite different from the other issue - which relates to the Court's jurisdiction - of whether a State's declaration excludes "disputes arising under multilateral treat[ies]" (United States reservation) from "the jurisdiction of the Court, [which by nature can only be voluntarily accepted] in all legal disputes concerning (a) the interpretation of a treaty, (b) any question of international law ..." (Statute, Art. 36, para. 2). The United States declaration of acceptance of the Court's jurisdiction excluded disputes arising under multilateral treaties subject to exceptions which do not qualify my reasoning and, in any event, have not materialized in the present case.

The persistent use of the term "reservation" to describe the exception clauses attached by States to their declarations under Article 36, paragraph 2, of the Statute, and more especially the attachment of the term "Vandenberg Reservation" to the exception in the United States declaration relating to disputes that arise under a multilateral treaty, have surely contributed to a misconception of the inherent scope of such declarations, and of that one in particular. Because of the idealism underlying the notion of a sovereign State submitting to be judged, the so-called "acceptance of the Optional Clause" has always been imagined in terms of the ideal case, where that submission is total and "unreserved". Nevertheless, the very structure of Article 36, paragraph 2, should make it clear that, in framing a declaration, a State, guided by the categories there suggested (the historical origins of which I shall explain in paras. 27-40), has simply to delineate the bounds of the area of legal disputes over which, subject to reciprocity, it is prepared to accept the Court's jurisdiction independently of treaty clauses or special agreements. If it is under no obligation to make any declaration at all, still less is it obliged to take the ideal case as its standard.

Hence the fact that exception clauses may frequently be useful as a means of delineation does not justify any presumption that a State employing them has retracted various parts of an *a priori* wholesale acceptance of the Court's jurisdiction; on the contrary, the instrument remains a positive indication that the State has unreservedly accepted that jurisdiction within a certain area which those exceptions have merely helped to define. Outside that area, there is simply no acceptance, not even an acceptance subject to a "reservation", and to reason as if there were is to yield to a kind of optical illusion.

In the present case, it seems that thinking about a certain exception in terms of a "reservation" has helped the Court to imagine that if multilateral treaties were ignored as a source of positive law, the "reservation" would lose its potency, so that the exception could be circumvented. I have explained above why I find this erroneous. The reference to multilateral treaties is merely a means of drawing the boundaries of jurisdiction so as to exclude certain disputes: there is no justification for supposing that a dispute "arising under" a multilateral treaty can nevertheless be brought under the Court's authority because (inevitably) it can also be analysed in terms of general international law. Having decided that the present dispute did "arise under" such a treaty or treaties, the Court should have concluded that only in the circumstances described by the exception itself, namely, the presence of all parties affected or specific waiver, could the boundary of acceptance of jurisdiction be widened to admit the dispute under Article 36, paragraph 2.

Thus, if the so-called Vandenberg Reservation is applicable in this case, and the United States acceptance of the Court's compulsory jurisdiction consequently does not extend to *disputes arising under* the Charter of the United Nations and the Charter of the Organization of American States, and if the Judgment yet declares that the Court can entertain the present case as admissible under Article 36, paragraph 2, as stated:

"The Court concludes that it should exercise the jurisdiction conferred upon it by the United States declaration of acceptance under Article 36, paragraph 2, of the Statute, to determine the claims of Nicaragua based upon customary international law notwithstanding the exclusion from its jurisdiction of disputes 'arising under' the United Nations and OAS Charters" (para. 182), the Court should have proved, not that it can apply customary and general international law independently, but that the dispute referred to it in the Applicant's claims had not arisen under these multilateral treaties. The Judgment, however, fails to do this. I must repeat my belief that. in so far as the Judgment holds the Vandenberg Reservation to be applicable, in my view, correctly, the Court should not, and indeed could not, on the basis of Article 36, paragraph 2, of the Statute, have entertained the whole dispute, which the United States has allegedly pursued.

[p. 529 **D.O. Jennings**] The jurisdiction of the Court is consensual, this requirement being an emanation of the independence of the sovereign State; which, it is in the present case not without pertinence to note, is also the basis of the principle of non-intervention. Consequently the Court, in the exercise under Article 36, paragraph 6, of its Statute of its competence to decide a dispute concerning its jurisdiction, must always satisfy itself that consent has in fact been accorded, before it can decide that jurisdiction exists. Moreover, the Court has to be mindful that a consent given in a declaration made under Article 36, paragraph 2, - the "Optional Clause" - is a consent that no State needs to make and that relatively very few have ever done so. Accordingly, any reservation qualifying such a consent especially demands caution and respect.

[pp. 533-534 **D.O. Jennings**] ... it is, in my view, not possible to circumvent the multilateral treaty reservation by resort to a residuary customary law; even supposing the latter could be disentangled from treaty and separately identified as to its content. The multilateral treaty reservation does not merely reserve jurisdiction over a multilateral treaty, where there is an "affected" party not a party to the case before the Court; it reserves jurisdiction over "disputes arising under a multilateral treaty".

Clearly the legal nature of a dispute is determined by the attitude of the parties between which the dispute is joined. Nicaragua eventually, though not originally, pleaded its case in the duplex form of a dispute under multilateral treaties or, in the alternative, a dispute under customary law. But there are at least two sides to a dispute. The United States did not countenance a dispute arising only under custom. Its response to the charge of the unlawful use of force, was based firmly on the terms of Article 51 of the Charter. One party cannot in effect redefine the response of the other party. If the Respondent relies on Article 51, there is a dispute arising under a multilateral treaty.

Consequently, I am unable to see how the main elements of this dispute - the use of force, and collective self-defence - can be characterized as other than disputes arising under a multilateral treaty. That being so, it follows from the multilateral treaty reservation, that the Court's jurisdiction is lacking, not merely in respect of a relevant multilateral treaty, but in respect of that dispute.

Accordingly, I have voted "No" to subparagraph (2) of paragraph 292; not at all on grounds of substance but on the ground of lack of jurisdiction. It follows also that I have had to vote "No" to subparagraph (4), dealing with certain direct attacks on Nicaraguan territory, and to subparagraph (5), dealing with unauthorized overflight of Nicaraguan territory; again because of lack of jurisdiction to decide one way or the other on the question of self-defence.

[p. 535 **D.O. Jennings**] One is, however, immediately faced with the difficulty that a plea of collective self-defence is obviously a possible justification of intervention and that this is the justification which the United States has pleaded. So it is again a dispute arising under Article 51 of the United Nations Charter. If one turns to the Inter-American system of law, the same problem arises. Article 18 of the Charter of the Organization of American States deals with intervention in peculiarly comprehensive terms, in that it prohibits intervention "for any reason whatever"; it also, in Article 21, deals with force and self-defence, but in specifically treaty terms. Thus, by that article, the American States "bind themselves in their international relations not to have recourse to the use of force, except in the case of self-defense *in accordance with existing treaties or in fulfillment thereof*" (emphasis added).

The latter phrase can only mean that self-defence in the inter-American system by definition requires recourse to multilateral treaties; such as, obviously, the Rio Treaty on Mutual Assistance, as well as the Principle of the OAS Charter (Art. 3 (*f*)) that: "An act of aggression against one American State is an act of aggression against all the other American States." In short, I am wholly unable to see how the issues of intervention raised in the instant case - intervention indeed by either Party, for each accuses the other of it - can be categorized as other than a dispute, or disputes, arising under multilateral treaties, and thus caught by the multilateral treaty reservation; at any rate where self-defence has formally been pleaded as a justification.

Applicability of Article VI, Section 22,
of the Convention on the Privileges and
Immunities of the United Nations,
Advisory Opinion of 15 December 1989
I.C.J. Reports 1989, p. 177

[pp.189-190] Romania however relies on its reservation to Section 30 [16] of the

16 Section 30 of the General Convention provides:

"All differences arising out of the interpretation or application of the present convention shall be referred to the International Court of Justice, unless in any case it is agreed by the parties to have recourse to another mode of settlement. If a

General Convention; but that Section operates on a different plane and in a different context from that of Article 96 of the Charter. When the provisions of the Section are read in their totality, it is clear that their object is to provide a dispute settlement mechanism. The first sentence of the Section provides for the case where a difference arises out of the interpretation or application of the General Convention between States parties to it, and contains two elements. The first is the treaty obligation to refer the difference to the Court, unless another mode of settlement is decided upon by the parties; the second is the object of the reference to the Court, namely to settle the difference.

The United Nations is itself intimately, and for the most part directly, concerned with the operation of the General Convention. Section 30 was therefore so framed as to take in also the settlement of differences between the United Nations and a State party to the General Convention. If such a difference arises,

"a request shall be made for an advisory opinion on any legal question involved in accordance with Article 96 of the Charter and Article 65 of the Statute of the Court. The opinion given by the Court shall be accepted as decisive by the parties."

This provision pursues the same intent as expressed in the first sentence of Section 30; the particular nature of the proceeding contemplated is attributable to the status as an international organization of one of the parties to the difference.

In case of a request for an advisory opinion made under Section 30, the Court would of course have to consider any reservation which a party to the dispute had made to that Section. In the particular case of Romania, the Court would have to consider whether the effect of its reservation could be to act as a bar to the operation of the procedure of request for advisory opinion, or merely to deprive any opinion given of the decisive effect attributed to such opinions by Section 30. But in the present case, the resolution requesting the advisory opinion made no reference to Section 30, and it is evident from the dossier that, in view of the existence of the Romanian reservation, it was not the intention of the Council to invoke Section 30. The request is not made under that Section, and the Court does not therefore need to determine the effect of the Romanian reservation to that provision.

Romania however contends that although the Council resolution 1989/75 dated 24 May 1989 does not allude to Section 30 of the General Convention as the basis of its request for advisory opinion, the question which it raises nevertheless relates to the applicability of a substantive provision of the General Convention "to a concrete case

---

difference arises between the United Nations on the one hand and a Member on the other hand, a request shall be made for an advisory opinion on any legal question involved in accordance with Article 96 of the Charter and Article 65 of the Statute of the Court. The opinion given by the Court shall be accepted as decisive by the parties."

considered to be a dispute between a State party to the Convention and the United Nations". It argues that

"If it were accepted that a State party to the Convention, or the United Nations, might ask for disputes concerning the application or interpretation of the Convention to be brought before the Court on a basis other than the provisions of Section 30 of the Convention, that would disrupt the unity of the Convention, by separating the substantive provisions from those relating to dispute settlement, which would be tantamount to a modification of the content and extent of the obligations entered into by States when they consented to be bound by the Convention."

However, the nature and purpose of the present proceedings are, as explained above, that of a request for advice on the applicability of a part of the General Convention, and not the bringing of a dispute before the Court for determination. Furthermore, the "content and extent of the obligations entered into by States" - and, in particular, by Romania - "when they consented to be bound by the Convention" are not modified by the request and by the present advisory opinion.

The Court thus finds that the reservation made by Romania to Section 30 of the General Convention does not affect the Court's jurisdiction to entertain the present request.

2.4. Jurisdiction on the Basis of a Special Agreement

Frontier Dispute, Judgment
(Burkina Faso/Republic of Mali)
I.C.J. Reports 1986, p. 554

[pp. 577-578] In the Chamber's opinion, it should first be recalled that there is a distinction between the question of the jurisdiction conferred upon it by the Special Agreement concluded between the Parties, and the question whether "the adjudication sought by the Applicant is one which the Court's judicial function permits it to give", a question considered by the Court in the case concerning the *Northern Cameroons*, among others (*I.C.J. Reports 1963*, p. 31). As it also stated in that case, "even if the Court, when seised, finds that it has jurisdiction, the Court is not compelled in every case to exercise that jurisdiction" (*ibid.*, p. 29). But in the absence of "considerations which would lead it to decline to give judgment" (*I.C.J. Reports 1974*, p. 271, para. 58), the Court is bound to fulfil the functions assigned to it by its Statute. Moreover, the Court has recently confirmed the principle that it "must not exceed the jurisdiction conferred upon it by the Parties, but it must also exercise that jurisdiction to its full extent" (*Continental Shelf (Libyan Arab Jamahiriya/ Malta), I.C.J. Reports 1985*, p. 23). In the present case, the Chamber finds it to be clear from the wording of the Special Agreement - including its preamble - that the common intention of the Parties was that the Chamber should indicate the frontier line between their respective territories throughout the whole of the "disputed area", and that this area was for them the whole of the frontier not yet delimited by joint agreement.

The Chamber also considers that its jurisdiction is not restricted simply because the end-point of the frontier lies on the frontier of a third State not a party to the proceedings. The rights of the neighbouring State, Niger, are in any event safeguarded by the operation of Article 59 of the Statute of the Court, which provides that "The decision of the Court has no binding force except between the parties and in respect of that particular case". The Parties could at any time have concluded an agreement for the delimitation of their frontier, according to whatever perception they might have had of it, and an agreement of this kind, although legally binding upon them by virtue of the principle *pacta sunt servanda*, would not be opposable to Niger. A judicial decision, which "is simply an alternative to the direct and friendly settlement" of the dispute between the Parties (*P.C.I.J., Series A, No. 22*, p. 13), merely substitutes for the solution stemming directly from their shared intention, the solution arrived at by a court under the mandate which they have given it. In both instances, the solution only has legal and binding effect as between the States which have accepted it, either directly or as a consequence of having accepted the court's jurisdiction to decide the case. Accordingly, on the supposition that the Chamber's judgment specifies a point which it finds to be the easternmost point of the frontier, there would be nothing to prevent Niger from claiming rights, vis-à-vis either of the Parties, to territories lying west of the point identified by the Chamber.

[pp. 579-580] The fact is, as the Parties seem to have realized towards the end of the proceedings, that the question has been wrongly defined. The Chamber is in fact required, not to fix a tripoint, which would necessitate the consent of all the States concerned, but to ascertain, in the light of the evidence which the Parties have made available to it, how far the frontier which they inherited from the colonial power extends. Certainly such a finding implies, as a logical corollary, both that the territory of a third State lies beyond the end-point, and that the Parties have exclusive sovereign rights up to that point. However, this is no more than a twofold presumption which underlies any boundary situation. This presumption remains in principle irrebuttable in the judicial context of a given case, in the sense that neither of the disputant parties, having contended that it possesses a common frontier with the other as far as a specific point, can change its position to rely on the alleged existence of sovereignty pertaining to a third State; but this presumption does not thereby create a ground of opposability outside that context and against the third State. Indeed, this is the whole point of the above-quoted Article 59 of the Statute. It is true that in a given case it may be clear from the record that the legal interests of a third State "would not only be affected by a decision, but would form the very subject-matter of the decision" (*Monetary Gold Removed from Rome in 1943, I.C.J. Reports 1954*, p. 32) so that the Court has to use its power "to refuse to exercise its jurisdiction" (*I.C.J. Reports 1984*, p. 431, para. 88). However, this is not the case here.

The Chamber therefore concludes that it has a duty to decide the whole of the *petitum* entrusted to it; that is, to indicate the line of the frontier between the Parties over the entire length of the disputed area. In so doing, it will define the location of the end-point of the frontier in the east, the point where this frontier ceases to divide the territories of Burkina Faso and Mali; but, as explained above, this will not amount to a decision by the Chamber that this is a tripoint which affects Niger. In accordance with Article 59 of the Statute, this Judgment will also not be opposable to Niger as regards the course of that country's frontiers.

2.5. Jurisdiction on the Basis of Treaties

2.5.1. General Questions

Military and Paramilitary Activities
(Nicaragua/United States of America)
Merits. J. 27.6.1986
I.C.J. Reports 1986, p. 14

[p. 136] It should however be emphasized that the Court does not consider that a compromissory clause of the kind included in Article XXIV, paragraph 2, of the 1956 FCN Treaty, providing for jurisdiction over disputes as to its interpretation or application, would enable the Court to entertain a claim alleging conduct depriving the treaty of its object and purpose. It is only because in the present case the Court has found that it has jurisdiction, apart from Article XXIV, over any legal dispute between the Parties concerning any of the matters enumerated in Article 36, paragraph 2, of the Statute, that it can proceed to examine Nicaragua's claim under this head.

[p. 142] Under the 1956 FCN Treaty, the Court has jurisdiction to determine "any dispute between the Parties as to the interpretation or application of the present Treaty" (Art. XXIV, para. 2); and as the Permanent Court of International Justice stated in the case concerning the *Factory at Chorzów*,

"Differences relating to reparations, which may be due by reason of failure to apply a convention, are consequently differences relating to its application." (*Jurisdiction, Judgment No. 8, 1927, P.C.I.J., Series A, No.9*, p. 21.)

[p. 539 **D.O. Jennings**] First, it should be noted that the 1956 Treaty creates, by Article XXIV, a title of jurisdiction under Article 36, paragraph 1, of the Court's Statute, being a treaty "in force" at the material time. It is a title of jurisdiction which is different from, and independent of, the question of jurisdiction under the United States Declaration made under Article 36, paragraph 2, of the Statute. It is, therefore, a title of jurisdiction which is not touched by the multilateral treaties reservation, which applies only to the Declaration made under Article 36, paragraph 2 and there is, accordingly, nothing to prevent the Court, when it is dealing with matters covered by the jurisdiction clause of the FCN Treaty, from considering and applying, for example, Articles 2, paragraph 4, and 51 of the United Nations Charter or any other relevant multilateral treaties. Indeed, the first part of Article XXI (*d*) of the FCN Treaty, to be considered below, clearly contemplates certain kinds of "obligations of a Party" arising from the United Nations Charter as being relevant to the interpretation and application of the treaty.

This does not mean that the principal dispute, the subject of the Nicaraguan Application, could be dealt with under the FCN Treaty jurisdiction clause; except indeed in so far as it may involve a dispute which directly concerns the "interpretation or application" of the provisions of the treaty. I am unable to accept the Nicaraguan argument, by which the treaty jurisdiction is supposed to comprise matters which could be said in general terms to be inconsistent with the "object and purpose" of an FCN treaty, but are not referred to specific articles of the treaty. The jurisdiction clause of such a treaty could not be regarded as conferring a jurisdiction to pass upon matters external to the actual provisions of the treaty, even though such matters may affect the operation of the treaty. Suppose hostilities, or even war, should arise between parties to an FCN treaty, then the Court under a jurisdiction clause surely does not have jurisdiction to pass upon the general question of the lawfulness or otherwise of the outbreak of hostilities or of war, on the ground only that this defeated the object and purpose of the treaty; though of course it might have jurisdiction for instance to decide whether there was a "war" or hostilities, for the purposes of interpreting and applying a war clause which was a term of the treaty. If it were otherwise, there would be no apparent limit to the kinds of dispute which might in certain circumstances be claimed to come under such a jurisdiction clause. The conferment of such a potentially roving jurisdiction could not have been within the intention of the parties when they agreed the jurisdiction clause; and if the Court had asserted such a jurisdiction, this would only have discouraged future mention of the Court in such FCN treaty jurisdiction clauses.

2.5.3. Specific Treaties

Border and Transborder Armed Actions
Nicaragua/Honduras),
Jurisdiction and Admissibility,
Judgment, I.C.J. Reports 1988, p. 69

[pp. 84-85] The first interpretation advanced by Honduras - that Article XXXI [17] must be supplemented by a declaration - is incompatible with the actual terms of the Article. In that text, the parties "declare that they recognize" the Court's jurisdiction "as compulsory *ipso facto*" in the cases there enumerated. Article XXXI does not subject that recognition to the making of a new declaration to be deposited with the United Nations Secretary-General in accordance with Article 36, paragraphs 2 and 4, of the Statute. It is drafted in the present indicative tense, and thus of itself constitutes acceptance of the Court's jurisdiction.

Turning to the second Honduran interpretation, the Court may observe at the outset that two possible readings of the relationship between Article XXXI and the Statute have been proposed by the Parties. That Article has been seen either as a treaty provision conferring jurisdiction upon the Court in accordance with Article 36, paragraph 1, of the Statute, or as a collective declaration of acceptance of compulsory jurisdiction under paragraph 2 of that same Article.

Honduras has advanced the latter reading. Nicaragua, after asserting in 1984, in the case concerning *Military and Paramilitary Activities in and against Nicaragua (Nicaragua v. United States of America)*, that Article XXXI constituted a declaration under Article 36, paragraph 2, of the Statute, has argued in the present case that Article XXXI falls under Article 36, paragraph 1, and therefore confers jurisdiction on the Court on a conventional basis.

There is however no need to pursue this argument. Even if the Honduran reading of Article XXXI be adopted, and the Article be regarded as a collective declaration of acceptance of compulsory jurisdiction made in accordance with Article 36, paragraph 2, it should be observed that that declaration was incorporated in the Pact of Bogotá as Article XXXI. Accordingly, it can only be modified in accordance with the rules provided for in the Pact itself. Article XXXI nowhere envisages that the undertaking entered into by the parties to the Pact might be amended by means of a unilateral

---

17 Article XXXI of the Pact of Bogotá, upon which Nicaragua relies to found jurisdiction, provides as follows:

"In conformity with Article 36, paragraph 2, of the Statute of the International Court of Justice, the High Contracting Parties declare that they recognize, in relation to any other American State, the jurisdiction of the Court as compulsory ipso facto, without the necessity of any special agreement so long as the present Treaty is in force, in all disputes of a juridical nature that arise among them concerning:

(a) The interpretation of a treaty;
(b) Any question of international law;
(c) The existence of any fact which, if established, would constitute the breach of an international obligation;
(d) The nature or extent of the reparation to be made for the breach of an international obligation."

declaration made subsequently under the Statute, and the reference to Article 36, paragraph 2, of the Statute is insufficient in itself to have that effect.

The fact that the Pact defines with precision the obligations of the parties lends particular significance to the absence of any indication of that kind. The commitment in Article XXXI applies *ratione materiae* to the disputes enumerated in that text; it relates *ratione personae* to the American States parties to the Pact; it remains valid *ratione temporis* for as long as that instrument itself remains in force between those States.

Moreover, some provisions of the Treaty restrict the scope of the parties' commitment. Article V specifies that procedures under the Pact "may not be applied to matters which, by their nature, are within the domestic jurisdiction of the State". Article VI provides that they will likewise not apply

"to matters already settled by arrangement between the parties, or by arbitral award or by decision of an international court, or which are governed by agreements or treaties in force on the date of the conclusion of the present Treaty".

Similarly, Article VII lays down specific rules relating to diplomatic protection.

Finally, Article LV of the Pact of Bogotá enables the parties to make reservations to that instrument which "shall, with respect to the State that makes them, apply to all signatory States on the basis of reciprocity". In the absence of special procedural provisions those reservations may, in accordance with the rules of general international law on the point as codified by the 1969 Vienna Convention on the Law of Treaties, be made only at the time of signature or ratification of the Pact or at the time of adhesion to that instrument.

These provisions together indicate that the commitment in Article XXXI can only be limited by means of reservations to the Pact itself. It is an autonomous commitment, independent of any other which the parties may have undertaken or may undertake by depositing with the United Nations Secretary-General a declaration of acceptance of compulsory jurisdiction under Article 36, paragraphs 2 and 4, of the Statute. Not only does Article XXXI not require any such declaration, but also when such a declaration is made, it has no effect on the commitment resulting from that Article.

Neither the first nor the second interpretation of the text advanced by Honduras is compatible with the actual terms of the Pact.

[p. 88] Under these circumstances, the Court has to conclude that the commitment in Article XXXI of the Pact is independent of such declarations of acceptance of compulsory jurisdiction as may have been made under Article 36, paragraph 2, of the Statute and deposited with the United Nations Secretary-General pursuant to paragraph

4 of that same Article. Consequently, it is not necessary to decide whether the 1986 Declaration of Honduras is opposable to Nicaragua in this case; it cannot in any event restrict the commitment which Honduras entered into by virtue of Article XXXI. The Honduran argument as to the effect of the reservation to its 1986 Declaration on its commitment under Article XXXI of the Pact therefore cannot be accepted.

[pp. 88-90] The second objection of Honduras to jurisdiction is based on Article XXXII of the Pact of Bogotá, which reads as follows:
"When the conciliation procedure previously established in the present Treaty or by agreement of the parties does not lead to a solution, and the said parties have not agreed upon an arbitral procedure, either of them shall be entitled to have recourse to the International Court of Justice in the manner prescribed in Article 40 of the Statute thereof. The Court shall have compulsory jurisdiction in accordance with Article 36, paragraph 1, of the said Statute."

It is the contention of Honduras that Articles XXXI and XXXII must be read together. The first is said to define the extent of the Court's jurisdiction and the second to determine the conditions under which the Court may be seised. According to Honduras it follows that the Court could only be seised under Article XXXI if, in accordance with Article XXXII, there had been a prior recourse to conciliation and lack of agreement to arbitrate, which is not the situation in the present case.

Nicaragua on the other hand contends that Article XXXI and Article XXXII are two autonomous provisions, each of which confers jurisdiction upon the Court in the cases for which it provides. It claims that Article XXXI covers all juridical disputes which, before the conclusion of the Pact, would have been subject to arbitration under the General Treaty of Inter-American Arbitration of 5 January 1929; and that Article XXXII relates to disputes, whatever their nature, previously in the domain of conciliation under the General Convention of Inter-American Conciliation of the same date. It maintains accordingly that the Court can be seised, under Article XXXI, in the cases covered by that text, without there being any requirement to ascertain whether the procedural conditions laid down, in other cases, by Article XXXII have or have not been satisfied.

Honduras's interpretation of Article XXXII runs counter to the terms of that Article. Article XXXII makes no reference to Article XXXI; under that text the parties have, in general terms, an entitlement to have recourse to the Court in cases where there has been an unsuccessful conciliation.

It is true that one qualification of this observation is required, with regard to the French text of Article XXXII, which provides that, in the circumstances there contemplated, the party has "le droit de porter *la question* devant la Cour". That expression might be thought to refer back to the question which might have been the subject of the dispute referred to the Court under Article XXXI. It should, however, be observed that the text uses the word "*question*", which leaves room for uncertainty, rather than the word "*différend* (dispute)", used in Article XXXI, which would have been perfectly clear. Moreover, the Spanish, English and Portuguese versions speak, in general terms, of an entitlement to have recourse to the Court and do not justify the conclusion that there is a link between Article XXXI and Article XXXII.

Moreover, Article XXXII, unlike Article XXXI, refers expressly to the jurisdiction which the Court has under Article 36, paragraph 1, of the Statute. That reference would be difficult to understand if, as Honduras contends, the sole purpose of Article XXXII were to specify the procedural conditions for bringing before the Court disputes for which jurisdiction had already been conferred upon it by virtue of the declaration made in Article XXXI, pursuant to Article 36, paragraph 2.

It is, moreover, quite clear from the Pact that the purpose of the American States in drafting it was to reinforce their mutual commitments with regard to judicial settlement. This is also confirmed by the *travaux préparatoires*: the discussion at the meeting of Committee III of the Conference held on 27 April 1948 has already been referred to in paragraph 37 above. At that meeting, furthermore, the delegate of Colombia explained to the Committee the general lines of the system proposed by the Sub-Committee which had prepared the draft; the Sub-Committee took the position "that the principal procedure for the peaceful settlement of conflicts between the American States had to be judicial procedure before the International Court of Justice" [18] (*translation by the Registry*). Honduras's interpretation would however imply that the commitment, at first sight firm and unconditional, set forth in Article XXXI would, in fact, be emptied of all content if, for any reason, the dispute were not subjected to prior conciliation. Such a solution would be clearly contrary to both the object and the purpose of the Pact.

In short, Articles XXXI and XXXII provide for two distinct ways by which access may be had to the Court. The first relates to cases in which the Court can be seised directly and the second to those in which the parties initially resort to conciliation.

In the present case, Nicaragua has relied upon Article XXXI, not Article XXXII. It is accordingly not pertinent whether the dispute submitted to the Court has previously been the subject of an attempted conciliation, nor what interpretation is given to Article XXXII in other respects, in particular as regards the nature and the subject-matter of the disputes to which that text applies. It is sufficient for the court to find that the second objection put forward by Honduras is based upon an incorrect interpretation of that Article and, for that reason, cannot be accepted.

---

18 "La Subcomisión estimó que el procedimiento principal para el arreglo pacífico de los conflictos entre los Estados Americanos ha de ser el procedimiento judicial ante la Corte Internacional de Justicia; ..." (*Novena Conferencia Internacional Americana, Actas y Documentos,* Vol. IV, p. 156).

Article XXXI of the Pact of Bogotá thus confers jurisdiction upon the Court to entertain the dispute submitted to it. For that reason, the Court does not need to consider whether it might have jurisdiction by virtue of the declarations of acceptance of compulsory jurisdiction by Nicaragua and Honduras set out in paragraphs 23 to 25 above.

Elettronica Sicula S.p.A. (ELSI)
Judgment of 20 July 1989
I.C.J. Reports 1989, p. 15

[pp. 41-42] It is common ground between the Parties that the Court has jurisdiction in the present case, under Article 36, paragraph 1, of its Statute, and Article XXVI of the Treaty of Friendship, Commerce and Navigation, of 2 June 1948 ("the FCN Treaty"), between Italy and the United States; which Article reads:
"Any dispute between the High Contracting Parties as to the interpretation or the application of this Treaty, which the High Contracting Parties shall not satisfactorily adjust by diplomacy, shall be submitted to the International Court of Justice, unless the High Contracting Parties shall agree to settlement by some other pacific means."

The jurisdiction is thus confined to questions of "the interpretation or the application" of the FCN Treaty and Protocols and of the Agreement Supplementing the Treaty between the United States of America and the Italian Republic, of 26 September 1951 (which Agreement is hereinafter called "the Supplementary Agreement"), Article IX of which provides that it is to "constitute an integral part" of the FCN Treaty. This same jurisdiction may accordingly be exercised by this Chamber, created by the Court to deal with this case by virtue of Article 26, paragraph 2, of its Statute, and Articles 17 and 18 of its Rules, at the request of and after consultation with the Parties.

2.7. Concurring Jurisdictions

Military and Paramilitary Activities
(Nicaragua/United States of America)
Merits. J. 27.6.1986
I.C.J. Reports 1986, p. 14

[p. 137] The Court has in this respect to note that the Treaty itself [19] provides in Article XXIV, paragraph 1, as follows:

"Each Party shall accord sympathetic consideration to, and shall afford adequate

19 Treaty of Friendship, Commerce and Navigation between Nicaragua and United States of America, signed at Managua on 21 January 1956.

opportunity for consultation regarding, such representations as the other Party may make with respect to any matter affecting the operation of the present Treaty."

Nicaragua claims that the conduct of the United States is such as drastically to "affect the operation" of the Treaty; but so far as the Court is informed, no representations on the specific question have been made. The Court has therefore first to be satisfied that a claim based on the 1956 FCN Treaty is admissible even though no attempt has been made to use the machinery of Article XXIV, paragraph 1, to resolve the dispute. In general, treaty rules being *lex specialis*, it would not be appropriate that a State should bring a claim based on a customary-law rule if it has by treaty already provided means for settlement of such a claim. However, in the present case, the operation of Article XXIV, paragraph 1, if it had been invoked, would have been wholly artificial. While Nicaragua does allege that certain activities of the United States were in breach of the 1956 FCN Treaty, it has also claimed, and the Court has found, that they were violations of customary international law. In the Court's view, it would therefore be excessively formalistic to require Nicaragua first to exhaust the procedure of Article XXIV, paragraph 1, before bringing the matter to the Court.

3. THE PROCEDURE OF THE INTERNATIONAL COURT OF JUSTICE

3.2. Procedure before a Chamber Dealing with a Particular Case (Article 26, Paragraph 2, of the Statute)

Land, Island and Maritime Frontier Dispute (El Salvador/Honduras) Constitution of Chamber, Order of 8 May 1987, I.C.J. Reports 1987, p. 10

[pp. 11-12] Whereas the Special Agreement, according to both existing translations into the official languages of the Court already referred to, defines in Article 2 the questions submitted for decision, and provides in Article 1 that the Parties submit those questions to a Chamber of the Court composed of three members, and further that in addition, the Chamber shall comprise two judges *ad hoc*, who may have the nationality of the Parties; and whereas the Court understands the Special Agreement as requesting the Court to form a Chamber to deal with the case in accordance with Article 26, paragraph 2, of its Statute;

Whereas the Parties were duly consulted, on 17 February 1987, as to the composition of the proposed Chamber of the Court in accordance with Article 26, paragraph 2, of the Statute and Article 17, paragraph 2, of the Rules of Court;

Whereas the Parties in the course of such consultation confirmed the indication, given in the Special Agreement, that as regards the number of judges to constitute such chamber, they approve, pursuant to Article 26 of the Statute, that number being fixed at five judges, including two judges *ad hoc* chosen by the Parties pursuant to Article 31, paragraph 3, of the Statute;

Whereas by a letter dated 7 March 1987 the Minister for Foreign Affairs of El Salvador notified the Court of its choice of Mr. Nicolas Valticos to sit as judge *ad hoc* in the Chamber; and whereas by a letter dated 8 April 1987, the Agent of Honduras notified the Court of its choice of Mr. Michel Virally to sit as judge *ad hoc* in the Chamber; and whereas no objection has been raised by either Party to the choice of judge *ad hoc* made by the other, and no objection to such choice appears to the Court itself;

the Court, unanimously,

1. Decides to accede to the request of the Governments of El Salvador and Honduras to form a special Chamber of five judges to deal with the present case;
2. Declares that at an election held on 4 May 1987 Judges Oda, Sette-Camara and Sir Robert Jennings were elected to form, with the above-named judges *ad hoc*, a Chamber to deal with this case, and that accordingly such a Chamber is duly constituted by the present Order, with the following composition:

Judges Oda, Sette-Camara, Sir Robert Jennings, Judges *ad hoc* Valticos, Virally;

[p. 13 **Decl. Oda**] In the case of a chamber provided for in Article 26, paragraph 2, of the Statute of the Court, the consent of the two parties is essential and, as that provision clearly states, the number of judges to constitute such a chamber shall be determined by the Court with the approval of the parties. At the same time, regarding the composition of the chamber, the views of the parties shall be ascertained by the President in accordance with Article 17, paragraph 2, of the Rules of Court. The Court, being sovereign in judicial proceedings, is free to choose any composition it likes; yet the possibility must also be borne in mind that sovereign States have the legal right to withdraw a case if they prefer a composition different from that determined by the Court. In practical terms, therefore, it is inevitable, if a chamber is to be viable, that its composition must result from a consensus between the parties and the Court. To ensure that viability, it accordingly behoves the Court to take account of the views of the parties when proceeding to the election. Nevertheless, the chamber is a component of the Court, bound by its Statute and Rules; and the process of election whereby it comes into being should be as judicially impartial as its subsequent functioning.

Land, Island and
Maritime Frontier Dispute
(El Salvador/Honduras)
Application to Intervene,
Order of 28 February 1990,
I.C.J. Reports 1990, p. 3

[pp. 4-6] Whereas under Article 26, paragraph 2, of the Statute the Court has power to form a chamber to deal with a particular case, and consequently to regulate matters concerning its composition; whereas it is for the tribunal seised of a principal issue to deal also with any issue subsidiary thereto; whereas a chamber formed to deal with a particular case therefore deals not only with the merits of the case, but also with incidental proceedings arising in that case (cf. *Frontier Dispute, Provisional Measures, Order of 10 January 1986, I.C.J. Reports 1986*, p. 3; *Elettronica Sicula S.p.A. (ELSI), I.C.J. Reports 1989,* p. 42, para. 49);

Whereas the rule of law that "every intervention is incidental to the proceedings in a case" (*Haya de la Torre, I.C.J. Reports 1951*, p. 76), applies equally whether the intervention is based upon Article 62 or Article 63 of the Statute;

Whereas the question whether an application for permission to intervene in a case under Article 62 of the Statute should be granted requires a judicial decision whether the State seeking to intervene "has an interest of a legal nature which may be affected by the decision" in the case, and can therefore only be determined by the body which will be called upon to give the decision on the merits of the case;

Whereas furthermore a State which has submitted a request for permission to intervene on which a decision has not yet been taken "has yet to establish any status in relation to the case" (*Continental Shelf (Tunisian/Libyan Arab Jamahiriya), Application to Intervene, Judgment, I.C.J. Reports 1981*, p. 6, para. 8), and therefore a State requesting such permission must, for the purposes of the decision whether that request should be granted, take the procedural situation in the case as it finds it;

Whereas in its Application for permission to intervene Nicaragua states that

"The practical consequence of a favourable response to the present request will be the reformation of the Chamber as presently constituted and the re-ordering of the written proceedings as arranged by the Order of 27 May 1987. Whilst my Government is bound to take all available steps in order to protect its legal interests, it is concerned to proceed in a spirit of goodwill and co-operation in face of a procedure which has already been initiated. Consequently, it is the intention of my Government to propose not a reformation of the Chamber and its jurisdictional basis *tout court* but only the making of those changes strictly necessary in order to maintain the minimum standards of efficacy and procedural fairness" (para. 23),

and that

"Nicaragua in the alternative would request that, for those reasons of elemental fairness explained above ..., the Court should, in any case, exclude from the mandate of the Chamber any powers of determination of the juridical situation of maritime areas both within the Gulf of Fonseca and also in the Pacific Ocean and, in effect, limit the Chamber's mandate to those aspects of the land boundary which are in dispute between El Salvador and Honduras" (para. 24);

Whereas, in the first place, while Nicaragua has thus referred to certain questions concerning the composition of the Chamber, it has done so only in contemplation of a favourable response being given to its request for intervention; whereas, in the second place, while Nicaragua contemplates a limitation of the mandate of the Chamber, its request to that effect is put forward only "in the alternative"; whereas the Court is thus not called upon to pronounce on any of these questions;

Whereas the mention in the Application of these questions, which are thus contingent on the decision whether the application for permission to intervene is to be granted, cannot lead the Court to decide in place of the Chamber the anterior question whether that application should be granted;

the Court, by twelve votes to three,

Finds that it is for the Chamber formed to deal with the present case to decide whether the application for permission to intervene under Article 62 of the Statute filed by the Republic of Nicaragua on 17 November 1989 should be granted.

[pp. 7-8 **Decl. Oda**] The competence of the Chamber formed under Article 26, paragraph 2, of the Statute to deal with any application to intervene is, in my view, unequivocally established by Article 62 of the Statute, read together with Article 90 of the Rules of Court which states that:

"Proceedings before the Chambers mentioned in Article[s] 26... of the Statute shall, subject to the provisions of the Statute and of these Rules relating specifically to the Chambers, be governed by the provisions of Parts I to III of these Rules applicable in contentious cases before the Court",

and by Article 27 of the Statute, which provides that "[a] judgment given by any of the chambers provided for in Article[s] 26 ... shall be considered as rendered by the Court". "Intervention" is one of the "Incidental Proceedings" for which provision is made in Section D of Part III of the Rules of Court ("Proceedings in Contentious Cases"). Permission to intervene in a case being dealt with by a chamber can properly be requested only of that chamber; and it is in the nature of the present case that any approach made to the full Court by a third State cannot, however labelled, be seen as constituting a proper application for permission to intervene. The Court was accordingly under no obligation to ascertain the views of the Parties to the case with regard to this aspect of Nicaragua's Application. The Application for permission to intervene that Nicaragua addressed to the Registrar of the Court on 17 November 1989 could have been dealt with by the Chamber at once.

Although Nicaragua, in its Application to the full Court, undoubtedly did request permission of the Court to intervene, making it clear that it thereby meant the full Court, it also referred to "[t]he practical consequence of a favourable response to the present request", namely, "the reformation of the Chamber as presently constituted". In other words, Nicaragua contemplates the "reformation" of the Chamber seised of the present case by the Order of 8 May 1987 (as complemented by the Order of 13 December 1989). In the alternative, Nicaragua contemplates suggesting that the Court should exclude from the mandate of the Chamber some of the powers with which it had previously been invested. In either event a request of this kind, addressed to the full Court by a State not party to the case, is not one which can be entertained under any of the provisions of the Statute or Rules of Court that govern the Court's procedures. Furthermore, to the extent that such "reformation" might involve a claim by the intervener, or would-be intervener, to be entitled to appoint a judge *ad hoc*, such a claim could only properly be considered by the Chamber, but not by the full Court, as is implied in Article 26, paragraph 2, of the Statute and Article 17, paragraph 2, of the Rules of Court (both of which are chiefly concerned with the initial or original constitution of a chamber), and as is apparent from the very character of intervention as an incidental proceeding. Once a chamber has been constituted, the powers of the full Court are, in my view, limited, so far as the composition of that chamber is concerned, to the filling of any vacancy in the original constitution that may arise as a result of the death, resignation or incapacity of an original member of the chamber. It would have been preferable in my view for the Court to have incorporated an explicit finding in that sense into the Order which it has found it necessary to make.

[p. 9 **D.O. Elias**] I wish to dissent from the Order made by the Court because I believe that Nicaragua's Application for permission to intervene should be heard and disposed of by the full Court and not by the Chamber.

My first reason is based on the main question of the scope of chamber jurisdiction: the scope of the jurisdiction of this Chamber, or of any other chamber composed by the Court under the present Rules, is neither definitive nor final, so that one cannot regard jurisdiction as being transferable *holus bolus* from the International Court of Justice itself to its affiliate envisaged in Article 26 of the Statute, or by any other text.

[pp. 9-10 **D.O. Elias**] My second reason is the almost absolute one that Article 27 of the Statute provides clearly that "A judgment given by any of the chambers provided for in Articles 26 and 29 shall be considered as rendered by the Court". It must follow that the Court and all its Members are bound by the judgment of a chamber, but not necessarily by a judgment arrived at by whatever means, or in defiance of a rule of justice overlooked or misconceived, or one subsequently overruled by the Court in the long run. This is so because, even though every Member of the court is bound by the decision of the chamber, no non-member of the chamber has the chance or indeed the right to take part or to intervene in the work of the chamber before its decision is handed down. This means that there is no opportunity for any Member to criticize, or to point out any lacunae before the case is ended by the particular chamber; nor has the Court any opportunity to intervene. Yet according to the present Statute the decision is one by which the Court must be regarded as also bound, without having had any opportunity of interference.

It is, however, invonceivable that the jurisdiction as conferred upon the Court by Article 36 of the Statute does not admit of any exception, and binds only the Court within the meaning of the law as envisaged by it. If, for any reason, a chamber exercises so-called jurisdiction which is vitiated by any rule of law or of justice, a judgment delivered by it may not be accepted in every respect as *ipso facto* binding, even though that judgment is apparently unexceptionable otherwise. It therefore follows that, unless Article 26 of the Statute itself, or the implementing Article of the Rules by which chambers are established, so define the scope and purpose of a chamber formed to deal with a particular matter referred to it, there cannot be a wholesale transfer of general jurisdiction of the Court by the assignment of a particular case to a particular chamber. It remains to be proved that a chamber is the equivalent of the Court in all respects. It may be noted that under Article 30 of the Statute the Court reserves the exclusive right to frame "rules for carrying out its functions. In particular, it shall lay down rules of *procedure*" (emphasis added). This shows that the chamber is not entirely its own master, and that it is possible that certain aspects of jurisdiction are residual or exerciseable only by the Court istself.

[p. 10 **D.O. Elias**] When the chamber procedure was conceived and framed - a process which may be regarded as having been somewhat hurried - not enough attention was paid to refining and considering its full implications in the administration of justice. That this has been so can easily be shown by going through the *arcanum* of decisions so far delivered under the chamber procedure since the wholesale adoption of the chamber procedure in the case concerning *Delimitation of the Maritime Boundary in the Gulf of Maine Area*. The entire machinery of chamber procedure has been shown time and again to be in need of a thorough overhaul, especially from the point of view of its implication in the declaration of general principles of international law, like that of intervention, which is necessarily wider than the narrow issues which Article 26 envisaged as the *only* work for a chamber. The chamber cannot be asked to undertake the finding of general principles of public international law, and is therefore not given the same authority and jurisdiction as the Court, unless specific provision is made in a particular case in the establishment or provenance of the chamber.

Finally, the present Order is too narrow, and seems consumed by preoccupation with a narrow conception of intervention, a concept which in all cases is wider than the Court Order itsell, or even its broader implications. The Order, in refusing to allow the request of Nicaragua to be dealt with by the Court fails to refer to the relevant consideration that it may raise problems such as the appointment of an *ad hoc* judge or other issues of the composition of the Chamber itself. If such problems were handled by the Court the matter could be dealt with by handing back the request of Nicaragua to the Chamber for disposal as appropriate. The Chamber cannot be expected to refer such matter or matters to the full Court for directions several times in succession in the course of its treatment of a single application. Clearly, a chamber of *equal* competence or jurisdiction cannot be expected to have matters referred in this way to "its" own organ within the ICJ system. The Chamber must also never be allowed to deal with such issues as appointment of an *ad hoc* judge, another problem of general international law the scope of which is too wide for the Chamber in any event.

[p. 12 **D.O. Tarassov**] All these statements make it quite clear that, in the Applicant's view, the present Chamber formed by the Court on the basis of a *compromis* between El Salvador and Honduras, without the participation of Nicaragua, can only become appropriate for the consideration of its Application if it is reformed, whether wholly or in part. Alternatively, the mandate of the present Chamber should be confined to the bilateral land frontier dispute between El Salvador and Honduras and a new chamber should be formed with the participation of Nicaragua on an equal footing with the initial Parties. It is obvious that all the proposed transformations, i.e., the full or partial reformation of the existing Chamber, or the modification or limitation of its mandate, cannot be effected by the existing Chamber itself. Only the full Court, which formed the present Chamber to deal with a land, island and maritime frontier dispute between El Salvador and Honduras and thus conferred upon it its mandate "to deal with the present case" (*I.C.J. Reports 1987, Order of 8 May 1987*, p. 12), has the power to undertake actions of that kind.

I believe that the Applicant, when making the above-mentioned submissions, was quite right to appeal to the body which is *fully empowered* to make the required changes. Moreover, the Applicant has opted for precisely this approach, emphasizing in its request that the matter raised by it is "exclusively within the procedural mandate of the full Court" (Nicaragua's Application, Preliminary Statements, last paragraph).

[pp. 12-13 **D.O. Tarassov**] There are no provisions either in the Statute or in the Rules of Court which can be seen as prohibiting the full Court from considering these submissions of the Applicant. Neither the Statute and Rules of Court nor the Court's own practice serve to deprive it entirely of functions relating to chambers, once those chambers have been formed. It is precisely the full Court that makes changes in the composition of a chamber, electing new members or approving new judges *ad hoc* to fill any vacancies that may arise and fixing time-limits for written proceedings. It is only natural that it should fall to the full Court to deal with a request for the *reformation* of the Chamber. It is a fact that Nicaragua's Application, intentionally addressed to the full Court, is also directly related to the composition of the Chamber. Of the five judges composing the Chamber, no more than a minority of two are currently Members of the Court. (The President of the Chamber, whose term of office in the Court has expired, continues to sit in the Chamber in accordance with Article 17 of the Rules of Court. The other two judges are judges *ad hoc* chosen by El Salvador and Honduras respectively.)

It is clear that the Court, which is responsible for the Chamber it has formed, has full confidence in the high professional skills of its members and in their judicial impartiality. It should be presumed that the Applicant has the same confidence. It is nonetheless very difficult to ignore the fact that the initial Parties have exercised a certain and by no means negligible influence on the composition of the Chamber, not only by choosing their respective judges *ad hoc* but also by giving the President of the Court their views "regarding the composition of the Chamber", in application of Article 17 of the Rules of Court, even though Article 26, paragraph 2, of the Statute expressly provides that the parties are only required to approve the Court's determination of "*The number of judges* to constitute such a chamber ..." (Emphasis added.)

Article 17, paragraph 2, of the Rules of Court permits a broader interpretation of this provision of the Statute, enabling the President to ascertain the views of the parties regarding those judges whom they would wish to be elected as members of a chamber. The Court, when forming a chamber, normally complies with those views. It follows that the initial parties do exercise an influence not only on the numerical, but also on the *personal* composition of the chamber.

The intervening State does not have this possibility and its procedural position before a chamber is not on a par with the position of the initial parties. Such an inequality might be especially harmful to the intervening party if it were to seek the reformation of the existing composition of a chamber or a modification of that chamber's mandate.

[pp. 14-15 **D.O. Tarassov**] What main conclusions can be drawn from these views of the initial Parties? In the first place, it is quite clear that their general attitude is not favourable to that aspect of Nicaragua's Application that relates to its request that the full Court, not the Chamber, should consider its suggestions regarding a possible reformation of the Chamber or reformulation of its mandate, and that they are, to put it bluntly, not in favour of any intervention by Nicaragua in the case. Could such a negative attitude have some impact upon the way in which the Applicant's request may be considered by the Chamber in its present composition? In theory, there could not be any such impact as all the members of a chamber, including the judges *ad hoc*, are independent of the parties and preserve their full impartiality during the whole of the proceedings in the case. Nobody, of course, should still be mindful of the procedural positions of the Parties during the formation of the chamber, and the various options available to them at that time. The same considerations hold good for all chambers and might be only slightly more specific in case of chambers formed on the basis of a *compromis*. Parties which have agreed by *compromis* to submit their dispute to a chamber may, if they both are not satisfied with the course of the proceedings or with the intermediate decisions of the chamber, put an end to it by a simple withdrawal of their *compromis* - although, in theory, the fact that this possibility exists can in no way exert pressure on the chamber. However, the problem is whether it is right that a State which has to protect what may be vital interests, and which finds itself in procedural circumstances like those currently affecting the procedural position of Nicaragua, should find itself entirely at the mercy of a theoretical construction of this kind. I am of the opinion that the Court, taking account of all the circumstances of the case and of the different submissions made in the Nicaraguan Application which, as was shown earlier, goes far beyond a simple request for permission to intervene and raises issues with which the Chamber is not competent to deal, should itself give the Applicant an opportunity to defend its own position before it in oral proceedings - or at least to defend its position with regard to the procedural issues. I think that such an attitude on the part of the Court would be particularly justified in that its governing documents provide it with no direct indications as to how to deal with an application for permission to intervene in a case pending before a chamber, in the event that such an application simultaneously makes a request for the reformation of that same chamber [20]. Any decision of the Court will accordingly establish an important precedent for future practice.

---

20 This lacuna in the guiding documents of the Court is quite understandable, however, as the Statute of the Court and the Rules of Court (even the most recent 1978 version) were elaborated and adopted at a time when *ad hoc* chambers for the most part did not exist. It is well known that, if procedural rules are to be both sound and helpful, they must be developed on the basis of prolonged practical experience and embody the sum total of such experience. The theoretical elaboration of the present rules in this field was mainly based on the good intention of making it easier for States to attain a peaceful settlement of their disputes while enhancing the activity of the International Court of Justice. It is significant that it is precisely the practical experience of recent chamber cases that has aroused interest in this useful and promising institution among the judges of the International Court of Justice (see dissenting opinion of Judge Shahabuddeen to this Order, p. 21, *infra*, footnote).

[pp. 16-17 **D.O. Tarassov**] According to Article 27 of the Statute, a judgment given by an *ad hoc* chamber is to be considered as rendered by the full Court. As a result of the present Order adopted by a majority of judges, the Applicant will have no more than two possible courses of action - it can either abandon its intention of preserving and defending its interests against possible violation as a result of judicial processes in the International Court of Justice or it can submit its Application to the Chamber. If it opts for the latter course, the Applicant will have to abide by the decision of five judges, only two of whom are Members of the Court, but whose decision will have the status of a judgment of the Court. In the event that permission to intervene is summarily rejected, or if the judgment on its merits fails to provide a proper safeguard of its lawful interests as an intervening Party, the Applicant will not be able to appeal, as the Court's judgment will have been rendered!

However, in theory, it might be possible in such a situation for the judgment to be adopted by a majority of non-members of the Court, with both Members of the Court voting against it. This possibility is no mere paradox - there are very important practical consequences for the Applicant. If the case were not to be considered by a chamber of the Court but by an Arbitration Tribunal, and if the decision of that Tribunal were to be seen by the third State as harmful to its interests, such a State would have the possibility of trying to defend those interests before the International Court of Justice, regardless of the fact that the Tribunal in question might have consisted entirely of Members of the International Court. However since, in the instant case, the Parties have decided not to submit their dispute to arbitration, but to refer it to a chamber of the Court, the third State is automatically deprived of that recourse to the full Court. Only as a result of hearings, with the full participation of all the States concerned and in which all those States would have had equal procedural rights, could the Court have properly arrived at a prima facie conclusion as to whether or not there were any possibilities of intrusion into the sphere of interests of the third State.

[p. 17 **D.O. Tarassov**] My vote against the present Order constitutes a reflection of my sincere hope that the decision of the Court, contained in this Order, will not be given the status of a precedent, serving to preclude - on purely formalistic grounds - any possibility of the Court considering questions relating to cases being dealt with by chambers but which those chambers are not able to resolve. Any such justification of future inaction could not only lead to a depreciation of the Court's own role, but might also bring about an unfortunate depreciation of the functioning of chambers by placing an insurmountable barrier between them and the full Court and, as a consequence, estranging them from the principal judicial organ of the United Nations. If that happened, *ad hoc* chambers would be transformed into some kind of hybrid between international judicial process and arbitration.

[p. 18 **D.O. Shahabuddeen**] Judged objectively and by universally accepted judicial standards, the selection of its members having been substantially determined or influenced by the Parties under the procedural arrangements referred to, the Chamber in this case cannot, in my respectful view, discharge the functions of the International Court of Justice, in its character as a court of justice, in relation to an application by a non-party for permission to intervene in the case pending before it. By itself disclaiming jurisdiction and instead leaving the Applicant with no recourse except to the Chamber, the Court effectively denies the Applicant its right to have its Application under Article 62 of the Statute judicially determined in the ordinary way.

[p. 19 **D.O. Shahabuddeen**] The finding of the Court that it is for the Chamber to deal with Nicaragua's Application is based essentially on the ground that the Chamber was formed to deal with the particular case and must also deal with proceedings incidental to it. In the normal case, I would agree. But, in the circumstances of this case, is the decision as logical as the Court suggests? Under the Court's own Rules, as amended in 1972 and revised in 1978, apart from two of the five members of the Chamber being *ad hoc* judges appointed as of right by the existing Parties, the remaining three were elected by the full Court to the Chamber after the Court had taken into account the views of the existing Parties as to the particular Members of the Court who should be so elected. Whether it is in fact so or not - and it is the Court which knows best - the Applicant is entitled to, and, as appears from its Application and written arguments, clearly does, entertain a reasonable apprehension that the three Members so elected were elected in conformity with the expressed wishes of the existing Parties. In substance, therefore, the Applicant is being told by the Court that it has no option but to submit to a Chamber all of whose five members it is reasonably entitled to feel have been practically hand-picked by the existing Parties. Conceivably, Nicaragua may nevertheless accept that option and go to the Chamber, and, if it does so, its Application may conceivably be granted by the Chamber. However, this possibility cannot affect the legal situation, as I see it. For it is not difficult to see why Nicaragua has not so far gone to the Chamber and why it has in fact come to the full Court - an attitude which is in itself the first practical illustration of how far an interested non-party State is likely to regard such a chamber as a legitimate manifestation of the Court. When its presentation is fairly read, Nicaragua obviously takes the view that the Chamber, as it stands, cannot discharge the functions of the International Court of Justice, considered as a court of justice, in relation to itself. That that is the central issue, inescapably presented, seems plain to me.

[p. 21 **D.O. Shahabuddeen**] The vice, then, in which the Court is held is this. Regardless of ultimate results, the Applicant has a right under Article 62 of the Court's

Statute to apply for permission to intervene. However, while closing its own doors to the Applicant, the full Court is unable, in my view, to indicate any judicially acceptable alternative forum to which the Applicant may turn. In consequence, the Applicant is effectively denied its right to have its Application for permission to intervene judicially considered.

[p. 34 **D.O. Shahabuddeen**] The material makes it clear that the concept of judges being selected by the parties was regarded as being a characteristic of arbitral procedures; that, as such, that concept was essentially opposed to the judicial character of the Court; that, on special grounds, it was, after anxious debate, nevertheless allowed a limited operation within the constitution of the Court in relation to *ad hoc* judges; but that this limited operation could not be extended consistently with the judicial character of the Court without an appropriate enabling amendment of its Statute.

[pp. 38-39 **D.O. Shahabuddeen**] Although considering that the names of members of an *ad hoc* chamber who were to be requested by the President to "step down" in favour of judges chosen by the parties could also be the subject of consultation between the President and the parties, Judge Jiménez de Aréchaga clearly recognized that what I would for convenience call the "standing-down procedure", as laid down by Article 31, paragraph 4, of the Statute, would continue to apply to such a chamber even after the 1972 amendments (Eduardo Jiménez de Aréchaga, *loc. cit.*, p. 3). A neglect in the Rules to reflect that fact was rightly cured by an appropriate change made in 1978 in Article 17, paragraph 2, of the Rules. As I sought to point out more fully in the separate opinion which I appended to the Order made in this case on 13 December 1989 (*I.C.J. Reports 1989*, pp. 165-167), the prescribed procedure was correctly observed in the case of the *Delimitation of the Maritime Boundary in the Gulf of Maine Area, Constitution of Chamber (I.C.J. Reports 1982*, pp. 4, 8 and 9). It was not applied in the case concerning *Elettronica Sicula S.p.A. (ELSI), Constitution of Chamber (I.C.J. Reports 1987*, pp. 3-4) for the reason that (however it came about) the elected judges included two serving national judges. It was not applied in the case concerning the *Frontier Dispute (Burkina Faso/Republic of Mali), Constitution of Chamber (I.C.J. Reports 1985*, pp. 6-7) nor in the case concerning the *Land, Island and Maritime Frontier Dispute (El Salvador/Honduras), Constitution of Chamber (I.C.J. Reports 1987*, p. 10). The Orders of Court in these two cases simply show the election of three serving judges and the addition of two named *ad hoc* judges. The Court did not, as it ought to have done under the prescribed procedure, elect five serving judges subject to two being asked to stand down in favour of *ad hoc* judges to be *later* chosen by the parties. Contrary to the laid down sequence, the two *ad hoc* judges were chosen by the parties *before* the election by the Court of any serving judges. The observance of the standing-down procedure prescribed by Article 31, paragraph 4, of the Statute made no practical sense in a situation in which the Court was in fact electing serving judges who had been previously designated by the parties (see Shabtai Rosenne, *Procedure in the International Court, A Commentary on the 1978 Rules of the International Court of Justice, 1983*, p. 43). The logic of allowing the parties a right to exercise "decisive influence" over selection would naturally lead to dispensation with that procedure. The question remains whether it was competent for the Court to confer such a right on them by Rules of Court.

A negative answer to that question is suggested by the inescapable fact that the standing-down procedure continues to apply to *ad hoc* chambers by virtue of the express provisions of Article 31, paragraph 4, of the Statute itself. Neither the Rules of Court nor any practice adopted by the Court can vary the scheme as laid down in those overriding provisions of the master law. Indeed, as has been noticed, the applicability of that scheme to *ad hoc* chambers was expressly and correctly recognized by an amendment made in Article 17, paragraph 2, of the Rules of Court in 1978. It applies to other chambers by virtue of Article 91, paragraph 2, of the Rules. What does therefore emerge is that the very decision to dispense with the standing-down procedure in relation to *ad hoc* chambers is an indication of the extent to which practical control over selection of serving judges as members of such chambers has been conceded to the parties; for it is only on this basis that the observance of a procedure still legally commanded both by the Statute and by the Rules would become the pointless ritual which presumably led to the decision to ignore its continuing existence in law.

[pp. 40-41 **D.O. Shahabuddeen**] The whole nature of the Court, as a court of justice, constitutes a prohibition, no less clear for being implied, against giving the parties any say in the selection of judges to hear a case, whether through the Rules of Court or otherwise, and whether in whole or in part, except in the case of *ad hoc* judges. So fundamental was that prohibition to the character of the Court as a court of justice, as distinguished from an arbitral body, that it was no more necessary to express it in its Statute than it would have been to do so in the constitution of any other "court of justice" within the normal acceptation of the meaning of this expression.

This implied prohibition is not neutralized by approaching the matter from the point of view of the doctrine of implied powers. True, the fact that specific powers are conferred on a body does not necessarily imply the non-existence of others. But the latter do not float around at large. In the last analysis, all the powers of a body must be conferred by its constituent instrument, whether expressly or impliedly.

[pp. 47-48 **D.O. Shahabuddeen**] To sum up, the field of operation of the rule-making power of the Court, as defined by Article 30 of the Statute, is wide but not unlimited. The Court, it may be said, has a certain autonomy in the exercise of its rule-making competence; but autonomy is not omnipotence, and that competence is not unbounded. Rules of Court could only be made in exercise of powers granted by the Statute, whether expressly or impliedly. The Statute did not expressly grant power to the Court to confer by Rules a right on the parties to have their views taken into account in the selection of serving judges to be members of an *ad hoc* chamber. Nor was any such power granted by the Statute impliedly: however generous may be the principle regulating the ascertainment of the extent of the Court's implied powers, such powers encounter an ultimate limit when they collide with the intrinsic nature of the Court itself. For the reasons given, the selection, whenever necessary, of serving judges to sit in any particular case is an integral part of the inalienable judicial power confided to the Court by the world community. The Court cannot, directly or indirectly, convey away that power in whole or in part, or share it with others, without destroying its essential character as a court of justice. A Rule of Court which purports to do so is contrary to the Statute.

[p. 48 **D.O. Shahabuddeen**] The foregoing considerations suggest that the requirement in Article 17, paragraph 2, of the Rules of Court 1978 for the President to ascertain the views of the parties regarding the "composition" of an *ad hoc* chamber should be construed harmoniously with the Statute, and that, when so construed, it is restricted to ascertainment of the views of the parties as to the "number" of members of the chamber. Failing that construction - a construction which does not correspond either with the general understanding of the provision or with the actual practice under it - it would seem that Article 17, paragraph 2, of the Rules is *pro tanto ultra vires* the Statute.

[p. 51 **D.O. Shahabuddeen**] Even if there is room for argument as to what is meant by the reference to "cases which they may have begun" in the governing provisions of Article 13, paragraph 3, of the Statute, it is not admissible to assign to that phrase one meaning in relation to cases heard before the full Court and another in relation to cases heard before a chamber. The form assumed by the Court in hearing a case has nothing to do with the question whether a case has been "begun" by a judge or not. The Court being in legal theory the same whether sitting *en banc* or in chamber, the question whether a judge has "begun" a case must be answered in the same way regardless of whether it is being heard before the one or the other. Whatever may be the meaning of the word "begun" as it appears in the Court's constituent text, that meaning can only be one and singular in relation to all judges. Different meanings may be given to the same word appearing in different places of an instrument or indeed in different places in the same provision of an instrument, but hardly to one and the same word appearing in a particular place in a particular provision, and certainly not where the meanings would be contradictory, as in this case [21].

21 Footnote omitted.

[p. 55 **D.O. Shahabuddeen**] In my opinion, reached with reluctance but with conviction, the methods by which the members of the Chamber have been selected do not satisfy the criteria required to enable it to discharge the judicial mission of the International Court of Justice, considered as a court of justice, in relation to the Applicant; and the fundamental reason for this is that the Chamber has been constituted not in accordance with the Statute, but in accordance with an unauthorized arrangement under which the Court has been essaying to transform itself into the Permanent Court of Arbitration, or something akin to it. This represents a major flaw which the Court, as the avowed guardian of its own judicial integrity, cannot correctly overlook. The existing practice may well continue unabated. My views may make no difference. It was nevertheless my duty to state them.

[pp. 56-57 **D.O. Shahabuddeen**] Viewing the matter at the level of general principles, I think it is first necessary to consider the relationship between the full Court and a chamber of any kind. No doubt, unless a chamber is indicated by the context, a reference in the Statute to the "Court" is a reference to the full Court, and evidently there are differences between these two bodies, but these differences are those between related and not mutually alien entities. In principle, the same Court is acting whether it acts through the full Court or through a duly established chamber. The first chamber judgment, given in 1924, began with the carefully chosen words, "The Court, sitting as a Chamber of Summary Procedure ...", and ended with a dispositif beginning significantly with the words, "For these reasons the Court decides..." (*Treaty of Neuilly, P.C.I.J., Series A, No. 3*, pp. 4 and 9 respectively). By Article 1 of the relevant Special Agreement, the case had been correspondingly submitted by the parties "to the Permanent Court of International Justice, in its Chamber for summary procedure ... (*P.C.I.J., Series C, No. 6*, p. 9). In effect, the functions of a chamber are as much the functions of the "Court" as are those of the full body. Thus, however desirable it may be for a chamber to be left to discharge its actual functions as autonomously as possible, the relationship between it and the full Court is not one between strangers. Nicaragua has drawn attention to significant instances of action taken by the full Court in relation to a chamber even after the latter has been established. The full Court, having set up a chamber, cannot interfere in its actual work; but I think it retains a continuing responsibility to ensure that the composition of the chamber is such as to enable it to function with a sufficient degree of procedural rectitude in order to qualify it as a convincing manifestation of the Court as a court of justice. If I mistake not, something of this view is implicit in the reference in the Court's Order to its "power to form a chamber to deal with a particular case, and consequently to regulate matters concerning its composition".

Under the system as it has so far worked, an *ad hoc* chamber, being composed of judges whose selection has been substantially influenced, if not determined, by the original parties (a proposition which cannot credibly be controverted), cannot function as a normal court of justice either in relation to an application for permission to intervene or, if the application is granted, in relation to the applicant as an intervening party to the case on the merits. A request for permission to intervene cannot but be coupled, as in this case, with a request for an appropriate reformation of the chamber. *Ex hypothesi*, the latter is beyond the competence of the chamber, which is thus incapable of dealing with either branch of the application.

[pp. 58-59 **D.O. Shahabuddeen**] The Court has cited the *Haya de la Torre* principle to the effect that "every intervention is incidental to the proceedings in a case" (*I.C.J. Reports 1951*, p. 76). In that case (decided under Article 63 of the Statute), the question was whether the purported intervention "actually relate[d] to the subject-matter of the pending proceedings" (*ibid.*). That is not the question here. While I accept that the principle would ordinarily mean that an application for permission to intervene under Article 62 of the Statute should be made to the tribunal dealing with the merits of the matter, this presupposes that the tribunal is one which can act judicially in relation to the application. That case was not concerned with the kind of issues arising here as to what should be done to give real effect to the applicant's right to apply where the tribunal, which should ordinarily act, does not satisfy the generally recognized criteria applicable to a court of justice in so far as the applicant at any rate is concerned. In particular, that case did not involve the concomitant application of the principle of equality of States which would ineluctably be breached if Nicaragua's only remedy was to go before a chamber composed of members selected as mentioned above.

[pp. 60-61 **D.O. Shahabuddeen**] Since, in my view, the Rules do not effectively provide for the case, the competence to deal with an application for permission to intervene in such a case falls to be considered as remaining with the full Court in keeping with the wording of Article 62 of the Statute. Under paragraph 1 of this, the request for permission to intervene is to be made to the "Court". Under paragraph 2, the decision is made by the "Court". Article 3 of the Statute makes it clear that references to the "Court" are references to the full Court. The Court may of course act through a chamber in proper instances. But where, as here, the Court cannot properly act through a chamber, the Court must of necessity act by itself. The jurisdiction belongs primarily to the Court and is retained by it to the extent that it has not, for any reason, become effectually exercisable by the chamber.

I appreciate that, by reason of the Special Agreement, it may be said that the case is pending before the Chamber and not before the Court. But if, as I consider, the right to apply for permission to intervene is applicable in relation to a case pending before such a chamber, this must be so because "the case" is in legal theory pending before the "Court" within the meaning of Article 62 of the Statute.

[pp. 61-62 **D.O. Shahabuddeen**] In sum, but with respect, I consider that the Court has misconceived Nicaragua's case. The essence of that case, as I understand it, is that the methods by which the Chamber has been formed entitle Nicaragua to take the view that the Chamber cannot exercise the judicial functions of the International Court of Justice in so far as Nicaragua is concerned. The Order of Court nowhere addresses this problem. *The Haya de la Torre* principle relied upon by the Court does not by itself suffice to provide a solution to that problem. A solution, if there is one, must, in the circumstances of this particular case, take account of the principle of equality of States, and there is no possibility of satisfying this principle without appropriate action taken by the full Court within the framework of the very special relationship existing between itself and the Chamber.

For these reasons, I would uphold the contention of Nicaragua that the full Court has jurisdiction to entertain its Application.

Land, Island and
Maritime Frontier Dispute
(El Salvador/Honduras)
Composition of Chamber,
Order of 13 December 1989,
I.C.J. Reports 1989, p. 162

[pp. 171-172 **S.O. Shahabuddeen**] The right to appoint an *ad hoc* judge touches the composition of the Court and consequently is directly governed by the Court's constituent instrument, namely, its Statute. Article 31 is the particular provision of the Statute concerned with the process of constituting a person as an *ad hoc* judge. It does not seem to offer the Court a role at any point in that process, either directly or indirectly through the other provisions referred to in it. The limits of the Court's rule-making power under Article 30 of the Statute (however generously construed) would not enable it, by making Rules of Court, to assume a role in that process not entrusted to it by the Statute. The Statute appears to leave the matter to the State concerned. This would accord with the fact that the institution of *ad hoc* judges as part of the composition of the Bench of the Court was effectively a limited carry-over from arbitral experience.

In sum, it is difficult to identify any acts of the Court from which an *ad hoc* judge may be said to derive his authority to act. Though recognizing the force of arguments to the opposite effect, on balance I prefer the view that the appointment of such a judge is constituted by the act of the State concerned in choosing him, the role of the Court being limited to the negative one of determining whether any ground (whether or not going to the validity of his appointment) exists for debarying him from sitting in the case. If this is correct, it leads to the view that the Order made today is not constitutive of an appointment made by the Court but is merely a formal judicial record of an appointment made by the State concerned. I would like in turn to record that it is on the basis of this understanding that I support the Order.

Elettronica Sicula S.p.A. (ELSI)
Judgement of 20 July 1989
I.C.J. Reports 1989, p. 15

[pp. 41-42] It is common ground between the Parties that the Court has jurisdiction in the present case, under Article 36, paragraph 1, of its Statute, and Article XXVI of the Treaty of Friendship, Commerce and Navigation, of 2 June 1948 ("the FCN Treaty"), between Italy and the United States; which Article reads:
"Any dispute between the High Contracting Parties as to the interpretation or the application of this Treaty, which the High Contracting Parties shall not satisfactorily adjust by diplomacy, shall be submitted to the International Court of Justice, unless the High Contracting Parties shall agree to settlement by some other pacific means."

The jurisdiction is thus confined to questions of "the interpretation or the application" of the FCN Treaty and Protocols and of the Agreement Supplementing the Treaty between the United States of America and the Italian Republic, of 26 September 1951 (which Agreement is hereinafter called "the Supplementary Agreement"), Article IX of which provides that it is to "constitute an integral part" of the FCN Treaty. This same jurisdiction may accordingly be exercised by this Chamber, created by the Court to deal with this case by virtue of Article 26, paragraph 2, of its Statute, and Articles 17 and 18 of its Rules, at the request of and after consultation with the Parties.

Frontier Dispute, (Burkina Faso/Republic of Mali),
Provisional Measures, Order of 10 January 1986
I.C.J. Reports 1986, p. 3

[p. 9] Whereas, in particular, when two States jointly decide to have recourse to a Chamber of the Court, the principal judicial organ of the United Nations, with a view to the peaceful settlement of a dispute, in accordance with Article 2, paragraph 3, and Article 33 of the Charter of the United Nations, and incidents subsequently occur which not merely are likely to extend or aggravate the dispute but comprise a resort to force which is irreconcilable with the principle of the peaceful settlement of international disputes, there can be no doubt of the Chamber's power and duty to indicate, if need be, such provisional measures as may conduce to the due administration of justice;

3.3. Judges *ad hoc*

Land, Island and
Maritime Frontier Dispute
(El Salvador/Honduras)
Composition of Chamber,
Order of 13 December 1989,
I.C.J. Reports 1989, p. 162

[pp. 171-172 **S.O. Shahabuddeen**] The right to appoint an *ad hoc* judge touches the composition of the Court and consequently is directly governed by the Court's constituent instrument, namely, its Statute. Article 31 is the particular provision of the Statute concerned with the process of constituting a person as an *ad hoc* judge. It does not seem to offer the Court a role at any point in that process, either directly or indirectly through the other provisions referred to in it. The limits of the Court's rule-making power under Article 30 of the Statute (however generously construed) would not enable it, by making Rules of Court, to assume a role in that process not entrusted to it by the Statute. The Statute appears to leave the matter to the State concerned. This would accord with the fact that the institution of *ad hoc* judges as part of the composition of the Bench of the Court was effectively a limited carry-over from arbitral experience.

In sum, it is difficult to identify any acts of the Court from which an *ad hoc* judge may be said to derive his authority to act. Though recognizing the force of arguments to the opposite effect, on balance I prefer the view that the appointment of such a judge is constituted by the act of the State concerned in choosing him, the role of the Court being limited to the negative one of determining whether any ground (whether or not going to the validity of his appointment) exists for debarring him from sitting in the case. If this is correct, it leads to the view that the Order made today is not constitutive of an appointment made by the Court but is merely a formal judicial record of an appointment made by the State concerned. I would like in turn to record that it is on the basis of this understanding that I support the Order.

3.5. Preliminary Objections

Cf. also: The Optional Clause, Reservations, supra III, 2.3.3.

Military and Paramilitary Activities
(Nicaragua/United States of America)
Merits. J. 27.6.1986
I.C.J. Reports 1986, p. 14

[pp. 29-31] The present case is the first in which the Court has had occasion to exercise the power first provided for in the 1972 Rules of Court to declare that a preliminary objection "does not possess, in the circumstances of the case, an exclusively preliminary character". It may therefore be appropriate to take this opportunity to comment briefly on the rationale of this provision of the Rules, in the light of the problems to which the handling of preliminary objections has given rise. In exercising its rule-making power under Article 30 of the Statute, and generally in approaching the complex issues which may be raised by the determination of appropriate procedures for the settlement of disputes, the Court has kept in view an approach defined by the Permanent Court of International Justice. That Court found that it was at liberty to adopt

"the principle which it considers best calculated to ensure the administration of justice, most suited to procedure before an international tribunal and most in conformity with the fundamental principles of international law" (*Mavrommatis Palestine Concessions, P.C.I.J., Series A, No. 2*, p. 16).

Under the Rules of Court dating back to 1936 (which on this point reflected still earlier practice), the Court had the power to join an objection to the merits "whenever the interests of the good administration of justice require it" (*Panevezys-Saldutiskis Railway, P.C.I.J., Series A /B, No. 75*, p. 56), and in particular where the Court, if it were to decide on the objection, "would run the risk of adjudicating on questions which appertain to the merits of the case or of prejudging their solution" (*ibid.*). If this power was exercised, there was always a risk, namely that the Court would ultimately decide the case on the preliminary objection, after requiring the parties fully to plead the merits, - and this did in fact occur (*Barcelona Traction, Light and Power Company, Limited, Second Phase, I.C.J. Reports 1970*, p. 3). The result was regarded in some quarters as an unnecessary prolongation of an expensive and time-consuming procedure.

Taking into account the wide range of issues which might be presented as preliminary objections, the question which the Court faced was whether to revise the Rules so as to exclude for the future the possibility of joinder to the merits, so that every objection would have to be resolved at the preliminary stage, or to seek a solution which would be more flexible. The solution of considering all preliminary objections immediately and rejecting all possibility of a joinder to the merits had many advocates and presented many advantages. In the *Panevezys-Saldutiskis Railway* case, the Permanent Court defined a preliminary objection as one

"submitted for the purpose of excluding an examination by the Court of the merits of the case, and being one upon which the Court can give a decision without in any way adjudicating upon the merits" (*P.C.I.J., Series A /B. No. 76*. p. 22).

If this view is accepted then of course every preliminary objection should be dealt with immediately without touching the merits, or involving parties in argument of the merits of the case. To find out, for instance, whether there is a dispute between the parties or whether the Court has jurisdiction, does not normally require an analysis of the merits of the case. However that does not solve all questions of preliminary objections, which may, as experience has shown, be to some extent bound up with the merits. The final solution adopted in 1972, and maintained in the 1978 Rules, concerning preliminary objections is the following: the Court is to give its decision

"by which it shall either uphold the objection, reject it, or declare that the objection does not possess, in the circumstances of the case, an exclusively preliminary character. If the Court rejects the objection, or declares that it does not possess an exclusively preliminary character, it shall fix time-limits for the further proceedings." (Art. 79, para. 7.)

While the variety of issues raised by preliminary objections cannot possibly be foreseen, practice has shown that there are certain kinds of preliminary objections which can be disposed of by the Court at an early stage without examination of the merits. Above all, it is clear that a question of jurisdiction is one which requires decision at the preliminary stage of the proceedings. The new rule enumerates the objections contemplated as follows:

"Any objection by the respondent to the jurisdiction of the Court or to the admissibility of the application, or other objection the decision upon which is requested before any further proceedings on the merits ..." (Art. 79. para. 1.)

It thus presents one clear advantage: that it qualifies certain objections as preliminary, making it quite clear that when they are exclusively of that character they will have to be decided upon immediately, but if they are not, especially when the character of the objections is not exclusively preliminary because they contain both preliminary aspects and other aspects relating to the merits, they will have to be dealt with at the stage of the merits. This approach also tends to discourage the unnecessary prolongation of proceedings at the jurisdictional stage.

Elettronica Sicula S.p.A. (ELSI)
Judgment of 20 July 1989
I.C.J. Reports 1989, p. 15

[p. 49] While the jurisdiction of the Chamber is not in doubt, an objection to the admissibility of the present case was entered by Italy in its Counter-Memorial, on the ground of an alleged failure of the two United States corporations, Raytheon and Machlett, on whose behalf the United States claim is brought, to exhaust the local remedies available to them in Italy. This objection, which the Parties agreed should be heard and determined in the framework of the merits, must, therefore, be considered at the outset.

**Aerial Incident of 3 July 1988 (Islamic Republic of Iran v. United States of America)
Order of 13 December 1989,
I.C.J. Reports 1989, p. 132**

[pp. 133-134] Whereas at a meeting between the President of the Court and the Agents of the Parties, convened by the President, pursuant to Article 31 of the Rules of Court, and held on 1 September 1989, the Agent of the United States of America stated that, as indicated in a letter filed in the Registry the same day, his Government intended to file preliminary objections to jurisdiction and admissibility prior to the filing of a Memorial by the Applicant;

Whereas at a further meeting between the President of the Court and the Agents of the Parties held on 12 September 1989 the Agent of the Islamic Republic of Iran stated that his Government contended that a preliminary objection should not be filed before the Memorial, and requested that appropriate time-limits be fixed for the written proceedings; and whereas the President of the Court then invited the Parties to state their respective positions more fully in writing with a view to a decision by the Court on the procedural question thus raised;

Whereas by a letter dated 26 September 1989 the Agent of the United States confirmed his Government's intention, and explained what was in the contention of the United States the legal basis in the Statute and Rules of Court for the filing of a preliminary objection prior to the filing of a Memorial by the Applicant;

Whereas by a letter dated 11 October 1989 the Agent of Iran contended on behalf of his Government that, for reasons explained in the letter, the United States was estopped and time-barred from raising jurisdictional questions; that even if the United States were still entitled to raise preliminary objections there was, for the reasons stated in the letter, no legal basis for the submission of preliminary objections prior to the filing of the Memorial in the present case; and whereas the Agent of Iran therefore requested the Court to fix time-limits for the written proceedings;

Whereas the time-limit for filing a preliminary objection is fixed by Article 79 of the Rules of Court, which provides that such an objection shall be made "within the time-limit fixed for the delivery of the Counter-Memorial"; whereas the Court is not at the present time seised of a preliminary objection by the United States; and whereas accordingly the Court is not called upon, at the present stage of the proceedings, to pronounce on the questions of preclusion and estoppel raised by Iran, whose views in this respect may be put forward later;

Whereas, in accordance with Article 79, paragraph 1, of the Rules of Court, while a respondent which wishes to submit a preliminary objection is entitled before doing so to be informed as to the nature of the claim by the submission of a Memorial by the Applicant, it may nevertheless file its objection earlier, the Court, unanimously,

Fixes the following time-limits for the written proceedings:

12 June 1990 for the Memorial of the Islamic Republic of Iran;
10 December 1990 for the Counter-Memorial of the United States of America.

[p. 135 **Decl. Oda**] As observed in the Order, "the Court is not at the present time seised of a preliminary objection by the United States". This being so, it seems to me that it is not required at this stage to take any decision on whether the preliminary objection may be submitted before the filing of the Memorial. Moreover, if the Court is to make such an important interpretation of its Rules as is given in the passage quoted above, this should, in my view, be dealt with in the operative part, not in the preambular part of the Order.

[pp. 136-137 **S.O. Schwebel**] There appears to be no difference in the Court about the tenor of the terms of the Rules, i.e., of the provisions of Article 79. Paragraph 1 of Article 79 provides:

"*Any* objection by the respondent to the jurisdiction of the Court ... the decision upon which is requested before *any* further proceedings on the merits, shall be made in writing within the time-limit fixed for the delivery of the Counter-Memorial.. ." (Emphasis added.)

Paragraph 3 provides:

"Upon receipt by the Registry of a preliminary objection, the proceedings on the merits *shall* be suspended and the Court ... shall fix the time-limit within which the other party may present a written statement of its observations and submissions ..." (Emphasis added.)

It follows that not only some but "any" - that is to say, "no matter which", "all", "every" (*Webster's New International Dictionary of the English Language*, 2nd ed., unabridged, 1945, p. 121) - objection by the respondent to the jurisdiction of the Court, the decision upon which objection is requested before "any" further proceedings on the merits, shall be dealt with as prescribed by Article 79. "Any" further proceedings on the merits must be understood to be just that: that is, all such proceedings, whether they be the Memorial (if the preliminary objection is filed before the Memorial has been filed), or subsequent pleadings, written or oral. The sole qualifications to this rule are that the objection shall be made "in writing" and "within the time-limit fixed for the delivery of the Counter-Memorial". The outer time-limit so fixed clearly embraces the period of time between the filing of the Application and the filing of the applicant's Memorial on the merits as well as the time between the filing of the Memorial and the delivery of the Counter-Memorial. Upon receipt by the Registry of a preliminary objection, the proceedings on the merits "shall" - i.e., must - be suspended; this is a mandatory provision to which the Court gives automatic effect.

That this interpretation of the rule is the correct interpretation is supported by the published references to the *travaux préparatoires* of Article 79 found in an authoritative article by Judge Jiménez de Aréchaga, then President of the Court.

[pp. 138-139 **S.O. Schwebel**] There are a number of cases in which the respondent did not appear but in which, nevertheless, it made manifest its objections to the jurisdiction on which the applicant relied. That is to say, while, because of its non-participation, the respondent could not and did not file a preliminary objection strictly so-called and so denominated by it, at the same time it brought to the attention of the Court its objections to the Court's jurisdiction. It is significant that, in these cases, the preliminary objections which, had the respondent been appearing in the case, could have been regularly filed and determined either before or after the filing of the applicant's Memorial, were in substance uniformly determined before the filing of any Memorial. While these cases are not dispositive, they accordingly support rather than counter the terms of the Rules.

[pp. 158-159 **S.O. Shahabuddeen**] Under the strict terms of Article 79, paragraph 1, of the Rules of Court, a respondent would be entitled as of right to file a preliminary objection before the disclosure of the merits of the applicant's claim through its Memorial. And that is a right not to be underestimated. But that right has to be balanced against possibly substantial injustice which an applicant might suffer if its case were dismissed on a preliminary objection before it had the opportunity, through its Memorial, of developing and supplementing its application on points of possible deficiency pursuant to a right to do so which it not unreasonably thought it had under the rule as interpreted and applied by the Court in the course of its own practice. Had it not been for the existence of the practice, such an applicant's application might have been more fully framed in the first instance. In my opinion, the balance when struck speaks with persuasive fairness in favour of the continuance of that practice and of the corresponding interpretation of the Rules which it portrays. If there is to be a change - and there may be good reason why there should be - it should be made by way of a formal amendment of the Rules designed to take effect prospectively, and not by way of a decision of the Court retrospectively invalidating a practice of its own creation upon which reasonable expectations have been founded.

[pp. 159-160 **S.O. Shahabuddeen**] Though not without hesitation - for the position is not quite tidy and the logic of development not fully revealed - I reach the conclusion that, while in principle a respondent has a right to file its preliminary objection before the applicant's Memorial is filed and while in some cases recourse to that right may be perfectly justifiable, the Court may exercise a discretion both to decline to recognize or treat with a preliminary objection so filed and to direct that it be filed after the filing of the Memorial. The terms and grounds of the proposed preliminary objections not having been disclosed, there is no apparent basis at this stage for considering a possible departure in this case from the usual way in which it is considered that that discretion should be exercised. In the result, the only course is to make an Order fixing time-limits for pleadings (including any preliminary objections). This has been done, and this I support. But, for the reasons given, I consider that the last recital of the Court's Order lacks internal balance in that -

(i) the recital focuses on the entitlement of a respondent to defer the filing of its preliminary objection until after it has been "informed as to the nature of the claim by the submission of a Memorial by the Applicant" but neglects to balance this by taking account of what, on the other hand, seems to be a recognized entitlement of an applicant to supplement its application through its Memorial on matters of fact or law which could help to protect it against an eventual preliminary objection; and

(ii) the recital focuses on the entitlement of a respondent to "file its objection earlier" (i.e., before the Memorial), but neglects to balance this by taking account of what, on the other hand, seems to be a discretion of the Court to decline to recognize or treat with an objection so filed and to direct that it be filed after the filing of the Memorial.

In sum, the recital in question approaches the procedural situation as if it were designed solely to confer options on a respondent. I am of opinion that the procedural regime actually in force (that is to say, the Rules of Court as well as the practice of the Court) is both more flexible and more balanced, and that, in particular, there are rights and expectations of an applicant which are also to be considered but which the recital does not take into account. I accept that, in law, a respondent has a right to file its preliminary objection before the filing of the Memorial. But that is not the whole picture, and the whole picture is not projected by the recital in question. Whence this reservation to that effect.

3.6. The Procedure in Default of Appearance

Military and Paramilitary Activities
(Nicaragua/United States of America)
Merits. J. 27.6.1986
I.C.J. Reports 1986, p. 14

[pp. 23-26] When a State named as party to proceedings before the Court decides not to appear in the proceedings, or not to defend its case, the Court usually expresses regret, because such a decision obviously has a negative impact on the sound administration of justice (cf. *Fisheries Jurisdiction, I.C.J. Reports 1973*, p. 7, para. 12; p. 54, para. 13; *I.C.J. Reports 1974*, p. 9, para. 17; p. 181, para. 18; *Nuclear Tests, I.C.J. Reports 1974*, p. 257, para. 15; p. 461, para. 15; *Aegean Sea Continental Shelf, I.C.J. Reports 1978*, p. 7, para. 15; *United States Diplomatic and Consular Staff in Tehran, I.C.J. Reports 1980*, p. 18, para. 33). In the present case, the Court regrets even more deeply the decision of the respondent State not to participate in the present phase of the proceedings, because this decision was made after the United States had participated fully in the proceedings on the request for provisional measures, and the proceedings on jurisdiction and admissibility. Having taken part in the proceedings to argue that the Court lacked jurisdiction, the United States thereby acknowledged that the Court had the power to make a finding on its own jurisdiction to rule upon the merits. It is not possible to argue that the Court had jurisdiction only to declare that it lacked jurisdiction. In the normal course of events, for a party to appear before a court entails acceptance of the possibility of the court's finding against that party. Furthermore the Court is bound to emphasize that the non-participation of a party in the proceedings at any stage of the case cannot, in any circumstances, affect the validity of its judgment. Nor does such validity depend upon the acceptance of that judgment by one party. The fact that a State purports to "reserve its rights" in respect of a future decision of the Court, after the Court has determined that it has jurisdiction, is clearly of no effect on the validity of that decision. Under Article 36, paragraph 6, of its Statute, the Court has jurisdiction to determine any dispute as to its own jurisdiction, and its judgment on that matter, as on the merits, is final and binding on the parties under Articles 59 and 60 of the Statute (cf. *Corfu Channel, Judgment of 15 December 1949 I.C.J. Reports 1949*, p. 248).

When Article 53 of the Statute applies, the Court is bound to "satisfy itself, not only that it has jurisdiction in accordance with Articles 36 and 37, but also that the claim" of the party appearing is well founded in fact and law. In the present case, the Court has had the benefit of both Parties pleading before it at the earlier stages of the procedure, those concerning the request for the indication of provisional measures and to the questions of jurisdiction and admissibility. By its Judgment of 26 November 1984, the Court found, *inter alia*, that it had jurisdiction to entertain the case ; it must however take steps to "satisfy itself" that the claims of the Applicant are "well founded in fact and law". The question of the application of Article 53 has been dealt with by the Court in a number of previous cases, referred to above, and the Court does not therefore find it necessary to recapitulate the content of these decisions. The reasoning adopted to dispose of the basic problems arising was essentially the same, although the words used may have differed slightly from case to case. Certain points of principle may however be restated here. A State which decides not to appear must accept the consequences of its decision, the first of which is that the case will continue without its participation; the State which has chosen not to appear remains a party to the case, and is bound by the eventual judgment in accordance with Article 59 of the Statute. There is however no question of a judgment automatically in favour of the party appearing, since the Court is required, as mentioned above, to "satisfy itself" that that party's claim is well founded in fact and law.

The use of the term "satisfy itself" in the English text of the Statute (and in the French text the term "s'assurer") implies that the Court must attain the same degree of certainty as in any other case that the claim of the party appearing is sound in law, and, so far as the nature of the case permits, that the facts on which it is based are supported by convincing evidence. For the purpose of deciding whether the claim is well founded in law, the principle *jura novit curia* signifies that the Court is not solely dependent on the argument of the parties before it with respect to the applicable law (cf. *"Lotus", P.C.I.J., Series A, No. 10*, p. 31), so that the absence of one party has less impact. As the Court observed in the *Fisheries Jurisdiction* cases:

"The Court ..., as an international judicial organ, is deemed to take judicial notice of international law, and is therefore required in a case falling under Article 53 of the Statute, as in any other case, to consider on its own initiative all rules of international law which may be relevant to the settlement of the dispute. It being the duty of the Court itself to ascertain and apply the relevant law in the given circumstances of the case, the burden of establishing or proving rules of international law cannot be imposed upon any of the parties, for the law lies within the judicial knowledge of the Court." (*I.C.J. Reports 1974*, p. 9, para. 17; p. 181, para. 18.)

Nevertheless the views of the parties to a case as to the law applicable to their dispute are very material, particularly, as will be explained below (paragraphs 184 and 185), when those views are concordant. In the present case, the burden laid upon the Court is therefore somewhat lightened by the fact that the United States participated in the earlier phases of the case, when it submitted certain arguments on the law which have a bearing also on the merits.

As to the facts of the case, in principle the Court is not bound to confine its consideration to the material formally submitted to it by the parties (cf. *Brazilian Loans, P.C.I.J., Series A, No. 20/21*, p. 124; *Nuclear Tests, I.C.J. Reports 1974*, pp. 263-264, paras. 31, 32). Nevertheless, the Court cannot by its own enquiries entirely make up for the absence of one of the Parties; that absence, in a case of this kind involving extensive questions of fact, must necessarily limit the extent to which the Court is informed of the facts. It would furthermore be an over-simplification to conclude that the only detrimental consequence of the absence of a party is the lack of opportunity to submit argument and evidence in support of its own case. Proceedings before the Court call for vigilance by all. The absent party also forfeits the opportunity to counter the factual allegations of its opponent. It is of course for the party appearing to prove the allegations it makes, yet as the Court has held:

"While Article 53 thus obliges the Court to consider the submissions of the Party which appears, it does not compel the Court to examine their accuracy in all their details; for this might in certain unopposed cases prove impossible in practice." (*Corfu Channel, I.C.J. Reports 1949*, p. 248.)

While these are the guiding principles, the experience of previous cases in which one party has decided not to appear shows that something more is involved. Though formally absent from the proceedings, the party in question frequently submits to the Court letters and documents, in ways and by means not contemplated by the Rules. The Court has thus to strike a balance. On the one hand, it is valuable for the Court to know the views of both parties in whatever form those views may have been expressed. Further, as the Court noted in 1974. where one party is not appearing "it is especially incumbent upon the Court to satisfy itself that it is in possession of all the available facts" (*Nuclear Tests, I.C.J. Reports 1974*, p. 263, para. 31 p. 468. para. 32). On the other hand, the Court has to emphasize that the equality of the parties to the dispute must remain the basic principle for the Court. The intention of Article 53 was that in a case of non-appearance neither party should be placed at a disadvantage; therefore the party which declines to appear cannot be permitted to profit from its absence, since this would amount to placing the party appearing at a disadvantage. The provisions of the Statute and Rules of Court concerning the presentation of pleadings and evidence are designed to secure a proper administration of justice, and a fair and equal opportunity for each party to comment on its opponent's contentions. The treatment to be given by the Court to communications or material emanating from the absent party must be determined by the weight to be given to these different considerations, and is not susceptible of rigid definition in the form of a precise general rule. The vigilance which the Court can exercise when aided by the presence of both parties to the proceedings has a counterpart in the special care it has to devote to the proper administration of justice in a case in which only one party is present.

[p. 320 **D.O. Schwebel**] ... considerations of burden of proof are beside the point, because the real point is that, where objections are raised to the appearing party's contentions, that party must convince the Court that those objections are unfounded if the Court is to meet the standard which Article 53 imposes.

In my view, the correct interpretation of Article 53 is that it affords the appearing State no advantage beyond that which it enjoys by reason of the non-appearing State's absence. If, in a given case, such as the one before the Court, the non-appearing party (or the Court or a judge) raise an affirmative defence to the claim, the appearing party must demonstrate that the defence is not good in order to prevail.

3.7. Evidence

Military and Paramilitary Activities
(Nicaragua/United States of America)
Merits. J. 27.6.1986
I.C.J. Reports 1986, p. 14

[p. 24] The use of the term "satisfy itself" in the English text of the Statute (and in the French text the term "s'assurer") implies that the Court must attain the same degree of certainty as in any other case that the claim of the party appearing is sound in law, and, so far as the nature of the case permits, that the facts on which it is based are supported by convincing evidence.

[pp. 39-41] The Court is bound by the relevant provisions of its Statute and its Rules relating to the system of evidence, provisions devised to guarantee the sound administration of justice, while respecting the equality of the parties. The presentation of evidence is governed by specific rules relating to, for instance, the observance of time-limits, the communication of evidence to the other party, the submission of observations on it by that party, and the various forms of challenge by each party of the other's evidence. The absence of one of the parties restricts this procedure to some extent. The Court is careful, even where both parties appear, to give each of them the same opportunities and chances to produce their evidence ; when the situation is complicated by the non-appearance of one of them, then *a fortiori* the Court regards it as essential to guarantee as perfect equality as possible between the parties. Article 53 of the Statute therefore obliges the Court to employ whatever means and resources may enable it to satisfy itself whether the submissions of the applicant State are well-founded in fact and law, and simultaneously to safeguard the essential principles of the sound administration of justice.

The Court should now indicate how these requirements have to be met in this case so that it can properly fulfil its task under that Article of its Statute. In so doing, it is not unaware that its role is not a passive one; and that, within the limits of its Statute and Rules, it has freedom in estimating the value of the various elements of evidence, though it is clear that general principles of judicial procedure necessarily govern the determination of what can be regarded as proved.

In this context, the Court has the power, under Article 50 of its Statute, to entrust "any individual, body, bureau, commission or other organization that it may select, with the task of carrying out an enquiry or giving an expert opinion", and such a body could be a group of judges selected from among those sitting in the case. In the present case, however, the Court felt it was unlikely that an enquiry of this kind would be practical or desirable, particularly since such a body, if it was properly to perform its task, might have found it necessary to go not only to the applicant State, but also to several other neighbouring countries, and even to the respondent State, which had refused to appear before the Court.

At all events, in the present case the Court has before it documentary material of various kinds from various sources. A large number of documents have been supplied in the form of reports in press articles, and some also in the form of extracts from books. Whether these were produced by the applicant State, or by the absent Party before it ceased to appear in the proceedings, the Court has been careful to treat them with great caution; even if they seem to meet high standards of objectivity, the Court regards them not as evidence capable of proving facts, but as material which can nevertheless contribute, in some circumstances, to corroborating the existence of a fact, i.e., as illustrative material additional to other sources of evidence.

However, although it is perfectly proper that press information should not be treated in itself as evidence for judicial purposes, public knowledge of a fact may nevertheless be established by means of these sources of information, and the Court can attach a certain amount of weight to such public knowledge. In the case of *United States Diplomatic and Consular Staff in Tehran*, the Court referred to facts which "are, for the most part, matters of public knowledge which have received extensive coverage in the world press and in radio and television broadcasts from Iran and other countries" (*I.C.J. Reports 1980*, p. 9, para. 12). On the basis of information, including press and broadcast material, which was "wholly consistent and concordant as to the main facts and circumstances of the case", the Court was able to declare that it was satisfied that the allegations of fact were well-founded (*ibid.*, p. 10, para. 13). The Court has however to show particular caution in this area. Widespread reports of a fact may prove on closer examination to derive from a single source, and such reports, however numerous, will in such case have no greater value as evidence than the original source. It is with this important reservation that the newspaper reports supplied to the Court should be examined in order to assess the facts of the case, and in particular to ascertain whether such facts were matters of public knowledge.

The material before the Court also includes statements by representatives of States, sometimes at the highest political level. Some of these statements were made before official organs of the State or of an international or regional organization, and appear in the official records of those bodies. Others, made during press conferences or interviews, were reported by the local or international press. The Court takes the view that statements of this kind, emanating from high-ranking official political figures, sometimes indeed of the highest rank, are of particular probative value when they acknowledge facts or conduct unfavourable to the State represented by the person who made them. They may then be construed as a form of admission.

However, it is natural also that the Court should treat such statements with caution, whether the official statement was made by an authority of the Respondent or of the Applicant. Neither Article 53 of the Statute, nor any other ground, could justify a selective approach, which would have undermined the consistency of the Court's methods and its elementary duty to ensure equality between the Parties. The Court must take account of the manner in which the statements were made public; evidently, it cannot treat them as having the same value irrespective of whether the text is to be found in an official national or international publication, or in a book or newspaper. It must also take note whether the text of the official statement in question appeared in the language used by the author or on the basis of a translation (cf. *I.C.J. Reports 1980*, p. 10, para. 13). It may also be relevant whether or not such a statement was brought to the Court's knowledge by official communications filed in conformity with the relevant requirements of the Statute and Rules of Court. Furthermore, the Court has inevitably had sometimes to interpret the statements, to ascertain precisely to what degree they constituted acknowledgments of a fact.

At the hearings in this case, the applicant State called five witnesses to give oral evidence, and the evidence of a further witness was offered in the form of an affidavit "subscribed and sworn" in the United States, District of Columbia, according to the formal requirements in force in that place. A similar affidavit, sworn by the United States Secretary of State, was annexed to the Counter-Memorial of the United States on the questions of jurisdiction and admissibility. One of the witnesses presented by the applicant State was a national of the respondent State, formerly in the employ of a government agency the activity of which is of a confidential kind, and his testimony was kept strictly within certain limits ; the witness was evidently concerned not to contravene the legislation of his country of origin. In addition, annexed to the Nicaraguan Memorial on the merits were two declarations, entitled "affidavits", in the English language, by which the authors "certify and declare" certain facts, each with a notarial certificate in Spanish appended, whereby a Nicaraguan notary authenticates the signature to the document. Similar declarations had been filed by Nicaragua along with its earlier request for the indication of provisional measures.

[pp. 42-45] As regards the evidence of witnesses, the failure of the respondent State to appear in the merits phase of these proceedings has resulted in two particular disadvantages. First, the absence of the United States meant that the evidence of the witnesses presented by the Applicant at the hearings was not tested by cross-examination; however, those witnesses were subjected to extensive questioning from the bench. Secondly, the Respondent did not itself present any witnesses of its own. This latter disadvantage merely represents one aspect, and a relatively secondary one, of the more general disadvantage caused by the non-appearance of the Respondent.

The Court has not treated as evidence any part of the testimony given which was not a statement of fact, but a mere expression of opinion as to the probability or otherwise of the existence of such facts, not directly known to the witness. Testimony of this kind, which may be highly subjective, cannot take the place of evidence. An opinion expressed by a witness is a mere personal and subjective evaluation of a possibility, which has yet to be shown to correspond to a fact; it may, in conjunction with other material, assist the Court in determining a question of fact, but is not proof in itself. Nor is testimony of matters not within the direct knowledge of the witness, but known to him only from hearsay, of much weight; as the Court observed in relation to a particular witness in the *Corfu Channel* case:

"The statements attributed by the witness... to third parties, of which the Court has received no personal and direct confirmation, can be regarded only as allegations falling short of conclusive evidence." (*I.C.J. Reports 1949*, pp. 16-17.)

The Court has had to attach considerable significance to the declarations made by the responsible authorities of the States concerned in view of the difficulties which it has had to face in determining the facts. Nevertheless, the Court was still bound to subject these declarations to the necessary critical scrutiny. A distinctive feature of the present case was that two of the witnesses called to give oral evidence on behalf of Nicaragua were members of the Nicaraguan Government, the Vice-Minister of the Interior (Commander Carrión), and the Minister of Finance (Mr. Huper). The Vice-Minister of the Interior was also the author of one of the two declarations annexed to the Nicaraguan Memorial on the merits, the author of the other being the Minister for Foreign Affairs. On the United States side, an affidavit was filed sworn by the Secretary of State. These declarations at ministerial level on each side were irreconcilable as to their statement of certain facts. In the view of the Court, this evidence is of such a nature as to be placed in a special category. In the general practice of courts, two forms of testimony which are regarded as prima facie of superior credibility are, first the evidence of a disinterested witness - one who is not a party to the proceedings and stands to gain or lose nothing from its outcome - and secondly so much of the evidence of a party as is against its own interest. Indeed the latter approach was invoked in this case by counsel for Nicaragua.

A member of the government of a State engaged not merely in international litigation, but in litigation relating to armed conflict, will probably tend to identify himself with the interests of his country, and to be anxious when giving evidence to say nothing which could prove adverse to its cause. The Court thus considers that it can certainly retain such parts of the evidence given by Ministers, orally or in writing, as may be regarded as contrary to the interests or contentions of the State to which the witness owes allegiance, or as relating to matters not controverted. For the rest, while in no way impugning the honour or veracity of the Ministers of either Party who have given evidence, the Court considers that the special circumstances of this case require it to treat such evidence with great reserve. The Court believes this approach to be the more justified in view of the need to respect the equality of the parties in a case where one of them is no longer appearing; but this should not be taken to mean that the non-appearing party enjoys *a priori* a presumption in its favour.

However, before outlining the limits of the probative effect of declarations by the authorities of the States concerned, the Court would recall that such declarations may involve legal effects, some of which it has defined in previous decisions (*Nuclear Tests, United States Diplomatic and Consular Staff in Tehran* cases). Among the legal effects which such declarations may have is that they may be regarded as evidence of the truth of facts, as evidence that such facts are attributable to the States the authorities of which are the authors of these declarations and, to a lesser degree, as evidence for the legal qualification of these facts. The Court is here concerned with the significance of the official declarations as evidence of specific facts and of their imputability to the States in question.

The declarations to which the Court considers it may refer are not limited to those made in the pleadings and the oral argument addressed to it in the successive stages of the case, nor are they limited to statements made by the Parties. Clearly the Court is entitled to refer, not only to the Nicaraguan pleadings and oral argument, but to the pleadings and oral argument submitted to it by the United States before it withdrew from participation in the proceedings, and to the Declaration of Intervention of El Salvador in the proceedings. It is equally clear that the Court may take account of public declarations to which either Party has specifically drawn attention, and the text, or a report, of which has been filed as documentary evidence. But the Court considers that, in its quest for the truth, it may also take note of statements of representatives of the Parties (or of other States) in international organizations, as well as the resolutions adopted or discussed by such organizations, in so far as factually relevant, whether or not such material has been drawn to its attention by a Party.

In addition, the Court is aware of the existence and the contents of a publication of the United States State Department entitled "*Revolution Beyond Our Borders*", *Sandinista Intervention in Central America* intended to justify the policy of the United States towards Nicaragua. This publication was issued in September 1985, and on 6 November 1985 was circulated as an official document of the United Nations General Assembly and the Security Council, at the request of the United States (A/40/858; 5/17612); Nicaragua had circulated in reply a letter to the Secretary-General, annexing *inter alia* an extract from its Memorial on the Merits and an extract from the verbatim records of the hearings in the case (A/40/907; 5/17639). The United States publication was not submitted to the Court in any formal manner contemplated by the Statute and Rules of Court, though on 13 September 1985 the United States Information Office in The Hague sent copies to an official of the Registry to be made available to anyone at the Court interested in the subject. The representatives of Nicaragua before the Court during the hearings were aware of the existence of this publication, since it was referred to in a question put to the Agent of Nicaragua by a Member of the Court. They did not attempt to refute before the Court what was said in that publication, pointing out that materials of this kind "do not constitute evidence in this case", and going on to suggest that it "cannot properly be considered by the Court". The Court however considers that, in view of the special circumstances of this case, it may, within limits, make use of information in such a publication.

In connection with the question of proof of facts, the Court notes that Nicaragua has relied on an alleged implied admission by the United States. It has drawn attention to the invocation of collective self-defence by the United States, and contended that "the use of the justification of collective self-defence constitutes a major admission of direct and substantial United States involvement in the military and paramilitary operations" directed against Nicaragua. The Court would observe that the normal purpose of an invocation of self-defence is to justify conduct which would otherwise be wrongful. If advanced as a justification in itself, not coupled with a denial of the conduct alleged, it may well imply both an admission of that conduct, and of the wrongfulness of that conduct in the absence of the justification of self-defence. This reasoning would do away with any difficulty in establishing the facts, which would have been the subject of an implicit overall admission by the United States, simply through its attempt to justify them by the right of self-defence. However, in the present case the United States has not listed the facts or described the measures which it claims to have taken in self-defence; nor has it taken the stand that it is responsible for all the activities of which Nicaragua accuses it but such activities were justified by the right of self-defence. Since it has not done this, the United States cannot be taken to have admitted all the activities, or any of them; the recourse to the right of self-defence thus does not make possible a firm and complete definition of admitted facts. The Court thus cannot consider reliance on self-defence to be an implicit general admission on the part of the United States; but it is certainly a recognition as to the imputability of some of the activities complained of.

[p. 49] In the view of the Court, the President's refusal to comment on the connection between covert activities and "what has been going on, or with some of the specific operations down there" can, in its context, be treated as an admission that the United States had something to do with the Corinto attack, but not necessarily that United States personnel were directly involved.

[p. 80] Reference was made during the hearings to the testimony of defectors from Nicaragua or from the armed opposition in El Salvador; the Court has no such direct testimony before it. The only material available in this respect is press reports, some of which were annexed to the United States Counter-Memorial on the questions of jurisdiction and admissibility. With appropriate reservations, the Court has to consider what the weight is of such material, which includes allegations of arms supply and of the training of Salvadoreans at a base near Managua. While the Court is not prepared totally to discount this material, it cannot find that it is of any great weight in itself. Still less can statements attributed in the press to unidentified diplomats stationed in Managua be regarded as evidence that the Nicaraguan Government was continuing to supply aid to the opposition in El Salvador.

The evidence or material offered by Nicaragua in connection with the allegation of arms supply has to be assessed bearing in mind the fact that, in responding to that allegation, Nicaragua has to prove a negative.

[pp. 82-83] The Court finds, in short, that support for the armed opposition in El Salvador from Nicaraguan territory was a fact up to the early months of 1981. While the Court does not possess full proof that there was aid, or as to its exact nature, its scale and its continuance until the early months of 1981, it cannot overlook a number of concordant indications, many of which were provided moreover by Nicaragua itself, from which it can reasonably infer the provision of a certain amount of aid from Nicaraguan territory.

[pp. 83-84] Secondly, even supposing it well established that military aid is reaching the armed opposition in El Salvador from the territory of Nicaragua, it still remains to be proved that this aid is imputable to the authorities of the latter country. Indeed, the applicant State has in no way sought to conceal the possibility of weapons en route to the armed opposition in El Salvador crossing its territory but it denies that this is the result of any deliberate official policy on its part. As the Court observed in 1949:

"it cannot be concluded from the mere fact of the control exercised by a State over its territory and waters that that State necessarily knew, or ought to have known, of any unlawful act perpetrated therein, nor yet that it necessarily knew, or should have known, the authors. This fact, by itself and apart from other circumstances, neither involves prima facie responsibility nor shifts the burden of proof." (*Corfu Channel, I.C.J. Reports 1949*, p. 18.)

[p. 320 **D.O. Schwebel**] ... considerations of burden of proof are beside the point, because the real point is that, where objections are raised to the appearing party's contentions, that party must convince the Court that those objections are unfounded if the Court is to meet the standard which Article 53 imposes.

In my view, the correct interpretation of Article 53 is that it affords the appearing State no advantage beyond that which it enjoys by reason of the non-appearing State's absence. If, in a given case, such as the one before the Court, the non-appearing party (or the Court or a judge) raise an affirmative defence to the claim, the appearing party must demonstrate that the defence is not good in order to prevail.

Frontier Dispute, Judgment
(Burkina Faso/Republic of Mali)
I.C.J. Reports 1986, p. 554

[p. 568] By becoming independent, a new State acquires sovereignty with the territorial base and boundaries left to it by the colonial power. This is part of the ordinary operation of the machinery of State succession. International law - and consequently the principle of *uti possidetis* - applies to the new State (as a State) not with retroactive effect, but immediately and from that moment onwards. It applies to the State as *it is*, i.e., to the "photograph" of the territorial situation then existing. The principle of *uti possidetis* freezes the territorial title; it stops the clock, but does not put back the hands. Hence international law does not effect any renvoi to the law established by the colonizing State, nor indeed to any legal rule unilaterally established by any State whatever; French law - especially legislation enacted by France for its colonies and *territoires d'outre-mer* - may play a role not in itself (as if there were a sort of *continuum juris*, a legal relay between such law and international law), but only as one factual element among others, or as evidence indicative of what has been called the "colonial heritage", i.e., the "photograph of the territory" at the critical date.

[pp. 582-583] At the present stage of its reasoning the Chamber can confine itself to the statement of a principle. Whether in frontier delimitations or in international territorial conflicts, maps merely constitute information which varies in accuracy from case to case; of themselves, and by virtue solely of their existence, they cannot constitute a territorial title, that is, a document endowed by international law with intrinsic legal force for the purpose of establishing territorial rights. Of course, in some cases maps may acquire such legal force, but where this is so the legal force does not arise solely from their intrinsic merits: it is because such maps fall into the category of physical expressions of the will of the State or States concerned. This is the case, for example, when maps are annexed to an official text of which they form an integral part. Except in this clearly defined case, maps are only extrinsic evidence of varying reliability or unreliability which may be used, along with other evidence of a circumstantial kind, to establish or reconstitute the real facts.

The actual weight to be attributed to maps as evidence depends on a range of considerations. Some of these relate to the technical reliability of the maps. This has considerably increased, owing particularly to the progress achieved by aerial and satellite photography since the 1950s. But the only result is a more faithful rendering of nature by the map, and an increasingly accurate match between the two. Information derived from human intervention, such as the names of places and of geographical features (the toponymy) and the depiction of frontiers and other political boundaries, does not thereby become more reliable. Of course, the reliability of the toponymic information has also increased, although to a lesser degree, owing to verification on the ground; but in the opinion of cartographers, errors are still common in the representation of frontiers, especially when these are shown in border areas to which access is difficult.

Other considerations which determine the weight of maps as evidence relate to the neutrality of their sources towards the dispute in question and the parties to that dispute. Since relatively distant times, judicial decisions have treated maps with a considerable degree of caution: less so in more recent decisions, at least as regards the technical reliability of maps. But even where the guarantees described above are present, maps can still have no greater legal value than that of corroborative evidence endorsing a conclusion at which a court has arrived by other means unconnected with the maps. In consequence, except when the maps are in the category of a physical expression of the will of the State, they cannot in themselves alone be treated as evidence of a frontier, since in that event they would form an irrebuttable presumption, tantamount in fact to legal title. The only value they possess is as evidence of an auxiliary or confirmatory kind, and this also means that they cannot be given the character of a rebuttable or *juris tantum* presumption such as to effect a reversal of the onus of proof.

[pp. 587-588] At this stage of its reasoning, the Chamber must emphasize that the present case is a decidedly unusual one as concerns the facts which have to be proven and the evidence which has been, or might have been, produced for this purpose. The Chamber has to ascertain where the frontier lay in 1932 in a region of Africa little known at the time and largely inhabited by nomads, in which transport and communications were very sketchy. In order to identify this the Chamber has to refer to the legislative and regulative texts, not all of which were even published; to the maps and sketch-maps compiled at the time, maps which are sometimes of doubtful accuracy and reliability and which contradict one another; and to administrative documents which, having been drawn up for the purposes of a system of government which ceased to exist nearly 30 years ago, have had to be obtained from various collections of archives. Although the Parties have provided it with a case file as complete as possible, the Chamber cannot however be certain of deciding the case on the basis of full knowledge of the facts. The case file shows inconsistencies and shortcomings. Some of these are already known; the Parties have informed the Chamber that they were unable to locate certain specific documents such as, for example, the cartographic documents mentioned in paragraph 57 above. But even if those documents had been located, the Chamber cannot preclude the possibility that the large body of archives from the French West Africa administration, now dispersed among several countries, may contain further documents of considerable relevance.

In these circumstances, it is clear that the Court cannot resolve the problem by means of any of its powers in the matter of evidence under Articles 48, 49 and 50 of its Statute. Nor can the solution be looked for in a systematic application of the rule concerning the burden of proof. For example, in respect of certain villages of which it is necessary to determine the administrative situation between 1927 and 1935, Mali claims that it is for Burkina Faso to demonstrate the Voltan character of the villages during that period. While it is true that "ultimately ... it is the litigant seeking to establish a fact who bears the burden of proving it" (*Military and Paramilitary Activities in and against Nicaragua, I.C.J. Reports 1984*, p. 437, para. 101), it is also for Mali to establish the facts underlying its claims, that is, to demonstrate that the villages were Sudanese at that time. The Special Agreement of 20 October 1983 by which the case was brought before the Court deals with the question of the burden of proof only in order to make it clear that it is not prejudged by the written procedure there provided for (Art. 3, para. 2). In any event, however, in a case such as this, the rejection of any particular argument on the ground that the factual allegations on which it is based have not been proved is not sufficient to warrant upholding the contrary argument. The Chamber has to indicate the line of the frontier on the basis of the documents and other evidence presented to it by the disputant Parties. Its task is further complicated by the doubts it has expressed above regarding the sufficiency of this evidence.

Elettronica Sicula S.p.A. (ELSI)
Judgment of 20 July 1989
I.C.J. Reports 1989, p. 15

[pp. 46-47] With such a deal of litigation in the municipal courts about what is in substance the claim now before the Chamber, it was for Italy to demonstrate that there was nevertheless some local remedy that had not been tried; or at least, not exhausted.

This burden Italy never sought to deny.

[p. 47] Where the determination of a question of municipal law is essential to the Court's decision in a case, the Court will have to weigh the jurisprudence of the municipal courts, and "If this is uncertain or divided, it will rest with the Court to select the interpretation which it considers most in conformity with the law" (*Brazilian Loans, P.C.I.J., Series A, Nos. 20/21*, p. 124). In the present case, however, it was for Italy to show, as a matter of fact, the existence of a remedy which was open to the United States stockholders and which they failed to employ. The Chamber does not consider that Italy has discharged that burden.

[p. 62] The Chamber has no need to go into the question of the extent to which it could or should question the validity of a finding of Italian law, the law governing the matter, by the appropriate Italian courts. It is sufficient to note that the conclusion above, that the feasibility of an orderly liquidation plan is not sufficiently established, is reinforced by reference to the decision of the courts of Palermo on the claim by the trustee in bankruptcy for damages for the injury caused by the requisition. Whether regarded as findings of Italian law or as findings of fact, the decisions of the courts of Palermo simply constitute additional evidence of the situation which the Chamber has to assess.

Land, Island and
Maritime Frontier Dispute
(El Salvador/Honduras)
Application to Intervene,
Judgment of 13 September 1990,
I.C.J. Reports 1990, p. 92

[pp. 117-118] There was in this connection some argument before the Chamber on the question of the extent of the burden of proof on a State seeking to intervene: how far such a State needs to demonstrate the elements required in order to satisfy Article 62. Nicaragua was of the view that it need only show a "provisional standard of proof"; and that it would be "inappropriate for the applicant to go too far on the question of the validity of the interests it claims". The Parties to the case took issue with these arguments. In the Chamber's opinion, however, it is clear, first, that it is for a State seeking to intervene to demonstrate convincingly what it asserts, and thus to bear the burden of proof; and, second, that it has only to show that its interest "may" be affected, not that it will or must be affected. What needs to be shown by a State seeking permission to intervene can only be judged *in concreto* and in relation to all the circumstances of a particular case. It is for the State seeking to intervene to identify the interest of a legal nature which it considers may be affected by the decision in the case, and to show in what way that interest may be affected; it is not for the Court itself - or in the present case the Chamber - to substitute itself for the State in that respect.

It needs, moreover, to be recalled in this connection that the present case raises a further problem, namely that the Parties to the case are in dispute about the interpretation of the very provision of the Special Agreement - paragraph 2 of Article 2 - which is invoked in Nicaragua's Application. This means that the legal interests of Nicaragua have to be assessed, in relation to the issues in the case, under two different possible situations: an eventual finding by the Chamber in favour of El Salvador's view of the meaning of Article 2, paragraph 2; or an eventual finding in favour of the view of Honduras. This difficulty is not only one for the Chamber in considering the present Application - for obviously, as mentioned above, it must not in any way anticipate its decision of these matters on the merits - but also for Nicaragua in framing its Application, even though it was given access to the pleadings under Article 53, paragraph 1, of the Rules of Court. Nevertheless, there needs finally to be clear identification of any legal interests that may be affected by the decision on the merits. A general apprehension is not enough. The Chamber needs to be told what interests of a legal nature might be affected by its eventual decision on the merits.

3.8. Duty of the Court to Seek Further Clarification

Military and Paramilitary Activities
(Nicaragua/United States of America)
Merits. J. 27.6.1986
I.C.J. Reports 1986, p. 14

[pp. 38-39] One of the Court's chief difficulties in the present case has been the determination of the facts relevant to the dispute. First of all, there is marked disagreement between the Parties not only on the interpretation of the facts, but even on the existence or nature of at least some of them. Secondly, the respondent State has not appeared during the present merits phase of the proceedings, thus depriving the Court of the benefit of its complete and fully argued statement regarding the facts. The Court's task was therefore necessarily more difficult, and it has had to pay particular heed, as said above, to the proper application of Article 53 of its Statute. Thirdly, there is the secrecy in which some of the conduct attributed to one or other of the Parties has been carried on. This makes it more difficult for the Court not only to decide on the imputability of the facts, but also to establish what are the facts. Sometimes there is no question, in the sense that it does not appear to be disputed, that an act was done, but there are conflicting reports, or a lack of evidence, as to who did it. The problem is then not the legal process of imputing the act to a particular State for the purpose of establishing responsibility, but the prior process of tracing material proof of the identity of the perpetrator. The occurrence of the act itself may however have been shrouded in secrecy. In the latter case, the Court has had to endeavour first to establish what actually happened, before entering on the next stage of considering whether the act (if proven) was imputable to the State to which it has been attributed.

A further aspect of this case is that the conflict to which it relates has continued and is continuing. It has therefore been necessary for the Court to decide, for the purpose of its definition of the factual situation, what period of time, beginning from the genesis of the dispute, should be taken into consideration. The Court holds that general principles as to the judicial process require that the facts on which its Judgment is based should be those occurring up to the close of the oral proceedings on the merits of the case. While the Court is of course very well aware, from reports in the international press, of the developments in Central America since that date, it cannot, as explained below (paragraphs 62 and 63), treat such reports as evidence, nor has it had the benefit of the comments or argument of either of the Parties on such reports.

3.9. Relevant Facts

Military and Paramilitary Activities
(Nicaragua/United States of America)
Merits. J. 27.6.1986
I.C.J. Reports 1986, p. 14

[p. 39] The Court holds that general principles as to the judicial process require that the facts on which its Judgment is based should be those occurring up to the close of the oral proceedings on the merits of the case.

3.10. Provisional Measures

3.10.1. General Questions

Military and Paramilitary Activities
(Nicaragua/United States of America)
Merits. J. 27.6.1986
I.C.J. Reports 1986, p. 14

[p. 144] When the Court finds that the situation requires that measures of this kind should be taken, it is incumbent on each party to take the Court's indications seriously into account, and not to direct its conduct solely by reference to what it believes to be its rights. Particularly is this so in a situation of armed conflict where no reparation can efface the results of conduct which the Court may rule to have been contrary to international law.

Frontier Dispute, (Burkina Faso/Republic of Mali),
Provisional Measures, Order of 10 January 1986
I.C.J. Reports 1986, p. 3

[pp. 9-10] Considering that, independently of the requests submitted by the Parties for the indication of provisional measures, the Court or, accordingly, the Chamber possesses by virtue of Article 41 of the Statute the power to indicate provisional measures with a view to preventing the aggravation or extension of the dispute whenever it considers that circumstances so require;

Whereas, in particular, when two States jointly decide to have recourse to a Chamber of the Court, the principal judicial organ of the United Nations, with a view to the peaceful settlement of a dispute, in accordance with Article 2, paragraph 3, and Article 33 of the Charter of the United Nations, and incidents subsequently occur which not merely are likely to extend or aggravate the dispute but comprise a resort to force which is irreconcilable with the principle of the peaceful settlement of international disputes, there can be no doubt of the Chamber's power and duty to indicate, if need be, such provisional measures as may conduce to the due administration of justice;

Whereas furthermore, according to the indications furnished by one of the Parties, armed actions within the territory in dispute could result in the destruction of evidence material to the Chamber's eventual decision;

Whereas the facts that have given rise to the requests of both Parties for the indication of provisional measures expose the persons and property in the disputed area, as well as the interests of both States within that area, to serious risk of irreparable damage; and whereas the circumstances consequently demand that the Chamber should indicate appropriate provisional measures in accordance with Article 41 of the Statute.

[p. 10] Whereas States remain at liberty to negotiate or resolve particular aspects of a dispute brought before the Court ; whereas their freedom to do so is not incompatible with the Court's exercise of its own functions ; and whereas the fact that the two Parties have entrusted another body with the task of defining the terms of the troop withdrawal in no way deprives the Chamber of the rights and duties pertaining to it in the case brought before it;

Whereas the Chamber, while welcoming the fact that the Parties have been able to reach agreement on a ceasefire, and have thus brought to an end the armed actions which gave rise to the requests for the indication of provisional measures, is nonetheless faced with its duty under Article 41 of the Statute to ascertain for itself what provisional measures ought to be taken to preserve the respective rights of either Party;

Frontier Dispute, Judgment
(Burkina Faso/Republic of Mali)
I.C.J.Reports 1986, p. 554

[p. 649] In its above-mentioned Order of 10 January 1986, the Chamber stated that the provisional measures therein set out were indicated "pending its final decision in the proceedings instituted on 20 October 1983 by the notification of the Special Agreement" concluded between the Parties. It follows that such Order ceases to be operative upon the delivery of the present Judgment, and that the provisional measures lapse at the same time. In accordance with Article 41 of the Statute of the Court, notice of the provisional measures indicated was given forthwith to the Security Council of the United Nations through the Secretary-General; the Chamber notes that the Secretary General will also receive a copy of the present Judgment, in accordance with Article 95 of the Rules of Court.

Applicability of the Obligation to Arbitrate
under Section 21 of the United Nations
Headquarters Agreement of 26 June 1947
Order of9 March 1988

[pp. 4-5] Whereas the preambular paragraphs of resolution 42/229 B indicated (inter alia) that "the constraints of time ... require the immediate implementation of the dispute settlement procedure in accordance with section 21 of the Agreement", that account should be taken of "the provisions of the Statute of the International Court of Justice, in particular Articles 41 and 68 thereof", and the decision to request an advisory opinion was made "taking into account the time constraint";

Whereas resolution 42/229 B, while it contains in its preamble a reference to Article 41 and 68 of the Statute, does not constitute a formal request for the indication of provisional measures;

Whereas it is not appropriate, in the circumstances of the case, for the Court to consider whether or not provisional measures may be indicated in proceedings on a request for advisory opinion;

Whereas the Court takes note that the General Assembly, at the meeting at which it adopted resolution 42/229 B requesting an advisory opinion of the Court also adopted resolution 42/229 A, by which it

"*Calls* upon the host country to abide by its treaty obligations under the Agreement and to provide assurance that no action will be taken that would infringe on the current arrangements for the official functions of the Permanent Observer Mission of the Palestine Liberation Organization to the United Nations in New York";

Whereas in the light of the indications given by the General Assembly in the resolution the Court finds that an early answer to the request would be desirable, as contemplated by Article 103 of the Rules of Court, and that accordingly all necessary steps should be taken to accelerate the procedure;

Arbitral Award of 31 July 1989
Provisional Measures
Order of 2 March 1990,
I.C.J. Reports 1990, p. 64

[pp. 79-80 **D.O. Thierry**] The measures have also a single aim. It is defined by Article 41 in a simple and straight forward manner that deserves the most careful attention. The aim of the measures is the preservation and therefore the protection *"du droit de chacun"*. Article 41 could have been formulated differently and more restrictively. It could, for example, have referred to the rights (in the plural [22]) of the parties, or to the rights claimed by the parties. This is not the case. The expression *"droit de chacun"* goes further. It invites the Court to exercise, in adopting provisional measures, its judicial function to the full.

But while the aim of the measures is the protection *"du droit de chacun"*, they can have different objects, as shown by the case-law of the Permanent Court of International Justice and of the present Court, depending on the circumstances of the cases which have been brought before them and on which they have pronounced. The object of the measures may be to prevent the aggravation of the dispute - this is obvious. They may be directed to preventing irreparable damage. Their object may be to preserve the exercise by the Court of its judicial function by preventing the parties from anticipating the subsequent decision of the Court on the merits. The latter concern has often been expressed by the Court. These objectives can be envisaged separately, but they are complementary. Regardless, however, of the immediate object of the measures, their aim is, in any event, the preservation *"du droit de chacun"*.

Finally, so far as their nature or substance is concerned, the measures may be diverse and, except for the need that they be suited to the circumstances and for their provisional character, there is no limit to the power of the Court to select the appropriate remedies. The measures may be the ones that the party asking for them requests; but they may be different "in whole" or in part, without it being necessary to rely in this respect on Article 75, paragraph 1, of the Rules of Court, which concerns the case where the Court acts *proprio motu*, that is to say, without having received a request for provisional measures.

Such are, in brief outline, the fundamental rules, deriving from the Statute and Rules of Court, that govern the power of the Court to indicate provisional measures.

---

22 The English version of Art. 41 ("to preserve the respective rights of either party") differs substantially from the French version.

[p. 81 **D.O. Thierry**] In short, although the circumstances do not require measures of the type the Security Council may take in connection with the maintenance of peace or for the settlement of disputes "the continuance of which is likely to endanger the maintenance of peace", they do call for provisional measures such as those that have been indicated by the Court in various cases where it has been requested to do so.

Such are the measures required by the circumstances if one considers that the incidents that have occurred are not altogether minor and without incidence on the rights of the Parties. By virtue of Article 41 of the Statute of the Court, if they are required by the circumstances the measures *ought* to be taken.

Given their provisional nature, such measures cannot, provided they are properly conceived, produce any negative effects on the rights of the Parties. On the other hand, the denial of a request for them involves some risk of aggravation of the dispute. It is therefore only if decisive legal reasons existed for not indicating provisional measures that a request for them should have been denied. But there are no such reasons here.

[p. 82 **D.O. Thierry**] The existence of irreparable damage (however defined) which has already been sustained is obviously not the precondition for granting provisional measures. These measures are intended (among other things) to *prevent* irreparable damage, i.e., to ensure that it does not occur. To require the existence of irreparable damage as the condition for the indication of provisional measures would be virtually an absurdity because, if the harm has already been done (i.e., irreparable damage has been caused), the provisional measures would not serve any useful purpose. Provisional measures are intended to counter the risk of any irreparable damage occurring. This is indeed the very clear meaning of the relevant jurisprudence, first expressed in 1927 by the Permanent Court of International Justice in the case concerning the *Denunciation of the Treaty of 2 November 1865 between China and Belgium (P.C.I.J., Series A, No. 8*, p. 7) and, more recently, by the Court in the *Fisheries Jurisdiction* case *(I.C.J. Reports 1972*, p. 16, para. 21). The commentators have however created an unfortunate confusion between the risk of irreparable damage and the damage resulting from events which have already taken place. A risk is by definition a matter of chance, and it is dangerous to rely for a decision on the absence of a risk or on its improbability. Moreover, the risk of irreparable damage must be viewed in the light of the situation of the State which is in danger of sustaining it. As is well known, Guinea-Bissau is a small State having very limited resources. To be deprived of maritime biological resources, and *a fortiori* of other maritime resources to which it might be entitled, can constitute an irreparable damage for that State. In that connection, the risk of irreparable damage in the present case can thus be regarded as comparable to the risk incurred by the applicant States in the cases where measures were actually indicated by the Court. In the *Anglo-Iranian Oil*

Co. case for example, irreparable damage would have been caused by the removal and sale of certain quantities of petroleum belonging to that company, while in the *Fisheries Jurisdiction* cases, the irreparable damage would have resulted from the exclusion of the British and German fishing fleets from the zone affected by the Icelandic regulations. It may well be questioned whether the damage in those cases was really "more irreparable" than that which Guinea-Bissau is threatened with.

3.10.3. Provisional Measures and Jurisdiction

Arbitral Award of 31 July 1989
Provisional Measures
Order of 2 March 1990,
I.C.J. Reports 1990, p. 64

[pp. 68-69] Whereas the Republic of Guinea-Bissau claims to found the jurisdiction of the Court to entertain the present case upon declarations made by the Parties accepting the compulsory jurisdiction of the Court under Article 36, paragraph 2, of the Statute of the Court; and whereas such declarations were made, by the Republic of Senegal on 22 October 1985, deposited with the Secretary-General of the United Nations on 2 December 1985, and by the Republic of Guinea-Bissau on 7 August 1989, deposited the same day with the Secretary-General of the United Nations; whereas the declaration made by Guinea-Bissau is without reservations, while the declaration of Senegal is subject to reservations, but Guinea-Bissau contends that none of them is relevant to the present dispute;

Whereas on a request for provisional measures the Court need not, before deciding whether or not to indicate them, finally satisfy itself that it has jurisdiction on the merits of the case, yet it ought not to indicate such measures unless the provisions invoked by the Applicant appear, *prima facie*, to afford a basis on which the jurisdiction of the Court might be founded;

Whereas the Court takes note of the statement made at the hearing by the Agent of Senegal that Senegal makes every reservation at this stage as to the jurisdiction of the Court with respect to the substance of the Application, and the statement of the Co-Agent of Senegal that it is not satisfied that the Court has jurisdiction to entertain the main Application, but does not wish to broach the issue of jurisdiction over the main Application at this stage; and whereas Senegal, while contending that the Court should decline to indicate provisional measures, has accordingly not based that contention on the ground of lack of jurisdiction on the merits of the case;

Whereas the Court considers that the two declarations made under Article 36, paragraph 2, of the Statute appear, *prima facie*, to afford a basis on which the jurisdiction of the Court might be founded;

Whereas the decision given in the present proceedings in no way prejudges the question of the jurisdiction of the Court to deal with the merits of the case or any questions relating to the merits themselves and leaves unaffected the right of the Respondent to submit arguments against such jurisdiction or in respect of such merits;

3.10.4. Provisional Measures and Merits

Frontier Dispute, (Burkina Faso/Republic of Mali),
Provisional Measures, Order of 10 January 1986
I.C.J. Reports 1986, p. 3

[p. 11] Whereas, so far as the administration of the dispute area is concerned, the Chamber does not, at the stage of provisional measures, consider itself empowered to modify the situation which prevailed before the armed actions leading to the filing of the Parties' requests; and whereas it is necessary at all events to avoid prejudging in that connection the existence of any specific line;

Whereas the decision rendered in these present proceedings must not prejudge any question relating to the merits of the case brought before the Chamber, and must leave intact the rights of the Parties in that respect.

Arbitral Award of 31 July 1989
Provisional Measures
Order of 2 March 1990
I.C.J. Reports 1990, p. 64

[pp. 69-70] Whereas Guinea-Bissau has requested the Court to exercise in the present proceedings the power conferred upon it by Article 41 of the Statute of the Court "to indicate, if it considers that circumstances so require, any provisional measures which ought to be taken to preserve the respective rights of either party"; whereas the purpose of exercising this power is to protect "rights which are the subject of dispute in judicial proceedings" (*Aegean Sea Continental Shelf, I.C.J. Reports 1976*, p. 9, para. 25; *Diplomatic and Consular Staff in Tehran, I.C.J. Reports 1979*, p. 19, para. 36); whereas such measures are provisional and indicated "pending the final decision" (Article 41, paragraph 2, of the Statute); and whereas therefore they are to be measures such that they will no longer be required as such once the dispute over those rights has been resolved by the Court's judgment on the merits of the case; Whereas Guinea-Bissau recognizes in its Application that the dispute of which it has seised the Court is not the dispute over maritime delimitation brought before the Arbitration Tribunal, but a "new dispute ... relating to the applicability of the text issued by way of award of 31 July 1989"; whereas however it has been argued by Guinea-Bissau that provisional measures may be requested, in the context of judicial proceedings on a subsidiary dispute, to protect rights in issue in the underlying dispute; that the only link essential for the admissibility of measures is the link between the measures contemplated and the conflict of interests underlying the question or questions put to the Court, - that conflict of interests in the present case being the conflict over maritime delimitation, - and that this is so whether the Court is seised of a main dispute or of a subsidiary dispute, a fundamental dispute or a secondary dispute, on the sole condition that the decision by the Court on the questions of substance which are submitted to it be a necessary prerequisite for the settlement of the conflict of interests to which the measures relate; whereas in the present case Guinea-Bissau claims that the basic dispute concerns the conflicting claims of the Parties to control, exploration and exploitation of maritime areas, and that the purpose of the measures requested is to preserve the integrity of the maritime area concerned, and that the required relationship between the provisional measures requested by Guinea-Bissau and the case before the Court is present;

Whereas the Application instituting proceedings asks the Court to declare the 1989 award to be "inexistent" or, subsidiarily, "null and void", and to declare "that the Government of Senegal is thus not justified in seeking to require the Government of Guinea-Bissau to apply the so-called award of 31 July 1989"; whereas the Application thus asks the Court to pass upon the existence and validity of the award but does not ask the Court to pass upon the respective rights of the Parties in the maritime areas in question; whereas accordingly the alleged rights sought to be made the subject of provisional measures are not the subject of the proceedings before the Court on the merits of the case; and whereas any such measures could not be subsumed by the Court's judgment on the merits;

Whereas moreover a decision of the Court that the award is inexistent or null and void would in no way entail any decision that the Applicant's claims in respect of the disputed maritime delimitation are well founded, in whole or in part; and whereas the dispute over those claims will therefore not be resolved by the Court's judgment;

Accordingly, the Court, by fourteen votes to one,

Dismisses the request of the Republic of Guinea-Bissau, filed in the Registry on 18 January 1990, for the indication of provisional measures.

[p. 74 **S.O. Shahabuddeen**] Accepting that the cases "have shown the need for a clear connection between the object of the incidental request and that of the principal one", Guinea-Bissau correctly submitted that the "establishment of the connection is necessary inasmuch as the subject of the request is to protect the rights in dispute, not other rights that are beyond the scope of the proceedings" (CR 90/1, p. 27,12 February 1990). These propositions reflect the traditional principle that provisional measures "should have the effect of protecting the rights forming the subject of the dispute submitted to the Court" (*Polish Agrarian Reform, P.C.I.J. Series A/B, No. 58*, p. 177).

In this case, it is clear that the maritime rights of the Parties, which are sought to be preserved by the requested provisional measures, will not be determined by a determination of the dispute pending before the Court as to the existence and validity of the award. In the result, as it has been argued in the Court's Order, the provisional measures requested are not directed to the preservation of the rights of the Parties in that particular and somewhat specialized dispute. Indeed, when the traditional principle is pressed to its logical conclusion, it is difficult to conceive of circumstances which could ground an indication of provisional measures relating to the substantive rights sought to be determined by an arbitral award where the dispute in the main case relates only to the existence and validity of the award.

[pp. 82-83 **D.O. Thierry**] It is likewise in the light of Guinea-Bissau's situation that the relationship between the Application and the subsidiary request must be viewed. The Application by Guinea-Bissau relates to the validity or the legal existence of the award of 31 July 1989; the request for the indication of provisional measures relates to rights which are the subject-matter of that award and which that award determines, at least with respect to the territorial sea, the contiguous zone and the continental shelf. It is, however, clear that Guinea-Bissau is defending only one right in the whole process of litigation on which it has embarked. This is the right to an equitable delimitation of maritime areas, and in particular of the continental shelf and the exclusive economic zone adjacent to its coasts and to those of Senegal. It is with a view to such an equitable delimitation, of which it feels it has been deprived by the 1960 agreement concluded by an exchange of letters between France and Portugal, that an Arbitration Agreement was concluded in 1985. Since however, in the view of Guinea-Bissau, the award rendered by the Tribunal is not valid, the question of the delimitation of the maritime frontier remains open. In the event (which it cannot rule out) of the Court pronouncing the nullity of the award, the question of the maritime frontier will have to be settled either by an agreement between the Parties - an eminently desirable solution - or by new arbitral proceedings, or else by the Court itself if it is seised of the matter. It is therefore in order to preserve the rights which would flow from the decision of the Court on the merits (i.e., on the validity of the award) that Guinea-Bissau has submitted a request for the indication of provisional measures. For indeed, if the Court renders a decision favourable to Guinea-Bissau, the question of whether the 1960 agreement can be opposed to it would be reopened and, by the same token, that of whether it is possible to oppose to it the definition of its maritime boundary and of its rights with regard to the territorial sea, the contiguous zone and the continental shelf on the one hand and to the exclusive economic zone on the other. It follows that the Court's decision on the merits will directly affect the respective rights of the Parties in the maritime zones in question. It is this effect that paragraph 26 of the Order disregards inasmuch as it merely notes that the Court is not called upon, for the moment, itself to determine the maritime boundary between Senegal and Guinea-Bissau.

Thus at every stage, that of the Arbitration Agreement, that of the arbitration proceedings, that of the challenging of the award or that of the request for the indication of provisional measures, it is the same rights of which Guinea-Bissau is trying to ensure the recognition, with a persistence which its economic condition explains and justifies. Accordingly, neither the "insufficiently irreparable" character of the damage incurred, nor the absence of a substantial and fundamental connection between the Application and the request, justifies the Court in abstaining from indicating the provisional measures which the circumstances require.

3.11. Intervention

3.11.1. General Questions (Article 62 and 63 of the Statute)

Land, Island and
Maritime Frontier Dispute
(El Salvador/Honduras)
Application to Intervene,
Order of 28 February 1990
I.C.J.Reports 1990, p. 3

[pp. 4-6] Whereas under Article 26, paragraph 2, of the Statute the Court has power to form a chamber to deal with a particular case; and consequently to regulate matters concerning its composition; whereas it is for the tribunal seised of a principal issue to deal also with any issue subsidiary thereto; whereas a chamber formed to deal with a particular case therefore deals not only with the merits of the case, but also with incidental proceedings arising in that case (cf. *Frontier Dispute, Provisional Measures, Order of 10 January 1986, I.C.J. Reports 1986*, p. 3; *Elettronica Sicula S.p.A. (ELSI), I.C.J. Reports 1989*, p. 42, para. 49);

Whereas the rule of law that "every intervention is incidental to the proceedings in a case" (*Haya de la Torre, I.C.J. Reports 1951*, p. 76), applies equally whether the intervention is based upon Article 62 or Article 63 of the Statute;

Whereas the question whether an application for permission to intervene in a case under Article 62 of the Statute should be granted requires a judicial decision whether the State seeking to intervene "has an interest of a legal nature which may be affected by the decision" in the case, and can therefore only be determined by the body which will be called upon to give the decision on the merits of the case;

Whereas furthermore a State which has submitted a request for permission to intervene on which a decision has not yet been taken "has yet to establish any status in relation to the case" (*Continental Shelf (Tunisian/Libyan Arab Jamahiriya), Application to*

Intervene, Judgment, I.C.J. Reports 1981, p. 6, para. 8), and therefore a State requesting such permission must, for the purposes of the decision whether that request should be granted, take the procedural situation in the case as it finds it;

Whereas in its Application for permission to intervene Nicaragua states that

"The practical consequence of a favourable response to the present request will be the reformation of the Chamber as presently constituted and the re-ordering of the written proceedings as arranged by the Order of 27 May 1987. Whilst my Government is bound to take all available steps in order to protect its legal interests, it is concerned to proceed in a spirit of goodwill and cooperation in face of a procedure which has already been initiated. Consequently, it is the intention of my Government to propose not a reformation of the Chamber and its jurisdictional basis *tout court* but only the making of those changes strictly necessary in order to maintain the minimum standards of efficacy and procedural fairness" (para. 23),

and that

"Nicaragua in the alternative would request that, for those reasons of elemental fairness explained above the Court should, in any case, exclude from the mandate of the Chamber any powers of determination of the juridical situation of maritime areas both within the Gulf of Fonseca and also in the Pacific Ocean and, in effect, limit the Chamber's mandate to those aspects of the land boundary which are in dispute between El Salvador and Honduras" (para. 24);

Whereas, in the first place, while Nicaragua has thus referred to certain questions concerning the composition of the Chamber, it has done so only in contemplation of a favourable response being given to its request for intervention; whereas, in the second place, while Nicaragua contemplates a limitation of the mandate of the Chamber, its request to that effect is put forward only "in the alternative"; whereas the Court is thus not called upon to pronounce on any of these questions;

Whereas the mention in the Application of these questions, which are thus contingent on the decision whether the application for permission to intervene is to be granted, cannot lead the Court to decide in place of the Chamber the anterior question whether that application should be granted; the Court, by twelve votes to three,

Finds that it is for the Chamber formed to deal with the present case to decide whether the application for permission to intervene under Article 62 of the Statute filed by the Republic of Nicaragua on 17 November 1989 should be granted.

[p. 9 **D.O. Elias**] I wish to dissent from the Order made by the Court because I believe that Nicaragua's Application for permission to intervene should be heard and disposed of by the full Court and not by the Chamber.

My first reason is based on the main question of the scope of chamber jurisdiction: the scope of the jurisdiction of this Chamber, or of any other chamber composed by the Court under the present Rules, is neither definitive nor final, so that one cannot regard jurisdiction as being transferable *holus bolus* from the International Court of Justice itself to its affiliate envisaged in Article 26 of the Statute, or by any other text.

[p. 12 **D.O. Tarassov**] All these statements make it quite clear that, in the Applicant's view, the present Chamber formed by the Court on the basis of a *compromis* between El Salvador and Honduras, without the participation of Nicaragua, can only become appropriate for the consideration of its Application if it is reformed, whether wholly or in part. Alternatively, the mandate of the present Chamber should be confined to the bilateral land frontier dispute between El Salvador and Honduras and a new chamber should be formed with the participation of Nicaragua on an equal footing with the initial Parties. It is obvious that all the proposed transformations, i.e., the full or partial reformation of the existing Chamber, or the modification or limitation of its mandate, cannot be effected by the existing Chamber itself. Only the full Court, which formed the present Chamber to deal with a land, island and maritime frontier dispute between El Salvador and Honduras and thus conferred upon it its mandate "to deal with the present case" (*I.C.J. Reports 1987, Order of 8 May 1987*, p. 12), has the power to undertake actions of that kind.

I believe that the Applicant, when making the above-mentioned submissions, was quite right to appeal to the body which is *fully empowered* to make the required changes. Moreover, the Applicant has opted for precisely this approach, emphasizing in its request that the matter raised by it is "exclusively within the procedural mandate of the full Court" (Nicaragua's Application, Preliminary Statements, last paragraph).

[p. 18 **D.O. Shahabuddeen**] Judged objectively and by universally accepted judicial standards, the selection of its members having been substantially determined or influenced by the Parties under the procedural arrangements referred to, the Chamber in this case cannot, in my respectful view, discharge the functions of the International Court of Justice, in its character as a court of justice, in relation to an application by a non-party for permission to intervene in the case pending before it. By itself disclaiming jurisdiction and instead leaving the Applicant with no recourse except to the Chamber, the Court effectively denies the Applicant its right to have its Application under Article 62 of the Statute judicially determined in the ordinary way.

[p. 19 **D.O. Shahabuddeen**] The finding of the Court that it is for the Chamber to deal with Nicaragua's Application is based essentially on the ground that the Chamber was formed to deal with the particular case and must also deal with proceedings incidental to it. In the normal case, I would agree. But, in the circumstances of this case, is the decision as logical as the Court suggests? Under the Court's own Rules, as amended in 1972 and revised in 1978, apart from two of the five members of the Chamber being *ad hoc* judges appointed as of right by the existing Parties, the remaining three were elected by the full Court to the Chamber after the Court had taken into account the views of the existing Parties as to the particular Members of the Court who should be so elected. Whether it is in fact so or not - and it is the Court which knows best - the Applicant is entitled to, and, as appears from its Application and written arguments, clearly does, entertain a reasonable apprehension that the three Members so elected were elected in conformity with the expressed wishes of the existing Parties. In substance, therefore, the Applicant is being told by the Court that it has no option but to submit to a Chamber all of whose five members it is reasonably entitled to feel have been practically hand-picked by the existing Parties. Conceivably, Nicaragua may nevertheless accept that option and go to the Chamber, and, if it does so, its Application may conceivably be granted by the Chamber. However, this possibility cannot affect the legal situation, as I see it. For it is not difficult to see why Nicaragua has not so far gone to the Chamber and why it has in fact come to the full Court - an attitude which is in itself the first practical illustration of how far an interested non-party State is likely to regard such a chamber as a legitimate manifestation of the Court. When its presentation is fairly read, Nicaragua obviously takes the view that the Chamber, as it stands, cannot discharge the functions of the International Court of Justice, considered as a court of justice, in relation to itself. That that is the central issue, inescapably presented, seems plain to me.

[p. 21 **D.O. Shahabuddeen**] The vice, then, in which the Court is held is this. Regardless of ultimate results, the Applicant has a right under Article 62 of the Court's Statute to apply for permission to intervene. However, while closing its own doors to the Applicant, the full Court is unable, in my view, to indicate any judicially acceptable alternative forum to which the Applicant may turn. In consequence, the Applicant is effectively denied its right to have its Application for permission to intervene judicially considered.

[p. 57 **D.O. Shahabuddeen**] Under the system as it has so far worked, an *ad hoc* chamber, being composed of judges whose selection has been substantially influenced, if not determined, by the original parties (a proposition which cannot credibly be controverted), cannot function as a normal court of justice either in relation to an application for permission to intervene or, if the application is granted, in relation to the applicant as an intervening party to the case on the merits. A request for permission to intervene cannot but be coupled, as in this case, with a request for an appropriate reformation of the chamber. *Ex hypothesi*, the latter is beyond the competence of the chamber, which is thus incapable of dealing with either branch of the application.

[pp. 58-59 **D.O. Shahabuddeen**] The Court has cited the *Haya de la Torre* principle to the effect that "every intervention is incidental to the proceedings in a case" (*I.C.J. Reports 1951*, p. 76). In that case (decided under Article 63 of the Statute), the question was whether the purported intervention "actually relate[d] to the subject-matter of the pending proceedings" (*ibid.*). That is not the question here. While I accept that the principle would ordinarily mean that an application for permission to intervene under Article 62 of the Statute should be made to the tribunal dealing with the merits of the matter, this presupposes that the tribunal is one which can act judicially in relation to the application. That case was not concerned with the kind of issues arising here as to what should be done to give real effect to the applicant's right to apply where the tribunal, which should ordinarily act, does not satisfy the generally recognized criteria applicable to a court of justice in so far as the applicant at any rate is concerned. In particular, that case did not involve the concomitant application of the principle of equality of States which would ineluctably be breached if Nicaragua's only remedy was to go before a chamber composed of members selected as mentioned above.

[pp. 60-61 **D.O. Shahabuddeen**] Since, in my view, the Rules do not effectively provide for the case, the competence to deal with an application for permission to intervene in such a case falls to be considered as remaining with the full Court in keeping with the wording of Article 62 of the Statute. Under paragraph 1 of this, the request for permission to intervene is to be made to the "Court". Under paragraph 2, the decision is made by the "Court". Article 3 of the Statute makes it clear that references to the "Court" are references to the full Court. The Court may of course act through a chamber in proper instances. But where, as here, the Court cannot properly act through a chamber, the Court must of necessity act by itself. The jurisdiction belongs primarily to the Court and is retained by it to the extent that it has not, for any reason, become effectually exercisable by the chamber.

I appreciate that, by reason of the Special Agreement, it may be said that the case is pending before the Chamber and not before the Court. But if, as I consider, the right to apply for permission to intervene is applicable in relation to a case pending before such a chamber, this must be so because "the case" is in legal theory pending before the "Court" within the meaning of Article 62 of the Statute.

[pp. 61-62 **D.O. Shahabuddeen**] In sum, but with respect, I consider that the Court has misconceived Nicaragua's case. The essence of that case, as I understand it, is that the methods by which the Chamber has been formed entitle Nicaragua to take the view that the Chamber cannot exercise the judicial functions of the International Court of Justice in so far as Nicaragua is concerned. The Order of Court nowhere addresses this problem. The *Haya de la Torre* principle relied upon by the Court does not by itself suffice to provide a solution to that problem. A solution, if there is one, must, in the circumstances of this particular case, take account of the principle of equality of States, and there is no possibility of satisfying this principle without appropriate action taken by the full Court within the framework of the very special relationship existing between itself and the Chamber.

For these reasons, I would uphold the contention of Nicaragua that the full Court has jurisdiction to entertain its Application.

3.11.2. Article 62, Prerequisites in General

Land, Island and
Maritime Frontier Dispute
(El Salvador/Honduras)
Application to Intervene,
Judgment of 13 September 1990,
I.C.J. Reports 1990, p. 92

[p. 111] First, El Salvador claims that the Application fails to fulfil the requirement in Article 81, paragraph 2 (*c*), of the Rules of Court that a State seeking to intervene is to set out in its application "any basis of jurisdiction which is claimed to exist as between the State applying to intervene and the parties to the case". Nicaragua does not set out any such basis in its Application but argues that Article 62 of the Statute "does not require a_separate title of jurisdiction" (para. 7). The Chamber does not see here any formal defect, justifying dismissal of the Application in *limine*, since the Rule only requires statement of "any basis of jurisdiction which is claimed to exist". El Salvador also advances the view that a "jurisdictional link" between the State seeking to intervene and the parties is a necessary condition for intervention. The Court, however, has observed in an earlier case that

"although this question is one of the Court's jurisdiction, it has no priority of the kind which attaches to a jurisdictional objection *stricto sensu* and need not be examined in advance of the other contentions put forward by the Parties either as objections to the admissibility of the Application, or as grounds for refusing it" (*I.C.J. Reports 1984*, p. 8, para. 11).

El Salvador's contentions on the question of the jurisdictional link will therefore be examined later (paragraphs 93-101).

[pp. 111-112] Second, El Salvador contends that Nicaragua's Application is defective because it does not comply with the requirement of Article 81, paragraph 2 (*b*), of the Rules of Court that a State applying to intervene indicate in its Application "the precise object of the intervention". Nicaragua's Application has two paragraphs (quoted in paragraph 38 above) stating the object of the intervention. El Salvador nonetheless contends (*inter alia*) that Nicaragua has not complied with the requirement to indicate "the precise object": it does not "indicate its position with respect to the fundamental issue in the case, which is to define the object of the litigation and consequently the scope of the powers of the Chamber", and "these omissions make the Application defective". In the Chamber's view, however, Nicaragua has given an indication of an object which could certainly be defined in a more precise way but is not so evidently lacking in precision as to justify the Chamber in rejecting the Application in *limine* for non-compliance with Article 81 of the Rules of Court.

[pp. 113-114] Finally, El Salvador relies on the fact that there has been "no discussion whatsoever between Nicaragua and either of the original Parties regarding the position of the Gulf of Fonseca". Therefore, it is argued, it is premature to bring such issues before the Chamber, and counter to the established rule "that before proceedings are brought in the Court, there must be a defined dispute which... has matured through the process of negotiation between the parties".

The Chamber does not consider that there is any requirement for the definition of a dispute in prior negotiations before an application can be made for permission to intervene. The function of intervention is, as indicated in the 1984 Judgment on the Application of Italy for permission to intervene in the case concerning the *Continental Shelf (Libyan Arab Jamahiriya/Malta)*, and as explained below, something wholly different from the determination of a further dispute between the State seeking to intervene and one or both of the parties. In that Judgment the Court found that that Application could not be granted because, *inter alia*, to give effect to it "the Court would be called upon... to determine a dispute, or some part of a dispute, between Italy and one or both of the principal Parties" (*I.C.J. Reports 1984*, p. 20, para. 31), without the consent of those parties. It would therefore be inappropriate to require, as a condition of intervention, the existence of such a dispute, defined by prior negotiations.

[p. 116] If in the present case the legal interests of Nicaragua would form part of "the very subject-matter of the decision", as Nicaragua has suggested, this would doubtless justify an intervention by Nicaragua under Article 62 of the Statute, which lays down a less stringent criterion. The question would then arise, however, whether such intervention under Article 62 of the Statute would enable the Chamber to pronounce upon the legal interests of Nicaragua which it is suggested by Nicaragua would form the very subject-matter of the decision. The Chamber will therefore first consider whether Nicaragua has shown the existence of an "interest of a legal nature which may be affected by the decision", so as to justify an intervention; and if such is the case, will then consider whether that interest may in fact form "the very subject-matter of the decision" as did the interests of Albania in the case concerning *Monetary Gold Removed from Rome in 1943*.

[pp. 117-118] There was in this connection some argument before the Chamber on the question of the extent of the burden of proof on a State seeking to intervene: how far such a State needs to demonstrate the elements required in order to satisfy Article 62. Nicaragua was of the view that it need only show a "provisional standard of proof"; and that it would be "inappropriate for the applicant to go too far on the question of the validity of the interests it claims". The Parties to the case took issue with these arguments. In the Chamber's opinion, however, it is clear, first, that it is for a State seeking to intervene to demonstrate convincingly what it asserts, and thus to bear the burden of proof; and, second, that it has only to show that its interest "may" be affected, not that it will or must be affected. What needs to be shown by a State seeking permission to intervene can only be judged *in concreto* and in relation to all the circumstances of a particular case. It is for the State seeking to intervene to identify the interest of a legal nature which it considers may be affected by the decision in the case, and to show in what way that interest may be affected; it is not for the Court itself - or in the present case the Chamber - to substitute itself for the State in that respect.

It needs, moreover, to be recalled in this connection that the present case raises a further problem, namely that the Parties to the case are in dispute about the interpretation of the very provision of the Special Agreement - paragraph 2 of Article 2 - which is invoked in Nicaragua's Application. This means that the legal interests of Nicaragua have to be assessed, in relation to the issues in the case, under two different possible situations: an eventual finding by the Chamber in favour of El Salvador's view of the meaning of Article 2, paragraph 2; or an eventual finding in favour of the view of Honduras. This difficulty is not only one for the Chamber in considering the present Application - for obviously, as mentioned above, it must not in any way anticipate its decision of these matters on the merits - but also for Nicaragua in framing its Application, even though it was given access to the pleadings under Article 53, paragraph 1, of the Rules of Court. Nevertheless, there needs finally to be clear identification of any legal interests that may be affected by the decision on the merits. A general apprehension is not enough. The Chamber needs to be told what interests of a legal nature might be affected by its eventual decision on the merits.

[p. 119] The Chamber concludes that, insofar as the dispute relates to sovereignty over the islands, it should not grant permission for intervention by Nicaragua, in the absence of any Nicaraguan interest liable to be directly affected by a decision on that issue. Any possible effects of the islands as relevant circumstances for delimitation of maritime spaces fall to be considered in the context of the question whether Nicaragua should be permitted to intervene on the basis of a legal interest which may be affected by a decision on the legal situation of the waters of the Gulf.

[pp. 121-122] The Chamber however notes that El Salvador in its pleadings has specifically claimed the existence of an "objective legal régime" of condominium in the waters of the Gulf (paragraph 67 above). Further, the fact that this regime was found to be applicable by the Central American Court of Justice in a case in which Nicaragua was the respondent party, appears to the Chamber to reinforce Nicaragua's assertion of a legal interest which may be affected by any decision in this matter. As appears from the above quotation, El Salvador's argument starts from the proposition that the 1917 Judgement of the Central American Court is *res judicata* between El Salvador and Nicaragua. The Chamber has noted above (paragraph 28) that in 1917 Nicaragua informed the States of Central America that it did not accept that Judgement. That very question of *res judicata*, even though not directly in issue before the Chamber since El Salvador does not contend that Honduras was a party to the case and as such bound by the decision, underlies the asserted opposability of the Judgement to Honduras, so that a decision on such opposability may affect the interests of Nicaragua.

Quite apart from the question of the legal status of the 1917 Judgement, however, the fact is that El Salvador now claims that the waters of the Gulf are subject to a condominium of the coastal States, and has indeed suggested that that régime "would in any case have been applicable to the Gulf under customary international law". Nicaragua has referred to the fact that Nicaragua plainly has rights in the Gulf of Fonseca, the existence of which is undisputed, and contends that

"The condominium, if it is declared to be applicable, would by its very nature involve three riparians, and not only the parties to the Special Agreement."

In the opinion of the Chamber, this is a sufficient demonstration by Nicaragua that it has an interest of a legal nature in the determination whether or not this is the régime governing the waters of the Gulf: the very definition of a condominium points to this conclusion. Furthermore, a decision in favour of some of the Honduran theses would equally be such as may affect legal interests of Nicaragua. The "community of interests" which is the starting-point of the arguments of Honduras is a community which, like the condominium claimed by El Salvador, embraces Nicaragua as one of the three riparian States, and Nicaragua must therefore be interested also in that question. Nicaragua contends that in this respect

"any decision taken by the Chamber - whether in deciding in favour of one Party or the other or by deciding otherwise - is necessarily a decision whose very subject-matter would be the determination of the rights of the three riparian States in respect of the Gulf of Fonseca, and of the waters outside the Gulf".

The Chamber, therefore, finds that Nicaragua has shown to the Chamber's satisfaction the existence of an interest of a legal nature which may be affected by its decision on these questions; and that this is so notwithstanding the fact that, as its Agent explained at the opening hearing, Nicaragua has "considered it unnecessary to allege or claim a specific right inside the Gulf of Fonseca".

[pp. 122] On the other hand, while the Chamber is thus satisfied that Nicaragua has a legal interest which may be affected by the decision of the Chamber on the question whether or not the waters of the Gulf of Fonseca are subject to a condominium or a "community of interests" of the three riparian States, it cannot accept the contention of Nicaragua that the legal interest of Nicaragua "would form the very subject-matter of the ",in the sense in which that phrase was used in the case concerning *Monetary Gold Removed from Rome in 1943* to describe the interests of Albania (see paragraphs 52-56 above). So far as the condominium is concerned, the essential question in issue between the Parties is not the intrinsic validity of the 1917 Judgement of the Central American Court of Justice as between the parties to the proceedings in that Court, but the opposability to Honduras, which was not such a party, either of that Judgement itself or of the régime declared by the Judgement. Honduras, while rejecting the opposability to itself of the 1917 Judgement, does not ask the Chamber to declare it invalid. If Nicaragua is permitted to intervene, the Judgment to be given by the Chamber will not declare, as between Nicaragua and the other two States, that Nicaragua does or does not possess rights under a condominium in the waters of the Gulf beyond its agreed delimitation with Honduras, but merely that, as between El Salvador and Honduras, the régime of condominium declared by the Central American Court is or is not opposable to Honduras. It is true that a decision of the Chamber rejecting El Salvador's contentions, and finding that there is no condominium in the waters of the Gulf which is opposable to Honduras, would be tantamount to a finding that there is no condominium at all. Similarly, a finding that there is no such "community of interests" as is claimed by

Honduras, between El Salvador and Honduras in their capacity as riparian States of the Gulf, would be tantamount to a finding that there is no such "community of interests" in the Gulf at all. In either event, such a decision would therefore evidently affect an interest of a legal nature of Nicaragua; but even so that interest would not be the "very subject-matter of the decision" in the way that the interests of Albania were in the case concerning *Monetary Gold Removed from Rome in 1943.* As explained above (paragraph 56), it follows from this that the question whether the Chamber would have power to take a decision on these questions, without the participation of Nicaragua in the proceedings, does not arise; but that the conditions for an intervention by Nicaragua in this aspect of the case are nevertheless clearly fulfilled.

[pp. 124-125] As for the arguments advanced by Nicaragua which might touch on this question of delimitation, the most general may be seen in its presentation, as a consideration supporting its assertion of a legal interest, of the "essential character of the legal principles, including relevant equitable principles, which would be relevant to the determination of the questions placed on the agenda by the Special Agreement" (Application, para. 2 (*d*)). The Chamber does not however consider that an interest of a third State in the general legal rules and principles likely to be applied by the decision can justify an intervention. Even when, as in the case of Malta's Application for permission to intervene in the case between Libya and Tunisia, the State seeking to intervene "does not base its request for permission to intervene simply on an interest in the Court's pronouncements in the case regarding the applicable general principles and rules of international law", but "bases its request on quite specific elements" in the case (*I.C.J. Reports 1981*, p. 17, para. 30), the interest invoked cannot be regarded as one which "may be affected by the decision in the case" (*I.C.J. Reports 1981*, p. 19, para. 33). The consideration urged in paragraph 2 (*d*) of the Application is thus insufficient to show the existence of an interest of a legal nature.

With specific reference to delimitation, Nicaragua's Application refers to:

"The leading role of coasts and coastal relationships in the legal régime of maritime delimitation and the consequence in the case of the Gulf of Fonseca that it would be impossible to carry out a delimitation which took into account only the coasts in the Gulf of two of the three riparian States" (para. 2 (*f*));

but the "role of coasts and coastal relationships" in maritime delimitation again involves general legal rules and principles. The contention that in the Gulf of Fonseca "it would be impossible to carry out a delimitation which took into account only the coasts in the Gulf of two of the three riparian States" would be more convincing were it not for the fact that in 1900 a maritime boundary was defined in the Gulf between Nicaragua and Honduras. In any event, the question is whether a legal interest of Nicaragua would be "affected" by such maritime delimitation. It occurs frequently in practice that a delimitation between two States involves taking account of the coast of a third State; but the taking into account of all the coasts and coastal relationships within the Gulf as a geographical fact for the purpose of effecting an eventual delimitation as between two riparian States - El Salvador and Honduras in the instant case - in no way signifies that by such an operation itself the legal interest of a third riparian State of the Gulf, Nicaragua, may be affected. In any case, it is for the Applicant State in the present proceedings to demonstrate to the satisfaction of the Chamber that this would be actually the case in the present instance. This Nicaragua has failed to do.

[p. 125] Accordingly the Chamber is not satisfied that a decision in the present case either as to the law applicable to a delimitation, or effecting a delimitation, between Honduras and El Salvador, of the waters of the Gulf (except as regards the alleged "community of interests"), would affect Nicaragua's interests. The Chamber therefore considers that although Nicaragua has, for purposes of Article 62 of the Statute, shown an interest of a legal nature which may be affected by the Chamber's decision on the question of the existence or nature of a régime of condominium or community of interests within the Gulf of Fonseca, it has not shown such an interest which might be affected by the Chamber's decision on any question of delimitation within the Gulf.

[pp. 126-127] Whether a State is entitled to a territorial sea, continental shelf, or exclusive economic zone is a question to be decided by application of the principles and rules of the law of the sea on those matters. As observed above (paragraph 76), an interest in the application of general legal rules and principles is not the kind of interest which will justify an application for permission to intervene. In the present case, the legal régime within the Gulf - whatever it may be found by the Chamber to be - will no doubt also be relevant to any decision delimiting the waters outside the Gulf; but this, in the view of the Chamber, tends solely to strengthen Nicaragua's claim to intervene in relation to the legal régime of the maritime spaces inside the Gulf, not to justify an intervention in relation to the legal situation of the maritime spaces outside.

[pp. 129-131] In order to be permitted to intervene, a State does not have to show that it has rights which need to be protected, but merely an interest of a legal nature which may be affected by the decision in the case. This matter of legal interests has however been dealt with and decided by the Chamber in the earlier part of this Judgment (paragraphs 72, 79 and 84); so it is in relation to those Nicaraguan interests of a legal nature which the Chamber has found to exist that the Chamber must now examine the declared object of the intervention. Nicaragua's substantive purpose appears to be to inform the Chamber of its rights or interests, and to protect them "by all legal means available", i.e., to prevent them being affected by the Chamber's decision, or to ensure that a decision affecting them is only taken after Nicaragua has been heard.

In its written observations on the Application for permission to intervene, El Salvador referred to this aspect of the Application and argued that

"[The] differing descriptions of the object of the intervention, oscillating between the purpose of protecting its rights by all legal means available and the conservative purpose of merely informing the Chamber of its rights, constitute an attempt to avoid the dilemma confronting a State seeking to intervene... If the object of the intervention is to inform the Court of its rights or claims, Nicaragua will have a full opportunity to do so (as Italy did) in the oral proceedings to be convened in accordance with Article 84, paragraph 2, of the Rules, without any need to allow its intervention. If, on the other hand, the object of the application is to protect its claims by all legal means, including that of seeking a favourable judicial pronouncement on these claims, then such a purpose will signify the introduction by Nicaragua of additional disputes, requiring a valid link of jurisdiction, which does not exist."

It appears to the Chamber that the consequence of that argument would be that intervention, not merely in the present case but in most cases, would have to be refused, if not for the one reason, then for the other, and that the purposes of Article 62 of the Statute would thus be frustrated. The Chamber cannot accept such a position. In the first place, with regard to the stated object of informing the Court of a third State's rights, it is evident that if it were necessary for a State which considered that its legal interests might be affected by the decision in a case to give an exhaustive account of these interests in its application for permission to intervene, or at the hearings held to consider whether permission to intervene should be granted, there would be no point in the institution of intervention and in the further proceedings to which it should give rise under the Rules of Court. It is true that in the circumstances of the case concerning the Continental Shelf (Libyan Arab Jamahiriya/Malta), the Court found itself able to take into account, in its decision on the merits, information about Italian claims presented to it during the proceedings on Italy's unsuccessful application to intervene. But the reason for the refusal of permission to intervene in that case was not that the Court was already sufficiently informed of Italy's interests by those proceedings. Nor was it a finding that Italy had not sufficiently indicated the interests to be protected or presented them in an inappropriate manner.

So far as the object of Nicaragua's intervention is "to inform the Court of the nature of the legal rights of Nicaragua which are in issue in the dispute", it cannot be said that this object is not a proper one: it seems indeed to accord with the function of intervention. It is true that Nicaragua in its Application went on to state that it has "the conservative purpose of seeking to ensure that the determinations of the Chamber did not trench upon the legal rights and interests of the Republic of Nicaragua.. .". The expression "trench upon the legal rights and interests" is language not to be found in Article 62 of the Statute, which refers to the possibility that an "interest of a legal nature" might be "affected" by the decision. If "trench upon" was intended perhaps to go further than the language of the Statute, then it should be borne in mind that it would hardly be possible, given Article 59 of the Statute and indeed the decision in the case concerning Monetary Gold Removed from Rome in 1943 (paragraphs 54-55 above), for a decision of the Court to "trench upon" the legal right of a third State. It seems to the Chamber however that it is perfectly proper, and indeed the purpose of intervention, for an intervener to inform the Chamber of what it regards as its rights or interests, in order to ensure that no legal interest may be "affected" without the intervener being heard; and that the use in an application to intervene of a perhaps somewhat more forceful expression is immaterial, provided the object actually aimed at is a proper one. Nor can the Chamber disregard in this connection the indication by the Agent of Nicaragua, quoted in paragraph 86 above, that Nicaragua seeks to protect its legal interest solely in such way as the Statute allows.

[p. 131] In the light of these statements, it appears to the Chamber that the object stated first in Nicaragua's Application, namely "generally to protect the legal rights of the Republic of Nicaragua in the Gulf of Fonseca and the adjacent maritime areas by all legal means available", is not to be interpreted as involving the seeking of a judicial pronouncement on Nicaragua's own claims. The "legal means available" must be those afforded by the institution of intervention for the protection of a third State's legal interests. So understood, that object cannot be regarded as improper.

3.11.3. Article 62, Jurisdictional Link

Land, Island and
Maritime Frontier Dispute
(El Salvador/Honduras)
Application to Intervene,
Judgment of 13 September 1990,
I.C.J. Reports 1990, p. 92

[pp. 132-133] The question is whether the existence of a valid link of jurisdiction with the parties to the case - in the sense of a basis of jurisdiction which could be invoked, by a State seeking to intervene, in order to institute proceedings against either or both of the parties - is an essential condition for the granting of permission to intervene under Article 62 of the Statute. In what follows, therefore, the expression "jurisdictional link" or "link of jurisdiction" is used in this sense. The question has been raised in previous cases before the Court in which permission has been sought to intervene under Article 62. In the case concerning the Continental Shelf (Tunisia/Libyan Arab Jamahiriya), the

Court found it unnecessary to decide the question, since it had reached the conclusion that, for other reasons, Malta's request for permission to intervene was not one to which it could accede (*I.C.J. Reports 1981*, p. 20, para. 36). In the case concerning the Continental Shelf (Libyan Arab Jamahiriya/Malta), the Court again found it possible "to reach a decision on the present Application without generally resolving the vexed question of the 'valid link of jurisdiction'" (*I.C.J. Reports 1984,* p. 28, para. 45). It did so however by stating two alternative lines of argument, one on the basis that such a link would be required, and one on the basis that it would not, and observing that in the circumstances of the case before it, "either of two approaches... must result in the Court being bound to refuse the permission to intervene requested by Italy" (*I.C.J. Reports 1984*, p. 22, para. 34). Although that Judgment contains a number of valuable observations on the subject, the question remains unresolved. Since in the present case the Chamber has reached the conclusion that Nicaragua has shown the existence of an interest of a legal nature which may be affected by the decision, and that the intervention of Nicaragua has a proper object, the only remaining question is whether a jurisdictional link is required; and since it is conceded that no such link exists, the Chamber is obliged to decide the point. In order to do so, it must consider the general principle of consensual jurisdiction in its relation with the institution of intervention.

[pp. 133-135] Normally, therefore, no other State may involve itself in the proceedings without the consent of the original parties.

Nevertheless, procedures for a "third" State to intervene in a case are provided in Articles 62 and 63 of the Court's Statute. The competence of the Court in this matter of intervention is not, like its competence to hear and determine the dispute referred to it, derived from the consent of the parties to the case, but from the consent given by them, in becoming parties to the Court's Statute, to the Court's exercise of its powers conferred by the Statute. There is no need to interpret the reference in Article 36, paragraph 1, of the Statute to "treaties in force" to include the Statute itself; acceptance of the Statute entails acceptance of the competence conferred on the Court by Article 62. Thus the Court has the competence to permit an intervention even though it be opposed by one or both of the parties to the case; as the Court stated in 1984, "the opposition [to an intervention] of the parties to a case is, though very important, no more than one element to be taken into account by the Court" (*I.C.J. Reports 1984*, p. 28, para. 46). The nature of the competence thus created by Article 62 of the Statute is definable by reference to the object and purpose of intervention, as this appears from Article 62 of the Statute.

Intervention under Article 62 of the Statute is for the purpose of protecting a State's "interest of a legal nature" that might be affected by a decision in an existing case already established between other States, namely the parties to the case. It is not intended to enable a third State to tack on a new case, to become a new party, and so have its own claims adjudicated by the Court. A case with a new party, and new issues to be decided, would be a new case. The difference between intervention under Article 62, and the joining of a new party to a case, is not only a difference in degree; it is a difference in kind. As the Court observed in 1984,

"There is nothing in Article 62 to suggest that it was intended as an alternative means of bringing an additional dispute as a case before the Court - a matter dealt with in Article 40 of the Statute - or as a method of asserting the individual rights of a State not a party to the case." (*Continental Shelf (Libyan Arab Jamahiriya/Malta), Application to Intervene, I.C.J. Reports 1984,* p. 23, para. 37.)

It is noteworthy that intervention is dealt with in Chapter III of the Court's Statute, which is headed "Procedure". This approach was adopted by the Court also when it drew up and revised its Rules of Court, where intervention appears in Section D of the Rules, headed "Incidental Proceedings". Incidental proceedings by definition must be those which are incidental to a case which is already before the Court or Chamber. An incidental proceeding cannot be one which transforms that case into a different case with different parties.

Intervention cannot have been intended to be employed as a substitute for contentious proceedings. Acceptance of the Statute by a State does not of itself create jurisdiction to entertain a particular case: the specific consent of the parties is necessary for that. If an intervener were held to become a party to a case merely as a consequence of being permitted to intervene in it, this would be a very considerable departure from this principle of consensual jurisdiction. That the incidental jurisdiction conferred by Article 62 of the Statute is circumscribed by the general principle of consensual jurisdiction over particular disputes was stated by the Court in its Judgment on the Italian Application to intervene in the case concerning the Continental Shelf (Libyan Arab Jamahiriya/Malta), when the Court was careful not to adopt a position in which

"it would be admitting that the procedure of intervention under Article 62 would constitute an exception to the fundamental principles underlying its jurisdiction; primarily the principle of consent, but also the principles of reciprocity and equality of States. The Court considers that an exception of this kind could not be admitted unless it were very clearly expressed." (*I.C.J. Reports 1984*, p. 22, para. 35.)

It is therefore clear that a State which is allowed to intervene in a case, does not, by reason only of being an intervener, become also a party to the case. It is true, conversely, that, provided that there be the necessary consent by the parties to the case, the intervener is not prevented by reason of that status from itself becoming a party to the case. That the competence given to the Court in Article 62 of the Statute is not extendable to making an intervener a party to the case unless the parties to the case have consented to the change appears also to be the view of Nicaragua, which stated during the oral proceedings that "Article 62 is a part of the incidental jurisdiction and there is no compelling logic requiring its provisions to be seen as an 'exception' to the principle of consent". There is furthermore in international law no process for joinder of a new party, or parties, whether as appellant or respondent, by move of the Court itself. The Court referred in 1984 to "the absence in the Court's procedures of any system of compulsory intervention, whereby a third State could be cited by the Court to come in as party..." *(Continental Shelf (Libyan Arab Jamahiriya/Malta), Application to Intervene, I.C.J. Reports 1984*, p. 25, para. 40) and again to the fact that the Court does not possess the power "to direct that a third State be made a party to proceedings" *(Military and Paramilitary Activities in and against Nicaragua (Nicaragua v. United States of America), I.C.J. Reports 1984*, p. 431, para. 88).

It thus follows also from the juridical nature and from the purposes of intervention that the existence of a valid link of jurisdiction between the would-be intervener and the parties is not a requirement for the success of the application. On the contrary, the procedure of intervention is to ensure that a State with possibly affected interests may be permitted to intervene even though there is no jurisdictional link and it therefore cannot become a party. Article 81, paragraph 2 (*c*), of the Rules of Court states that an application under Article 62 of the Statute shall set out "any basis of jurisdiction which is claimed to exist as between the State applying to intervene and the parties to the case"; the use of the words "any basis" (and in French the formula "toute base de compétence ... existerait") shows that a valid link of jurisdiction is not treated as a sine qua non for intervention (cf. also *Continental Shelf (Tunisia/Libyan Arab Jamahiriya), Application to Intervene, I.C.J. Reports 1981*, p. 16, para. 27).

The Chamber therefore concludes that the absence of a jurisdictional link between Nicaragua and the Parties to this case is no bar to permission being given for intervention.

3.11.4. Procedural Rights of the Intervening State

Land, Island and
Maritime Frontier Dispute
(El Salvador/Honduras)
Application to Intervene,
Judgment of 13 September 1990,
I.C.J. Reports 1990, p. 92

[pp. 135-136] Since this is the first case in the history of the two Courts in which a State will have been accorded permission to intervene under Article 62 of the Statute, it appears appropriate to give some indication of the extent of the procedural rights acquired by the intervening State as a result of that permission. This is particularly desirable since the intervention permitted relates only to certain issues of the many submitted to the Chamber. In the first place, as has been explained above, the intervening State does not become party to the proceedings, and does not acquire the rights, or become subject to the obligations, which attach to the status of a party, under the Statute and Rules of Court, or the general principles of procedural law. Nicaragua, as an intervener, has of course a right to be heard by the Chamber. That right is regulated by Article 85 of the Rules of Court, which provides for submission of a written statement, and participation in the hearings. Time-limits will be fixed for a written statement by Nicaragua, and observations thereon by the Parties, in accordance with Article 85, so soon after the delivery of the present Judgment as the appropriate consultations can be held.

The scope of the intervention in this particular case, in relation to the scope of the case as a whole, necessarily involves limitations of the right of the intervener to be heard. An initial limitation is that it is not for the intervener to address argument to the Chamber on the interpretation of the Special Agreement concluded between the Parties on 24 May 1986, because the Special Agreement is, for Nicaragua, *res inter alios acta*.

4. JUDGMENTS OF THE INTERNATIONAL COURT OF JUSTICE

4.1. General Questions

Aerial Incident of 3 July 1988 (Islamic Republic of Iran v. United States of America) Order of 13 December 1989, I.C.J.Reports 1989, p. 132

[pp. 157-258 **S.O. Shahabuddeen**] For the reasons given, it may be contended that the practice referred to is not strictly consistent with the terms of the existing rule, in the sense that it tends to inhibit a respondent in the exercise of a seemingly absolute right available under the strict terms of the rule to file a preliminary objection before the filing of the Memorial. But, however arguable that might be, the possibility of a different interpretation of the rule could not be wholly excluded, and of course the competence to interpret the Rules lay with the Court. It is general experience that formal rules of procedure - at any rate where no conflict with an overriding constituent instrument is involved (a caveat to which I attach importance in this field) - develop through the way in which they are interpreted and applied by the court concerned as evidenced by its practice.

The real question then is, should this Court at this stage overrule the interpretation of Article 79 of the Rules, which is implicit in its practice, on the ground that it is erroneous? The Court is not committed to any doctrine of binding precedent, but it does respect its own jurisprudence. Consequently, though competent to reverse its previous holdings on the law, the Court is not expected to exercise that competence lightly and without good reason (Sir Hersch Lauterpacht, The Development of International Law by the International Court, 1958, p. 19). It may be too general a way of putting the position merely to say that the Court should act cautiously. But what then should be the criteria guiding the prudence of the Court in a procedural matter of this kind? In the absence of any clear guidelines having been adopted by the Court, it seems to me that, in a case of this particular kind, it would be reasonable for the Court to apply something corresponding to the twin tests of clear error and public mischief as known to the upper levels of judicial activity in many jurisdictions. There should, I think, be clear error in the sense that the Court must be satisfied that the opposing arguments are not barely persuasive but are conclusively demonstrative of manifest error in a previous holding. And there should be public mischief, or something akin to it, in the sense that the injustice created by maintaining a previous but erroneous holding must decisively outweigh the injustice created by disturbing settled expectations based on the assumption of its continuance; mere marginal superiority of a new ruling should not suffice.

Land, Island and Maritime Frontier Dispute (El Salvador/Honduras) Application to Intervene, Order of 28 February 1990, I.C.J. Reports 1990, p. 3

[pp. 16-17 **D.O. Tarassov**] According to Article 27 of the Statute, a judgment given by an *ad hoc* chamber is to be considered as rendered by the full Court. As a result of the present Order adopted by a majority of judges, the Applicant will have no more than two possible courses of action - it can either abandon its intention of preserving and defending its interests against possible violation as a result of judicial processes in the International Court of Justice or it can submit its Application to the Chamber. If it opts for the latter course, the Applicant will have to abide by the decision of five judges, only two of whom are Members of the Court, but whose decision will have the status of a judgment of the Court. In the event that permission to intervene is summarily rejected, or if the judgment on its merits fails to provide a proper safeguard of its lawful interests as an intervening Party, the Applicant will not be able to appeal, as the Court's judgment will have been rendered!

However, in theory, it might be possible in such a situation for the judgment to be adopted by a majority of non-members of the Court, with both Members of the Court voting against it. This possibility is no mere paradox - there are very important practical consequences for the Applicant. If the case were not to be considered by a chamber of the Court but by an Arbitration Tribunal, and if the decision of that Tribunal were to be seen by the third State as harmful to its interests, such a State would have the possibility of trying to defend those interests before the International Court of Justice, regardless of the fact that the Tribunal in question might have consisted entirely of Members of the International Court. However since, in the instant case, the Parties have decided not to submit their dispute to arbitration, but to refer it to a chamber of the Court, the third State is automatically deprived of that recourse to the full Court. Only as a result of hearings, with the full participation of all the States concerned and in which all those States would have had equal procedural rights, could the Court have properly arrived at a prima facie conclusion as to whether or not there were any possibilities of intrusion into the sphere of interests of the third State.

4.2. Res judicata

Frontier Dispute, Judgment
(Burkina Faso/Republic of Mali)
I.C.J. Reports 1986, p. 554

[pp. 577-578] The Chamber also considers that its jurisdiction is not restricted simply because the end-point of the frontier lies on the frontier of a third State not a party to the proceedings. The rights of the neighbouring State, Niger, are in any event safeguarded by the operation of Article 59 of the Statute of the Court, which provides that "The decision of the Court has no binding force except between the parties and in respect of that particular case". The Parties could at any time have concluded an agreement for the delimitation of their frontier, according to whatever perception they might have had of it, and an agreement of this kind, although legally binding upon them by virtue of the principle *pacta sunt servanda*, would not be opposable to Niger. A judicial decision, which "is simply an alternative to the direct and friendly settlement" of the dispute between the Parties (*P.C.I.J., Series A, No. 22*, p. 13), merely substitutes for the solution stemming directly from their shared intention, the solution arrived at by a court under the mandate which they have given it. In both instances, the solution only has legal and binding effect as between the States which have accepted it, either directly or as a consequence of having accepted the court's jurisdiction to decide the case. Accordingly, on the supposition that the Chamber's judgment specifies a point which it finds to be the easternmost point of the frontier, there would be nothing to prevent Niger from claiming rights, vis-à-vis either of the Parties, to territories lying west of the point identified by the Chamber.

[pp. 579-580] The fact is, as the Parties seem to have realized towards the end of the proceedings, that the question has been wrongly defined. The Chamber is in fact required, not to fix a tripoint, which would necessitate the consent of all the States concerned, but to ascertain, in the light of the evidence which the Parties have made available to it, how far the frontier which they inherited from the colonial power extends. Certainly such a finding implies, as a logical corollary, both that the territory of a third State lies beyond the end-point, and that the Parties have exclusive sovereign rights up to that point. However, this is no more than a twofold presumption which underlies any boundary situation. This presumption remains in principle irrebuttable in the judicial context of a given case, in the sense that neither of the disputant parties, having contended that it possesses a common frontier with the other as far as a specific point, can change its position to rely on the alleged existence of sovereignty pertaining to a third State; but this presumption does not thereby create a ground of opposability outside that context and against the third State. Indeed, this is the whole point of the above-quoted Article 59 of the Statute. It is true that in a given case it may be clear from the record that the legal interests of a third State "would not only be affected by a decision, but would form the very subject-matter of the decision" (*Monetary Gold Removed from Rome in 1943, I.C.J. Reports 1954*, p. 32) so that the Court has to use its power "to refuse to exercise its jurisdiction" (*I.C.J. Reports 1984*, p. 432, para. 88). However, this is not the case here.

The Chamber therefore concludes that it has a duty to decide the whole of the *petitum* entrusted to it; that is, to indicate the line of the frontier between the Parties over the entire length of the disputed area. In so doing, it will define the location of the end-point of the frontier in the east, the point where this frontier ceases to divide the territories of Burkina Faso and Mali; but, as explained above, this will not amount to a decision by the Chamber that this is a tripoint which affects Niger. In accordance with Article 59 of the Statute, this Judgment will also not be opposable to Niger as regards the course of that country's frontiers.

[p. 649] The Chamber also notes that the Parties, having concluded a Special Agreement for the settlement of their disputes by a Chamber of the Court, did not merely by doing so undertake to comply with the Court's decisions pursuant to Article 94, paragraph 1, of the Charter of the United Nations, but also declared expressly in that Special Agreement that they "accept the Judgment of the Chamber given pursuant to the Special Agreement as final and binding upon them" (Art. IV, para 1). Having completed its task, the Chamber is happy to record the adherence of both Parties to the international judicial process and to the peaceful settlement of disputes.

Military and Paramilitary Activities
(Nicaragua/United States of America)
Merits. J. 27.6.1986
I.C.J. Reports 1986, p. 14

[pp. 174 **S.O. Ruda]** I fully agree with the statement of the Court in paragraph 27 that a State party to proceedings before the Court may decide not to participate in them. But I do not think that the Court should pass over in silence a statement whereby a State reserves its rights in respect of a future decision of the Court.

Article 94, paragraph I, of the United Nations Charter says in a clear and simple way: "Each Member of the United Nations undertakes to comply with the decision of the International Court of Justice in any case to which it is a party."

No reservation made by a State, at any stage of the proceedings, could derogate from this solemn obligation, freely entered into, which is, moreover, the cornerstone of the system, centred upon the Court, for the judicial settlement of international disputes. The United States, like any other party to the Statute, is bound by the decisions taken by the Court and there is no right to be reserved but the right to have them complied with by such other parties as they may bind.

[p. 198 **S.O. Sette-Camara]** We should abide by the categoric provision of Article 59 of the Statute, which confines the binding force of the res judicata to the parties in the case, and consequently bear in mind the fact that the expansion of the effects of the Judgment, so as to affect a third party, constitutes a departure from the general rule, and, like any exception, must therefore be founded in indisputable evidence.

5. ADVISORY OPINIONS OF THE INTERNATIONAL COURT OF JUSTICE

5.2. Request for Advisory Opinion

Applicability of the Obligation to Arbitrate under Section 21 of the United Nations Headquarters Agreement of 26 June 1947
Advisory Opinion of 26 April 1988
I.C.J. Reports 1988, p. 12

[pp. 26-27] In the present case, the Court is not called upon to decide whether the measures adopted by the United States in regard to the Observer Mission of the PLO to the United Nations do or do not run counter to the Headquarters Agreement. The question put to the Court is not about either the alleged violations of the provisions of the Headquarters Agreement applicable to that Mission or the interpretation of those provisions. The request for an opinion is here directed solely to the determination whether under section 21 of the Headquarters Agreement the United Nations was entitled to call for arbitration, and the United States was obliged to enter into this procedure. Hence the request for an opinion concerns solely the applicability to the alleged dispute of the arbitration procedure provided for by the Headquarters Agreement. It is a legal question within the meaning of Article 65, paragraph 1, of the Statute. There is in this case no reason why the Court should not answer that question.

[p. 30] The Court has next to consider whether the dispute is one which concerns the interpretation or application of the Headquarters Agreement. It is not however the task of the Court to say whether the enactment, or the enforcement, of the United States Anti-Terrorism Act would or would not constitute a breach of the provisions of the Headquarters Agreement; that question is reserved for the arbitral tribunal which the Secretary-General seeks to have established under section 21 of the Agreement.

Applicability of Article VI, Section 22,
of the Convention on the Privileges and
Immunities of the United Nations,
Advisory Opinion of 15 December 1989
I.C.J. Reports 1989, p. 177

[p. 187] The present request for advisory opinion is the first request made by the Council, pursuant to paragraph 2 of Article 96 of the Charter. That paragraph provides that organs of the United Nations, other than the General Assembly and the Security Council,
"which may at any time be so authorized by the General Assembly, may also request advisory opinions of the Court on legal questions arising within the scope of their activities".

Such authorization in respect of the Council was given by General Assembly resolution 89 (I) of 11 December 1946. The question which is the subject of the request, involving as it does the interpretation of an international convention in order to determine its applicability, is a legal question. Furthermore it is one arising within the scope of the activities of the Council. As indicated in paragraph 10 above, Mr. Mazilu's assignment was pertinent to a function and programme of the Council. The Commission is a subsidiary organ of the Council, and the Sub-Commission, of which he was appointed special rapporteur, is in turn a subsidiary organ of the Commission. Accordingly, the request before the Court fulfils the conditions of Article 96, paragraph 2, of the Charter of the United Nations.

5.3. Jurisdictional Questions and Denial of the Request for Advisory Opinion

Cf. also: Equality of Parties, supra III, 1.3.

Applicability of Article VI, Section 22, of the Convention on the Privileges and Immunities of the United Nations, Advisory Opinion of 15 December 1989 I.C.J. Reports 1989, p. 177

[pp. 188-190] The jurisdiction of the Court under Article 96 of the Charter and Article 65 of the Statute, to give advisory opinions on legal questions, enables United Nations entities to seek guidance from the Court in order to conduct their activities in accordance with law. These opinions are advisory, not binding. As the opinions are intended for the guidance of the United Nations, the consent of States is not a condition precedent to the competence of the Court to give them. As the Court observed in 1950,
"The consent of States, parties to a dispute, is the basis of the Court's jurisdiction in contentious cases. The situation is different in regard to advisory proceedings even where the Request for an Opinion relates to a legal question actually pending between States. The Court's reply is only of an advisory character: as such, it has no binding force. It follows that no State, whether a Member of the United Nations or not, can prevent the giving of an Advisory Opinion which the United Nations considers to be desirable in order to obtain enlightenment as to the course of action it should take. The Court's Opinion is given not to the States, but to the organ which is entitled to request it; the reply of the Court, itself an 'organ of the United Nations', represents its participation in the activities of the Organization, and, in principle, should not be refused." (*Interpretation of Peace Treaties with Bulgaria, Hungary and Romania, First Phase, Advisory Opinion, I.C.J. Reports 1950*, p. 71.)

This reasoning is equally valid where it is suggested that a legal question is pending, not between two States, but between the United Nations and a member State.

Romania however relies on its reservation to Section 30 of the General Convention; but that Section operates on a different plane and in a different context from that of Article 96 of the Charter. When the provisions of the Section are read in their totality, it is clear that their object is to provide a dispute settlement mechanism. The first sentence of the Section provides for the case where a difference arises out of the interpretation or application of the General Convention between States parties to it, and contains two elements. The first is the treaty obligation to refer the difference to the Court, unless another mode of settlement is decided upon by the parties; the second is the object of the reference to the Court, namely to settle the difference.

The United Nations is itself intimately, and for the most part directly, concerned with the operation of the General Convention. Section 30 was therefore so framed as to take in also the settlement of differences between the United Nations and a State party to the General Convention. If such a difference arises,
"a request shall be made for an advisory opinion on any legal question involved in

accordance with Article 96 of the Charter and Article 65 of the Statute of the Court. The opinion given by the Court shall be accepted as decisive by the parties."

This provision pursues the same intent as expressed in the first sentence of Section 30; the particular nature of the proceeding contemplated is attributable to the status as an international organization of one of the parties to the difference.

In case of a request for an advisory opinion made under Section 30, the Court would of course have to consider any reservation which a party to the dispute had made to that Section. In the particular case of Romania, the Court would have to consider whether the effect of its reservation could be to act as a bar to the operation of the procedure of request for advisory opinion, or merely to deprive any opinion given of the decisive effect attributed to such opinions by Section 30. But in the present case, the resolution requesting the advisory opinion made no reference to Section 30, and it is evident from the dossier that, in view of the existence of the Romanian reservation, it was not the intention of the Council to invoke Section 30. The request is not made under that Section, and the Court does not therefore need to determine the effect of the Romanian reservation to that provision.

Romania however contends that although the Council resolution 1989/75 dated 24 May 1989 does not allude to Section 30 of the General Convention as the basis of its request for advisory opinion, the question which it raises nevertheless relates to the applicability of a substantive provision of the General Convention "to a concrete case considered to be a dispute between a State party to the Convention and the United Nations". It argues that

"If it were accepted that a State party to the Convention, or the United Nations, might ask for disputes concerning the application or interpretation of the Convention to be brought before the Court on a basis other than the provisions of Section 30 of the Convention, that would disrupt the unity of the Convention, by separating the substantive provisions from those relating to dispute settlement, which would be tantamount to a modification of the content and extent of the obligations entered into by States when they consented to be bound by the Convention."

However, the nature and purpose of the present proceedings are, as explained above, that of a request for advice on the applicability of a part of the General Convention, and not the bringing of a dispute before the Court for determination. Furthermore, the "content and extent of the obligations entered into by States" - and, in particular, by Romania - "when they consented to be bound by the Convention" are not modified by the request and by the present advisory opinion.

The Court thus finds that the reservation made by Romania to Section 30 of the General Convention does not affect the Court's jurisdiction to entertain the present request.

[pp. 190-191] While, however, the absence of the consent of Romania to the present proceedings can have no effect on the jurisdiction of the Court, it is a matter to be considered when examining the propriety of the Court giving an opinion. It is well settled in the Court's jurisprudence that when a request is made under Article 96 of the Charter by an organ of the United Nations or a specialized agency for an advisory opinion by way of guidance or enlightenment on a question of law, the Court should entertain the request and give its opinion unless there are "compelling reasons" to the contrary.

[p. 191] In view of the emphasis placed by Romania on its reservation to Article 30 of the General Convention and the absence of its consent to the present request for advisory opinion, the Court must consider whether in this case "to give a reply would have the effect of circumventing the principle that a State is not obliged to allow its disputes to be submitted to judicial settlement without its consent". The Court considers that in the present case to give a reply would have no such effect. Certainly the Council, in its resolution requesting the opinion, did conclude that a difference had arisen between the United Nations and the Government of Romania as to the *applicability* of the Convention to Mr. Dumitru Mazilu. But this difference, and the question put to the Court in the light of it, are not to be confused with the dispute between the United Nations and Romania with respect to the *application* of the General Convention in the case of Mr. Mazilu.

In the present case, the Court thus does not find any compelling reason to refuse an advisory opinion.

5.4. Procedure

Applicability of the Obligation to Arbitrate under Section 21 of the United Nations Headquarters Agreement of 26 June 1947 Order of 9 March 1988

[pp. 4-5] Whereas the preambular paragraphs of resolution 42/229 B indicated (*inter alia*) that "the constraints of time ... require the immediate implementation of the dispute settlement procedure in accordance with section 21 of the Agreement", that account should be taken of "the provisions of the Statute of the International Court of Justice, in particular Articles 41 and 68 thereof", and the decision to request an advisory opinion was made "taking into account the time constraint";

Whereas resolution 42/229 B, while it contains in its preamble a reference to Article 41 and 68 of the Statute, does not constitute a formal request for the indication of provisional measures;

Whereas it is not appropriate, in the circumstances of the case, for the Court to consider whether or not provisional measures may be indicated in proceedings on a request for advisory opinion;

Whereas the Court takes note that the General Assembly, at the meeting at which it adopted resolution 42/229 B requesting an advisory opinion of the Court also adopted resolution 42/229 A, by which it

"*Calls* upon the host country to abide by its treaty obligations under the Agreement and to provide assurance that no action will be taken that would infringe on the current arrangements for the official functions of the Permanent Observer Mission of the Palestine Liberation Organization to the United Nations in New York";

Whereas in the light of the indications given by the General Assembly in the resolution the Court finds that an early answer to the request would be desirable, as contemplated by Article 103 of the Rules of Court, and that accordingly all necessary steps should be taken to accelerate the procedure;

...

5.5. Review of Decisions of the United Nations Administrative Tribunal

Application for Review of Judgement No. 333 of the United Nations Administrative Tribunal, Advisory Opinion Advisory Opinion 27.5.1987

[pp. 29-30] The competence of the Court to give an advisory opinion at the request of the Committee on Applications for Review of Administrative Tribunal Judgements (hereinafter called "the Committee") derives immediately from Article 11, paragraphs 1 and 2, of the Statute of the United Nations Administrative Tribunal, which provides as follows:

"1. If a Member State, the Secretary-General or the person in respect of whom a judgement has been rendered by the Tribunal (including any one who has succeeded to that person's rights on his death) objects to the judgement on the ground that the Tribunal has exceeded its jurisdiction or competence or that the Tribunal has failed to exercise jurisdiction vested in it, or has erred on a question of law relating to the provisions of the Charter of the United Nations, or has committed a fundamental error in procedure which has occasioned a failure of justice, such Member State, the Secretary-General or the person concerned may, within thirty days from the date of the judgement, make a written application to the Committee established by paragraph 4 of this article asking the Committee to request an advisory opinion of the International Court of Justice on the matter.

2. Within thirty days from the receipt of an application under paragraph I of this article, the Committee shall decide whether or not there is a substantial basis for the application. If the Committee decides that such a basis exists, it shall request an advisory opinion of the Court, and the Secretary-General shall arrange to transmit to the Court the views of the person referred to in paragraph 1."

The fundamental text in this respect is however Article 96 of the United Nations Charter:

"1. The General Assembly or the Security Council may request the International Court of Justice to give an advisory opinion on any legal question.

2. Other organs of the United Nations and specialized agencies, which may at any time be so authorized by the General Assembly, may also request advisory opinions of the Court on legal questions arising within the scope of their activities."

Similarly, Article 65, paragraph 1, of the Statute of the Court provides that

"The Court may give an advisory opinion on any legal question at the request of whatever body may be authorized by or in accordance with the Charter of the United Nations to make such a request."

In two previous advisory opinions (*Application for Review of Judgement No. 158 of the United Nations Administrative Tribunal, I.C.J. Reports 1973*, p. 166; *Application for Review of Judgement No. 273 of the United Nations Administrative Tribunal, I.C.J. Reports 1982*, p. 325), the Court has examined the question of its competence under these provisions. In one of these cases the request for opinion originated, as in the present case, from an application by a staff member; in the other the request originated from an application to the Committee by a member State. In the first of those cases, the Court concluded that "the Committee on Applications for Review of Administrative Tribunal Judgements is an organ of the United Nations, duly constituted under Articles 7 and 22 of the Charter, and duly authorized under Article 96, paragraph 2, of the Charter to request advisory opinions of the Court for the purpose of Article 11 of the Statute of the United Nations Administrative Tribunal. It follows that the Court is competent under Article 65 of its Statute to entertain a request for an advisory opinion from the Committee made within the scope of Article 11 of the Statute of the Administrative Tribunal." (*Application for Review of Judgement No. 158 of the United Nations Administrative Tribunal, I.C.J. Reports 1973*, p. 175, para. 23.)

That conclusion presupposes that in any specific case the conditions laid down by the Charter, the Statute, and the Statute of the Administrative Tribunal are complied with, and in particular that a question on which the opinion of the Court is requested is a "legal question" and one "arising within the scope of [the] activities" of the requesting organ. The question whether a judicial body failed to exercise jurisdiction is clearly a legal question, as is also the question whether it erred on a question of law. Furthermore, the questions put to the Court by the Committee in the present case

"clearly arise out of the performance of [its] primary function of screening the applications presented to it. They are therefore questions which, in the view of the Court, arise within the scope of the Committee's own activities; for they arise not out of the judgements of the Administrative Tribunal but out of objections to those judgements raised before the Committee itself." (*Application for Review of Judgement No. 158 of the United Nations Administrative Tribunal, I.C.J. Reports 1973*, p. 174, para. 21.)

[pp.32-33] When a request was first made to the Court for an advisory opinion pursuant to Article 11 of the Statute of the Administrative Tribunal, the Court subjected the machinery established by that Article to critical examination, in order to satisfy itself that it would be right to give an opinion in such a case. Inspired by its own previous approach to the question of reviewing in an advisory opinion a decision of the ILO Administrative Tribunal, it was reluctant to "imperil the working of the régime established by the Statute of the Administrative Tribunal for the judicial protection of officials" and concluded that

"although the Court does not consider the review procedure provided by Article 11 as free from difficulty, it has no doubt that, in the circumstances of the present case, it should comply with the request by the Committee on Applications for Review of Administrative Tribunal Judgements for an advisory opinion" (*Application for Review of Judgement No. 158 of the United Nations Administrative Tribunal, I.C.J. Reports 1973*, p. 183, para. 40).

This conclusion is qualified by a reservation as to the merits of the procedure established by Article 11 of the Tribunal's Statute. In its 1973 Advisory Opinion the Court examined a number of criticisms addressed to this procedure, and in particular the fact that "being composed of member States, the Committee is a political organ", yet discharged "functions which, in the Court's view, are normally discharged by a legal body" (*I.C.J. Reports 1973*, p. 176, para. 25). Ultimately the Court however considered that it should give an advisory opinion at the request of the Committee established under Article 11; it noted that

"A refusal by the Court to play its role in the system of judicial review set up by the General Assembly would only have the consequence that this system would not operate precisely in those cases in which the Committee has found that there is a substantial basis for the objections which have been raised against a judgement." (Ibid., p. 177, para. 28.)

Similarly in the present case it is clear from the request made by the Committee, from the written statements submitted to the Court by the Government of Italy and the Government of the United States of America, and from the statement of views of the Applicant transmitted to the Court, that objections have been raised against Judgement No. 333, and that their examination is appropriate to secure "the judicial protection of officials" of the United Nations. Accordingly, while renewing reservations made in previous cases as to the procedure established by Article 11, the Court concludes that it should give an advisory opinion in the present case.

[p. 36] A preliminary point arises from the wording of the first question put to the Court by the Committee, whereby the Court is asked specifically whether the Administrative Tribunal failed to exercise jurisdiction "by not responding to the question whether a legal impediment existed" to the Applicant's further employment. It has been suggested that the Committee intended the Court to take as established that the Tribunal did in fact not respond to that question, and to give its opinion solely on the legal question whether the Tribunal thus failed to exercise jurisdiction. This problem is one of interpretation, in the sense that it is appropriate to ascertain what the Committee intended to ask of the Court; but it is also one relating to the respective competences of the Committee and of the Court. In the view of the Court, it is in fact the latter consideration which prevails. Such a restrictive interpretation of the Committee's question as suggested above seems prima facie unlikely, and "It is not to be assumed" that the body requesting an opinion of the Court "would thus seek to fetter or hamper the Court in the discharge of its judicial functions" (Certain Expenses of the *United Nations, I.C.J. Reports 1962*, p. 157). Even if such had been the intention of the Committee, however, in the view of the Court it would nevertheless be bound to examine the question in all its aspects: "the Court must have full liberty to consider all relevant data available to it in forming an opinion on a question posed to it for an advisory opinion" (ibid.). The Court cannot therefore simply assume that the Tribunal did in fact fail to respond to the question of the alleged legal impediment, and consider solely whether by not doing so it failed to exercise jurisdiction.

[pp. 42-43] The Court would recall that in appropriate cases it is entitled to look behind the strict terms of the question as presented to it. In its Advisory Opinion concerning the Interpretation of the Agreement of 25 March 1951 between the WHO and Egypt, the Court, following the line of its earlier jurisprudence, observed that

"if it is to remain faithful to the requirements of its judicial character in the exercise of its advisory jurisdiction, it must ascertain what are the legal questions really in issue in questions formulated in a request" (*I.C.J. Reports 1980*, p. 88, para. 35).

The Court in that case, as to some extent also in other cases, found it necessary to reformulate the question submitted for advisory opinion in order to deal with "the questions really in issue". As the Court made clear in a later case, such reformulation must remain within the limits on the powers of the requesting body: the Court cannot, by reformulating the question put, respond to a question which that body could not have submitted, for example because it was not a legal question "arising within the scope of the activities" of the requesting body. In the case concerning the Application for Review of Judgement No. 273 of the United Nations Administrative Tribunal, where the Court had occasion to reformulate the question put by the Committee, it observed that its jurisdiction under Article 11 of the Tribunal's Statute is limited to the four specific grounds of objection there specified and recalled its previous dictum that

"Consequently, the Committee is authorized to request, and the Court to give, an advisory opinion only on legal questions which may properly be considered as falling within the terms of one or more of those four 'grounds'." (*Application for Review of Judgement No. 158 of the United Nations Administrative Tribunal, I.C.J. Reports 1973*, p. 184, para. 41.)

In considering what questions are "really in issue", the Court must of course have regard also to the intentions of the requesting body as they emerge from such records as may be available of the discussions leading up to the decision to request an opinion. This was the course which the Court followed in 1980 in its Advisory Opinion on the Interpretation of the Agreement of 25 March 1951 between the WHO and Egypt (*I.C.J. Reports 1980*, pp. 85 to 88, paras. 28 to 34), in order to define "the true legal question submitted to the Court" (ibid., p. 89, para. 36). In the present case, as noted above (paragraph 22), application was made to the Committee on all four of the grounds set out in Article 11 of the Statute of the Tribunal; and the Committee took a formal decision on each of those grounds as a separate question. It decided that there was no substantial basis for the Application on the ground either that the Tribunal had exceeded its jurisdiction, or that it had committed a fundamental error in procedure which had occasioned a failure of justice (A/AC.86/XXIV/PV.5, pp. 2-3). The Court accordingly concludes that it is not open to it to enter into these grounds, by reformulating the question put to it or otherwise, because it cannot be said that it was the intention or wish of the Committee to have an opinion of the Court on these points.

On the other hand, it was the intention of the Committee to have the opinion of the Court on the question whether the Administrative Tribunal failed to exercise jurisdiction vested in it, one of the four grounds of objection contemplated by Article 11 of the Tribunal's Statute. Without going beyond the limits of this ground, it is open to the Court to redefine the point on which it is asserted that the Tribunal failed to exercise its jurisdiction, if this will enable it to give guidance on "the legal questions really in issue". It thus seems to the Court essential to examine whether the Tribunal addressed its mind to both the questions defined at the end of the paragraph 42 of this Opinion.

[p. 44] Similarly in the present case, the Judgement of the Tribunal does not state specifically that it was the view of the Tribunal that, while a fixed-term appointment on secondment cannot be renewed or extended without the consent of the seconding Government, there is no automatic bar to the holder of such appointment being given a career appointment on its expiration. Nor does the Tribunal ever specifically reject or uphold the contention that the Secretary-General, because he was convinced that there was such a bar, could not have given "every reasonable consideration" to the Applicant's application for appointment. If however it can be established with sufficient certainty that "the Tribunal addressed its mind" to the matters on which these contentions were based, "and drew its own conclusions therefrom", then, whatever view be taken of the conclusion reached by the Tribunal on the evidence available, there was no failure to exercise jurisdiction in that respect.

[p. 45] In order to interpret or elucidate a judgement it is both permissible and advisable to take into account any dissenting or other opinions appended to the judgement. Declarations or opinions drafted by members of a tribunal at the time of a decision, and appended thereto, may contribute to the clarification of the decision. Accordingly the wise practice of the Tribunal, following the example of the Court itself, has been not only to permit such expressions of opinion but to publish them appended to the judgement. It is therefore proper in the present case, in order better to grasp the position of the Tribunal on the point now under examination, to refer not only to the Judgement itself, but also to the "Statement" of Mr. Endre Ustor and the dissenting opinion of Mr. Arnold Kean.

[p. 52] In the statement of his views transmitted to the Court the Applicant has expressed his objections to the Judgement of the Tribunal in terms of "principles" of the Charter rather than as breaches of specific provisions; he contends that "a failure [by the Tribunal] to reconcile its conclusions with principles of the Charter constitutes no less of an error of law than an erroneous interpretation of a Charter provision". In the view of the Court, however, there was good reason for the wording chosen for the relevant passage in Article 11 of the Tribunal's Statute, referring to an error on "a question of law relating to the provisions of the Charter". A claim of error of law in a Judgement of the Tribunal based on alleged lack of respect for principles, without reference to any specific texts, might well serve as a cover for a generalized attack on the merits of the Tribunal's decision, and an invitation to the Court to "retry the case and to attempt to substitute its own opinion on the merits for that of the Tribunal" (*I.C.J. Reports 1982*, p. 356, para. 58), which the Court has declared is not its proper role.

[p. 63] It is clear that the expression "the paramount consideration" (in French, la consideration dominante) in Article 101 of the Charter is not synonymous with "the sole consideration"; it is simply a consideration to which greater weight is normally to be given than to any other. Nor does it mean that "efficiency, competence and integrity" together constitute a sufficient consideration, in the sense that a high enough standard of each gives rise to an entitlement to appointment. It is also clear, since paragraph 1 of the Article provides that "The staff shall be appointed by the Secretary-General under regulations established by the General Assembly", that the task of balancing the various considerations, in cases where they incline in different directions, is for the Secretary-General, subject to any general directions which might be given to him by the General Assembly. Resolution 37/126 itself constitutes such a direction, and one which operated in favour of the Applicant as compared with any outside candidate, or one without his record of more than "five years' continuing good service". Both on this basis, and on the basis of Article 101, paragraph 3, of the Charter, it is material to observe that the Applicant's efficiency and competence were highly spoken of by his superiors. The Tribunal did not make any finding reflecting on his integrity; it did however discuss the consequences of a change of nationality by a staff member in another connection to be considered below.

The decision was that of the Secretary-General; and it was not for the Tribunal, nor indeed for the Court, to substitute its own appreciation of the problem for that of the Secretary-General. The Court could only find that the Tribunal had in this respect "erred on a question of law relating to the provisions of the Charter" if it found that the Tribunal had upheld a decision of the Secretary-General which could not be reconciled with the relevant article of the Charter. That does not appear to the Court to be the case. The decision of the Secretary-General cannot be said to have failed to respect the "paramount" character of the considerations mentioned in Article 101, paragraph 3, simply because he took into account "all the circumstances" enumerated in his Answer (paragraph 80 above) in order to give effect to "the interests of the Organization".

[p. 66] It is the Judgement of the Tribunal, not the action of the Secretary-General giving rise to the application to the Tribunal, which has to be reviewed by the Court; and it is the Court's duty to point out any error "on a question of law relating to the provisions of the Charter" in a judgement of the Tribunal referred to it on that ground, whether or not such error affected the disposal of the case. This is clear from the wording of Article 11 of the Tribunal's Statute: it is only where what is alleged is "a fundamental error in procedure" - the fourth ground specified in that Article - that there exists the additional requirement that that error should have "occasioned a failure of justice". The other errors mentioned therefore constitute grounds of objection in themselves, regardless of their impact on the operative part of the Tribunal's decision.

Having considered the passage in question carefully, the Court is however unable to find that the Tribunal there committed an error of law "relating to the provisions of the Charter". The question is of course not whether the Judgement in the Fischman case contained such an error, but whether the reasoning of the Tribunal in Judgement No. 333, in support of which it quoted its decision in the earlier case, erred on such a question of law. The Secretary-General had in effect argued that the retention of the Applicant in service notwithstanding his severance of his ties with his own government did not imply that a "new contractual relationship" had come into existence. For the Secretary-General, the change of nationality was an act having no specific legal or administrative consequences. The Tribunal upheld the Secretary-General's main contention, but at the same time pointed out that, according to one view, the change of nationality was not necessarily such an act, but one which in some circumstances "may adversely affect the interests of the United Nations" (ST/AFS/SER.A/238 quoted in the Judgement in the Fischman case). This is very far from saying that a change or attempted change of nationality may be treated as a factor outweighing the "paramount" consideration defined by Article 101, paragraph 3, of the Charter, which is what the Applicant accuses the Secretary-General of having done.

[pp. 113-114 **D.O. Schwebel**] The terms of Article 11 of the Statute of the Tribunal, as well as its travaux préparatoires, make clear that an error of law "relating to" provisions of the United Nations Charter need not squarely and directly engage a provision of the Charter. It is sufficient if such an error is "in relationship to" the Charter, "has reference to" the Charter, or "is connected with" the Charter.

[p. 114 **D.O. Schwebel**] When the Secretary-General fails to apply a provision of a resolution binding upon him which the General Assembly has adopted in pursuance of its authority under Article 101, paragraph 1, of the Charter, which provides that, "The staff shall be appointed by the Secretary-General under regulations established by the General Assembly", and when the Administrative Tribunal omits to recognize that failure - and consequently accepts a failure to apply the governing regulation - the Tribunal errs on a question of law "relating to" the Charter. That is exactly the instant case. It is exactly the kind of case which the General Assembly had in mind when it adopted Article 11 of the Statute of the Administrative Tribunal, as the foregoing quotations from the *travaux préparatoires* show.

[p. 122 **D.O. Schwebel**] But since the Court, as the Court acknowledges, is obliged to assign error relating to a Charter provision regardless of its impact on the operative part of the Tribunal's decision, and whether or not it "has occasioned a failure of justice", the Court should have held that, in this respect, the Administrative Tribunal erred on a question of law relating to a provision of the Charter. The Court's failure to do so is the more regrettable in view of the importance of upholding a principle of the Charter which is vital to the maintenance of the independence and exclusively international responsibility of the Secretariat.

[pp. 140-141 **D.O. Jennings**] The relevant provisions of the Charter are to be found in Chapter XV, and in Articles 100 and 101; but these Charter provisions lay down general principles. They are not expressed in self-executing language, but need to be implemented by the Staff Regulations and Rules, and indeed by the jurisprudence of the Administrative Tribunals acting under the terms of their statutes. Moreover it is clear from the preparatory work of the UNAT Statute that

"The words 'relating to the provisions of the Charter' covered not only interpretations of the provisions of the Charter but also the interpretation or application of staff regulations deriving from Chapter XV of the Charter" (statement on behalf of the sponsors of the text; see *A/AC.78/SR.10*, p. 3, and also *I.C.J. Reports 1982*, p. 469).

There must also be included in this corpus of applicable law the General Assembly's decision in paragraph 5, section IV, of resolution 37/126, which the Respondent acknowledges to have been binding on him at the material time. The question is, therefore, whether the Tribunal in its Judgement No. 333, erred in interpreting and/or applying the relevant parts of this body of law to the facts of the present case? In so adjudging the Court is entitled to render an opinion which "is to have a conclusive effect with regard to matters in litigation in that case" before the Administrative Tribunal

(*I.C.J. Reports 1973*, p. 182, para. 39).

[pp. 172-173 **D.O. Evensen**] There may exist an inherent conflict between the provisions in Article 100 of the United Nations Charter on the independence and integrity of the Secretariat and the practice of secondment if the principle of secondment is too rigidly applied. At least in cases of career appointments, lack of secondment cannot constitute a legal impediment for further employment in the United Nations. In my opinion, it must also be open to a staff member, whose appointment is based on a contract of secondment, to apply for a new stint in the Secretariat on the basis of a career contract.

In view of the foregoing, I find that the Administrative Tribunal in its Judgement No. 333 of 8 June 1984 erred on questions of law relating to provisions of the Charter of the United Nations. It erred in acquiescing in the Secretary-General's apparent failure to apply regulations binding upon him under Article 101, paragraph 1, of the Charter. It erred in not finding that the administrative measures taken against Mr. Yakimetz were inconsistent with Article 100 of the Charter. And it erred under Article 101, paragraph 3, of the Charter in treating government consent to Secretariat appointments as a paramount consideration.

[p. 82 **S.O. Elias**] One can hardly escape the feeling that the criticism that the Administrative Tribunal has too easily accepted the decision of the Secretary-General in approving the exercise of his discretion seems to imply that the Tribunal, and even this Court, should substitute its own discretion for that of the Secretary-General in concluding that the Applicant's employment should not be renewed. This would of course amount to requiring the Court to go into the merits of the entire case under the guise of the review asked of it under the present Statute. As we have pointed out earlier in this opinion the Court should not do that. In Application for Review of Judgement No. 273 of the United Nations Administrative Tribunal (*I.C.J. Reports 1982*, p. 356, para. 58), the Court warns against the procedure when it said that its proper role in the review proceedings is not to retry the case or "to attempt to substitute its own opinion on the merits for that of the Tribunal".

The Court, therefore, has no other choice than to affirm the judgement of the Administrative Tribunal and to answer the two questions put to it by the Committee in the negative.

[p. 107 **S.O. Ago**] I must say that I have always felt some dissatisfaction - although no more in the case now in question than in previous ones - whenever the Court has been called upon to give an opinion in the context of proceedings for review of a decision of the United Nations Administrative Tribunal or of other similar tribunals. This is because such requests, or so I cannot help feeling, place the Court in an uncomfortable position. It is, so to speak, caught between two conflicting requirements. On the one hand, it must scrupulously avoid the temptation to carry out any of the functions which might be proper to an administrative appeal court, but which would be wholly incompatible with its nature as the supreme judicial organ of the United Nations, whose role is to settle international legal disputes between States. On the other hand, given the narrow limits to which its powers of appraisal in such cases are confined - and quite rightly, let me hasten to say - by the governing texts, including the Statute of the United Nations Administrative Tribunal, it can scarcely be denied that the Court has very little scope for exercising any decisive concrete influence in the interest of ensuring that administrative justice is genuinely done.

That something had to be done to counteract the drawbacks which might result from the decisions of the Administrative Tribunal, established in order to ensure observance of the law in the mutual relations between the United Nations administration and its staff, was clear from the outset to those responsible for setting up this essential judicial body. This was the reason why a review procedure was devised and put into operation. But it may be wondered whether this procedure, which is undeniably complex, requiring as it does the successive and combined intervention of two high-level bodies, is the most appropriate one for the particular ends in view. Under this system, the forum which is immediately available to an individual considering himself injured by a judgement of the Administrative Tribunal is the Committee on Applications for Review of Administrative Tribunal Judgements. The members of this Committee are the representatives of all the member States on the General Committee of the most recent regular session of the General Assembly. This extremely broad composition, and the type of procedure followed by the Committee in reaching its decisions, do not correspond very closely to the sort of composition and procedure one expects of a body entrusted with judicial functions. And yet the functions entrusted to it are certainly judicial, or at least quasi-judicial. It has to (a) sift and examine the applications received for review of judgements of the Administrative Tribunal; (b) decide whether or not there is a "substantial basis" for each application; (c) select, among the various grounds for review laid down in the Statute of the Administrative Tribunal, those which it considers applicable to the case in hand, thereby taking the responsibility of excluding the others outright; (d) request, in such cases, an advisory opinion of the International Court of Justice on the grounds not rejected. Moreover, the competence bestowed upon the Court for the rendering of an advisory opinion to that Committee following such a request is necessarily confined to certain clearly-defined legal aspects, and nobody anxious to avoid distorting the Court's proper functions would seriously contemplate widening these limits. Then again, I leave unuttered all that might be said about the, to say the least, curious aspects, in legal logic, of a procedure which consists of requesting a tribunal to rule by means of an advisory opinion upon a decision handed down by another tribunal.

[p. 89 **S.O. Oda**] As the Statute of UNAT provides that an advisory opinion may be sought of the Court because of the objection of a staff member to the Tribunal's judgement on four grounds, including ground III that "the Tribunal ... has erred on a question of law relating to the provisions of the Charter of the United Nations" (Art. 11 (1)), I would suggest that the Court is expected in this case to function in substance similarly to an appellate court vis-à-vis UNAT, to review the actual substance of the Secretary-General's decision and, if necessary, to substitute its own opinion on the merits for that of UNAT.

[pp. 117-118 **D.O. Schwebel**] In view of the terms of the Tribunal's Statute and the foregoing intentions of its draftsmen, and in view of the Court's proper holding that it may examine "in full liberty the facts of the case" and check "the Tribunal's appreciation of the facts" (*I.C.J. Reports 1973*, p. 207, para. 85), I believe that today's opinion of the Court, and previous opinions to like effect, are on weak ground when they shelter behind the conclusion that, "the Court's proper role is not to retry the case and to attempt to substitute its own opinion on the merits for that of the Tribunal" (*I.C.J. Reports 1982*, p. 356, para. 58, adopted in this opinion in paras. 27 and 89). On the contrary, the Court, when seised of a case of this kind, exercises "judicial review... The opinion of the Court is to be given a reformatory character." Since an objection on the ground that the Tribunal has erred on a question of law relating to a provision of the Charter "relates not to the validity of the judgment but to the merits of the judgment" of the Tribunal, this ground affords the Court "true appellate jurisdiction" (Leo Gross, "Participation of Individuals in Advisory Proceedings before the International Court of Justice: Question of Equality between the Parties", 52 American Journal of International Law (1958), p. 36.)

This is the conclusion which Judge Oda, in his separate opinion, and which I, in my dissenting opinion, reached in 1982 in the Mortished case, after an examination of the drafting history of Article 11 of the Statute of the Administrative Tribunal; it remains correct today (see *I.C.J. Reports 1982*, pp. 393-397,468-470,471, and Judge Oda's separate opinion in the current case, paras. 14-18). It is fully justified by the intent of the General Assembly in adopting Article 11 of the Statute of the Administrative Tribunal, as that intent is shown by the quotations from the travaux préparatoires set out above and in the cited Mortished opinions. In such a case, the Court is entitled - if not required - to substitute its opinion for that of the Tribunal on the merits; and both the Secretary-

General and the Tribunal are bound to conform their judgments to the Court's opinion. What is at issue in the Yakimetz case is the Administrative Tribunal's "interpretation or application" - or misinterpretation or misapplication - "of staff regulations deriving from Chapter XV of the Charter", an issue explicitly declared by the drafters of Article 11 of the Statute to be within the Court's competence. The Court is fully empowered to give an opinion on the merits of that issue. Its failure to do so constitutes a failure to exercise a responsibility validly entrusted to it by the General Assembly.

Summary of the Decisions and Advisory Opinions

Frontier Dispute

(Burkina Faso v. Mali)

By a Special Agreement of 16 September 1983 filed with the Registry of the Court on 20 October 1983 the Republic of Burkina Faso and the Republic of Mali had submitted a dispute to the Court concerning the delimitation of their common frontier. According to Article II of this Special Agreement the case was to be decided by a Chamber of the Court constituted according to Article 26(2) of the Statute. After having duly consulted the Parties as to the composition of the Chamber, the Court decided by an order of 3 April 1985 that the Chamber was to be composed of the Judges Lachs, Ruda and Bedjaoui as well as Judge *ad hoc* Luchaire to sit for Burkina Faso and Judge *ad hoc* Abi-Saab to sit for Mali.

Requests for the Indication of Provisonal Measures, Order of 10 January 1986

Before the Chamber had the opportunity to decide the question, the dispute flared up into war on Christmas Day 1985 apparently because of a census carried out by Burkinabe authorities allegedly violating Malian sovereignty. Both Parties then asked the Chamber to indicate provisional measures in order to preserve their respective rights although, at the same time, they were engaged, since 1977, in a political mediation endeavour within a regional West African group under the *Accord de non-agression et d'assistance en matière de dèfense* (A.N.A.D.). On 30 December 1985, this group reached a common declaration made by Burkina Faso and Mali containing the terms of a cease-fire but postponing the question of troop withdrawal which, according to Burkina Faso, should be ordered by the Court. With a view to the common declaration and the negotiation process under the auspices of A.N.A.D., Mali objected to the request. In its Order of 10 January 1986, the Chamber stated that the negotiations between the Parties were not incompatible with the functions of the Court but concluded, with regard to this special item, that an order concerning the withdrawal of the troops required geographical and strategic expertise which the Chamber lacked so that the regulation of this point was left to the A.N.A.D. process. Among the provisional measures indicated by the Chamber there may be mentioned the order to re-establish, as regards the administration of the disputed areas, the status quo ante the armed conflict.

Judgment on the Merits of 22 December 1986

Since both Parties had agreed that at the moment of independence there existed a definite frontier and that no modification had taken place since 1959 to 1960, it was the task of the Chamber to define this frontier line in the disputed area.

As regards the applicable law, the Parties had stated in the preamble to the Special Agreement that the settlement of the dispute should be "based in particular on the respect for the principle of the intangibility of frontiers inherited from colonization". Thus, the Chamber could not disregard the principle of *uti possidetis juris* which it declared to be a firmly established principle of international law where decolonization is concerned. Its obvious purpose was to prevent the independence and stability of new States being endangered by the challenging of frontiers subsequent to the withdrawal of the administering power by upgrading former administrative frontiers to international frontiers. This principle, therefore, might represent the wisest course to preserve stability; it might, however, be wondered that the principle had been able to withstand the new attitudes to international law that had developed, since at first sight it conflicted outright with the right of peoples to self-determination. But as African States had selected the principle of *uti possidetis* among all other classic principles, the Chamber could not challenge it merely because in 1960, when both Parties achieved independence, this principle had not yet been proclaimed by the African Heads of State and Government.

The Chamber then considered whether equity could be invoked and decided that only equity *infra legem* was to be considered; this is shown by the application which the Chamber made of equity in delimitating the frontier on the basis of the rules and principles applicable in the case. These considerations of equity *infra legem* had to come into play in order to guide the Chamber in the exercise of its functions of interpreting and applying the law and the legal titles involved, since it had to draw a delimitation line and not only to indicate the principles on the basis of which the Parties would themselves proceed to delimitation.

As a last consideration concerning the applicable law, the Chamber had regard to the French colonial law, *droit d'outre-mer*, since both Parties had been part of French West Africa. As the frontier between the Parties became an international frontier upon independence, French law, according to the Chamber, could no longer play a role in itself but only as one factual element among others, or as evidence indicative of what has been called the "colonial heritage", because international law did not contain any renvoi to the law of the colonizing States.

The Chamber had two preliminary questions to examine, the first of which concerned the argument of acquiescence, the second the classic problem of interference into the rights of third States not party to the dispute.

As regards acquiescence, Burkina Faso had argued that Mali had accepted as binding the solution to the dispute outlined by the OAU Mediation Commission. If this objection were well-founded there would have been no need for the Chamber to establish the frontier inherited from the colonial period. The Chamber, however, disposed of this objection because, on the one hand, both Parties had agreed that the Commission had not been a judicial organ competent to issue legally binding decisions and, on the other hand, the Commission had never completed its work. As to the official declarations of Mali concerning the acceptance of the binding character of the solution to be found by the Commission, the Chamber stated that those declarations had not been made during negotiations between the two Parties and thus could at most be regarded as unilateral acts not intended to create legal obligations. As to the argument that Mali had acquiesced to the application of the principles of delimitation approved by the sub-commission and intended to serve as a basis for the final report of the Mediation Commission, the Chamber found that Mali's approach to those principle was of little significance: Since the Chamber had to decide on the basis of international law the principles found by the sub-commission had to be applied as such if they were elements of law; if not, they were of no importance since the Special Agreement did not refer to them.

As regards the problem of possible interference into rights of third States not party to the dispute, Mali had argued that the Chamber was not competent to fix the tripoint Mali-Niger-Burkina Faso, forming the end-point of the frontier between the parties, without Niger's agreement. Burkina Faso in turn considered that according to the Special Agreement the Chamber had to determine definitively the entire common frontier and thus to determine the tripoint. The Chamber disposed of this preliminary objection by finding that its jurisdiction was not restricted only because of the fact that the disputed area was adjacent to a third State, Niger, not party to the proceedings, whose rights, incidentally, were protected under Article 59 of the Statute.

As to the second aspect of the question whether the need of safeguarding the interests of a third State concerned would require the Chamber to refrain from determining the whole course of the frontier line as requested in the Special Agreement, the Chamber found that this would presuppose that those legal interests of the third State would form the very subject-matter of the decision which, however, was not the case: In the present case, the Chamber had not so much to define a tripoint, as to indicate the ultimate point of the frontier which ceases to divide the territories of Burkina Faso and Mali, which implied logically that the territory of a third State (Niger) lies beyond the end-point of that frontier.

The Chamber then proceeded to examine the abundant evidence produced by the parties, in particular legislative and regulative texts and administrative documents, the legal force of which was in dispute. As to the maps submitted, the Chamber departed from the principle that they merely constitute information, and never territorial titles in themselves. They were given the effect of "corroborative evidence endorsing a conclusion at which the Court has arrived by other means unconnected with the maps". However, two of the maps produced appeared to be of special significance, one of which, issued between 1958 and 1960 by the French *Institut géographique national (IGN),* a neutral body in relation to the parties, must be viewed as compelling where other evidence is lacking. Besides this material, also the colonial "*effectivités*", that is the conduct of the colonial administrative authorities, had to be taken into account as proof of the effective exercise of territorial jurisdiction in the region, although the role of these "*effectivités*" was rather complex and in need of careful evaluation.

Despite the abundance of evidence submitted there were some shortcomings and inconsistencies which rendered the task of determining the frontier a rather complex one, because the Chamber had to find out "where the frontier lay in 1932 in a region of Africa little known at the time by reference to legislative and regulative texts, not all of which were even published and maps which were sometimes of doubtful accuracy and reliability". Thus, finally, the Chamber could not be certain that it was deciding upon the basis of full knowledge of the facts.

After having examined all evidence in detail and having determined what weight to attach to each aspect, the Chamber determined the frontier in the disputed area beginning with the endpoint of the frontier already established between the parties. Although not even this point had been clearly indicated by the parties, the Chamber could conclude that there was such a point accepted by both parties. The Chamber then proceeded by drawing a series of straight lines in eight different sectors of the disputed area. The actual delimitation line was reproduced on a map annexed to the judgment.

Nomination of Experts

The final act of the Chamber in this dispute consisted in the order of 9 April 1987 in which it nominated, according to Article IV of the Special Agreement, three experts to assist the parties in the operation of the demarcation of the frontier.

Military and Paramilitary Activities in and against Nicaragua

Nicaragua v. USA

Judgment of the Court of June 27,1986

On April 9,1984, Nicaragua had initiated proceedings against the United States of America in the International Court of Justice. The action was based on the allegation that the United States had supported by its policy and actions a mercenary army, the contras, in launching attacks on the territory of Nicaragua, with the purpose of overthrowing the (Sandinista) Government of Nicaragua. By funding and assisting, covertly and overtly, the "contra" movement, the United States was using - according to Nicaragua - armed force against Nicaragua in violation of the international obligations of the United States under general international law as well as under the United Nations Charter, the OAS Charter and the bilateral United States-Nicaragua Treaty of Friendship and Commerce. In particular, it was submitted by Nicaragua that the United States was violating the prohibition of the use of force in international relations and the parallel rule on prohibition of intervention.

As a first step, the Court had decided on the interim measures requested by Nicaragua. By Order of 10 May 1984, the Court had indicated some provisional measures. By Order of 15 August 1984, the Court had then rejected the declaration to intervene under Article 63 of the Statute made by El Salvador. At the end of the first phase, the Court finally had decided in its judgment on jurisdiction and admissibility of 26 November 1984 that it had jurisdiction under Article 26 para. 2 of the Statute.

Having lost in the jurisdiction and admissibility phase, however, the United States did not cease to continue in contesting the Court's jurisdiction and decided not to appear before the Court in the proceedings on the merits. That decision made the dispute even more complicated to resolve for the Court, but the Court came to the conclusion that the United States' non-appearance did not prevent it from giving a decision in the case. A requirement to be respected in such a situation was only established by Article 53 of the Statute, according to which the Court has to satisfy itself that the claim of the party appearing is well founded in fact and law. There exists no possibility of a judgment automatically in favor of the applicant State, but the Court also has to ensure that the party which declines to appear should not be permitted to profit from its absence. This leads to a result in which a particular emphasis is placed on the active role of the Court in establishing the facts and the law relevant for deciding the case. As to determination of the facts and the production of evidence, the Court further stressed that it had freedom in estimating the value of the various elements of evidence. Although the Court found it necessary to treat these sources with caution, some types of alleged evidence like certain documentary material, evidence of witnesses presented by the applicant and certain governmental publications can contribute to corroborate the existence of a fact and can be taken into account to show whether facts are matters of public knowledge, even when they do not constitute evidence capable of proving facts.

Concerning the United States' preliminary objection that the questions of the use of force and collective self-defence raised in the case were not justiciable, the Court argued that as a "legal dispute" the case did not necessarily involve it in evaluation of political or military matters, but that the issues raised of collective self-defence were legal questions which it had competence to determine. The multilateral treaty reservation invoked by the United States, however, was confirmed by the Court to be a relevant obstacle to further exercise of its jurisdiction, at least in part. In the first (procedural) phase the Court had declared that the objection to jurisdiction based on the reservation did "not possess, in the circumstances of the case, an exclusively preliminary character" since it contained both preliminary aspects and other aspects relating to the merits and that, accordingly, it had to be dealt with at the stage of the merits. The reservation had excluded from the jurisdiction of the Court all "disputes arising under a multilateral treaty" which could affect third States which are parties to the treaty but which are not participating in the proceedings before the Court. Now, after a careful examination of the reservation, the Court concluded that it would be impossible to say that a ruling on the alleged breaches of the Charter of the United Nations as well as of the OAS Charter would not "affect" third parties, in particular El Salvador as the supposed beneficiary of the claimed actions of collective self-defence. Therefore, the jurisdiction conferred on the Court by the United States declaration under Article 36 para. 2 of the Statute did not permit the Court to entertain the claims based on violations of multilateral treaties such as the United Nations Charter and the OAS Charter. But the effect of the reservation was confined to barring the applicability of these two multilateral treaties as multilateral treaty law; as far as the application was based on principles of international customary law enshrined also in treaty law provisions, the multilateral treaty reservation did not exclude the Court's jurisdiction under the United States optional clause.

As to the facts, the Court found it established that some incidents were directly imputable to the United States. For example it was clear, after examining the facts, that, on a date in late 1983 or early 1984, the President of the United States had authorized a U.S. Government agency to lay mines in Nicaraguan ports. Accordingly, in early 1984 mines had been laid in or close to several ports of Nicaragua, either in Nicaraguan internal waters or in its territorial sea or both, and they had been laid by persons in the pay and acting on the instructions of the U.S. agency, under the supervision and with the logistic support of United States agents. Directly to be attributed to the United States were also several operations against Nicaraguan oil installations, a naval base and other facilities of the State of Nicaragua, carried out as direct actions of United States personnel, or of persons in its pay. Although it could not be proved that any United States military personnel took a direct part in the operations, United States agents undoubtedly participated in the planning, direction and support of these operations.

Quite to the contrary, the question of imputability of operations created numerous difficulties in the case of the field activities of the 'contra' force. In contrast to the Nicaraguan allegation that the 'contra' forces were a mercenary army created and controlled by the United States, the Court, on the basis of the available information, was notable to satisfy itself beyond doubt that the United States had "created" the 'contra' force; the Court only held it established that the United States largely financed, trained, equipped, armed and organized the FDN, one main element of the force. In the light of the evidence and material available to it, the Court was not satisfied that all the operations launched by the 'contra' force, at every stage of the conflict, reflected strategy and tactics solely devised by the United States. Despite all the evidence of logistic support, the supply of intelligence information, the use of United States military advisers etc., the evidence did not warrant a finding that the United States gave direct combat support (in the sense of a direct intervention by United States combat forces) nor did it warrant a finding that the 'contras' could be equated, for legal purposes, with an organ of the United States Government, or as acting on behalf of that Government. Such a direct attribution of 'contra' forces to the United States Government as an organ acting on behalf of that Government would have required an extreme degree of control over the rebel forces, a degree of control that could have been inferred only from the fact of total dependence of the 'contras' on United States aid; that the United States exercised such a degree of control, however, could not be deduced from the evidence collected by the Court. In conclusion, the Court took the view that the 'contras' remained responsible for their acts, and in particular for the alleged violations by them of humanitarian law. United States participation, even if preponderant or decisive, in the financing, organizing, training, supplying and equipping of the 'contras', the selection of its military or paramilitary targets, and the planning of the whole of its operation, in the view of the Court was still insufficient in itself for the purpose of attributing to the United States the acts committed by the 'contras' in the course of their military or paramilitary operations in Nicaragua.

Concerning the measures of an economic nature complained of by Nicaragua as an indirect form of intervention in its internal affairs, the Court centred its attention on the suspension (and subsequent termination) of economic aid in the spring of 1981, the

American actions to block loans to Nicaragua from international financial bodies, the reduction of the sugar import quota in September 1983 and the total trade embargo declared by executive order in May 1985.

As to the reverse factual allegations brought up by the United States in order to justify its actions as an exercise of collective self-defence, the Court had to cope with the difficulties created by the non-participation of the applicant side. There was no evidential material presented by the United States in the proceedings on the merits, and it was not easy to substantiate the alleged assistance of Nicaragua to armed rebel forces operating in neighbouring countries, particularly in El Salvador. Confined to rudimentary investigations of the facts by the Court itself, the factual basis of the allegations could not really be clarified. Evidence of military aid from or through Nicaragua to rebel forces in El Salvador remained weak, although the Court could not conclude that no transport of or traffic in arms had taken place. Thus, the Court could only take note "that the allegations of arms-trafficking are not solidly established" and that it "has not, in any event, been able to satisfy itself that any continuing flow on a significant scale took place after the early months of 1981", the date until which support for the armed opposition in El Salvador could be established as a fact by the Court.

But the Court went even further by raising the question of imputability of deliveries to the Government of Nicaragua: it noted that, having regard to the circumstances characterizing this part of Central America, it is scarcely possible for Nicaragua's responsibility for an arms traffic taking place on its territory to be automatically assumed. On the contrary, the Court considered it more realistic, and consistent with the probabilities, to recognize that an activity like arms-trafficking, if on a limited scale, may very well be pursued unbeknown to the territorial government". Accordingly, the Court came to the result that the evidence was insufficient to satisfy it that the Government of Nicaragua was responsible for any flow of arms at either period. The fact that certain trans-border military incursions into Honduras and Costa Rica were imputable to Nicaragua, however, was considered by the Court to be established.

As to the law applicable to the dispute, the Court confined its reasoning in principle to the body of customary international law. Given its approach to the United States multilateral treaty reservation, the Court had to analyze the scope and content of the customary law rules parallel to the multilateral treaty norms excluded by the American reservation. Even in cases where a treaty norm and a customary norm were to have exactly the same content, the Court did not see that as a reason to judge the customary norm as being necessarily deprived of its separate applicability. Consequently, the Court felt in no way bound to uphold customary rules only in so far as they differ from the treaty rules which it was prevented by the United States reservation from applying. The Court held that in the field in question customary law continues to exist alongside treaty law. The areas governed by the two sources of law often do not overlap exactly, and in many cases the rules also do not have the same content.

In its analysis of the concrete rules of customary law to be applied in the dispute, however, the Court decisively relied on the treaty law of the UN Charter in establishing the content of the applicable law, despite its theoretical emphasis on 'opinio juris' and actual practice.

Concerning the substance of the customary rules relating to the use of force in international relations, the Court stated that the principles as to the use of force incorporated in the United Nations Charter correspond, in essentials, to those found in customary international law. In order to be satisfied that there exists in customary law an 'opinio juris' as to the binding character of the obligation to refrain from the threat or use of force, the Court mainly dealt with the practice in the United Nations. The Court argued that an 'opinio juris' may, though with all due caution, be deduced from the attitude of the Parties and the attitude of other States towards certain General Assembly resolutions, in this case particularly the "Friendly Relations Declaration" of 1970. Consent to such resolutions is, as the Court stressed, not to be understood as merely a "reiteration or elucidation" of the treaty commitment undertaken in the Charter, but has to be qualified as an acceptance of the validity of the rule declared by the resolution, here: as one of the forms of expression of 'opinio juris' with regard to the principle of non-use of force.

Even more reliance on the set of rules created by the system of the United Nations Charter characterized the considerations of the Court relating to the right of self-defence. That the general rule of customary law prohibiting force allows for certain exceptions was viewed as undisputed by the Court. Already the terms of Article 51 of the United Nations Charter demonstrate that the State community starts from the assumption that there exists an "inherent right" of self-defence based in customary law which, in principle, covers both collective and individual self-defence. In defining, however, the specific conditions which may have to be met for its exercise, in addition to the conditions of necessity and proportionality, the Court distinguished "the most grave forms of the use of force" (those constituting an armed attack) from "other less grave forms". Without further attempting to base this distinction in an analysis of State practice, the Court erected its subsequent argumentation on the crucial concept of "armed attack" established by Article 51 of the UN Charter. Whether self-defence be individual or collective, its exercise is, according to the Court, subject to the State concerned having been the victim of an armed attack. To the Court there appeared to be general agreement on the nature of the acts which can be treated as constituting armed attacks. An armed attack in the construction of the Court must be understood as including not merely action by regular armed forces across an international border, but also the sending by a State of armed bands or groups on to the territory of another State, if such an operation, because of its scale and effects, would have been classified as an armed attack had it been carried out by regular armed forces. In this respect the Court quoted the definition of aggression annexed to General Assembly resolution 3314 (XXIX), which in the view of the Court may be taken to reflect customary law. Not to be included in the concept of "armed attack", however, are acts of mere assistance to rebels in the form of the provision of weapons or logistical or other support. Such assistance may, the Court believed, be regarded as a threat or use of force, or may amount to intervention in the internal or external affairs of other States, but it may not justify an action of self-defence.

Furthermore, the Court found it to be clear that it is the State which is the victim of an armed attack which must form and declare the view that it has been so attacked. The Court stated that there is no rule in customary international law permitting another State to exercise the right of collective self-defence on the basis of its own assessment of the situation; what is always required is a formal request by the State which is a victim of the alleged attack, a requirement mainly deduced by the Court from Article 3 of the OAS Charter.

Also the principle of non-intervention, which involves the right of every sovereign State to conduct its affairs without outside interference, was construed by the Court with particular reference to the numerous declarations and resolutions on that subject-matter adopted by international organizations and conferences. As regards the content of the principle, the Court noted that a prohibited intervention must be one bearing on matters in which each State is permitted, by the principle of State sovereignty, to decide freely (for example the choice of a political, economic, social and cultural system). Intervention is regarded to be wrongful when it uses, in regard to such choices, methods of coercion. The element of coercion, which in the view of the Court forms the very essence of prohibited intervention, is particularly obvious in the case of an intervention which uses force, either in the direct form of military action, or in the indirect form of support for subversive or terrorist armed activities within another State. With regard to the second question raised by the Court, namely the question whether the practice is sufficiently in conformity with the principle of non-intervention for this to be a rule of customary international law, the Court concluded, notwithstanding the fact that there had been in recent years a number of instances of foreign intervention for the benefit of opposition groups, that the practice of States does not justify the view that any general right of intervention in support of an opposition within another State exists in contemporary international law.

As a consequence of its ruling that collective self-defence requires the existence of an armed attack, the Court then had to deal with the question whether there exists a right to take counter-measures (individually as well as collectively) in response to conduct not amounting to armed attack but in breach of the principle of non-intervention. Such a right to take collective counter-measures would be analogous to the right of self-defence in the case of armed attack, but the act giving rise to the reaction, as well as the reaction itself, would be less grave, not amounting to armed attack. In the view of the Court, however, under international law in force today, States do not have a right of "collective" armed response to acts which do not constitute an "armed attack"; at the same time the Court left open the question what direct reactions are lawfully available to a State which considers itself the victim of another State's acts of intervention, possibly involving the use of force.

In dealing with the principle of respect for State sovereignty, which extends, as the Court recalled, to the internal waters and territorial sea of every State and to the airspace above its territory, the Court noted that the laying of mines within the ports as well as in the territorial sea necessarily affects the sovereignty of the coastal State. Besides, the customary right of innocent passage and the right of free access to ports, which both follow from the freedom of communications and of maritime commerce, are also infringed by such mining operations. Accordingly, the Court found it certain that interference with navigation by the laying of mines prejudices both the sovereignty of the coastal State over its internal waters, and the right of free access enjoyed by foreign ships. It was further observed by the Court that the absence of any warning or notification with regard to the mining was not only an unlawful act but also a breach of the principles of humanitarian law underlying the Hague Convention No. VIII of 1907.

Since the evidence available was insufficient for the purpose of attributing to the United States the acts committed by the 'contras', the Court could not judge the alleged violations by the 'contra' forces of the principles of international humanitarian law. What remained as a question, however, according to the construction of the Court, was the law applicable to the acts of the United States in relation to the activities of the 'contras'. The Court analyzed that question not from the perspective of the treaty law laid down in the four Geneva Conventions of 12 August 1949, but as a question of the "fundamental general principles of humanitarian law" stated in Article 3 common to the four Geneva Conventions; in the Court's view, the Geneva Conventions are in some respects a development, and in other respects no more than the expression, of such principles. For the Court there was no doubt that these rules constitute a minimum yardstick, reflecting what the Court already in 1949 had called "elementary considerations of humanity". The Court therefore found them applicable to the dispute, with the effect that the United States was seen to be under an obligation to "respect" the Conventions and even to "ensure respect" for them, and thus not to encourage persons or groups engaged in the conflict in Nicaragua to act in violation of these "fundamental general principles".

The Court ultimately used as a legal yardstick the bilateral Treaty of Friendship, Commerce and Navigation signed at Managua on 21 January 1956. In its Judgment on jurisdiction and admissibility of 26 November 1984, the Court had concluded that it had jurisdiction also on the basis of the 1956 Treaty of Friendship, Commerce and Navigation, concerning disputes as to the interpretation or application of the treaty. The Court now found that it had to determine the meaning of the various relevant provisions, in particular the derogation clause of Article XXI para. 1 (c) and 1 (d) of the treaty.

In the final part of the Judgment, the Court then related its abstract statements on the applicable law to the factual findings it had made earlier. Beginning with the question of the lawfulness of the use of force and the alleged justification of the American actions under the right of self-defence, the Court appraised the facts as proved by the available evidence to constitute infringements of the principle of non-use of force, unless justified by circumstances which exclude their uniawfulness. The laying of mines in the internal waters and territorial sea of Nicaragua, the attacks on Nicaraguan ports, oil installations and naval bases directly imputable to the United States, but also the arming and training of the 'contras' were judged by the Court to be a *prima facie* violation of the prohibition of the use of force, unless these actions could be justified as an exercise of the right of self-defence. To fulfil the requirements of a lawful action of collective self-defence, the Court would have had to find that Nicaragua engaged in an armed attack against El Salvador, Honduras or Costa Rica, since only such an attack could have justified reliance on the right of self-defence according to the Court's construction of the relevant principles of customary international law. With regard to El Salvador, however, the Court considered that the provision of arms to the opposition in another State did not constitute an armed attack on that State; concerning Honduras and Costa Rica, the Court stated that, in the absence of sufficient information as to the transborder incursions into the territory of those two States from Nicaragua, it was difficult to decide whether they amounted to an armed attack by Nicaragua. The Court found that neither these incursions nor the alleged supply of arms might be relied on as justifying the exercise of the right of self-defence. The Court also came to the conclusion that the procedural requirements put up for the exercise of this right, namely that the States allegedly attacked believed themselves that they were the victim of an armed attack, and expressly requested the assistance of the State claiming to act in collective self-defence, were not present. In addition, the Court regarded the United States activities as not satisfying the criteria of necessity and proportionality. The Court thus decided, by 12 votes to 3, that it had to reject the justification of collective self-defence maintained by the United States in connection with the military and paramilitary activities in and against Nicaragua, and that accordingly the United States had acted in breach of its customary law obligation not to use force against another State.

As regards the principle of non-intervention, the Court found it clearly established that the United States intended, by its support of the 'contras', to coerce Nicaragua in respect of matters in which each State is permitted to decide freely. It considered that if one State, with a view to the coercion of another State, supports and assists armed bands in that State whose purpose is to overthrow its government, that amounts to an intervention in its internal affairs, whatever the political objective of the State giving support. Basing its further reasoning on the conclusion that intervention in the internal affairs of another State does not produce an entitlement to take collective counter-measures involving the use of force, and that the acts of intervention of which Nicaragua was accused could only have justified proportionate counter-measures on the part of the State which had been the victim of these acts, the Court stated that there was no justification for counter-measures taken by a third State, the United States. The Court therefore found, by 12 votes to 3, that the support given by the United States to the military and paramilitary activities of the 'contras' in Nicaragua, by financial support, training, supply of weapons, intelligence and logistic support, constituted a clear breach of the obligation under customary law not to intervene in the affairs of another State. With regard to the form of "indirect" intervention which Nicaragua saw in the taking of certain economic sanctions, however, the Court felt unable to regard such action as a breach of the customary law principle of non-intervention.

Also by 12 votes to 3, the Court decided that the direct attacks on Nicaraguan ports, oil installations etc., the unauthorized overflights of Nicaraguan territory and the mining operations in Nicaraguan ports infringed the principle of respect for territorial sovereignty. The laying of mines in or near Nicaraguan ports additionally was qualified as constituting an infringement, to Nicaragua's detriment, of the freedom of communications and of maritime commerce. Concerning the mining operations, the Court further decided, by 14 votes to 1, that the United States, by failing to give notice of the existence and location of the mines laid by it, was responsible for a breach of customary principles of international humanitarian law. Also constituting a breach of its obligations under the general principles of humanitarian law was the publication and dissemination in 1983 of a manual entitled "Operaciones sicológicas en guerra de guerrillas", since by virtue of the general principles of humanitarian law the United States was bound to refrain from encouragement of groups engaged in conflict to commit violations of the humanitarian minimum standard laid down in Article 3 common to the four Geneva Conventions.

As to the other grounds mentioned by the United States in justification of its acts, the Court reaffirmed that there does not exist a new rule opening up a right of intervention by one State against another on the ground that the latter has opted for some particular ideology or political system; that alleged violations of human rights could not be taken as a justification for the use of force, since the use of force could not be the appropriate method to monitor or ensure respect for human rights; and that the alleged militarization of Nicaragua may not be accepted as justifying the use of force, since in international law there are, according to the Court, no rules, other than such rules as may be accepted by the State concerned, whereby the level of armaments of a sovereign State can be limited.

Finally, the Court turned to the claims of Nicaragua based on the Treaty of Friendship, Commerce and Navigation. Nicaragua had accused the United States of depriving the Treaty of its object and purpose and of emptying it of real content. Although the Court felt unable to regard all the acts complained of in that light, it considered that there were certain activities of the United States which were such as to undermine the whole spirit of the agreement. These were, according to the Court, the mining of Nicaraguan ports, the direct attacks on ports, oil installations etc., and the general trade embargo. By 12 votes to 3, the Court thus decided that these were acts calculated to deprive of its object and purpose the Treaty of Friendship, Commerce and Navigation of 21 January 1956. Also by 12 votes to 3, the Court decided that by the attacks on Nicaraguan ports and oil installations as well as by the declaration of a general trade embargo, the United States had acted in breach of the clause on freedom of commerce and navigation contained in Article XIX of the Treaty. The contention that by the mining of Nicaraguan ports the United States had acted in manifest contradiction with the freedom of navigation and commerce guaranteed by Article XIX of the Treaty, was upheld by the Court with 14 votes to 1.

The remaining task of the Court was to adjudge on the Nicaraguan claim concerning reparation. Alter satisfying itself that it had jurisdiction to order reparation, the Court declared as appropriate the request of Nicaragua for the nature and amount of the reparation to be determined in a subsequent phase of the proceedings, and considered only the fundamental question whether Nicaragua had a legal claim to demand compensation at all. The Court decided that the United States is under an obligation to make reparation for all injury caused to Nicaragua by the breaches of obligations under customary law and the 1956 Treaty on Friendship, Commerce and Navigation, and that the form and amount of such reparation, failing agreement between the parties, will be settled by the Court, which reserved for this purpose the subsequent procedure in the case. Finally, the Court unanimously recalled to both parties to the case the need to co-operate with the Contadora efforts in seeking a definitive and lasting peace in Central America, in accordance with the customary law principle of peaceful settlement of international disputes.

Review of Judgment No. 333 of the United Nations Administrative Tribunal, Advisory Opinion of May 27,1987

The central problem with which the Court had to deal in its Advisory Opinion concerning the review of Judgment No.333 of the United Nations Administrative Tribunal was the discretion of the Secretary-General in decisions on the employment of staff members. The Court had to ask itself how far the Secretary-General's discretion in that regard is structured by legal principles derived from the provisions of the UN Charter, and to what degree the Administrative Tribunal (and in the consequence also the International Court of Justice in its task of reviewing the Administrative Tribunal's judgments) should control the content of the Secretary-General's decisions in staff matters. Article 101 para.3 of the Charter gives some basic guidelines on recruitment and service conditions in providing: "The paramount consideration in the employment of the staff and in the determination of the conditions of service shall be the necessity of securing the highest standards of efficiency, competence, and integrity." More concrete shape was given to these rules on employment of staff by several General Assembly resolutions. Resolution 37/126 provided, inter alia, "that staff members on fixed-term appointments upon completion of five years of continuing good service shall be given every reasonable consideration for a career appointment", a rule the benefits of which were claimed by the applicant before the Administrative Tribunal in the proceedings leading to Judgment No. 333.

Mr. Yakimetz, the applicant, had served in the United Nations secretariat from 1969-1974 on the basis of a secondment from the Soviet Government. Alter some years back in the USSR he again entered the service of the United Nations in 1977 as a reviser in the Russian Translation Service, with a five-year appointment, and again on the basis of a secondment. Before the end of his fixed-term contract, he was transferred in 1981 as Programme Officer to the Programme Planning and Co-Ordination Office, with his contract later extended for one year until the end of 1983.

On 9 February 1983, one day after the applicant had been informed by his superiors that they intended to request a further extension of his contract, he applied for asylum in the United States, informing the Representative of the USSR about his resigning from all positions in the Soviet civil service. After Mr. Yakimetz had addressed a memorandum to his superior in the Programme Planning and Co-Ordination Office in which he requested an extension of his contract, he was informed in November 1983 by the Deputy Chief of Staff Services "upon instruction by the Office of the Secretary-General" that it was not the intention of the organization to extend his fixed-term contract beyond its expiration date, i.e. 26 December 1983. The applicant's protests, invoking inter alia General Assembly resolution 37/126, and a request to the Secretary-General for review of the decision proved fruitless, since the Secretary-General informed Mr.Yakimetz of maintaining his decision. Concerning the motivation of that decision, the New York Times in an article of January 1984 quoted the Executive Assistant to the Secretary-General as having said that "to have the contract extended... Soviet consent was essential". And the Under-Secretary-General for Administration and Management, commenting on that report in a letter to the New York Times, pointed out that "a person who is on loan returns to his government unless that government agrees otherwise".

The Administrative Tribunal, which then was seised with the case by Mr.Yakimetz, found in its Judgment No. 333 that the applicant, contrary to his contention, did not have a legal expectancy of continued United Nations employment. Regarding the principle established by General Assembly resolution 37/126, the Tribunal considered the Secretary-General to have given "the required (i.e. 'every reasonable') consideration for a career appointment". The Secretary-General "apparently decided", stated the Tribunal, "in the background of secondment of the Applicant..., that the Applicant could not be given a probationary appointment. He thus exercised his discretion properly, but he should have stated explicitly... that he had given 'every reasonable consideration' to the Applicant's career appointment". At the same time, however, the Tribunal expressed "its dissatisfaction with the failure of the Respondent to record sufficiently early and in specific terms the fact that he had given the question of the Applicant's career appointment 'every reasonable consideration' as enjoined by the General Assembly resolution" - a statement severely attacked by the President of the Tribunal. The President, Mr. Endre Ustor, annexed a statement that in his view the doctrine of the Tribunal on secondment precluded not only the extension of a seconded fixed-term appointment but also its conversion to any other type of appointment without the consent of the Government concerned. The Tribunal's Vice-President, Mr. Arnold Kean, on the other hand dissented completely from the Judgment in expressing the view that the Secretary-General's decision "was flawed by fundamental mistakes of fact or law and requires to be set aside" and declared "that the Tribunal should accept the Applicant's plea that he was illegally denied his right to reasonable consideration for a career appointment".

The applicant did not accept the Judgment and applied to the Committee on Applications for Review of Administrative Tribunal Judgments which is the competent organ to request an advisory opinion of the Court. The Committee came to the conclusion that there was (at least in part) a substantial basis for the application and submitted two questions to the Court. It asked whether the Administrative Tribunal had failed to exercise jurisdiction vested in it by not responding to the question whether a legal impediment existed to the further employment of the applicant, and it asked the Court whether the Tribunal had erred on questions of law relating to provisions of the Charter of the United Nations.

The Court examined first the question of its competence to give an advisory opinion, and the propriety in doing so. Recalling its previous jurisprudence, the Court concluded that the questions addressed to it were clearly legal questions arising within the context of the Committee's activities, questions which undoubtedly fall within the scope of the Court's competence under Article 11, paras. 1 and 2 of the Statute of the United Nations Administrative Tribunal, Article 96 of the UN Charter and Article 65 para. 1 of the Statute of the Court. As for the propriety of giving an opinion, the Court again emphasized the discretionary character of its power under Article 65 of its Statute, but found that there was a clear legal justification for replying to the two questions put to it by the Committee. The Court, however, qualified its conclusion by a reservation as to the merits of the procedure established by Article 11 of the Tribunal's Statute. It recalled that in its 1973 advisory opinion on the Fasla case it had subjected the machinery established by Article 11 of the Tribunal's Statute to critical examination, and had expressed severe doubts as to the propriety of this procedure. While renewing in principle these reservations, the Court, which showed itself anxious "to secure the judicial protection of officials" of the United Nations, concluded nevertheless that it should give an opinion in the case.

The Court also recalled in general the principle established in its advisory opinions of 1973 and 1982 that its role in review proceedings was not "to retry the case and to attempt to substitute its own opinion on the merits for that of the Tribunal"; in particular, it is not, in the view of the Court, its task to express a view on the correctness of any finding of the Tribunal, unless this is necessary in order to reply to the questions put to it.

With regard to the first question - whether the Tribunal had failed to exercise jurisdiction vested in it by not examining the question of a possible legal impediment to further employment of the applicant - the Court stated that the Tribunal's handling of the question of the "legal impediment" was not entirely clear. In the view of the Court an analysis of the Tribunal's Judgment shows that, for the Tribunal, there could be no legal expectancy, but neither was there any legal impediment to "reasonable consideration" being given to an application for a career appointment. According to the Tribunal there would have been no legal impediment to such an appointment if the Secretary-General, in the exercise of his discretion, had seen fit to offer one. But, such was held by the Tribunal, having given reasonable consideration to the applicant's case, the Secretary-General had decided against a new appointment.

In the Court's perspective, however, with that finding the question was not really exhausted. The Court noted that the real complaint of the applicant against the Tribunal was not so much an alleged failure of the Tribunal to respond to the question whether there was a legal impediment to his further employment, but that the Tribunal paid insufficient attention to the indications that the Secretary-General had thought that there was a legal impediment, so that the "reasonable consideration" either never took place or was vitiated by a basic assumption - namely that there was an impediment - which was later conceded to be incorrect. In recalling the need to look in some cases behind the strict terms of the question put to it, the Court stated it essential not only to put under scrutiny whether the Tribunal failed to examine the question of the legal impediment to the applicant's further employment, but also whether the Tribunal omitted to examine the Secretary-General's belief in that regard, and the possible impact of that belief on his ability to give "every reasonable consideration" to a career appointment. If it could be established with sufficient certainty that the Tribunal addressed its mind to the matters on which the applicant's contentions were based, "then, whatever view be taken of the conclusion reached by the Tribunal on the evidence available, there was no failure to exercise jurisdiction in that respect".

The fact that the text of the Tribunal's Judgment does not take up specifically the question of the existence of a "legal impediment" does not justify, according to the Court, the conclusion that the Tribunal failed to address this question. What the Tribunal stated was that the Secretary-General could take the decision to offer the applicant a career appointment, but was not bound to do so. From this it follows for the Court that the Tribunal was clearly deciding, although by implication, that there was no absolute legal impediment to further employment. In that regard the Court also refers to the statement of the Tribunal's President Ustor and to the dissenting opinion of the Tribunal's Vice-President Kean, which the Court found advisable to take into account in order to elucidate the Tribunal's Judgment. In view of these opinions appended to the Judgment, the Court found it impossible to conclude that the Tribunal did not address its mind to the issues specifically mentioned by Mr. Ustor and Mr. Kean as the grounds for their disagreement with part of the Judgment. The "Tribunal as a body, represented by the majority which voted in favour, must also have drawn its conclusions on these issues, even if those conclusions were not spelled out as clearly in the Judgement as they ought to have been". Finally, as to the question whether 'every reasonable consideration' was in fact given, the Court affirmed that it was in any event one for the Tribunal to decide, and one which the Tribunal did decide, in the affirmative. The Court, recalling that it is not entitled to substitute its own opinion for that of the Tribunal on the merits of the case, did not find it possible to uphold the contention that the Secretary-General did not give "every reasonable consideration" to the applicant's case, in implementation of resolution 37/126. "The fact of the matter is however that the Tribunal found that the consideration given was reasonable, and to accuse the Tribunal of being wrong in that decision is not to convict it of failure to exercise its jurisdiction, but rather to complain of the way in which it did exercise it." The Court, accordingly, considered that the Tribunal did not fail to exercise jurisdiction vested in it.

With regard to the second question - whether the Tribunal erred on questions of law relating to provisions of the Charter of the United Nations - the Court began its analysis with a remark concerning the nature of its task. Alter recalling that the interpretation, in general, of Staff Regulations and Rules is not the Court's business, but that it is, on the contrary, very much the business of the Court to judge whether there is a contradiction between a particular interpretation or application of them by the Tribunal and any of the provisions of the Charter, the Court emphasized that it is also open to the Court to judge whether there is any comparable contradiction between the Charter and the Tribunal's interpretation of any other relevant texts such as, in that case, General Assembly resolution 37/126.

The allegation that the Tribunal erred on a question of law relating to the Charter when affirming that the appointment decision was based on "reasonable consideration" of the applicant's case, although no proposal had ever reached the Appointment and Promotion Board, was refuted by the Court. Art. 101, para. 1 of the Charter, which provides that "The staff shall be appointed by the Secretary-General under regulations established by the General Assembly", does not specify which procedures are to be followed in such a case. The Tribunal had found that it was left to the Secretary-General "to decide how every reasonable consideration for a career appointment should be given to a staff member" and that the Secretary-General had "the sole authority to decide what constituted 'reasonable consideration'". But the Tribunal had, as the Court remarked, nowhere stated that the Secretary-General possesses unfettered discretion. Although the Tribunal had accepted as sufficient a statement by the Secretary-General that the 'reasonable consideration' required by resolution 37/126 had been given, and had not required the Secretary-General to furnish any details of when and how it was given, let alone calling for evidence to that effect, the Court felt unable to regard the interpretation given by the Tribunal to resolution 37/126 as in contradiction with Article 101, para.1, of the Charter. Additionally, the Court also dismissed the allegation that the Tribunal should have regarded the statements quoted by the applicant as evidence that the problem of secondment and the lack of government consent had been allowed to dominate more than the Secretary-General was ready to admit. The Tribunal had taken the opposite position, in stating that the Secretary-General had "exercised his discretion properly". Whether or not this was an error of judgment on the Tribunal's part, the Court was certain that it was not an error on a question of law relating to Article 101, para. 1, of the Charter. "Whatever view be taken as to the way in which the Tribunal examined the exercise by the Secretary-General of his discretion, taking into account the apparent inconsistency between the Secretary-General's pleading and the reported statements of his senior officials, the essential point is that the Tribunal did not abandon all claim to test such exercise against the requirements of the Charter. On the contrary, it re-affirmed the need to check any 'arbitrary or capricious exercise' of a discretionary power."

The decisive provision of the Charter to be dealt with by the Court, however, was Article 101, para. 1, which declares that the "paramount consideration" in the employment of the staff should be "the necessity of securing the highest standards of efficiency, competence, and integrity". The Court stressed that the expression "the paramount consideration" is not synonymous with "the sole consideration", and that it is for the Secretary-General to balance the various considerations; it was not for the Tribunal, nor was it for the Court, to substitute its own appreciation of the problem for his. In the view of the Court, the Secretary-General's decision could not be said to have failed to respect the "paramount" character of the considerations mentioned in Article 101 para.3, simply because he took into account all the circumstances of the case in order to give effect to the interests of the organization. The fact that the Tribunal referred in its Judgment to its own jurisprudence established previously by the Fischman case was viewed by the Court to be not essential to the reasoning of the decision. The Tribunal had criticized the Secretary-General for not respecting the "widely-held belief' that staff members who break their ties with their home countries can no longer claim to fulfil the conditions governing employment in the United Nations; the Tribunal had found in its Judgment that this position must provide an essential guidance in this matter. The Court here observed that this "widely-held belief" amounts merely to the views expressed by some delegates to the Fifth Committee in 1953, which never materialized in a General Assembly resolution. However, since the Tribunal, in the Court's opinion, had not established that the "essential guidance" referred to in the Fischman decision was determinative of the question of reasonable consideration, it had not erred on the interpretation of Article 101, para.3 when verifying whether 'reasonable consideration' had taken place.

The Court found thus, by 11 votes to 3, that the Tribunal had not erred on any question of law relating to the provisions of the Charter of the United Nations and, unanimously, that it had not failed to exercise jurisdiction vested in it by not responding to the question whether a legal impediment existed to the further employment of the applicant.

Applicability of the Obligation to Arbitrate under Section 21 of the United Nations Headquarters Agreement of 26 June 1947, Advisory Opinion of 9 March 1988

On 2 March 1988 the General Assembly of the United Nations adopted resolution 42/229 B whereby it requested the International Court of Justice to give an advisory opinion on the question whether the United States of America, as a party to the Agreement between the United Nations and the United States of America regarding the Headquarters of the United Nations, is under an obligation to enter into arbitration in accordance with section 21 of the Agreement. In the light of the indication given by the General Assembly in the resolution, the Court found that an early answer to the request would be desirable, as contemplated by Article 103 of the Rules of Court, and that accordingly all necessary steps should be taken to accelerate the procedure. The Court delivered the Advisory Opinion, after the application of an accelerated procedure, in response to a request submitted by the General Assembly of the United Nations under resolution 42/229 B, adopted on 2 March 1988. The General Assembly's request had arisen from the situation which had developed following the signing of the Anti-Terrorism Act adopted by the U.S. Congress in December 1987, a law which was specifically aimed at the Palestine Liberation Organization and inter alia declared illegal the establishment or maintenance of an office of the Organization within the jurisdiction of the United States. The law thus concerned in particular the office of the PLO Observer Mission to the United Nations, established in New York after the General Assembly had conferred observer status on the PLO in 1974. The maintenance of the office was held by the Secretary-General of the United Nations to fall within the ambit of the Headquarters Agreement concluded with the United States on 26 June 1947. The General

Assembly put the following question to the Court: "In the light of facts reflected in the reports of the Secretary-General, is the United States of America, as a party to the Agreement between the United Nations and the United States of America regarding the Headquarters of the United Nations, under an obligation to enter into arbitration in accordance with section 21 of the Agreement?". The relevant part of section 21 referred to in the question is worded as follows: "(a) Any dispute between the United Nations and the United States concerning the interpretation or application of this agreement or of any supplemental agreement, which is not settled by negotiation or other agreed mode of settlement, shall be referred for final decision to a tribunal of three arbitrators...". The Court was thus obliged to determine whether there existed a dispute between the United Nations and the United States. To that end, the Court recalled that the existence of a dispute, that is to say, a disagreement on a point of law, is a matter for objective determination and cannot depend upon the mere assertion or denials of parties. The United States had never expressly contradicted the Secretary-General's view, but had taken measures against the PLO Mission and indicated that they were being taken irrespective of any obligations it might have under the Headquarters Agreement. However, in the Court's view, the mere fact that a party accused of the breach of a treaty did not advance any argument to justify its conduct under international law did not prevent the opposing attitudes of the parties from giving rise to a dispute concerning the treaty's interpretation or application. Neither could the Court accept that the United States undertaking not to take any other action to close the Mission before the decision of a domestic Court had prevented a dispute from arising. Thus, the Court found that the opposing attitudes of the United Nations and the United States revealed the existence of a dispute. This dispute also concerned "the interpretation or application of this Agreement" in the sense of section 21 of the Headquarters Agreement. The United States had given precedence to the Anti-Terrorism Act over the Agreement, and that had been challenged by the Secretary-General. Furthermore, the United States had taken a number of measures against the PLO Observer Mission. Those had been regarded by the Secretary-General as contrary to the Agreement. Without disputing that point, the United States had stated that the measure in question had been taken "irrespective of any obligations the United States may have under the Agreement". Those two positions were irreconcilable; thus there existed a dispute between the United Nations and the United States concerning the application of the Headquarters Agreement. The Court then considered whether the dispute was one "not settled by negotiation or other agreed mode of settlement" in the terms of section 21 (a). The Court found that, taking into account the United States attitude, the Secretary-General had in the circumstances exhausted such possibilities of negotiation as were open to him, nor had any "other agreed mode of settlement" been contemplated by the United

Nations and the United States. In particular, the current proceedings before the United States courts could not constitute an "agreed method of settlement" within the meaning of section 21. The Court had therefore to conclude that the United States was bound to respect the obligation to enter into arbitration. For those reasons, the Court was unanimously of the opinion: "that the United States of America, as a party to the Agreement between the United Nations and the United States of America regarding the Headquarters of 26 June 1947, is under an obligation, in accordance within section 21 of that Agreement, to enter into arbitration for the settlement of the dispute between itself and the United Nations".

Border and Transborder Armed Actions

(Nicaragua v. Honduras)

On 28 July 1986, the Republic of Nicaragua filed in the Registry of the Court an Application instituting proceedings against the Republic of Honduras in respect of a dispute concerning the alleged activities of armed bands, said to be operating from Honduras, on the border between Honduras and Nicaragua and in Nicaraguan territory. At the suggestion of Honduras, agreed to by Nicaragua, the present 'phase of the proceedings was devoted, in accordance with an Order made by the Court on 22 October 1986, solely to the issues of the jurisdiction of the Court and the admissibility of the Application.

Judgment on the Jurisdiction of the Court and Admissibility of the Application of 20 December 1988

As the basis of the jurisdiction of the Court, Nicaragua referred to the provisions of Article XXXI of the Pact of Bogotá and to the Declarations made by Nicaragua and Honduras accepting the compulsory jurisdiction of the Court as provided for in Article 36 (1) and (2) of the Statute of the Court. Nicaragua claimed to be entitled to found jurisdiction on a Honduras Declaration of 20 February 1960, while Honduras asserted that that Declaration had been modified by a subsequent Declaration, made on 22 May 1986 and deposited with the Secretary-General of the United Nations prior to the filing of the Application by Nicaragua.

Since in relations between the States parties to the Pact of Bogotá, that Pact is governing, the Court first examined the question whether it had jurisdiction under Article XXXI of that Pact.

Honduras maintained that the Pact did not provide any basis for the jurisdiction of the Court putting forward two series of arguments supporting this statement.

First, Honduras interpreted Article XXXI of the Pact to the effect that, for a State party to the Pact which has made a declaration under Article 36 (2) of the Statute, the extent of the jurisdiction of the Court under Article XXXI of the Pact was determined by that declaration, and by any reservation appended to it. It also maintained that any modification or withdrawal of such a declaration which was valid under Article 36 (2) of the Statute was equally effective under Article XXXI of the Pact. Honduras had, however, given two successive interpretations of Article XXXI, claiming initially that to afford jurisdiction it was to be supplemented by a declaration of acceptance of compulsory jurisdiction and subsequently that it could be so supplemented but did not have to be.

The Court considered that the first interpretation advanced by Honduras was incompatible with the actual terms of Article XXXI of the Pact. As to the second interpretation, the Court noted the two readings of Article XXXI of the Pact proposed by the Parties: As a treaty provision conferring jurisdiction in accordance with Article 36 (1) of the Statute or as a collective declaration of acceptance of compulsory jurisdiction under Article 36 (2) of the Statute. Even on the latter interpretation, however, the declaration, having been incorporated into the Pact of Bogotá, could only be modified in accordance with the rules provided for in the Pact itself. However, Article XXXI nowhere envisaged that the undertaking entered into by the parties to the Pact might be amended by means of a unilateral declaration made subsequently under the Statute, and the reference to Article 36 (2) of the Statute was insufficient in itself to have that effect.

The fact that the Pact defines with precision the obligations of the parties lent particular significance to the absence of any indication of that kind. The commitment in Article XXXI applied *ratione materiae* to the disputes enumerated in that text; it related *ratione personae* to the American States parties to the Pact; it remained valid *ratione temporis* for as long as that instrument itself remained in force between those States. Moreover, the commitment in Article XXXI could only be limited by means of reservations to the Pact itself; it constituted an autonomous commitment, independent of any other which the parties might have undertaken or might undertake by accepting the compulsory jurisdiction of the Court under Article 36 (2) and (4) of the Statute. The Court found further confirmation of its reading of Article XXXI in the *travaux préparatoires* of the Pact. From these it followed that, in their relations with the other parties to the Pact, States which wished to maintain reservations included in a declaration of acceptance of compulsory jurisdiction would have to restate them as reservations to the Pact. That interpretation corresponded, moreover, to the subsequent practice of the parties to the Pact.

The Court concluded that the commitment in Article XXXI of the Pact was independent of such declarations of acceptance of compulsory jurisdiction as might have been made under Article 36 (2) of the Statute. Therefore, the Court dismissed the pertinent Honduran argument.

The second objection of Honduras was based upon its contention that Articles XXXI and XXXII of the Pact were to be read together from which it followed that the Court could only be seised under Article XXXI if there had been a prior recourse to conciliation and lack of agreement to arbitrate, a situation which did not arise in the present case. Nicaragua contended that Articles XXXI and XXXII each conferred, independently of each other, jurisdiction upon the Court.

The Court held that the Honduran interpretation of Article XXXII ran counter to the terms of that Article. A confirmation of this holding was to be found in the *travaux préparatoires* of the Pact. The Honduran interpretation would, moreover, imply that Article XXXI would be emptied of all content if, for any reason, the dispute were not subjected to prior conciliation; such a solution, however, would be clearly contrary to both the object and the purpose of the Pact.

Thus, the Court found that Article XXXI of the Pact of Bogotá conferred jurisdiction upon the Court to entertain the dispute submitted to it. Therefore, it did not need to consider whether it might have jurisdiction by virtue of the declaration of acceptance of compulsory jurisdiction by Nicaragua and Honduras.

Honduras had raised four objections as to the admissibility of the Nicaraguan Application, two of which were general in nature whereas the remaining two were based upon provisions of the Pact of Bogotá.

As to the first ground of inadmissibitity, the alleged political motivation of the proceedings, the Court observed that it could not concern itself with the potitical motivation underlying a State's decision to choose judicial settlement. The Court recalled, moreover, that, while there was no doubt that the issues of which the Court had been seised might be regarded as part of a wider regional problem, "no provision of the Statute or Rules contemplated that the Court should decline to take cognizance of one aspect of a dispute merely because that dispute has other aspects, however important".

As to the second ground of inadmissibility, the alleged vagueness of the Application, the Court found that the Nicaraguan Application met the requirements of the Statute and the Rules of the Court, namely that an Application was to indicate the subject of the dispute, to specify the precise nature of the claim and in support thereof to give no more than a succinct statement of the facts and grounds on which the claim was based.

The third ground of inadmissibitity put forward by Honduras was based upon Article II of the Pact of Bogotá which Honduras interpreted to the effect that the precondition of recourse to the procedures established by the Pact was not merely that both parties should hold the opinion that the dispute could not be settled by negotiation, but that they should have manifested that opinion. The Court, noting a discrepancy between the four texts of Article II of the Pact (the reference in the French text being to the opinion of only one of the Parties), proceeded on the hypothesis that the stricter interpretation should be used, i.e. that it would be necessary to consider whether the opinion of both Parties was that it was not possible to settle the dispute by negotiation. In order to ascertain the opinion of the Parties, the Court analysed in detail the sequence of events in their diplomatic relations, in particular the development of what had become to be known as the *Contadora process*. Since that process was, as a result of the presence and action of third States, markedly different from a "direct negotiation through the usual diplomatic channels", it did not fall within the relevant provisions of Article II of the Pact of Bogotá. Consequently, Honduras could not plausibly maintain, at the date of the filing of the Nicaraguan Application, that the dispute between the Parties was at that time capable of being settled by direct negotiation. The Court, therefore, considered that the provisions of Article II of the Pact of Bogotá did not constitute a bar to the admissibility of Nicaragua's Application.

The fourth ground of inadmissibility put forward by Honduras was based upon the contention that the *Contadora process* was to be considered as a "special procedure" in the meaning of Article II of the Pact of Bogotá, and that therefore Nicaragua was precluded both by Article IV of the Pact and by elementary considerations of good faith from commencing any other procedure for pacific settlement, such as the present procedures before the Court, until such time as the *Contadora process* had been concluded, which had not been the case at the date of the filing of the Nicaraguan Application. In order to decide the issue as to whether the *Contadora process* had been concluded, the Court resumed its survey of the *Contadora process* and considered that this process had come to a standstill on 28 July 1986, the date on which Nicaragua filed its Application. Since, however, the *Contadora process* had been set in train again in February 1987, the Court had to decide upon the question whether this latter procedure should be regarded as having ensured the continuation of the *Contadora process* without interruption, or whether on 28 July 1986 that process should be regarded as having been "concluded" for the purposes of Article IV of the Pact of Bogotá, and a process of a different nature as having got under way thereafter. Relying upon the fundamentally different character of the two parts of the *Contadora process* mentioned above, the Court concluded that the procedures employed in that process up to the date of the filing of the Nicaraguan Application had been "concluded"; therefore, the submissions of Honduras based upon Article IV of the Pact of Bogotá had to be rejected. As to the further contention of Honduras that Nicaragua was precluded also by elementary considerations of good faith from commencing any other procedure for pacific settlement, the Court considered that the "conclusion" of the *Contadora process* had freed Nicaragua also in relation to any other obligation to exhaust that procedure which might had existed independently of the Pact of Bogotá.

Therefore, the Court found, unanimously, that it had jurisdiction to entertain the Application filed by Nicaragua and, unanimously, that that Application was admissible. Judge Lachs appended a declaration, and Judges Oda, Schwebel and Shahabuddeen appended separate opinions to the Judgment.

Elettronica Sicula S.p.A. (ELSI) case

(United States of America v. Italy)
Judgment of 20 July 1989

On July 20, 1989, the International Court of Justice delivered its judgment in the case concerning Elettronica Sicula S.p.A. (ELSI) between the United States of America and Italy.

Raytheon-ELSI S.p.A. (ELSI), an Italian corporation wholly owned by the United States corporations Raytheon Company (Raytheon), which held 99.16 per cent of the shares, and its subsidiary The Machlett Laboratories (Machlett), which held the remaining 0.83 per cent, was established in Palermo, Italy, where it produced electronic components.

ELSI had been in economic trouble since the 1960s. In 1967, representatives of ELSI and Raytheon held numerous meetings with officials of the Italian Government and of the Sicilian region in an attempt to secure governmental support for ELSI. When it became apparent that these discussions were unlikely to be successful, Raytheon prepared to close the plant. The balance sheet for the end of September 1967 showed that under Italian law and accounting principles the book value of ELSI's assets still exceeded its liabilities. However, internal accounting adjustments in accordance with Rayhteon's accounting policy showed ELSI insolvent. Raytheon therefore formally declared that it would not subscribe to any additional loans made to ELSI. It was, however, ready to financially support an orderly liquidation. The Italian authorities pressed ELSI not to close the plant and promised help. The final decision to close the plant was taken in March 1968.

On April 1, 1968, the Mayor of Palermo issued an order, effective immediately, requisitioning ELSI's plant and related assets for six months. An administrative appeal brought against the order was not decided by the Prefect of Palermo until August 22, 1969. It was then held that the Mayor had exceeded his powers and that the requisition had been unlawful. In the meantime, the plant had been occupied and production had ceased. On April 26, 1968, ELSI filed petition in bankruptcy. A trustee was appointed. In July 1969, ELSI was purchased for far less than book value by a subsidiary of the State-controlled IRI. An action for damages resulting from the requisition was dismissed by the Court of Palermo. On appeal, the Court of Appeal of Palermo granted a small portion of the claims. This decision was upheld by the Court of Cassation in 1975. In 1974, the United States transmitted a note to Italy enclosing a claim on behalf of Raytheon, based on several alleged violations of the Treaty of Friendship, Commerce and Navigation concluded between Italy and the United States (FCN Treaty).

The United States application before the International Court of Justice was filed in 1987. According to the wishes of the parties, the case was submitted to and decided by a Chamber of the Court under Article 26(2) of the Statute of the Court.

Italy entered an objection to the admissibility of the present case on the ground of an alleged failure of the two United States corporations to exhaust local remedies. The United States questioned whether the rule of the exhaustion of local remedies could apply at all, as Article XXVI of the FCN Treaty was unqualified by any reference to the local remedies rule. The United States further argued that the local remedies rule was inapplicable in so far as its claim was for a declaratory judgment of a direct injury to the United States by infringement of its rights under the FCN Treaty. The Chamber rejected these arguments. The United States also observed that Italy, until the filing of the Counter-Memorial, had at no time suggested that Raytheon should sue in the Italian courts on the basis of the Treaty, and argued that this amounted to an estoppel. The Chamber, however, found that an estoppel cannot be derived from a mere failure to mention a matter at a particular point in diplomatic exchanges.

After examining the actions taken against the requisition order, the Chamber considered that the municipal courts had been fully seized of the matter which was the substance of the Applicant's claim before the Chamber. Furthermore, since it was for Italy to show the existence of a local remedy, and since Italy had not been able to satisfy the Chamber that there clearly remained some remedy which Raytheon, independently of ELSI, ought to have pursued and exhausted, the Chamber rejected the objection of non-exhaustion of local remedies.

As to the merits, the majority found that it had not been sufficiently established that an orderly liquidation of ELSI's assets would still have been feasible at the time of the requisition. The Chamber first observed that Article III of the Treaty, the right "to control and manage corporations", had not been violated, since it had not been established that the creditors would have given the company enough time for an orderly liquidation, or that the price obtainable on a quick sale would have been sufficient. The Chamber felt that since the feasibility of an orderly liquidation had not been sufficiently established, the requisition order could not interfere with control and management in any real sense. Thus the requisition, while unlawful, was not the cause of ELSI's bankruptcy.

The Chamber also dismissed the claim that Article V, paragraphs 1 and 3, of the FCN Treaty, which were concerned with the protection and security of nationals and their property, had been violated. According to the Chamber the toleration of the occupation of the plant by the workers did not cause any material harm to ELSI. The delay in the administrative appeal was not regarded as a denial of justice, since, under the Italian Law, there had been a means of requesting a quick decision.

The judgment further found that no taking without a due process of law had occurred contrary to Article V, paragraph 2, of the Treaty. The Chamber left the question open, whether the Italian term "espropriazione" should be interpreted in a stricter sense than the English term "taking". In that respect, the Chamber found that although a requisition could be an expropriation, it was not in the present case, since ELSI was already under an obligation to file for bankruptcy.

The Chamber also concluded that the requisition order had not violated Article I of the Supplementary Agreement to the FCN Treaty, which prohibited "arbitrary or discriminatory measures". According to the Chamber arbitrariness would require more than mere unlawfulness. But since the order was "consciously made in the context of an operating system of law and of appropriate remedies of appeal", it could hardly be an arbitrary act. Finally, the Chamber stated that the right to dispose of property and interests, guaranteed by Article VII of the FCN Treaty, had not been violated, since what really deprived the United States shareholders of their right to dispose of ELSI's real property was the precarious financial state of ELSI, which ultimately led to bankruptcy and thus prevented the shareholders from disposing of the company's property.

Having thus found that the Respondent, Italy, had not violated the FCN Treaty in the manner asserted by the Applicant, it follows that the Chamber rejected the claim for reparation made by the Applicant.

Case Concerning the Aerial Incident of 3 July 1988

(Islamic Republic of Iran v. United States of America),
Order of 13 December 1989.

On 17 May 1989, the Islamic Republic of Iran filed in the registry of the Court an Application instituting proceedings against the United States of America in respect of a dispute concerning the interpretation and application of the 1944 Convention on International Civil Aviation and the 1971 Convention for the Suppression of Unlawful Acts against the Safety of Civil Aviation. The dispute arose from the destruction of an Iranian aircraft, and the killing of 290 passengers and crew, on 3 July 1988. The United States intended to find preliminary objections to jurisdiction and admissibility prior to the filing of a memorial by the Applicant. The Court stated that whereas, in accordance with Article 79, para. 1, of the Rules of Court, while a respondant which wishes to submit a preliminary objection is entitled before doing so to be informed as to the nature of the claim by the submission of a Memorial by the Applicant, it may nevertheless file its objection earlier. The Court unanimously fixed the following time-limits for the written proceedings: 12 June 1990 for the Memorial of the Islamic Republic of Iran: 10 December 1990 for the Counter-Memorial of the United States of America.

Applicability of Article VI, Section 22, of the Convention on the Privileges and Immunities of the United Nations, Advisory Opinion of December 15, 1989

On December 15, 1989 the International Court of Justice delivered an advisory opinion on a request brought by the United Nations Economic and Social Council concerning the applicability of Article VI, Section 22, of the Convention on the Privileges and Immunities of the United Nations in the case of Mr. Mazilu.

On March 13, 1984 the Commission on Human Rights - a subsidiary organ of the Economic and Social Council - elected Mr. Mazilu, a Romanian national nominated by Romania, to serve as a member of the Sub-Commission on Prevention of Discrimination and Protection of Minorities. The Sub-Commission on August 29, 1985 requested Mr. Mazilu to prepare a report on "Human Rights and Youth" and further requested the Secretary-General to provide him with all necessary assistance for the completion of his task.

The thirty-ninth session of the Sub-Commission, at which Mr. Mazilu's report was to be presented, was not convened in 1986 but was postponed until 1987. The three-year mandate of its members - originally due to expire on December 31, 1986 - was extended by a Council decision for an additional year. When the° session of the Sub-Commisson opened in Geneva on August 10, 1987, no report had been received from Mr. Mazilu, nor was he present. By a letter the Permanent Mission of Romania informed the United Nations Office at Geneva that Mr. Mazilu had suffered a heart-attack and was still in hospital. A telegram signed "D. Mazilu" was received in Geneva on August 18, 1987 and informed the Sub-Commission of his inability, due to heart illness, to attend the current session. In these circumstances, the Sub-Commission deferred consideration of Mr. Mazilu's report until 1988.

After the 1987 session of the Sub-Commission, the Centre for Human Rights of the United Nations Secretariat in Geneva made various attempts to contact Mr. Mazilu. In December 1987, Mr. Mazilu informed the Under-Secretary-General for Human Rights that he had not received previous communications of the Centre. In January 1988, Mr. Mazilu informed the Under-Secretary-General for Human Rights that he had been twice in hospital in 1987 and that he had been forced to retire, as of December 1, 1987, from his various governmental posts. He also stated that the Romanian authorities were refusing him a travel permit. In April and May 1988, Mr. Mazilu, in a series of letters, complained that strong pressure had been exerted on him and on his family. On December 31, 1987 the terms of all members of the Sub-Commission, including Mr. Mazilu, expired. Nevertheless, all the rapporteurs and special rapporteurs of the Sub-Commission were invited to attend its 1988 session, but Mr. Mazilu again did not appear. A special invitation was cabled to him, but the telegram was not delivered and the United Nations Information Centre in Bucharest was unable to locate Mr. Mazilu. The Under-Secretary-General for Human Rights informed the Sub-Commission that the Romanian Government took the position that any intervention by the United Nations Secretariat and any form of investigation in Bucharest would be considered interference in Romania's internal affairs. On September 1, 1988, the Sub-Commission adopted resolution 1988/37 by which it requested the Secretary-General of the United Nations to approach the Government of Romania and invoke the applicability of the Convention on the Privileges and Immunities of the United Nations. It also requested the Commission to urge the Council to request from the International Court of Justice an advisory opinion on the applicability of the relevant provisions of the Convention on the Privileges and Immunities of the United Nations to the present case. Pursuant to that resolution the Secretary-General, on October 26, 1988 addressed a Note Verbale to the Permanent Representative of Romania to the United Nations in New York, in which he invoked the General Convention in respect of Mr. Mazilu. On January 6, 1989, the Permanent Representative of Romania handed to the Legal Council of the United Nations an Aide-Mémoire. Romania stated that Mr. Mazilu had in 1987 become gravely ill and that he had been placed on the retired list on grounds of ill-health. Romania expressed the view that the Convention "does not equate rapporteurs with experts on missions" and that "even if rapporteurs are given some of the status of experts, they can enjoy only functional immunities and privileges". Romania stated expressely that it was opposed to a request for an advisory opinion from the Court on any aspect of the case.

The Council, however, on May 24, 1989 adopted its resolution 1989/75, by which it requested the Court to render an opinion.

The Court, having considered the question which is the subject of the request, took the view that it was a legal question in that it involved the interpretation of an international convention in order to determine its applicability and, moreover, that it was a question arising within the scope of the activities of the Council, as Mr. Mazilu's assignment was pertinent to a function and programme of the Council.

Romania claimed that, because of the reservation made by it to Section 30 of the General Convention, the United Nations could not, without Romania's consent, submit a request for an advisory opinion in respect of its difference with Romania. The Court in that respect began by referring to its earlier jurisprudence, recalling that the consent of States is not a condition precedent to its competence under Article 96 of the Charter and Article 65 of the Statute to give advisory opinions. This applied even when the request for an opinion was seen as relating to a legal question pending between the United Nations and the Member State. The Court then noted that Section 30 of the General Convention operated on a different plane and in a different context from that of Article 96 of the Charter as, when the provisions of that Section are read in their totality, it was clear that their object was to provide a dispute settlement mechanism. The Court found that the request was not made under Section 30 and that it accordingly did not need to determine the effect of the Romanian reservation to that provision. The Court recalled that the nature and purpose of the present proceedings were those of a request for advice on the applicability of a part of the General Convention, and not the bringing of a dispute before the Court for determination. It added that the content and extent of the obligations entered into by States when they consented to be bound by the

Convention are not modified by the request and by the present advisory opinion. The Court thus found that the reservation made by Romania to Section 30 of the General Convention did not affect the Court's jurisdiction to entertain the request submitted to it.

On the other hand, the Court found that the absence of the consent of Romania to the proceedings before the Court was a matter to be considered when examining the propriety of its giving an opinion. The Court stated that in certain circumstances the lack of consent of an interested State might render the giving of an advisory opinion incompatible with the Court's judicial character. It observed that an instance of this would be when to give a reply would have the effect of circumventing the principle that a State is not obliged to allow its disputes to be submitted to judicial settlement without its consent. The Court considered that in the present case to give a reply would have no such effect. In that respect it distinguished between the question of the applicability of the Convention in the case of Mr. Mazilu on the one hand and its application on the other hand. Accordingly, the Court did not find any compelling reason to refuse to give an advisory opinion.

The Court then considered what was meant by "experts on missions" for the purposes of Section 22 on the Convention of the Privileges and Immunities of the United Nations. The Court found that the purpose of Section 22 was to enable the United Nations to entrust missions to persons who do not have the status of an official of the Organization and to guarantee them such privileges and immunities as are necessary for the independent exercise of their functions. The Court noted that the practice of the United Nations showed that the persons so appointed and in particular the members of committees and commissions of the United Nations, have been regarded as experts on mission within the meaning of Section 22.

The Court then turned its attention to the meaning of the phrase "during the period of their missions" which is part of that Section. In this connection the question arose whether experts on missions are also covered by Section 22 when there is no travel or apart from travel. To answer this question, the Court considered it necessary to determine the meaning of the word "mission" in English and "mission" in French, the two languages in which the General Convention was adopted. The Court considered that Section 22, in its reference to experts performing missions for the United Nations, uses the word "mission" in a general sense. According to the Court, the intent of Section 22 was to ensure the independence of such experts in the interest of the Organization by according them the privileges and immunities necessary for the purpose. The Court accordingly concluded that Section 22 is applicable to every expert on mission, whether or not he travels.

The Court finally took up the question whether experts on missions could invoke the privileges and immunities provided for in Section 22 against the States of which they are nationals or on the territory of which they reside. It found that the privileges and immunities of Article VI were conferred with the view to ensuring the independence of international officials and experts in the interest of the Organization; this independence must be respected by all States, including the State of nationality and the State of residence. The Court noted, that some States have entered reservations to certain provisions of Article VI itself, as regards their nationals or persons resident on their territory. In its view, the very fact that it was felt necessary to make these reservations confirms that in the absence of such reservations, experts on missions enjoy the privileges and immunities provided for under the General Convention in their relations with the States of which they are nationals or on the territory of which they reside.

The Court observed that members of the Sub-Commission are elected by the Commission as experts in their individual capacity. The Court therefore found that, since their status was neither that of a representative of a Member State nor that of a United Nations official, and since they perform functions independently for the Sub-Commission, the members of the Sub-Commission must be regarded as experts on missions within the meaning of Section 22. The Court further noted that rapporteurs or special rapporteurs are entrusted by the Sub-Commission with a research mission. Their status was neither that of a representative of a Member State nor that of a United Nations official. Since they carry out their research independently on behalf of the United Nations, they must be regarded as experts on missions within the meaning of Section 22, even in the event that they are not, or are no longer, members of the Sub-Commission.

Regarding the case of Mr. Mazilu, the Court found that at no time had he ceased to have the status of an expert on mission within the meaning of Section 22, or ceased to be entitled to enjoy for the exercise of his functions the privileges and immunities provided for therein. The Court further pointed out that it was for the United Nations to decide whether in the circumstances it wished to retain Mr. Mazilu as special rapporteur and took note that decisions to that effect had been taken by the Sub-Commission.

The Court therefore was of the opinion that in these circumstances Mr. Mazilu continued to have the status of a special rapporteur, and that as a consequence he had to be regarded as an expert on mission within the meaning of Section 22 of the General Convention and that the Section was accordingly applicable in the case of Mr. Mazilu.

Land, Island and Maritime Frontier Dispute

(El Salvador v. Honduras)

On 11 December 1986 El Salvador and Honduras jointly notified to the Court a Special Agreement concluded between them on 24 May 1986 whereby a dispute referred to as land, island and maritime frontier dispute would be submitted for decision to a chamber to be constituted according to Article 26 para. 2 of the Statute. The Chamber should consist of three Members of the Court and two judges *ad hoc* chosen by each Party.

By an *Order of 8 May 1987* the Court elected Judges Oda, Sette-Camara and Sir Robert Jennings to sit as members in the Chamber; El Salvador appointed Mr. Valticos and Honduras Mr. Virally to sit as judges *ad hoc*. After the death of Judge *ad hoc* Virally, Honduras, on 9 February 1989, appointed Mr. Torres Bernárdez as judge *ad hoc*. Since after a number of communications it appeared that El Salvador had no objection to the choice of Mr. Torrez Bernárdez, the Court, by an *Order of 13 December 1989* took note of the new composition of the Chamber which was presided by Judge Sette-Camara.

Application for Permission to Intervene

(Order of 28 February 1990)

On 17 November 1989 Nicaragua filed an Application for permission to intervene under Article 62 of the Statute. This application was addressed to the Court, not to the Chamber, since Nicaragua was of the opinion that its request was a matter exclusively within the procedural mandate of the full Court.

In its Order of 28 February 1990 the Court found that it was for the Chamber formed to deal with the case to decide whether the application for permission to intervene should be granted, stating as the reason that the tribunal seised of a principal issue has to deal also with any issue subsidiary thereto. Furthermore, the Court argued, an application for permission to intervene under Article 62 of the Statute required a judicial decision on whether the State seeking to intervene "has an interest of a legal nature which may be affected by the decision" on the merits and this question could only be determined by the body which had to give the decision on the merits.

This view was not shared by Judges Elias, Tarassov and Shahabuddeen who each appended a dissenting opinion. Their concern was essentially that the methods by which the members of the Chamber were selected did not satisfy the criteria required to enable it to discharge the judicial mission of the International Court of Justice, considered as a court of justice, in relation to Nicaragua. They expressed severe doubts as to whether a Chamber constituted according to the wishes of the Parties would be prepared to permit the intervention of a third State against the will of the main Parties.

Application of Nicaragua for Permission to Intervene
Judgment of the Chamber of 13 September 1990

By its Judgment of 13 September 1990 the Chamber unanimously decided to permit the intervention of Nicaragua.
According to Article 62 of the Statute a request to intervene should be permitted if a State considers that it has "an interest of a legal nature which may be affected by the decision in the case". In the present case the Chamber found that Nicaragua had shown such an interest to exist, limited, however, exclusively to the part of the case concerning the legal régime of the waters of the Gulf of Fonseca. These findings were based essentially on the fact that El Salvador claimed that the waters of the Gulf should be subject to a condominum of the coastal States while Honduras' arguments started from the "community of interests". According to the Chamber both arguments thus embraced Nicaragua as one of the three riparian States of the Gulf.

Besides the legal interest which may be affected, the request for permission to intervene has to indicate the precise object of the intervention (Article 81 para. 2 b) of the Rules of Procedure). The Chamber found that, even though the request of Nicaragua might not have been formulated sufficiently clearly in this respect, it had to take into account the object actually aimed at. This object, namely generally to protect the legal rights of Nicaragua in the Gulf of Fonseca and the adjacent maritime areas by all means available, was not to be interpreted as involving a judicial pronouncement

Case Concerning the Arbitral Award of 31 July 1989

(Guinea-Bissau v. Senegal) Order of 2 March 1990

In 1960 France and Portugal concluded an Agreement for the purpose of defining the maritime boundary between Senegal - at that time an autonomous State within the Communauté - and the Portuguese Province of Guinea. After the accession to independance of Senegal and Guinea-Bissau a dispute arose between the two States concerning the delimitation of their maritime territories. The two States submitted this dispute to an Arbitration Tribunal which had to decide on the following questions:
1) whether the Agreement of 1960 had the force of law between the Parties; and

2) in the event of a negative answer, to define the course of the line delimiting the maritime territories of the two States.

By its decision of 31 July 1989 the Arbitration Tribunal stated that the Agreement of 1960 had force of law in relation to the Parties.

Interim measures of Protection,
Order of 2 March 1990

By a request of 23 August 1989 Guinea-Bissau had instituted proceedings against Senegal concerning the existence and validity of the arbitral award of 31 July 1989. The main reason advanced by Guinea-Bissau was the fact that one of the two arbitrators making up the appearance of a majority in favour of the text of the award had, by a declaration appended to it, expressed a view in contradition with the one apparently adopted by the vote.

On 18 January 1990, Guinea-Bissau, on the ground of actions stated to have been taken by Senegal in a maritime area which Guinea-Bissau regarded as an area disputed between the Parties, requested the Court to indicate the following provisional measures:

> "In order to safeguard the rights of each of the Parties, they shall abstain in the disputed area from any act or action of any kind whatever during the whole duration of the proceedings until the decision given by the Court."

By fourteen votes to one the Court dismissed the request for the reason that the subject matter of the request for provisional measures was not the same as that of the proceedings before the Court on the merits of the case. By the provisional measures Guinea-Bissau sought to protect the respective rights of the Parties in the maritime areas in question while the Application asked the Court to declare the 1989 award to be inexistent or, subsidiarily, null and void and thus inapplicable. Thus, the requested measures could not be subsumed under the Court's judgment on the merits as is required by Article 41 of the Statute of the Court. Moreover, as the decision of the Court on the merits stating the invalidity of the award would not entail any decision as to the Applicant's claim in respect of the disputed maritime delimination, the necessary link between the subject matter of the request for interim measures and the request on the merits was lacking.

While the proceedings on the merits were still pending before the Court, Guinea-Bissau brought a new claim against Senegal on 12 March 1991 concerning the delimination of the maritime territories between the two States.

The Judges of the International Court of Justice
1986 - 1990

Roberto AGO	Italy	6. 2.1979-(5. 2.1997)
Mohammed BEDJAOUI	Algeria	19. 3.1982-(5. 2.1997)
Taslim Olawale ELIAS	Nigeria (President 1982-1985)	6. 2.1976-14. 8.1991(+)
Jens EVENSON	Norway	6. 2.1985-(5. 2.1994)
Gilbert GUILLAUME	France	14. 9.1987-(5. 2.2000)
Sir Robert Yewdall JENNINGS	United Kingdom	6. 2.1982-(5. 2.2000)
Manfred LACHS	Poland (President 1973-1976)	6. 2.1967-(5. 2.1994)
Guy LADREIT DE LACHARRIERE	France (Vice-President 1985-1987)	6. 2.1982-10. 3.1987(+)
Kéba MBAYE	Senegal (Vice-President 1988-1991)	6. 2.1982- 5. 2.1991
Mohammed SHAHABUDDEEN	Guyana	6. 2.1988-(5. 2.1997)
NAGENDRA SINGH	India (Vice-President 1976-1979, President 1985-1988)	6. 2.1973-11.12.1988(+)
NI ZHENGYU	China	6. 2.1985-(5. 2.1994)
Shigeru ODA	Japan	6. 2.1976-(5. 2.1994)
Raghunandan Swarup PATHAK	India	18. 4.1989- 5. 2.1991
José Maria RUDA	Argentina (President 1988-1991)	6. 2.1973-(5. 2.1991)
Stephen M. SCHWEBEL	USA	15. 1.1981-(5. 2.1997)
José SETTE-CAMARA	Brazil (Vice-President 1982-1985)	6. 2.1979- 5. 2.1988
Nikolai Konstantinovitch TARASSOV	USSR	9.12.1985-(5. 2.1997)

Judges ad hoc

Georges ABI-SAAB	Mali	Frontier Dispute (Burkina Faso v.Republic of Mali)
François LUCHAIRE	Burkina Faso	Frontier Dispute (Burkina Faso v. Republic of Mali)
Claude-Albert COLLIARD	Nicaragua	Military and Paramilitary Activities in and against Nicaragua (Nicaragua v. United States of America)
Nicolas VALTICOS	El Salvador	Case concerning the Land, Island and Maritime Frontier Dispute (El Salvador v. Honduras)
Michel VIRALLY	Honduras (died 27. 2. 1989)	Case concerning the Land, Island and Maritime Frontier Dispute (El Salvador v. Honduras)
Paul Henning FISCHER	Denmark	Case concerning Maritime Delimitation in the Area between Greenland and Jan Mayen (Denmark v. Norway)
Santiago TORRES BERNARDEZ	Honduras	Case concerning the Land, Island and Maritime Frontier Dispute (El Salvador v. Honduras)
Hubert THIERRY	Guinea-Bissau	Arbitral Award of 31 July 1989 (Guinea-Bissau v. Senegal)

General Index

Abuse of rights see Diplomatic and consular relations, abuse of diplomatic functions
Acquiescence 128
Ad hoc judges 32 f., 117 f., 171 f., 175 f., 178, 181 f., 189
Administrative boundaries 5 f., 95 ff.
Administrative Tribunal of the United Nations see United Nations
Advisory Opinions of the International Court of Justice
- - discretionary character 245
- jurisdictional questions and denial of the request for advisory opinion 242 ff.
- procedure 245 f.
- - equality of the "parties" 242 ff.
- - provisional measures 212, 246
- request for the advisory opinion 213, 241 f.
- - interpretation of the request 241 f., 250
- - right to request 242
Affidavit 201 f.
Aggression 3, 7 f., 18, 22 f., 33 f., 41 ff., 50 f., 53, 58 f.
Alabama case 27
Aliens 104 ff.
Alliances, military and political 67 f.
American Convention on Human Rights 107
Arbitrariness 1 f., 28, 86 f.
Arbitration procedures 71, 111 ff., 121, 168, 180, 182
Armaments, limitation of 31
Armed attack 10, 22 f., 41 ff., 46, 48 ff., 53 ff., 56 f., 58, 60 f., 78
Armed bands see Sending of armed bands
Arms, deliveries to insurgents 46, 51, 54, 56 f. , 60 f., 65, 90 f., 205
Assistance to rebels 42 ff., 46, 48, 50 f., 54, 56 f., 58, 60 f., 64 ff., 88 f.

Belligerents, rights and duties 108 f.
Blockade-like measures 60
Bogotá Conference 1948 69 ff.
Bogotá Pact of 1948 1, 69 ff., 132, 140 ff., 147 f., 166 ff.
Boundaries 5 f., 32, 92 ff., 97 f., 128, 206
- respect for 42, 95 f.
- see also Maritime boundaries
Burden of proof 131, 136, 198 f., 205 ff., 208 f., 227, 231

Chambers of the International Court of Justice 171 ff.
- constitution (Art. 26 para. 2 of the Statute) 117 f., 171 f., 173, 179, 181 ff., 187 f.
- jurisdiction 174 ff., 188
- reform of the Chamber procedure 177 ff., 186 f.
Charter of the United Nations see United Nations, Charter
Civil strife, instigation of acts of 42 ff., 56 f., 61,

- see also Assistance to rebels; Support for subversive or terrorist armed activities
Civil war see Non-international armed conflict
Clean hands doctrine 3 ff.
Coexistence, principle 24, 42
Collective security 53 f., 61 f.
Collective self-defence 22 f., 43, 48 f., 52 ff., 60 f., 204
"Colonial heritage" 97 f., 102, 206
Compensation for expropriations 105 f.
"Compétence de la compétence" 120 ff.
Conciliation 71, 145, 168
Condominium 228 ff., 231
Conference on Security and Co-operation in Europe
- Declaration on principles governing the mutual relations of CSCE-States 7, 17
- Final Act of Helsinki (1975) 20, 24, 41, 64
Contadora process 1, 31 f., 142 ff., 148, 149 ff.
Continental shelf 99 f.
Convention on the Law of the Sea 29, 100
Counter-measures involving the use of force 44 f., 53, 56, 61, 67, 84
Covert actions 89 f., 92
Customary international law 7 ff.
- codification 47, 93
- and conventional law 9 ff., 13, 16 ff., 22 ff., 28 f., 45 ff., 52, 55, 69, 171
- - see also Customary international law, determination of rules of customary international law through treaties
- - see also Treaties, treaty embodiment of customary international law
- determination of rules through treaties 10 f., 14, 16 ff., 22 ff., 51
- influence of treaty law on its formation 13, 16 ff., 46 f., 52,
- "instant" custom 14
- opinio juris 7 f., 13, 15 ff., 19 ff., 33 f., 40 f., 62 f.
- regional customary law 95 ff.
- role of UN General Assembly resolutions in its formation 17, 19, 24, 33 f., 43, 50, 63
- State practice 13, 15 ff., 18, 20 f., 24, 32, 64, 95 ff.

Decolonisation 5 f., 69, 94, 95 ff., 102 ff., 206
Default, procedure in default of appearance 119 f., 129, 153 f., 195 ff., 199 ff., 201 ff., 206, 210 f.
Delict, international see Violations of international law; Responsibility of States
Denunciation see Treaties
Diplomatic protection 15, 104 f., 134 ff.
Discretion, of the Secretary-General in appointing staff members 35 f., 37 ff., 252 ff., 255
Dispute settlement 111 ff.
Domestic law, relationship to international law 27 f., 112 ff., 125, 136 f.

Due process of law 1 f.

Economic sanctions 66, 81, 115 f.
Effective possession, as a basis of sovereignty 96
"Effectivités coloniales" 97 f.
Elementary considerations of humanity 78, 84, 101, 109 f.
Equality, sovereign 19, 63
Equity 5 ff., 94
Estoppel 6 f., 135 f., 192 f.
European Convention on Human Rights 77, 108
Evidence see Procedure of the International Court of Justice
Ex aequo et bono decisions 5 f., 94
Exhaustion of local remedies 111, 133 ff., 192
Exclusive economic zone 99 f.
"Experts on mission" for International Organizations 74 ff.
Exploration, as a territorial title 96, 98, 207
Expropriation 105 f.
Extinction and suspension of international treaties
- see also Treaties, denunciation

Family life, protection of its integrity 107 f.
Force, prohibition of the use of force 7 ff., 10 ff., 16 ff., 25, 28 f., 33 f., 40 ff., 52 f., 56, 65, 68, 107, 122 f., 212
Freedom of navigation 82 f., 84, 100 f.
Friendly Relations-Declaration 17, 19, 24, 33, 41 f., 43 f., 49 f., 63
Frontiers see Boundaries
Fundamental rights see Human rights
Fundamental rights of States 28 ff., 62 f., 68

General Agreement on Tariffs and Trade (GATT) 66, 80, 115
General Assembly of the United Nations
- resolutions 17, 19, 33 f., 43, 63
General principles of law 3, 15, 107 f.
General Treaty of Inter-American Arbitration of 1929 71
Geneva Conventions on the Protection of Victims of War of 1949
- as an expression of fundamental general principles of humanitarian law 78 f., 92, 109 f.
- common Art.3 78 f., 109 f.
- minimum rules for all types of armed conflicts 109 f.
Good faith 1 ff., 127, 143 f., 147 f., 152
Good offices 145

Hague Convention No.VIII of 1907 101, 108 f.
High seas 100
Human rights 107 f.
- mechanism of protection 107
- specific rights 107 f.
Humanitarian aid to insurgents 65 f., 110
Humanitarian law 108 ff.

- fundamental general principles 78. 92, 108 ff.
- Geneva Conventions 78 f., 92, 109 f.

Implied powers 32 f., 118, 184
Injury see Responsibility of States; Violations of international law
Innocent passage 100, 108 f.
Interim measures of protection see Procedure of the International Court of Justice
Internal waters 28 f.; 99 f.
International Court of Justice 117 ff.
- admissibility of an application 143, 146 ff.
- - date of assessment 143, 147 ff.
- - potential problems 151
- Advisory Opinions see Advisory Opinions of the International Court of Justice
- applicable law 5, 128 f.
- determination of the existence of a dispute 120 ff., 123 ff., 140, 146 f.
- ex aequo et bono decisions 5 f., 94
- exhaustion of local remedies 133 ff.
- function 32 f., 94, 111, 117 f., 127 f., 146 f., 162 f., 182 ff., 212, 255 f.
- judgments see Judgments of the International Court of Justice
- jurisdiction see Jurisdiction of the International Court of Justice
- political questions 120 ff., 146 f.
- procedure see Procedure of the International Court of Justice
- Rules of Court 117 f., 119 f., 147, 172, 174 f., 177 f., 181 ff., 189 f., 192 ff., 212 f., 214, 225 f., 232 f., 235, 237
- selection of judges 32, 117 f., 185, 189
- simultaneous seizing of the International Court of Justice and of the Security Council 120, 122 f.
- Statute
- - Art. 26 para. 2 171 ff., 174 f., 178
- - Art. 27 238
- - Art. 30 176, 183 f., 189 f.
- - Art. 31 para. 4 182
- - Art. 36 para. 1 70 f., 132, 165, 166, 234
- - Art. 36 para. 2 70, 118 f., 120 ff., 130, 132, 157, 166
- - Art. 36 para. 4 132, 166
- - Art. 36 para. 6 130, 159, 196
- - Art. 38 14, 129 f., 147, 156
- - Art. 41 212 f., 214, 217
- - Art. 50 200
- - Art. 53 119, 129, 156, 196, 198, 199, 201, 206, 210
- - Art. 59 128, 130, 147, 163, 197, 233, 240
- - Art. 60 130
- - Art. 62 173 f., 181 f., 209, 220 ff.
- - Art. 63 224, 234
- - Art. 65 242 f., 247

International courts see International Court of Justice; United Nations Administrative Tribunal
International economic law 115 f.
International jurisdiction see International Court of Justice; United Nations Administrative Tribunal
International law

- and municipal law 27 f., 112 ff., 125, 136 f.
- violation see Responsibility of States; Violations of international law

International Law Commission 8 f., 18, 41, 68, 74, 91

International organizations
- privileges and immunities of its officials 73 ff.
- relationships between the organization and its staff members 34 ff.,
- seat
- - host agreements 111 ff., 124 ff., 133 f., 138, 213, 241
- - and relations to the host State 111 ff., ff.
- specific organizations see United Nations; World Health Organization (WHO)

International organs see International organizations

International responsibility see Responsibility of States

International treaties see Treaties

Interpretation, of international treaties see Treaties, interpretation

Intervention before the International Court of Justice see Procedure of the International Court of Justice

Intervention, prohibition 8 f., 10, 16, 18 ff., 28 f., 42 ff., 49, 51, 53, 56, 58, 60, 62 ff.

Investments, protection of 104 ff.

Irregular forces, organizing of see Sending of armed bands

Judgments of the International Court of Justice
- binding force 196, 237 ff., 241
- judgments of a chamber 238 f.
- res judicata 88, 128, 147, 163, 228 ff., 239 ff.
- - and third States 164, 239 f., 241

Judicial control of administrative discretion 37 ff., 255

Judicial notice 203, 249 f.

Jura novit curia 129 f., 197

Jurisdiction, international see International Court of Justice; United Nations Administrative Tribunal

Jurisdiction of the International Court of Justice 130 ff.
- concurring jurisdictions 170 f.
- consent of States 118 f., 122, 131 ff., 140, 153, 158, 162 f., 234 ff., 239 f., 243, 245
- in case of continuing negotiations 140 ff.
- to decide upon the own jurisdiction "competence de la competence" 120 ff., 123 ff., 130 ff., 142, 159, 196
- jurisdiction of a chamber 171 f.
- necessity of diplomatic negotiations 138 ff.
- optional clause 70, 118 f., 121 ff., 130, 152 ff., 164, 189 ff., 216 f.
- - denunciation or later modification of a declaration (notice period in particular) 70, 130,
- - form of declarations made under Art. 36 para. 2 of the Statute
- - reciprocity 158
- - reservations 9 ff., 13 f., 70, 119, 153 ff., 216

- - - of participation of other parties to multilateral treaties 9 ff., 13 f., 16, 22, 59, 66, 69, 70, 78, 109, 119, 153 ff., 156 ff., 165
- on the basis of a special aggreement 6, 93, 94, 162 ff., 171 f., 177 ff., 208, 210, 227, 240
- and third States 154 ff., 156 f., 163 f., 240
- on the basis of treaties 70 ff., 123 ff., 132, 164 ff.
- - General Act for the Pacific Settlement of International Disputes of 1949 132
- - General Convention on the Privileges and Immunities of the United Nations of 1946 160 ff.
- - Headquarters Agreement of the United Nations of 1947 123 ff., 138 f.
- - Pact of Bogotá of 1948 69 ff., 132, 140 ff., 148 ff., 151, 166 ff.
- - Treaty of Friendship, Commerce and Navigation between the United States and Italy of 1948 15, 170
- - Treaty of Friendship, Commerce and Navigation between the United States and Nicaragua of 1956 79 f., 164 f., 171

Jus cogens 7 ff., 18, 41, 68

Law of the sea see Continental shelf; Exclusive Economic zone; Internal waters; Maritime boundaries; Territorial sea;
Law of the Sea Convention 29, 100
Lex specialis, treaty rules as 171
Liberation movements 124
Local remedies rule 15, 11, 133 f., 192

Maps, legal significance 93 f., 206 ff.
Maritime boundaries, delimitations 99 f., 219 f., 228 ff.
Martens clause 109 f.
- see also Elementary considerations of humanity

Mediation 142, 145, 148
Mercenaries 42, 50
Military assistance 66 f., 90, 205
Mines, laying in territorial waters 29, 44 f., 57, 60, 100 f., 108 f., 116
Montevideo Convention on Rights and Duties of States of 1933 7, 17, 19, 63
Most-favoured-nation treatment 104
Multilingual treaties 71 ff., 75, 80, 105, 141 f., 168 f., 171, 199, 214
Municipal law, and international law 27 f., 112 ff., 125, 136 f.
Mutual security arrangements 62

National liberation, wars of 69
National security exception in FCN Treaties 54, 79 f.
National treatment 104 f.
Navigation, freedom of 82 f., 84, 100 f.
Necessity 55 f., 57, 116
Neutral powers, rights and duties 108 f.
Non-international armed conflict 78 f., 109 f.
Nuremberg trials 45

Objection see Procedure of the International Court of Justice
Observer missions to the United Nations 111 ff., 124 f., 213, 241
Optional clause see Competence of the International Court of Justice
Organs, international see International organizations
Organization of African Unity 95 ff., 128
- Charter 95
Organization of American States 24 f., 42 f., 53, 68, 80, 107
- Charter 14, 16, 22 f., 24 f., 48, 51, 60, 62, 69, 155 f., 160
Organizations, international see International organizations
Overflights, unauthorized 29, 45, 67

Pacta sunt servanda, principle 85, 163
Peaceful settlement of disputes 31, 42, 70 f., 88 188, 212
Political commitments 24 ff., 30,
Political questions 120 ff., 146 f.
Ports, access to 29, 100 f., 108
Preclusion 192
Preliminary objection see Procedure of the International Court of Justice
Preparatory work "Travaux préparatoires" 69 ff., 74 f.
Privileges and immunities, of officials of international organizations 73 ff.
Procedure of the International Court of Justice
- ad hoc judges 32 f., 171 f., 175 f., 178, 181 f., 187 f., 189
- chamber 171 ff.
- - constitution (Art. 26 para. 2 of the Statute) 171 f., 175 f., 181 ff., 185, 187 f.
- - effects of its judgments 128 f., 176, 180
- - competence to indicate provisional measures 212
- - relationship to the Full Court 184 ff.
- default 119 f., 129, 153 f., 195 ff., 199 ff., 201 ff., 206, 210 f.
- duty to seek further clarification 196 ff., 199 ff., 203, 210 f., 212, 249 f.
- equality of the parties 88, 119 f., 187, 198, 199, 201, 203, 235, 242 ff.
- evidence 6 f., 119, 128, 128, 197, 198 f., 199 ff., 212
- - burden of proof 131, 136, 198 f., 205 ff., 208 f.
- - case files 208
- - documentary material 200
- - maps as evidence of boundaries 93 f., 206 ff.
- - matters of public knowledge 200
- - presentation of evidence 199
- - press reports 205
- - statements by representatives of States 200 ff.
- - witnesses 201 ff., 205
- interim measures of protection 188, 211 ff.
- - irreparable damage 215 f., 217 f., 220
- - and jurisdiction 216 f.
- - and merits 213 f., 217
- intervention (Arts. 62 and 63 of the Statute) 140, 173 ff., 176, 178, 220 ff.
- - Art. 62 179, 181, 225 ff.

- - - jurisdictional link 173, 220 ff., 225, 233 ff., f.
- - organ competent to decide upon an application to intervene 221 ff.
- - Art. 63 224, 234
- - procedure 236 f.
- judicial notice 203, 249 f.
- jura novit curia 129 f., 197
- preliminary objections 189 ff., 198
- jurisdiction and the merits 190 f.
- proof see Procedure of the International Court of Justice, evidence
- provisional measures see Procedure of the International Court of Justice, interim measures of protection
- questions of admissibility 189 ff.

Proof see Procedure of the International Court of Justice

Property, international protection 105 f.

Proportionality 10, 44, 49 f., 55 f., 57, 59, 116

Protection of investments, principles 15

Protectorate 32, 96

Provisional measures see Interim measures of protection

Public international law see International law

Reasonable expectations 195

Red Cross 65 f., 110

Reparation 87 f.

Reprisals, armed 42, 45, 47

Request for actions of collective self-defence 51 f., 55, 61

Res judicata 88, 128, 147, 163, 228 ff., 239 ff.
- and third States 164, 239 f., 241

Reservations 76, 167, 243 ff.

Resolutions of the General Assembly of the United Nations 17, 19, 33 ff., 43, 63

Responsibility of States 27, 56 f., 85 ff., 101
- imputability of acts of private persons 54, 88 ff., 203, 205, 210
- lawful reactions by the State claiming to be a victim 53, 56
- obligation to make reparation 87 f.
- participation 92
- treaty violations 85 ff., 113

Rio Treaty (Inter-American Treaty of Reciprocal Assistance) of 1947 14, 22 f., 51, 54, 77 f., 80, 160

Sea, law of the see Continental shelf; Exclusive fishery zone; Territorial sea; Maritime boundaries;

Seat of international organizations see International organizations

Security Council of the United Nations 23, 33 f., 52 f., 55, 57, 59, 78, 80, 122 f.

Self-defence 8, 10 ff., 13, 22 f., 43, 45 ff., 48 ff., 77 f., 80, 84, 122 f., 204

Self-determination
- principle of self-determination of peoples 8, 30 f., 42, 97, 102 ff.
- attempt to deactivate the principle by preeminence of uti possidetis 97, 102

Sending of armed bands 3, 42 ff., 50 f., 56 ff., 89 f.

Shareholders, rights of foreign 15, 105 f.
"Soft law" see Political commitments
Sources of international law 9 ff.
Sovereign equality 19
Sovereignty
- principle 20, 28 ff., 44 f., 62, 64, 67 f., 90, 93, 95, 97, 101, 205 f., 228
- territorial limits 28 f.

States
- equality 19, 63, f.
- exclusive jurisdiction 30 f.
- fundamental rights 28 ff., 62 f., 68
- responsibility see Responsibility of States
- territory see Territory of States

Stimson doctrine 17, 41
Succession of States 32, 95 f., 97 f., 104, 206
Support for subversive or terrorist armed activities 20, 42 ff., 56 ff., 64 f., 89 f.

"Terra nullius" 98
Territorial sea 29, 99 f.
Territorial title 93, 96 f., 206
Territory of States
- acquisition
- - modes of acquisition 96
- - acquisition by force 17, 41,
- determination of boundaries 32, 92 ff., ff., ff.
- extension 28 f.
- - air space 29
- - internal waters 28 f.
- - territorial sea 28 f.

Terrorist activities, support see Support for subversive or terrorist armed activities
Trade embargo 81 ff., 115 f.
"Travaux préparatoires" 69 ff., 74 f., 169, 194, 257
Treaties
- concept and form of a treaty 27
- and customary international law 9 ff., 13, 16 ff., 22 ff., 28 f.,
- - see also Customary international law, determination of rules of customary international law through treaties
- denunciation 78
- interpretation 11, 14, 69 ff.
- - context 71
- - in the consideration of general law 134 f.
- - intention of the parties 132 f., 165
- - multilingual treaties 71 ff., 75, 80, 105, 141 f., 168 f., 199, 214
- - object and purpose 71 f., 73, 81, 85
- - in the consideration of other treaties 71, 80
- - preamble 81
- - preparatory work 69 ff., 74 f., 169, 194, 257
- - systematic interpretation 71, 76, 80, 168
- Maps as annex to treaties 93 f.
- preamble 81
- reservations 76, 167, 243 ff.
- specific treaties
- - Charter of the Organization of American States 14, 16, 22 f., 24 f., 30, 48, 60, 62, 69, 155 f., 160
- - Chicago Convention on Civil Aviation of 1944 29

- - General Convention on the Privileges and Immunities of the United Nations of 1946 73 ff., 160 ff., 243 f.
- - Geneva Conventions on the Protection of Victims of War of 1949 78 f., 109 f.
- - Geneva Convention on the Territorial Sea of 1958 29
- - Hague Convention No.VIII of 1907 101, 108
- - Headquarters Agreement between the United Nations and the United States of 1947 111 ff., 123 f..
- - Law of the Sea Convention of 1982 29, 100
- - Montevideo Convention on the Rights and Duties of States of 1933 3, 17, 19, 41, 63
- - Pact of Bogota of 1948 1, 69 ff., 132, 140 ff., 147 f., 166 ff.
- - Rio Treaty (Inter-American Treaty of Reciprocal Assistance) of 1947 14, 22 f., 51, 54, 77 f., 80, 160
- - Treaty of Friendship, Commerce and Navigation between the United States and Italy of 1948 15, 28, 73, 86 f., 104 ff., 134 ff., 170
- - Treaty of Friendship, Commerce and Navigation between the United States and Nicaragua of 1956 54, 66, 79 ff., 115 f., 130, 164 f.
- - - see also Jurisdiction of the International Court of Justice, on the basis of treaties
- - Vienna Convention on the Law of Treaties 9, 11, 68, 73, 85, 93, 105
- termination and suspension of treaties 11, 82 f.
- - see also Treaties, denunciation
- treaty embodiment of customary international law 10 ff., 46 f.,
- violation 10, 15, 28, 86 ff., 113, 124, 126

Treaty of Friendship, Commerce and Navigation between the United States and Italy of 1948 15, 28, 73, 86, 104 ff., 134 ff.

Treaty of Friendship, Commerce and Navigation between the United States and Nicaragua of 1956 54, 66, 79 ff., 115 f., 130, 164 f.

Unfriendly acts 86

Unilateral acts of States 24 ff.

Uninhabited territories 96

United Nations
- Administrative Tribunal , 34 ff., 37 ff., 246 ff.
- - Committee on Applications for Review of United Nations Administrative Tribunal Judgments 39 f., 256
- - defects in the procedure 38 ff., 255 f.
- - revision of decisions by the International Court of Justice 35 f., 246 ff.
- Charter 9 ff., 16, 23, 34 ff.
- - Art.2 para.4 (Prohibition of the Use of Force) 8 f., 10 ff., 14, 18 ff., 41, 46 f.,
- - Art.6 para.2 (obli-gations of non-members) 13
- - Art.33 (Peaceful settlement of disputes) 31
- - Chapter VII 53, 61, 80

- - Art.51 (Self-Defence) 8, 10 ff., 14, 23, 43, 46 f., 48 ff., 52, 55, 57, 60, 77, 101,160
- - Art.96 (Advisory Opinions of the ICJ) 161, 242 f., 247
- - Art. 100 (Independence of the Agents) 153, 313
- - Art. 101 para. 1 (Competence of the General Assembly in Staff Matters) 34 ff., 252 ff.
- - Art. 102 (Registration of Treaties) 132
- General Assembly 33 f.
- - Resolutions 17, 19, 33 f., 43, 63
- Human Rights Commission 76 f.
- Human Rights Committee 75
- Secretary-General 34 ff., 37 ff., 246 f., 252 ff.
- - discretionary powers of the Secretary-General under the Charter 37 ff., 252 ff.
- Status of non-member states 14
- Status of officials 76 f.

Universal Declaration of Human Rights of 1948 77, 108

Use of force
- justification 44, 48 ff., 53, 55 ff., 61
- prohibition 7 ff., 10 ff., 16 ff., 25, 28 f., 33 f., 40 ff., 52 f., 56, 65, 68, 107, 122 f., 212

Uti possidetis 6, 32, 94, 95 ff., 206

Violations of international law 29 ff.,

War, state of 60, 101, 108, 165

GPSR Compliance

The European Union's (EU) General Product Safety Regulation (GPSR) is a set of rules that requires consumer products to be safe and our obligations to ensure this.

If you have any concerns about our products, you can contact us on ProductSafety@springernature.com

In case Publisher is established outside the EU, the EU authorized representative is:

Springer Nature Customer Service Center GmbH
Europaplatz 3
69115 Heidelberg, Germany

Batch number: 10682211

Printed by Printforce, the Netherlands